Palgrave Studies in the History of Emotions

Series Editors
David Lemmings
School of History and Politics
University of Adelaide
Adelaide, Australia

William Reddy
Department of History
Duke University
Durham, North Carolina, USA

Palgrave Studies in the History of Emotions includes work that redefines past definitions of emotions; re-conceptualizes theories of emotional 'development' through history; undertakes research into the genesis and effects of mass emotions; and employs a variety of humanities disciplines and methodologies. In this way it produces a new interdisciplinary history of the emotions in Europe between 1100 and 2000.

More information about this series at
http://www.springer.com/series/14584

Laura Kounine • Michael Ostling
Editors

Emotions in the History of Witchcraft

palgrave
macmillan

Editors
Laura Kounine
University of Sussex
Falmer, Brighton
United Kingdom

Michael Ostling
Arizona State University
Tempe, Arizona
USA

Palgrave Studies in the History of Emotion
ISBN 978-1-137-52902-2   ISBN 978-1-137-52903-9   (eBook)
DOI 10.1057/978-1-137-52903-9

Library of Congress Control Number: 2016958278

Cover illustration: Frans Hals, *Malle Babbe* or *The Witch of Haarlem* (detail), 1633

Printed on acid-free paper

This Palgrave Macmillan imprint is published by Springer Nature
The registered company is Macmillan Publishers Ltd.
The registered company address is: The Campus, 4 Crinan Street, London, N1 9XW, United Kingdom

ACKNOWLEDGEMENTS

This book originated in a conversation over coffee—a conversation made possible by an Early Career International Research Fellowship at the ARC Centre of Excellence for the History of Emotions at the University of Melbourne and by the Centre for the History of European Discourses (now Institute for Advanced Studies in the Humanities), University of Queensland. Further collaborations on the theme of 'Witchcraft and Emotions' were made possible by the generous support of the ARC Centre of Excellence for the History of Emotions at the University of Melbourne and the Center for the History of Emotions at the Max Planck Institute for Human Development in Berlin. The editors would like to thank those institutions, and in particular Ute Frevert, Charles Zika, Kiran Sande, Phil Almond, Peter Cryle, and Karin Sellberg.

CONTENTS

NOTES ON CONTRIBUTORS

Edward Bever is a Professor of History at the State University of New York College at Old Westbury and the author of *The Realities of Witchcraft and Popular Magic in Early Modern Europe: Culture, Cognition, and Everyday Life*. He has also published numerous shorter works on early modern witchcraft and popular magic.

Robin Briggs is Emeritus Senior Research Fellow, All Souls College, Oxford, and a Fellow of the British Academy. His research interests have been in the social and religious history of France between the sixteenth and the eighteenth centuries, and the history of European witchcraft. He is currently writing a general study of north-western Europe over a very long time span. Major publications include *Early Modern France, 1560–1715* (1977, revised ed. 1998), *Communities of Belief* (1989), *Witches and Neighbours* (1996, revised ed. 2002), and *The Witches of Lorraine* (2007).

Sarah Ferber is Professor of History at the University of Wollongong, Australia. Her books include: *Demonic Possession and Exorcism in Early Modern France* (2004) and *Bioethics in Historical Perspective* (2013). She is a member of the editorial advisory board of the journal *Preternature*. With legal scholar, Adrian Howe, she researches the ways in which modern law and medicine address acts of violent exorcism.

Malcolm Gaskill is Professor of Early Modern History at the University of East Anglia. He is the author of *Crime and Mentalities in Early Modern England* (2000); *Hellish Nell: Last of Britain's Witches* (2001); *Witchfinders* (2005); and *Witchcraft: a Very Short Introduction* (2010). His most recent book is *Between Two Worlds: How the English Became Americans* (2014). Currently, he is working on a case study of witchcraft accusations in the Connecticut Valley in the 1640s and 50s.

Peter Geschiere is Professor of African Anthropology at the University of Amsterdam and co-editor of the journal *Ethnography*. Since 1971 he has undertaken historical-anthropological field-work in various parts of Cameroon and elsewhere in West Africa. His publications include *The Modernity of Witchcraft: Politics and the Occult in Post-colonial Africa* (1997), *Perils of Belonging: Autochthony, Citizenship and Exclusion in Africa and Europe* (2009), and *Witchcraft, Intimacy and Trust: Africa in Comparison* (2013).

Tamar Herzig is Associate Professor of Early Modern History at Tel Aviv University, where she also serves as Director of the Curiel Institute for European Studies. Her books include *Savonarola's Women* (2008) and *Christ Transformed into a Virgin Woman* (2013). She has also published numerous articles on fifteenth and sixteenth-century demonology and on the prosecution of witches in early modern Italy.

E.J. Kent is a graduate of the University of Melbourne who now works as an Independent Researcher. Her research into masculinity and witchcraft in the early modern Transatlantic English world has been published as *Cases of Male Witchcraft in Old and New England, 1692–1592* (2013), as well as a variety of articles. She is currently pursuing research on masculinity in the Salem witch trials, and in ideas of evil in early modern English culture.

Valerie A. Kivelson is Thomas N. Tentler Collegiate Professor and Arthur F. Thurnau Professor of History at the University of Michigan. Her most recent book is *Desperate Magic: The Moral Economy of Witchcraft in Seventeenth-Century Russia* (2013). She is also the author of *Autocracy in the Provinces* (1997), and of *Cartographies of Tsardom* (2006). She has co-edited four volumes of essays on subjects ranging from Muscovite visual culture to the cultural history of Russian Orthodoxy. Her current work uses visual sources to understand Russia's early modern imperial expansion.

Laura Kounine is Lecturer in Early Modern History at the University of Sussex, and was previously a research fellow at the Centre for the History of Emotions at the Max Planck Institute for Human Development, Berlin. She is the co-editor of *Cultures of Conflict Resolution in Early Modern Europe* (2016) and author of the forthcoming *Imagining the Witch: Emotions, Gender and Selfhood in Early Modern Germany*.

Charlotte-Rose Millar is a Postdoctoral Fellow in the Institute for Advanced Studies in the Humanities at the University of Queensland and an Associate Investigator with the ARC Centre of Excellence for the History of Emotions. Her book, *The Devil is in the Pamphlets: Witchcraft and Emotion in Early Modern England* is forthcoming in 2017. She is also the author of numerous works on witchcraft, diabolism, emotions and sexual practices in early modern England and has won two prizes for her published work.

Michael Ostling is an Honors Faculty Fellow at Barrett, The Honors College of Arizona State University, and an Honorary Fellow of the Institute for Advanced Studies in the Humanities, University of Queensland. He is the author of *Between the Devil and the Host* (2011) and the editor of the forthcoming *Fairies, Demons, and Nature Spirits* (2017). He also writes about ethnobotany, popular culture, and critical pedagogy.

Rita Voltmer is Senior Lecturer and researcher in Medieval and Early modern History at the University of Trier. Her books include *Wie der Wächter auf dem Turm* (2005), *Hexen. Wissen was stimmt* (2008), and *Hexen und Hexenverfolgung in der Frühen Neuzeit* (2012, with Walter Rummel). She has also published numerous articles and book chapters and has curated several exhibitions on the topic of witchcraft. Current research interests include European and transatlantic witch hunts; the history of criminality and poverty; and the cultural transmission/ translation of knowledge.

Charles Zika is a Professorial Fellow in the School of Historical and Philosophical Studies, University of Melbourne, and Chief Investigator in the ARC Centre of Excellence for the History of Emotions. His interests lie in the intersection of religion, emotion, visual culture and print in early modern Europe, and focus on pilgrimage, communal integrity, natural disaster and witchcraft in this period. His most recent books include *The Appearance of Witchcraft* (2007); *The Four Horsemen: Apocalypse, Death & Disaster* (2012, with Cathy Leahy and Jenny Spinks); and *Celebrating Word and Image 1250–1600* (2013, with Margaret Manion).

Laurel Zwissler is an Assistant Professor of Religion at Central Michigan University, and author of the forthcoming *Cosmologies of Interconnection* (2017). She received her doctorate from the University of Toronto in the Centre for the Study of Religion and the Collaborative Program in Women and Gender Studies. Her ethnographic work focuses on global justice activists and investigates contemporary interrelations between religion, gender, and politics, relating these to theoretical debates about empirical and ideal roles of religion in the public sphere. She is now building on this work with ethnographic research within the North American fair-trade movement.

LIST OF FIGURES

CHAPTER 1

Introduction: 'Unbridled Passion' and the History of Witchcraft

Michael Ostling and Laura Kounine

> *Wiem, że to grzech jest wielki, wiem, że wszelkie czary*
> *Szkodliwe, ale żal mój nie ma żadnej miary.*
>
> *I know witchcraft is harmful, that in practicing it I fall*
> *Into great sin, but there's no limit to my bitter gall.*
>
> —Szymon Szymonowic, Sielanki, 1614

In Thomas Dekker's *Witch of Edmonton* (1658), Mother Sawyer is a quarrelsome old woman, 'shunned/And hated like a sickness'.[1] But she is no witch, until the hatred of her neighbours drives her to become one:

M. Ostling
Arizona State University

L. Kounine
University of Sussex

© The Author(s) 2016
L. Kounine, M. Ostling (eds.), *Emotions in the History of Witchcraft*, DOI 10.1057/978-1-137-52903-9_1

1

> Some call me witch,
> And being ignorant of myself, they go
> About to teach me how to be one, urging
> That my bad tongue—by their bad usage made so—
> Forspeaks their cattle, doth bewitch their corn,
> Themselves, their servants, and their babes at nurse.[2]

Insulted by a neighbour, she curses him (impotently, her malediction not yet empowered by the Devil). The neighbour beats her and leaves her bleeding, and in the desperate fullness of her rage against a cruel world, she invokes 'some power, good or bad' to 'Instruct me which way I might be revenged/Upon this churl.' When she declares her willingness to 'give this fury leave to dwell within/This ruined cottage' of her ageing body, the Devil appears in the form of a dog. He promises her his love and the power of revenge in exchange for her soul, and Mother Sawyer, not yet a witch when she had been beaten for witchcraft, becomes a witch in fact.[3]

Scholars of witchcraft are rightfully reluctant to equate fictitious depictions of witchcraft with the actual practices of accused witches or their accusers.[4] And yet the depiction of Mother Sawyer's trajectory towards diabolism closely parallels stories from the trials of accused witches. For example that of Mengeatte Grand Jacques in Lorraine, of whom a witness recalled that 'she wished she could be a witch for two hours to do as she wanted'—in order to harm those who wrongly called her witch.[5] And Dekker's play well illustrates the central conundrum of any attempt to recover a history of emotions from literature *or* from trials: witches were identified by their negative emotions, but these negative emotions were themselves inspired by suspicions or allegations of witchcraft.

Witchcraft is a crime of 'headie and unbridled passion', an overflowing of 'bitter gall' with 'no limit'.[6] Witches are 'fit to burst from enormous resentment', or 'exasperated with a wrathfull and unruly passion of revenge, or transported by unsatiable love'.[7] Witch trials themselves unfold as dramas of emotional expression and repression, wherein the 'unbridled passions' on view belong to accusers, witnesses, and officers of the court—such as the bailiff who, according to the testimony of one accused witch, 'with gruesome and shocking torture took out his anger on me'.[8] Jurisprudential convention required accusers to present their case in coolly dispassionate language, such as when Stanisław Gałek, in early eighteenth-century Poland, assured the court that his accusation arose 'not out of hatred, or rancour, or spite, or wrath … but because of the facts and the truth'.[9] But such accusations arose from almost unbearable grief and fear—at the loss of a cow or a child or one's sexual potency, at the notion that one's neighbour could be responsible for that loss. Meanwhile accused witches, under conditions ranging from intimidation at best to prolonged and brutal torture at worst, tried to maintain their emotional composure. But not too much composure—rant and rave and they proved themselves full of the 'unbridled passion' expected of witches, but if they failed to shed remorseful tears they displayed a culpable dispassion. As was noted in the record of a witch trial in the Lutheran duchy of Württemberg, which took place in 1616, 'the prisoner, with her behaviour, without shedding a single tear, cheekiness, and lack of fear' should not be let out of prison, even though she had confessed to nothing.[10] Witches were either all too emotionally human or inhumanly cool under pressure, and were damned either way.

As Lyndal Roper has recently noted, 'witchcraft is fundamentally about physical harm caused by emotions … [W]ishing evil may well actually have caused harm, for emotional conflicts can make people ill'.[11] However, the challenge for historians is to untangle *whose* emotions caused *what* harm: the accused witch, whose envy induced illness; or the accuser, torturer, and executioner, driven by grief or fear to dunk an alleged witch in the local pond, hang her from the strappado, or burn her at the stake. While curses or the evil eye *might lead* to a witchcraft victim's sickness, the emotions of accusers and magistrates indubitably *have led* to the deaths of thousands of alleged witches. Roper has argued that 'without an understanding of the emotional dynamics of witchcraft, we cannot comprehend the intensity and bitterness of the witch trials'.[12] The unbridled passions discoverable in the history of witchcraft might belong primarily to the accusers.

The present volume attempts to take on this challenge, discriminating between the several emotional registers that both promise to illuminate and threaten to obscure any account of emotions in the history of witchcraft. Part I, 'In Representation', explores discourses *about* the emotional lives of witches. These chapters focus on the witch imagined, depicted, and contested in authoritative and influential works of demonology and visual art. Tamar Herzig revisits the notorious *Malleus maleficarum*, among the earliest and most reprinted of demonological manuals. Through an examination of the full corpus of works by its author Heinrich Institoris, Herzig complicates the standard reading of the *Malleus* as misogynistic rant: she shows that for Institoris the ungovernable emotionalism of women leads in one direction towards witchcraft, in another, towards sainthood. Charles Zika offers a detailed case study of a small set of prints and sketches by Jacques de Gheyn II, using these to explicate a Europe-wide visual script, drawing on humoral theory, which locates the affectless cruelty of witches as the flipside of the Virgin's mercy and compassion. In contrast, Laura Kounine's provocative reading of Nicolas Remy's *Daemonolatria*, one of the most influential demonological texts during the height of the witch craze, turns away from the alleged emotions of female witches to depictions of their supposed master, the Devil, whose rage and jealousy drove people—both men and women—to witchcraft. Finally, E.J. Kent examines the male witch in old and New England, showing how his depiction is modelled on and reflects seventeenth-century concerns about masculine tyranny. Together, these four chapters integrate representations of witchcraft into contemporaneous theories of the emotions and of gender.

Part II, 'On Trial', would seem to move from representation to reality, from literary or visual or intellectual history to the history of experience. Rita Voltmer's chapter on torture immediately dashes any such naïve hope, as she calls into question the possibility of recovering 'authentic' emotions from witch-trial records, arguing that these represent carefully constructed emotionological scripts, intended to justify the brutality of early modern courts. The other four chapters in this section express a cautious hope that trial records might provide a window onto the actual emotions of accused witches and their alleged victims. Valerie Kivelson resituates the often beautifully romantic love spells deployed by Muscovite women as part of a larger discourse negotiating relationships of hierarchy and dependency in a harsh feudal society where beatings and torture were routine. Robin Briggs draws on his decades-long immersion in the witch-trial records of Lorraine to consider the emotional landscapes of entire villages: the disruptive love that could move a woman to bewitch, the overwhelming grief that engendered suspicion, the hatred and fear necessary to overcome peasant solidarity and trigger formal accusations before courts of law. Michael Ostling looks to accounts of demon lovers in Polish witch trials to find evidence for marital affection in the least likely of places. Finally, Charlotte-Rose Millar makes use of a very full corpus of English witch-trial pamphlets to highlight the emotional underpinnings of what is often understood in terms of legal contract or theological covenant—the witches' pacts with their familiar devils. Taken together, these five chapters emphasize the problems and prospects of mining the trial records to reconstruct early modern emotions.

Part III, 'In the Mind', turns inward, seeking explanations for the phenomenon and experience of witchcraft in the workings of the mind. Edward Bever takes an approach grounded in neurobiology and evolutionary psychology, suggesting that anger, hatred, and jealousy can trigger strong stress reactions in those to whom they are directed—reactions culturally explained as witchcraft. Peter Geschiere's comparative ethnography of Africa and Europe explores the complex therapeutics of practices related to witchcraft: the gossip that turns grief or rage into an actionable accusation, allowing one to mediate and express the dangers of intimacy. Sarah Ferber's contribution historicizes psychological approaches, juxtaposing nineteenth-century classifications of witchcraft as delusion, twentieth-century historiographies of the emotional childishness supposedly revealed in the witch trials, and twenty-first-century legal cases of exorcism assault. Together, these three chapters provide an overview of psychological approaches to witchcraft and the emotions while also subjecting such approaches to critique.

This leads us towards a reflection on our own emotions about the emotions discovered in the history of witchcraft. Part IV, 'In History', moves from the history of emotions to the emotions of history: the uses of the past for the arousal and maintenance of emotional dispositions today. For at least the last two centuries, memorializations of the witch trials have been deployed to inculcate outrage against their perpetrators—a moving target ranging from fanatical priests to scheming medical doctors to patriarchy in general. While such memorializations often depend on tendentious, ahistorical readings of the past, the emotions they arouse are no less real or powerful. Laurel Zwissler's case study explores this issue sensitively, through an ethnographic analysis of contemporary pagans and the emotions aroused through remembrance of the 'Burning Times'. Finally, Malcolm Gaskill's Afterword reflects on the importance of getting the history of the emotions of witchcraft right, and provides some recommendations towards that goal.

Models for the History of Emotions

While the chapters fall neatly into the categories above, they also draw extensively on each other across such neat divisions. To take just one example, Geschiere's interest in the therapeutics of counter-magic (Part III) places him in conversation with Briggs (Part II), who in turn speaks to Kounine (Part I) through their shared focus on the demonologist Nicolas

Remy. Indeed, the chapters could have been ordered entirely differently to bring out different sets of connections. Below, we examine the chapters in this volume through the framework of the burgeoning literature on the history of emotions. This has a twofold purpose: first, to show how the history of emotions can provide guidance into examining the emotions in witchcraft; and second, to explore the ways in which scholars have approached emotions in witchcraft in order to provide further avenues for the history of emotions.[13] As befits a young field, the history of emotions has proven fertile ground for the production of neologisms, and its theoretical elaboration has proceeded through the delineation of multiple overlapping, rival terms—emotives, emotionology, emotional regimes, or practices, or communities or arenas.

Emotives

William Reddy has perhaps done more than any other to shape the field of the history of emotions, with his highly influential work on 'emotional regimes' and in particular 'emotives'. Reddy's term 'emotives' denotes gestures and speech acts at once 'descriptive and performative', both reflecting and constructing emotional experience.[14] This productively ambiguous term can be used in a variety of ways. On the one hand, emotives are the words used to translate ephemeral, inchoate feelings into stable, public, analysable (and thus historical) emotions: they facilitate the 'attempt to feel what one says one feels'.[15] The term thus clarifies the process of coming to feel particular emotions by having a language in which to express them—a process explored especially in Zwissler's ethnography of the motivating anger cultivated by contemporary pagan activists, Millar's discussion of the affection and rage expressible through devil familiars, and in Ostling's and Kivelson's exploration of love magic.[16] Kivelson also takes the term 'emotive' in a different direction, exploiting its affinity with the linguistic category of performatives. Just as performative speech acts such as promises or baptisms 'do things in the world', so to with emotives: they are words and gestures with effects beyond their semantic meaning. Kivelson comments that 'This eureka moment [that words are actions] comes as no surprise to anyone who studies witchcraft.'[17] Historians and anthropologists of witchcraft have long known that a muttered malediction can bring illness or death, and that even unspoken emotions do harm: as John Aubrey argued long ago, 'the glances of envy and malice do shoot also subtilly; the eye of the malicious person does really infect and make sick the spirit of the other'.[18] A witch's curse or angry glance can be explicated in terms of such emotives; it expressed her rage or envy and induced answering feelings in her victim, with real-world consequences ranging from the victim's illness to the witch's death at the stake. Although he does not use the term, Edward Bever's account of the 'neurobiology of emotional aggression' can be recast in terms of emotives in this extended sense.[19]

Emotionology and Emotional Regimes

Emotionology (a term whose coinage in 1985 marks the arrival of the 'history of emotions' as a coherent discipline) denotes 'the attitude or standards that a society … maintains toward basic emotions and their appropriate expression [and] the way that institutions reflect and encourage these attitudes in human conduct'.[20] The rival 'emotional regime' covers similar territory, but emphasizes the workings of power—emotional regimes uphold and are upheld by wider discourses of gender, class (or estate), and ethnicity (or nation).[21] Both terms intend to bypass the problems involved in historicizing internal emotional experience in favour of theories about emotion, representations of emotion, emotional discourses, and norms.

The 'unbridled passion' through which witchcraft has been imagined constitutes one such emotionological tradition: quite independently of whether any witch ever felt such passion, the theory that she did so shaped demonological discourse and the assumptions of magistrates presiding over witch trials. An inverted version of the same emotionology informed the historiography of witchcraft from the late eighteenth century well into the twentieth. Historians have resembled demonologists precisely in their preferences for accounting for witchcraft in terms of emotional excess, but this excess has belonged to the demonologist and magistrate rather than the accused witch. Enlightenment theories of witchcraft have sought explanations for the 'witch craze' in the 'sadomasochistic fantasies and infanticidal impulses' of demonologists.[22] As Sarah Ferber shows, such an attitude towards the emotions of witchcraft is fossilized in the classificatory systems of contemporary law, psychology, and even library science—the Dewey Decimal system places witchcraft together with 'delusions' in ways which prejudge its rationality while also keeping it safely distant from conceptually relevant categories such as 'Christianity'.[23] Laurel Zwissler explores a different preservation of a similar emotionology among feminist activists and contemporary pagans, who use it to stoke their own resistance to the cold anti-emotionalisms inherent to monotheism and patriarchy.[24]

Despite their outdated adherence to the notion of the 'Burning Times' as a genocide directed against women, Zwissler's pagans have a point. For decades now, feminist historians have read misogynist demonology as a sort of inverted mirror, a flipped image by which one can reconstruct early modern patriarchal standards of female emotional comportment. Sigrid Brauner, for example, reverse-engineered the femmes fatales of Hans Baldung Grien's artwork and the gynophobic bombast of the *Malleus maleficarum* to discover the 'proper' emotional range of the ideal German woman: subdued, self-contained, keeping a civil tongue in her head, maintaining, with the help of her husband's benign oversight, a check on her natural female tendency to emotional outbursts.[25] Nor was this mere emotionology, mere theory. As Louise Jackson has argued, witch trials and stories of witch trials enforced emotional norms: as an anti-model for loving mothers, dutiful wives, chaste and modest widows, 'the witch was a warning to women as to what would happen if they behaved in a way which could be counted as subversive'.[26] 'The witch defined the virtuous woman in the negative', holding up 'a dark mirror to feminine quietude'.[27]

There can be no doubt that the imagination of the witch's emotional excess was profoundly gendered. A seventeenth-century Polish critique of the witch trials explains that witches tended to be women because they are 'full of affect and unchecked passion'.[28] But the same notion was widespread in contexts entirely divorced from the witch trials, such as in the sermons of the Polish historian-priest Szymon Starowolski: 'If [women] love someone, they love without measure. If they hate someone, their hatred and wrath is measureless; when they begin to be good, they become saints.'[29] Although Starowolski might have borrowed this commonplace from the *Malleus maleficarum* (which copies it from Johannes Nider's *Formicarius*), he more likely took it from Seneca: 'a woman either loves or hates, there is no third'.[30]

Several chapters in the present volume seek not so much to contest the feminist reading of gendered emotional regimes as to qualify and complicate it. Tamar Herzig's radical rereading of the *Malleus* in the light of Institoris's reverence for embodied female piety demonstrates that he took quite seriously both sides of women's alleged emotionalism—' unrestrained emotionality was essentially a female trait; but it could turn contemporary women not only into wicked witches, but also into reincarnated Christs'.[31]

At the other end of the book, Zwissler notes an ironically similar valoriza-
tion of female emotionalism among Progressive-era feminists and some of
their twenty-first century sisters, for whom 'women's stronger emotionality makes them more authentic, wise and positioned to govern justly'.[32]
Charles Zika provides close visual reading of several works by Jacques de
Gheyn the Younger, to suggest that he depicts not his own understanding
of the practices of actual witches but of those alleged witches' deluded
fantasies. We are thus usefully reminded that opponents of the witch trials
such as Johannes Weyer and Reginald Scot preserved the *Malleus'* sense of
emotionally overwrought female witches while robbing them of any claim
to diabolism *or* holiness, rendering them merely melancholy and entirely
powerless.[33] E.J. Kent's comparison of the language used to describe male
witches and male tyrants shows that men, too, could be envisioned as
emotionally out of control, though the emotions unleashed tended to
be pride and wrath rather than envy or spite.[34] Finally, Laura Kounine's
emphasis on the 'inconsistency and fragility inherent in the category of the
"witch", the "feminine", and the "masculine"' in Remy's *Daemonolatria*
shows that, at least among those demonologists in close contact with
actual witch trials, the abstract emotionological gender classifications tend
to blur and crumble.[35] In practice, both emotions and gender norms tend
to overflow the neat categories into which demonologists and historians
try to confine them.

Emotional Practices

So far we have mostly explored the representation of emotions; we turn
now to their embodiment in practice. Cognitive scientists and neurobi-
ologists continue to debate about the number and nature of the 'basic
emotions', which are presumably universal and uniform across the human
species.[36] Smiling, weeping, and blushing may be universal physiological
expressions of emotion, typically experienced as uncognized and involun-
tary. However, the frequency, distribution among genders or age groups
or classes, and appropriateness to specific situations or relations—indeed
the meaning and practice—of smiling, weeping, or blushing vary widely
across time and culture. So too with emotional practices more generally. Emotions are both internal, private, ahistorical feelings we *have* and
external, public, historically embedded actions we *do*: smiling or weeping
expresses but also incites emotion in culturally variable ways. Emotions
thus bridge Cartesian gaps between the body and language, between the

longue durée of human evolution and the discontinuities and sudden shifts of human history. They are 'both physical and mental; they are expressed in words but they also have a physiological component'.[37] As Monique Scheer suggests in a foundational article, emotions have a history because they are practices, shaping and shaped by the embodied habitus of specific cultures, discourses, and regimes of power.[38]

Although the term 'emotional practice' is new, scholars of witchcraft have been describing such practices and their effects for nearly eighty years. E.E. Evans-Pritchard's *Witchcraft, Oracles and Magic among the Azande* (1937) is best remembered for defending the rationality of witchcraft belief—a defence that made possible its serious study in the intervening decades.[39] But it is easy to forget that this rationality had an emotional motivation. Witchcraft turns the indifferent natural world, with its meaningless coincidences, into a social world peopled by others towards whom one might feel and act. The victim of witchcraft gained, not just an explanation, but an enemy: a person towards whom to direct one's anger and fear; a person to punish or from whom to seek reparation. Through the complex procedures of divination, accusation, denial, confession, and apology typical of many witch-believing traditional societies, both 'victim' and 'witch' could express and resolve otherwise unavowable conflicts and hatreds; in Jacqueline van Gent's words, witchcraft and magic 'provide people with the discourse and the ritual practice to express socially unacceptable emotions'.[40] Evans-Pritchard's insight came into the historical study of European witchcraft via the work of Alan Macfarlane, who explicated English witchcraft accusation in terms of 'charity refused'. Householders, at once guilty for refusing charity to a beggar-woman and resentful of her envious request, projected their guilt and resentment outwards onto the woman who incited it, constructing her as a witch.[41] Lyndal Roper has, influentially, brought Macfarlane's account of projection into the bedchamber and especially into the emotionally charged atmosphere of childbed: she contends that young women's fear of the post-menopausal bodies of older women, and the envy such older women were assumed to bear against the young and fertile, 'provided the emotional fuel of the witch craze'.[42] Perhaps most explicitly, the devil familiars which populated English witchcraft pamphlets, as discussed by Millar in this volume, can be seen as physical manifestations of such projected and externalized emotions: not only were they devils from hell sent *to* the witch to tempt her, they were also external embodiments of witches' internal thoughts and desires, sent *from* her to act out those desires and thoughts in the world.[43]

Peter Geschiere discovers similar therapeutics in twentieth- and twenty-first-century Cameroon, South Africa, and rural France. His chapter emphasizes that such emotional practices must be grasped holistically, within their total context. This might complicate neat understandings of the emotions of witchcraft, but will ultimately deepen our understandings of why witchcraft beliefs were—and continue to be—so powerful. As Geschiere notes, 'One way or another, the full weight of the context has to be taken into account if we want to understand people's obsessions and anxieties.'[44] In the present volume, Briggs depicts the generation and management of emotion accomplished in early modern Lorraine through witchcraft suspicion, accusation, and counter-magical assault. Meanwhile, suspected witches could internalize their alleged abilities, 'empowering them to turn their emotions of the moment into actions, aligning their psychic life with a version of external reality'.[45] We have returned to the world of *The Witch of Edmonton*, in which suspicion of witchcraft could incite the suspect to come to believe herself a witch.

In a rather different way, Kivelson and Ostling explore the emotional practices associated with love magic in early modern Muscovy and Poland. Surprisingly, they find it has little to do with love. In a now classic essay, John Winkler described the ancient Mediterranean emotionology of love as 'a diseased state', a 'pathology' or 'mental disturbance'—and related this emotionology to ancient Greek love and curse magic. In ways tantalizingly similar to Macfarlane's model of witchcraft accusation, the user of love magic *himself* felt burning pangs of desire and lust, but through the spell he (it usually was a he) projected these desires onto the love object, thus ameliorating his own passion.[46] In Poland and Muscovy, one finds very similar spells used for a very different purpose: despite their language of burning love and insatiable desire, they were usually used to seek mere kindness—to soften the edges of brutal feudal hierarchies. Love magic performs emotional work, but the emotions involved have little to do with love.[47]

Emotional Communities and Emotional Arenas

And yet accused witches did sometimes speak of love, seemingly sincerely. That they did so in the context of interrogation under torture raises issues both methodological and ethical. Pioneering work in the emotional history of witchcraft has focused on this queasy nexus of invaluable source material and its abominable context of collection. Lyndal Roper's now classic *Oedipus and the Devil* relied on close readings of interrogations under torture to reconstruct the love lives of early modern German women.[48] Similarly, Diane Purkiss has controversially suggested that

> Some of the stories told by accused witches may have been stories which perhaps could not be told until released by the court procedure, stories that expressed a powerful mixture of memory and desire, stories that could be paradoxically liberating, though told under terrible duress.[49]

In this sense, the torture chamber constitutes what Mark Seymour has recently dubbed an 'emotional arena', a place or occasion (like a church, a wedding-feast, a funeral, a seedy motel) that evokes and makes possible the expression of particular emotions appropriate to it—emotions that might not otherwise ever find expression.[50] Ostling's chapter, for example, takes advantage of this model to hear words of love and longing in the confession of a seventeenth-century accused witch about her demon lover.[51] Rita Voltmer, in her important and impassioned contribution, hears in such testimony nothing but the voices of the torturer, the magistrate, the scribe.[52] For Voltmer, the court comprised what Barbara Rosenwein has called an 'emotional community', a social group defining and defined by the 'modes of emotional expression that they expect, encourage, tolerate, and deplore'.[53] Scribal convention and the interests of the court ensured that those emotions allowed to enter into the historical record conformed to accepted demonological scripts predetermining the emotions expressed by the accused witch. She could be appropriately spiteful, appropriately cold-hearted and dry-eyed, appropriately contrite and repentant after confession, but these represented emotions provide no window into the witch's heart—on the contrary, they are just as much emotionological, just as much mere representations, as are demonological treatises or works of art.[54] To pretend otherwise is to allow the torturer to get the final word, erasing the accused witch utterly and finally. Although most contributors to the present volume come to different conclusions, Voltmer's warning about the value of tortured testimony must be kept constantly in mind.

Malcolm Gaskill has recently emphasized that in witch trials, as in few other early modern sources, we hear the 'expressions of feeling made by humble people'.[55] The temptation (indeed the duty) to heed such expressions is very strong indeed, but so is the responsibility to hear them right—

to avoid mistaking the ventriloquized voices of torturers, magistrates, and demonologists for the authentic expressions of the people. We enter into this tangled forest in trepidation and with care, aware that the stakes are high in every sense.

NOTES

1. Thomas Dekker, John Ford, and William Rowley, *Witch of Edmonton* [1658], Act 2 scene 2.
2. Ibid.
3. Ibid.
4. *The Witch of Edmonton* draws on an actual case, as depicted in Henry Goodcole's pamphlet *Wonderfull discoverie of Elizabeth Sawyer* [1621]. But as Marion Gibson has argued, such pamphlets bent and distorted trial testimony to their own polemical ends. See Gibson, 'Understanding Witchcraft?' For further discussion of the problems and prospects of using pamphlets for witchcraft history, see Millar's chapter, this volume.
5. See Briggs's chapter, this volume.
6. Cotta, *Triall of Witch-craft* [1616], 96. Szymon Szymonowic, *Sielanki* [1614], 15 vv. 21–2.
7. Swizralus [pseud.], *Peregrinacya dziadowska* [1614], 97.
8. Hauptstaatsarchiv Stuttgart, A209 Bü 144, Anna Murschel 1598–1600, 6r.
9. Wawrzeniecki, 'Proces o czary'. For discussion of this and similar oaths, see Ostling, *Between the Devil and the Host*, 70–1.
10. Hauptstaatsarchiv Stuttgart, A209 Bü 999, Anna Müller, 10 December 1616, 3r. See also the discussion in Zika's and Voltmer's chapters, this volume.
11. Roper, *The Witch*, 112.
12. Confino et al., 'Forum: History of Emotions', 74.
13. For useful entries into this rapidly growing field, see e.g. Boddice, 'Affective Turn'; Matt and Stearns, eds., *Doing Emotions History*; Plamper, 'History of Emotions', 237–65; Plamper, *History of Emotions*; Sullivan, 'History of the Emotions', 93–102.
14. Reddy, *Navigation of Feeling*; Sullivan, 'History of the Emotions', 96.
15. Reddy, in Plamper, 'History of Emotions', 240.
16. See Chapters 7, 9, 10, 14 of this volume.

17. Kivelson, this volume, p. 132.
18. Aubrey, *Miscellanies*, 242.
19. Bever, this volume; see also Bever, 'Witchcraft Fears'; Bever, *Realities of Witchcraft*. Bever's analysis builds on but goes further than classical anthropological accounts such as Cannon, '"Voodoo" Death'; Lester, 'Voodoo Death'. But it should be noted that his neurobiological model updates even older explanations of witchcraft, such as Francesco Maria Guazzo's contention that the faculty of imagination can excite 'fear or shame or anger or sorrow, and these emotions so affect a man with heat or cold that his body either grows pale or reddens, and he consequently becomes joyful and exultant, or torpid and dejected.' See Guazzo, *Compendium Maleficarum* [1626], bk. 1 ch. 1.
20. Stearns and Stearns, 'Emotionology', 813.
21. Reddy, *Navigation of Feeling*.
22. Haliczer, 'The Jew as Witch', 148–9; see also Trevor-Roper, 'European Witch-craze', 153–4. In its extreme form, this position has found few adherents among historians for many decades, and has been entirely untenable since Nicholas Spanos's devastating critique: see Spanos, 'Witchcraft in Histories of Psychiatry'. Nevertheless, it remains alive and well in popular accounts.
23. Ferber, this volume. Note that the Library of Congress system follows Dewey on this point; most materials on early modern European witch trials being classified in BF (Psychology) rather than in such other possible categories as BL (Religion and Mythology), BR (Christianity), GR (Folklore), or HV (Criminology).
24. Zwissler, this volume.
25. Brauner, *Fearless Wives and Frightened Shrews*.
26. Jackson, 'Witches, Wives, and Mothers', 314.
27. Kamensky, *Governing the Tongue*, 152.
28. Anon., *Czarownica powołana* [1639], 37.
29. Starowolski, *Świątnica Pańska* [1645], 471.
30. Bailey, *Battling Demons*, 51. See also Institoris, *Malleus maleficarum* [1487], ed. Mackay, vol. 2, 116 (Latin original in ibid., vol. 1, 285); and Herzig's chapter, this volume. On the commonplace construction of women's emotionalism outside the context of witch trials, see Maclean, *Renaissance Notion of Women*; Reeser, *Moderating Masculinity*, 1–48.

31. Herzig, this volume, p. 30. For a tantalizingly similar understanding of women's greater 'openness' to both demons and God among contemporary Pentecostals, see Lawless, "The Night I Got the Holy Ghost".
32. Zwissler, this volume, p. 254.
33. Zika, this volume.
34. Kent, this volume.
35. Kounine, this volume, p. 70.
36. See discussion of the voluminous literature in Bever's chapter, this volume. See also Elster, *Strong Feelings*.
37. Confino et al., 'History of Emotions', 70. This bridge-building potential of emotions—between mind and body, cultural studies and cognitive science, neurobiology and history—forms a leitmotif of the programmatic literature. See e.g. Elster, *Strong Feelings*, 4, 98–114; Reddy, *Navigation of Feeling*.
38. Scheer, 'Are Emotions a Kind of Practice?'
39. Evans-Pritchard, *Witchcraft, Oracles and Magic*, esp. 63–83.
40. Van Gent, *Magic, Body and the Self*, 193.
41. Macfarlane, *Witchcraft in Tudor and Stuart England*, 196. For a refreshingly non-Freudian account of how emotions such as envy can generate beliefs, which in turn generate new and more comfortable emotions such as indignation or anger, see Elster, *Strong Feelings*, 34, 108–11.
42. Roper, *The Witch*, 112.
43. See Millar, this volume.
44. Geschiere, this volume.
45. Briggs, this volume, p. 138.
46. Winkler, 'Constraints of Desire', quotations at 82, 84. For an update and partial critique of Winkler's model, see Frankfurter, 'Social Context of Women's Erotic Magic'.
47. Kivelson, this volume; Ostling, this volume.
48. Roper, *Oedipus and the Devi*.
49. Purkiss, 'Sounds of Silence', 82.
50. Seymour, 'Emotional Arenas'.
51. Ostling, this volume.
52. Voltmer, this volume.
53. Rosenwein, 'Worrying about Emotions', 842.
54. Voltmer, this volume.
55. Gaskill, 'Witchcraft, Emotions and Imagination', 174.

PART I

In Representation

.

CHAPTER 2

Fear and Devotion in the Writings of Heinrich Institoris

Tamar Herzig

In 1486 Heinrich Institoris (also known as Kramer, d. *c.*1505) turned his notes from the reports that he had written to Bishop Georg II Golser (*c.*1420–89) about the witch prosecutions at Innsbruck into the *Malleus maleficarum* (*The Hammer of* [*Female*] *Witches*), a lengthy handbook for judges in cases of witchcraft. By the end of that year, his manuscript had been delivered to the printing house of Peter Drach in Speyer.[1] Appearing in almost thirty editions before the end of the seventeenth century, the *Malleus* was a bestseller by early modern standards.[2] It played a pivotal role in shaping demonological discourse, and its influence proved far more lasting than that of any other early witchcraft tract.[3] Still the best-known premodern witchcraft treatise to date, the *Malleus* has often been regarded as embodying the anxiety that kindled the great European witch-hunts.[4]

Arguably the most misogynistic text published in the premodern era, the *Malleus* owes much of its notoriety to its attack on women's

T. Herzig
Tel Aviv University

© The Author(s) 2016
L. Kounine, M. Ostling (eds.), *Emotions in the History of Witchcraft*, DOI 10.1057/978-1-137-52903-9_2

unbridled emotionality.[5] Following Jean Delumeau, Institoris's dia-tribe on the female sex has been explained as reflecting a chaste friar's fear of female sexuality.[6] Moreover, for radical second-wave feminists from the 1960s onwards the hatred of women, which they regarded as the main cause of the witch craze, was manifested first and foremost in the *Malleus*.[7] Thus, Andrea Dworkin underscored the *Malleus*'s 'frenzied and psychotic woman-hating' as emblematic of the Church's fear of female sexuality that underlay the large-scale persecution of witches.[8]

In more recent years, scholars of early modern Europe have offered more nuanced and historically accurate interpretations of the *Malleus*'s construction of women as slaves to their desires. Hans Peter Broedel proposes that whenever social order and masculinity are defined against a powerfully sexualized and rigidly controlled notion of femininity, 'anxi-ety about the stability of these structures expresses itself … , as in the *Malleus*, in terms of fears of occult harm and deviant sexuality'.[9] Walter Stephens, on the other hand, has provocatively argued that Institoris's demonological tract 'betrays no fear of feminine power, but rather a will to prove such power exists; not a simple hatred of female sexuality, but rather a desire to appropriate and exploit women's real or imagined potential'.[10] In the last two decades, historians have also shifted their attention from Institoris's feelings about female sexuality to his attitude towards women's spiritual powers, explaining the *Malleus*'s configura-tion of witchcraft as the culmination of escalating clerical anxiety over the somatic mysticism and social prestige of saintly women in late medi-eval Europe. In the *Malleus*'s invective against the female sex, it has been suggested, the apprehension of male ecclesiastics vis-à-vis the increased political influence of charismatic holy women in the last centuries of the Middle Ages reached its apotheosis.[11] The current chapter brings together these two concerns, namely the fear of women's sexuality and the preoccupation with female mysticism, and shows that Institoris's attitude towards charismatic religious women was in fact characterized by fascination, rather than by anxiety. As this chapter demonstrates, as far as Institoris was concerned women's frightening proclivity to witch-craft and the admirable experiences of ascetic women mystics were two sides of one, singularly somaticized and emotional understanding of the female nature.

DOMINICAN FRIARS AND EMBODIED FEMALE SPIRITUALITY IN THE LATE MIDDLE AGES

To understand Institoris's interest in ascetic female mystics, we must take into consideration the attitudes of prominent Dominican writers towards women's affective piety in the late Middle Ages. Dominican preachers and anti-heretical polemicists began singling out mystically gifted women— whom they regarded as 'proofs' of Catholic doctrines to be employed for the confutation of heretical contentions—already in the thirteenth century.[12] Nonetheless, as Dyan Elliott demonstrates, during the troubled years of the Avignon papacy (1309–77), the public visibility of influential holy women such as Catherine of Siena (1347–80) and Birgitta of Sweden (1303–73) also came to be regarded as a threat to clerical authority.[13] When the pope's return to Rome, which both Catherine and Birgitta had actively sought to facilitate, was followed by the Great Schism (1378–1415), those who opposed the growing influence of women mystics blamed them for this calamity. An offensive against affective female piety was initiated during the Council of Constance (1414–18), and was spearheaded by the chancellor of the University of Paris, Jean Gerson (d. 1429), who censured all forms of spirituality that depended on the body and the senses.[14]

The preoccupation with women's somatic spirituality was especially pronounced among fifteenth-century Dominican preachers active in Swiss and German lands, such as Johannes Mulberg (d. 1414) and Eberhard Mardach (d. 1428).[15] Mardach asserted that the experiences of women who, when contemplating the crucifix, were rapt in ecstasy and claimed to relive the suffering of Christ's Passion, smacked of heresy.[16] In the same vein, the Dominican Johannes Meyer (1422–85) posited the ideal of an anonymous, communal life and of nuns' strict obedience to male Dominican officials as an alternative to women's ecstatic visionary spirituality and extravagant asceticism.[17]

The suspicion of women's affective mysticism found its most notable expression in the Dominican theologian Johannes Nider's work, *Formicarius* (*The Anthill*, c.1438).[18] Writing shortly after the trial and execution of Jeanne d'Arc (d. 1431), Nider (1380–1438) expressed an acute concern over the problem of discerning genuine mystical experiences from those that originated in diabolic fraud. Although he admitted that saintly women such as Catherine of Siena were capable of attaining high levels of religious devotion, Nider stressed the inherent depravity of the female sex.[19]

According to Nider, women's weak nature renders them more susceptible to the exploitation of astute men who lead them astray; it also turns some of them into deceivers. He pointed specifically to fraudulent women's reliance on visible bodily proofs of their contact with the divine, in order to convince their devotees of the authenticity of their apparitions. Nider recounted the story of Magdalena Beutler (1407–58), a Clarissan nun of Freibourg, who was famous for her spectacular raptures and once foretold the time of her death, but when the fixed date had passed and she remained alive, her deception was discovered.[20] He also reported the case of an unnamed ecstatic recluse who had prophesied that the wounds of the stigmata would appear on her body. When discussing the aftermath of this false prediction, Nider did not dismiss the possibility of saintly individuals' stigmatization, and referred to the reception of the stigmata by St Francis (d. 1226).[21] It is therefore telling that in his eulogy of St Catherine of Siena he mentioned neither her stigmatization, nor any of her other ecstatic or visionary experiences, although these were emphasized in her official *vita*, with which he was undoubtedly familiar.[22]

Nider's discussion of female nature profoundly influenced Heinrich Institoris's own treatment of women's greater propensity for witchcraft in his *Malleus*.[23] Nonetheless, a close reading of the entire corpus of Institoris's writings makes it clear that the two Dominicans' opinions concerning somatic female spirituality diverged significantly. In contrast with Nider and with other fifteenth-century Dominican authors such as Mulberg, Mardach, and Meyer, Institoris maintained that God favoured women's bodies as vessels through which he performed great miracles. This chapter argues that Institoris was no more fearful of female witches than he was of learned men who strayed from Catholic orthodoxy.[24] It proposes that the Dominican inquisitor construed the female heresy of witchcraft as an inherently physical, as opposed to doctrinal, heresy; but that, as far as he was concerned, women's holiness was also essentially embodied. Hence, he presented the visible manifestations of female devotion as the most effective means of warding off the doctrinal threats posed by male-led heterodox groups.

FEMALE WITCHES AND MALE HERETICS IN THE DEVIL'S SERVICE

The mere title of the most successful work that Institoris was to ever author, *Malleus maleficarum* (*The Hammer of [Female] Witches*), already expresses his notion that witchcraft is essentially a female crime, and an entire *quaestio* of the book is dedicated to explaining the predominance of women in the diabolic sect of witches. Institoris argues that the crime of witchcraft is primarily the result of women's inability to restrain their passions. He contends that women are by nature not only physically, but also intellectually and morally weaker than men. Reiterating medieval medical views, he presents women's carnal appetite as far greater than that of men and argues that it is, in fact, insatiable. Women's inability to keep their lasciviousness within proper boundaries, he asserts, is the main reason for their predominance among members of the diabolic sect of witches.[25]

The *Malleus* affirms that women's minds are also naturally more impressionable than the minds of men, and are therefore more ready to receive the influence of a disembodied spirit. This contention is based on the presumption that, because of their cool and moist bodily humours, women receive impressions more easily, retain them better, and are less capable of critically evaluating them than are men.[26] Institoris acknowledges that not all the impressions that women uncritically receive have a diabolical origin. As a matter of fact, he remarks that pious women actually use the quality of their greater impressionability *well*, noting that women 'are by nature more easily impressed upon to receive revelations through the impression of the disembodied spirits, and when they use this temperament well, they are very good, but when they use it badly, they are worse'.[27]

Scholars have often underscored the first part of this contention, dismissing Institoris's assertion that women tend to be either very good or extremely evil as mere rhetoric.[28] However, Institoris's praise of women's supernatural experiences in the works that he published after the composition of the *Malleus* indicates that his acknowledgment, in this anti-witchcraft tract, of devout women's ability to become 'very good' when they receive the influence of a disembodied (divine) spirit was anything but rhetorical. Furthermore, whereas the infamous inquisitor doubtlessly held that witchcraft was a predominantly female heresy, he assumed that men were the ones primarily guilty of doctrinal heterodoxy.[29]

Institoris's first extant published work is a short treatise that he wrote against the Dominican Archbishop Andrea Jamometić of the Craina (d. 1484), who attempted to summon a Church council in Basel.[30] The *Epistola contra quendam conciliistam archiepiscopem videlicet Crainensem* (*Epistle against a certain Conciliarist Archbishop, namely Archbishop of the Craina*), which Institoris completed in 1482, is a virulent attack on Jamometić. Stressing the menacing threat posed by the Dominican archbishop, the

Epistola attests to Institoris's preoccupation with men who espoused heretical Conciliarist views.[31]

In the *Tractatus novus de miraculoso eucharistie sacramento* (*A new tract concerning the miraculous sacrament of the Eucharist*), which the witch-hunter issued in Augsburg in 1493—seven years after the publication of his *Malleus*—he condemned the doctrinal errors of Berengar of Tours (d. 1088), another man who had been accused of heresy.[32] In a subsequent publication, the *Tractatus varii contra errores adversus eucharistie sacramentum exortos* (*Various tracts against the errors appearing against the sacrament of the Eucharist*, 1496), Institoris explained that all European heterodox groups originated with intellectual male founders, who rebelled against the church and withdrew from it to form their own sects. In this work, the friar once again decried the doctrinal errors of Berengar, alongside the views attributed to the thirteenth-century heretic Guido Lacha of Brescia, and of several other, unnamed, male heretics.[33]

In the *Opusculum in errores 'Monarchie'* (*Small work against the errors of the 'Monarchia'*), which Institoris published in Venice in 1499, he censured the heretical views of yet another learned man, the renowned jurist Antonio de' Roselli (1381–1466), who had challenged papal supremacy. In this work, Institoris reiterated his anti-Conciliarist notions and labelled as a heretic any man who wished to detract from the pope's absolute authority and power, either in spiritual or in temporal matters. Moreover, he associated Roselli with other notorious heterodox men, notably with the philo-Hussite 'Waldensian bishop' Friedrich Reiser (d. 1458).[34]

Institoris was certainly aware of women's attraction to contemporary heretical groups, such as the one led by Reiser in Strasburg.[35] In fact, in 1480 he was personally involved in interrogating the female followers of Johannes Molitoris (d. 1482), a canon of St Moritz in Augsburg suspected of having administered communion daily, in an unorthodox manner, to a group of lay devotees.[36] Nonetheless, in the polemical works that he published Institoris strove to downplay women's presence in dissenting religious groups. As far as he was concerned, doctrinal heresy, which involved learning, preaching, or writing, was unequivocally a male affair; as such, it was radically different from diabolic witchcraft, which he presented in his writings as an inherently female heresy.

Shortly after the publication of the *Opusculum*, Pope Alexander VI (r. 1492–1503) appointed Institoris inquisitor and papal nuncio of the Kingdom of Bohemia, which in those years included Bohemia, Moravia, and Silesia. The pope charged the indefatigable friar with prosecuting members of the Hussite sects that flourished in these regions, and espe-cially the group known as the Bohemian Brethren (*Unitas fratrum*) or 'Pikarts', who had split off from the Utraquists a few decades earlier, and whom Catholic polemicists regarded as a Waldensian offshoot.[37] By early 1501 Institoris had settled in Olomouc, the bishopric see and administra-tive centre of Moravia, where on 20 April he published his most influ-ential attack on religious dissent, *Sancte Romane ecclesie fidei defensionis clippeum adversus Waldensium seu Pikardorum heresim* (*A shield to defend the Holy Roman Church against the heresy of the Pikards or Waldensians*).[38] The *Clippeum* was out of print within a year of its publication, and Institoris issued a second edition in Olomouc on 20 March 1502. Of the Dominican inquisitor's seven published works, the *Clippeum* was second in popularity only to the *Malleus*,[39] and in the early sixteenth century it circulated widely in Central Europe.[40]

In the *Clippeum*, Institoris presents the Bohemian Brethren as a het-erodox group that is intimately linked to witches, because both sects form part of the diabolic conspiracy to undermine the church. The Alsatian friar argues that whereas the Devil uses (female) witches to perform demonic deeds, he relies on (male) heretics such as the Bohemian Brethren for spreading heterodox doctrines that weaken the Christian faith.[41] While this gendered division of labour reflects Institoris's presumptions about women's greater propensity to witchcraft, it also attests to his enduring fear of the menace posed by heterodox men and male-led heretical groups.

Institoris contends that the Bohemian Brethren learned their heretical doctrines while being demonically possessed, a possession that had clear visible signs.[42] He provides the readers of his *Clippeum* with a detailed description of the process during which the Brethren obtain their demonic doctrines. According to the Alsatian friar, those who wish to join the heretical sect have to attend a Catholic Mass and renounce the Christian faith by asserting that everything the priest says is a lie. They then stand with their mouths open and await flies that would enter them. Once they had swallowed a fly, heretics who had previously been illiterate immedi-ately know how to read.[43] The description of how the heretics gain their demonic knowledge is reminiscent of the notion—formulated in Nider's *Formicarius* and reiterated in the *Malleus*—that recruits to the witches' sect learn the diabolic arts by drinking a potion made from the flesh of unbaptized babies. Since Institoris was careful to distinguish the male-led sect of the Bohemian heretics from the predominantly female sect of witches, though, he refrained from accusing the Brethren of cannibalism, preferring instead to emphasize the connection between their heterodox knowledge and flies, a *topos* that can be traced back to early Christianity.[44]

DEVOUT RELIGIOUS WOMEN AGAINST FRIGHTFUL HERETICS

Institoris contrasted the feigned holiness of the Bohemian heretics with the genuine sanctity of three Italian women who were still alive at that time. These were the Dominican tertiaries Colomba of Rieti (1467–1501), Stefana Quinzani (1457–1530), and—most importantly—the acclaimed stigmatic Lucia Brocadelli of Narni (1476–1544), with whom Institoris first established ties in 1500, when he visited her in Ferrara on his way from Rome to Olomouc.[45] An *instrumentum publicum* that was drafted in Ferrara on 2 March 1500 indicates that Institoris was present during an inquisitorial examination that certified the authenticity of Brocadelli's miraculous stigmatization, and which was conducted at his request.[46] In the *Clippeum*, the Alsatian inquisitor recalled his visit to Ferrara, and remarked that seeing Brocadelli's bleeding stigmata wounds had such a profound emotional effect on him that he actually knelt down and kissed them.[47]

Institoris dedicated more than twelve pages of his *Clippeum* to a detailed discussion of the spiritual experiences of Brocadelli, Quinzani, and Colomba of Rieti, presenting the mystical gifts of these three holy women—rather than the preaching powers of saintly friars or priests—as the most valuable means of warding off the doctrinal threats posed by male-led heterodox groups. He argues that as members of the female sex, deprived as they are of the capability to critically evaluate the images that influence their minds, women can actually reach a perfect degree of *imitatio Christi*. In this manner, thinking of Christ's Passion during prayer had such an impact on Brocadelli's mind that she received the signs of the stigmata on her own members. Similarly Quinzani, who every Friday used to contemplate a crucifix, entered a state of ecstasy, in which she physically relived the suffering of Christ's Passion and death on the Cross. Finally, contemplating the real presence of Christ in the host consecrated during Mass had such a profound impression on Colomba of Rieti's mind that she immediately fell into a mystical rapture.[48]

Institoris provided his readers with two documents that authenticated the supernatural experiences of the Italian mystics, namely a notarial document attesting to the examination of Lucia Brocadelli's stigmatization in 1497 and another one certifying Stefana Quinzani's ecstasies of the Passion from the same year. These texts were followed by a letter that the inquisitor had received from Ercole I d'Este (1431–1505), duke of Ferrara, in the course of his visit to northern Italy, in praise of the divine gifts of Brocadelli, Quinzani, and Colomba of Rieti. Duke Ercole's letter ends with the affirmation that the Italian mystics' miraculous experiences alone 'suffice as a proof for the truth of the faith of the Holy Roman Church' (*sufficiant in approbationem veritatis fidei sancte Romane ecclesie*).[49] Institoris, who published Ercole's letter in his anti-heretical tract, evidently shared the duke's admiration for the three holy women.

Although the Dominican demonologist was doubtlessly familiar with the writings of early fifteenth-century Dominican authors such as Nider, who warned of the potential diabolic origins of the flamboyant manifestations of affective female piety, he entirely ignored their caveats. In fact, in discussing the somatic holiness of the three Italian Dominican tertiaries, Institoris disregarded the possibility of diabolic fraud and expressed unqualified credulity in the authenticity of their mystical experiences. Resuming the support of visionary and ecstatic women that had been favoured by thirteenth- and fourteenth-century Dominican friars involved in the struggle with heresy, Institoris praised the Italian mystics not only in writing, but also in a public disputation that he held in Olomouc. In this disputation, Institoris strove to convince the leaders of the Bohemian Brethren that Catholicism was the only true faith, by arguing that God manifested his powers by the miraculous deeds of pious Italian women whose embodied experiences imitated the suffering of Christ's Passion and crucifixion.[50] Thomas of Prelouc (Tůma Přeloučký, 1435–1518), who participated in the disputation, later described it in a letter addressed to Lord Albrecht of Sternberg (or Šternberk, d. *c.*1530).[51] His remarks are worth quoting at length:

Herr Doktor, the old inquisitor of the heretics, told me in Olomouc, when I was visiting him with my comrade, that there were some [persons] of such wonderful holiness in Italy. He also told me about the female sex, that in Italy some sisters in the cloisters were leading such holy lives as has never been heard of since the beginning of the world—neither before the Law [of Moses], nor under the Old Law, nor under the New Law until our own times. Neither Abraham, nor Moses nor any of the other Prophets nor even John the Baptist, of whom the Lord himself gave witness that no holier man born of a woman had appeared, nor even the Virgin Mary nor the Lord her son, nor any of the apostles, were anything in holiness compared with these women. None of those mentioned was so holy that he neither ate nor drank for six or eight years and yet lived and did not die, while only receiving the Body of God, like one of these sisters [namely, Colomba of Rieti]. Furthermore, not one of the saints, except for the monk [*sic*] Francis, bore on his body the marks of the wounds of the Passion of the son of God like another sister [Lucia Brocadelli]—wounds that are renewed every Friday in her saintly body, until blood flows from them. ... The prayers of such holy persons are known and trusted before God. When they pray, God the Lord hears and gives victory.[52]

The tone of this letter makes it clear that the Bohemian Brethren jeered at Institoris's overt attempts to propagate the fame of the Italian holy women in Moravia. To counter their ridicule, the inquisitor published his last known work, which was titled *Stigmifere virginis Lucie de Narnia aliarumque spiritualium personarum feminei sexus facta admiracione digna* (*Deeds of the stigmatic virgin Lucia of Narni and of other spiritual persons of the female sex that are worthy of admiration*). A pamphlet of nine unpaginated leaves, the *Stigmifere* was issued in Olomouc on 16 September 1501 and several other editions soon appeared in print. Institoris himself published a German translation of the *Stigmifere* in Olomouc, and an abridged Latin rendition and its German translation were both printed in Nuremberg, also in 1501. Another abbreviated German edition was published in Strasburg in 1502.[53]

The title page of the Strasburg edition is adorned with a woodcut attributed to the artist and printer Bartholomäus Kistler (d. 1525) and depicts three scenes from Quinzani's ecstasy of the Passion, as described in all versions of the pamphlet.[54] In this woodcut, hints of flames at the contours of Quinzani's figure indicate that she is undergoing an ecstatic rapture, and she appears so absorbed in her spiritual experience that she does not seem to notice the demons who attempt to scourge her. The woodcut's unusual iconography has led art historians to surmise that it depicts an episode of demonic possession.[55] However, readers familiar with the pamphlet's contents surely realized that the female figure portrayed in the title page was the holy woman Stefana Quinzani, battling with her demonic tempters. Whether or not Institoris was involved in selecting this particular image for the Strasburg pamphlet cannot be determined, but the image was undoubtedly in line with his own view of pious women mystics as the mirror image of fearsome diabolic witches. Whereas the latter were to be hated for knowingly entering a pact with the Devil, the former inspired religious devotion by heroically resisting demonic attempts and by vanquishing the Evil One with their unyielding faith.

The *Stigmifere*'s various Latin and German editions rehearsed some of the information about Quinzani, Brocadelli, and Colomba of Rieti that already appeared in the *Clippeum*. Institoris also had the full texts of several documents that had been sent to him from Ferrara incorporated into the *Stigmifere*. These included a lengthy poem, titled *Carmen theocasticon de Lucia Narniensis tercii habitus Cherubici Dominici virgine stygmifera* (*A saintly-godly poem about the stigmatic virgin Lucia of Narni of the Third Order of the Seraphic Dominic*). Written by an unknown Italian humanist, the poem was never published in the Italian peninsula, and the text that Institoris published in Olomouc is its only known version. The *Carmen* is the earliest text known to date to describe in detail the mystical raptures that preceded Brocadelli's reception of the stigmata, and the first account in praise of her stigmatization ever to appear in print. It features lengthy monologues attributed to Brocadelli herself, and recounts her rapturous visions just before and immediately after the miraculous occurrence in 1496, thereby providing a unique testimony of this Dominican tertiary's spiritual experiences.[56]

Another text that Institoris published in the *Stigmifere* was a letter penned by Duke Ercole d'Este's son, Cardinal Ippolito d'Este (1479–1520). In his missive, the cardinal expressed his astonishment at the miracle of Brocadelli's stigmatization, and affirmed, 'What am I saying? [that] with these holy wounds and admirable stigmata, which He suffered in His own body for the redemption of humanity, Jesus Christ transformed Himself into a virgin woman.'[57] This statement alluded to the portrayals of both Francis of Assisi and Catherine of Siena as saintly individuals who were transfigured into Christ at the moment of their stigmatization. Just like St Francis and St Catherine, Brocadelli was united to Jesus in soul and body, becoming one and the same as Him. Nonetheless, in the cardinal's letter it is not the holy woman who is being transformed into Christ; rather, the Saviour is the one being transformed, as He turns Himself into a live female virgin. This affirmation contrasted with the predominant late medieval notion that Jesus had been incarnated as a man, and not as a woman, because the male sex was the more honourable one.[58] Remarkably, although Institoris omitted other sentences from Ippolito d'Este's missive when he incorporated it into the *Stigmifere*, he decided to leave this astounding statement intact.[59] Hence, by publishing the cardinal's letter, the infamous witchhunter propagated the notion that a live woman should be revered as a reincarnated Christ.

The inquisitor who attacked women's unbridled emotionality in the *Malleus*, then, also viewed women's inability to restrain their religious devotion as a gendered trait that enabled them to become one with Christ, in a mystical union to which no man could aspire. Betraying no fear of women's supernatural powers, Institoris's documented fascination with their bodies can also not be reduced solely to a chaste friar's hatred of female sexuality, and clearly goes beyond simple categorizations. While there can be no doubt that he assumed women to be more carnal than their male counterparts, Institoris perceived diabolic witchcraft and female holiness as two sides of the same coin, both closely related to the gendered specificity of the female body, and to women's inability to control their emotions.

CONCLUSION

The entire corpus of Institoris's works makes it clear that his anxiety over women's greater proclivity to witchcraft went hand in hand with his profound admiration for the traditional features of somatic female spirituality, which he in turn valued as the ultimate proof confuting erroneous beliefs. Fearful of the persistence of male-led heretical groups at the turn of the fifteenth and sixteenth centuries, the adamant inquisitor placed his hopes in the emaciated bodies of ascetic women mystics. His publication of the *Clippeum* and the *Stigmifere* as part of the campaign that he led against the Bohemian Brethren indicates that his promotion of Italian holy women was based on the same gendered presumptions as his configuration of diabolic witchcraft in the *Malleus*. As far as the Alsatian demonologist was concerned, the very qualities that rendered wicked women more susceptible to meddling in witchcraft could turn devout women into the privileged conduits for divine revelations that confirmed the tenets of Catholicism. Institoris construed the fear-provoking female heresy of witchcraft as an inherently physical, as opposed to doctrinal, heresy; yet the sanctity of devout women in his own times, which he not only openly admired but also actively propagated, was also inherently embodied. Furthermore, it was in the uncontrollable affective piety typical of saintly female mystics that he placed his hopes for warding off the Devil's conspiracy to spread hetero-doxy and undermine Christendom. As Institoris argued in the *Malleus*, unrestrained emotionality was essentially a female trait; but it could turn contemporary women not only into wicked witches, but also into reincarnated Christs.

NOTES

1. Behringer, '*Malleus Maleficarum*', 717–23. In 1487, Institoris added a foreword to the book, in which he presented the *Malleus* as co-written by himself and by his fellow inquisitor Jakob Sprenger (c. 1436/38–1492). The work has subsequently been attributed to both Dominicans, but in the last three decades, it has been definitively established that Institoris was its sole author (ibid.).
2. Rob-Santer, '*Malleus Maleficarum*', 155–72.
3. Williams, 'Demonologies', 74; Broedel, 'Fifteenth-Century Witch Beliefs'.
4. Jerouschek, '500 Years of the *Malleus Maleficarum*', xxxi–xxxvii. See also Roper, 'Witchcraft and the Western Imagination', 121–8.
5. Broedel, *The Malleus Maleficarum and the Construction of Witchcraft*, 177–9.
6. See Delumeau, *La peur en occident*, 308, 322–3; Camerlynck, 'Féminité et sorcellerie', 13–25; Jerouschek, '500 Years of the *Malleus Maleficarum*', xxxvii.
7. For the influence of these radical feminist writings on perceptions of early modern witch-hunting outside academia see Rowlands, 'Witchcraft and Gender', 450–3.
8. Dworkin, *Woman Hating*, 134–6.
9. Broedel, *The Malleus Maleficarum and the Construction of Witchcraft*, 167–84, quotation at 180.
10. Stephens, 'Witches Who Steal Penises', 496.
11. See Elliott, 'Physiology of Rapture', 172–3; Klaniczay, 'Miraculum and Maleficium', 64–5; Vauchez, 'Between Virginity', 359; Caciola, *Discerning Spirits*, 274–319.
12. McNamara, 'Rhetoric of Orthodoxy', 9–27.
13. Elliott, *Proving Woman*, 180–93, 297–300.
14. Elliott, 'Flesh and Spirit', 28–31.

15. Schiewer, 'Auditionen und Visionen', 289–317. On Mulberg's life see von Heusinger, *Johannes Mulberg*.
16. Williams-Krapp, '*Dise ding sint dennoch nit ware zeichen der heiligkeit*', 61–71; Williams-Krapp and Ulla Williams, 'Dominikaner im Kampf', 427–46.
17. See Hamburger, *Visual and the Visionary*, 444–59; Poor, *Mechthild of Magdeburg*, 141–51.
18. Elliott, 'Physiology of Rapture', 167–8.
19. Klaniczay, 'Learned Systems', 58–62; Caciola, *Discerning Spirits*, 317.
20. Nider, *Formicarius* [*c*.1475], lib. 3, cap. 8. On Beutler see Klaniczay, 'Process of Trance', 9–14.
21. Nider, *Formicarius* [*c*.1475], lib. 3, cap. 11.
22. See Herzig, *Christ Transformed into a Virgin Woman*, 107–8.
23. Bailey, 'Feminization of Magic', 120–1.
24. This argument is further elaborated in Herzig, *Christ Transformed into a Virgin Woman*, on which the brief treatment of Institoris's attitude towards female spirituality in this chapter draws.
25. Institoris (Kramer), *Malleus maleficarum*, ed. Mackay [2006], vol. 1, 282–94 (lib. 1 quaest. 6); English translation in ibid., vol. 2, 111–25. For a perceptive reading of this section of the *Malleus*, see Brauner, *Fearless Wives and Frightened Shrews*, 31–49.
26. Cf. Maclean, *Renaissance Notion of Woman*, 42; Bornstein, 'Spiritual Kinship and Domestic Devotions', 176.
27. Institoris, *Malleus Maleficarum*, ed. Mackay, vol. 2, 116 (Latin original in ibid., vol. 1, 285).
28. See for example Broedel, *The Malleus Maleficarum and the Construction of Witchcraft*, 176.
29. Herzig, 'Flies, Heretics and the Gendering of Witchcraft', 51–80.
30. On Jamometić see Burckhardt, *Erzbischof Andreas von Krain*; Schlecht, *Andrea Zamometić*; Petersohn, *Kaiserlicher Gesandter und Kurienbischof*.
31. Institoris, *Epistola contra quendam conciliistam archiepiscopem* [1482]. For the responses to Institoris's attack on Jamometić see Numagen, *Tertia editio invectiva responsalis* [1657], 422–425.
32. Institoris, *Tractatus novus de miraculoso eucharistie sacramento* [1493], unpaginated.

33. Institoris, *Sermones de corpore Christi* ..., in *Tractatus varii* [1496], pars 1, sermo 1; Ibid., pars 2, sermo 13; ibid., pars 2, sermo 17. See also idem, *Tractatus erroneus*, in *Tractatus varii*.

34. Institoris, *Opusculum in errores* [1499], 12ᵛ and passim.

35. In his last anti-heretical work, Institoris dryly notes that a woman who numbered among Reiser's female followers was burned at the stake with him: Institoris, *Sancte Romane* [1501], 69ʳ, 106ᵛ. However, he perceived the woman merely as a follower of the male heretic Reiser, whom he presented as the main culprit. See de Lange, 'La fin tragique', 12–18. In the two other works in which Institoris discusses Reiser's death at the stake, he completely disregards the public execution of his female follower.

36. The protocol of Institoris's proceedings against Molitoris was published in Koeniger, *Inquisitionsprozess*, 5–57. See also Schröder, 'Tägliche Laienkommunion', 609–29.

37. See Cegna, 'I valdesi di Moravia', 392–95; Müller, 'Bohemian Brethren', vol. 2, 214; Audisio, *Waldensian Dissent*, 73–6; Cameron, *Waldenses*, 148–50. For an analysis of the doctrinal differences between the Waldensians and the Bohemian Brethren see ibid., 226–31. Augustinus Moravus, who issued a tract against the Bohemian Brethren, also associated them with the Waldensians: Moravus, *Tractatus de secta waldensium* [1500], sig. a 2ʳ. On Institoris's presentation of the Bohemian 'Waldensians' see Molnàr, 'Autour des polémiques antivaudoises', 115–36.

38. Schnyder, *Malleus Maleficarum. Kommentar*, 64–7; Říčan, *History of the Unity of the Brethren*, 91–4.

39. Herzig, 'Witches, Saints, and Heretics', 43.

40. Zeman, *Hussite Movement*, 99; Vobr, *Catalogus librorum*, vol. 2, 248–52.

41. Institoris, *Sancte Romane ecclesie* ..., 88ʳ.

42. Ibid., 10ᵛ, 14ᵛ–15ᵛ, 88ʳ. On the Brethren's heterodox views see Holeton, 'Bohemian Eucharistic Movement', 42–3; idem, 'Church or Sect?' 21; Atwood, *Theology of the Czech Brethren*, 179–81. That heretics who disseminated erroneous doctrines were, in fact, demonically possessed was a widely held view; see Goodich, *Miracles and Wonders*, 23.

43. Institoris, *Sancte Romane ecclesie* ..., 15ᵛ.

44. Herzig, 'Flies, Heretics and the Gendering of Witchcraft', 51–80.

45. Institoris, *Sancte Romane ecclesie* ..., 18–22ʳ, 50ʳ, 78ʳ–79ᵛ.

46. Two copies of this *instrumentum publicum* are preserved in the Archivio Generale dell'Ordine dei Predicatori, Rome, Sez. XIV, lib. GGG, Pt. I, cc. 332^r–332^v and cc. 333^r–335^v.

47. Institoris, *Sancte Romane ecclesie* ..., 79^v. This passage has been noted in passing by Riezler, *Geschichte der Hexenprozesse*, 101; Schnyder, *Malleus Maleficarum. Kommentar*, 64.

48. Institoris, *Sancte Romane ecclesie* ..., 10^r, 18^r–22^v, 50^r, 78^r–79^v.

49. Ibid., 22^v.

50. As noted in the later account of the disputation in Camerarius, *De ecclesiis fratrum* [1605], 96.

51. On Thomas and his ties with Albrecht of Sternberg see Brock, *Political and Social Doctrines*, 230–1.

52. Thomas of Prelouc's letter of 10 April 1502, cited (in German) in Schnyder, *Malleus Maleficarum. Kommentar*, 71–2.

53. Two additional versions in Latin, followed by a Castilian translation, were printed in Seville and in Valladolid in 1502. On the publication and propagation of this pamphlet see Herzig, *Christ Transformed into a Virgin Woman*, 157–271; for a critical edition of the *Stigmifere*'s original Latin version see ibid., 293–320.

54. *Wunderbarlithe* [*sic*] *geschichten* [1502?]), title page.

55. See Dupeux (ed.), *Gravure d'illustration en Alsace*, 22. Because of the unusual iconography of its title page, the pamphlet is also included in a survey of German publications dealing with demonic and divine possession: Blackwell, 'German Narratives', 250.

56. Herzig, *Christ Transformed into a Virgin Woman*, 191–227, 313–20.

57. A copy of Cardinal Ippolito d'Este's letter of 24 July 1501 is kept at the Archivio Storico Diocesano, Ferrara, fondo Santa Caterina di Siena, busta 3/25 (*Processi della Beata Lucia da Narni*). The letter was published in Institoris (ed.), *Stigmifere virginis Lucie de Narnia* [1501] (unpaginated).

58. See Gibson, 'Could Christ Have Been Born a Woman?' 65–82. In the *Malleus*, Institoris echoed this notion when he concluded his discussion of women's greater propensity for witchcraft by expressing his gratitude to the Almighty for privileging the male sex and affirming that God, who had been born and had suffered on behalf of humankind in the guise of a man, preserved men from the nefarious crimes of witches (Institoris, *Malleus maleficarum*, ed. Mackay, vol. 1, 292). For the increasingly positive attitude towards female

spirituality that the inquisitor expressed in the subsequent treatises that he published see Herzig, *Christ Transformed into a Virgin Woman*, 74–6, 123–36.

59. On the discrepancies between the cardinal's original letter and the version that Institoris published in the *Stigmifere* see Herzig, *Christ Transformed into a Virgin Woman*, 175–7.

CHAPTER 3

The Cruelty of Witchcraft: The Drawings of Jacques de Gheyn the Younger

Charles Zika

During the first decade of the seventeenth century, the renowned Dutch painter and printmaker Jacques de Gheyn II designed and drew a whole series of images depicting witchcraft. From the mid-1590s when de Gheyn moved to Leiden, he had directed his artistic skills to the recording of closely observed nature and the exciting new world of scientific observation and discovery. Much of this came to fruition in the delicate and exquisitely crafted watercolours that he painted in subsequent years—of flowers, plants, insects, fishes and crabs—all specimens meant to represent the art of nature. But de Gheyn was also fascinated by the nature of the imagination, and especially the fertile and deluded human imagination. His scenes of witchcraft, of which he produced many, were depictions of what many contemporaries imagined witches did: overturning divinely ordered nature; crippling communities through natural disasters such as storms, lightning, and avalanches; harvesting and cooking up body parts for their ghastly magical salves. Yet he applied to these witchcraft images

C. Zika
Centre for the History of Emotions, University of Melbourne

© The Author(s) 2016
L. Kounine, M. Ostling (eds.), *Emotions in the History of Witchcraft*, DOI 10.1057/978-1-137-52903-9_3

the same technical skill and virtuosity as he did to images representing the natural world.[1]

It is generally acknowledged that de Gheyn's witches drew on a long sixteenth-century iconographical tradition, and in particular the work of Hans Baldung Grien and Pieter Brueghel the Elder.[2] But a novel element in the depiction of witchcraft by de Gheyn is its harsh and cruel nature. The figures of de Gheyn's witches display hard and unfeeling features, they exercise terrible violence on the bodies of their victims, and they are often located in dank subterranean surroundings that reek of mutilation and death. A graphic example is a little-known drawing entitled *Three Witches in an Archway* (Fig. 3.1). The drawing depicts three elderly witches, partly naked and displaying their distended breasts, fully engaged in extracting something from the nose or mouth of a corpse. The corpse, clearly a male body, is draped over one woman's knee, with the head cradled by the left hand of another, as the women perform what seems to be the grisly task of harvesting body parts, presumably for one of their malefic potions. The women are intent on their task, their united purpose emphasized by the central woman's hands on the shoulders of her two companions. Their gaze is fixed on their victim, and their wrinkled faces, sunken eyes, the rigid line of their noses, and unkempt hair communicate a lack of compassion in their work. The whole scene is enshrined in a series of archways, providing a strong sense of an underground location where evil acts can be carried out secretly, hidden from the eyes of others.

Many of these features can be found in de Gheyn's other witchcraft images. In a drawing held by the Ashmolean (Fig. 3.2), a group of witches are located in a vaulted cellar with a male corpse that has been disembowelled.[3] A large shadow cast by one of the witches pointing at the corpse helps to create an ominous atmosphere. On the ground there are bones and a human skull, a frog that has been nailed to the floor; in the background there is a desiccated hand (the so-called Hand of Glory procured from a criminal who has been hanged), and mounted on the wall a horse's skull. In a drawing customarily called *Witches' Kitchen* (Fig. 3.3), which depicts a group of witches around a boiling cauldron assisted by monstrous spirits, a curious procession of female seductresses takes place, as well as other activities visible through archways, while an opening in the floor reveals a dead male body whose hand is being gnawed by rats.[4] In *Witches Cooking Body Parts* (Fig. 3.4), de Gheyn depicts a naked witch with distended breasts about to tip different human body parts displayed on a plate in front of her—a hand, a foot, two small human heads—into a cauldron stirred by one of her colleagues. A series of sketches (Fig. 3.5)

Fig. 3.1   Jacques de Gheyn II, *Three Witches in an Archway*, c. 1600–1610, pen and brown ink, National Gallery of Victoria, Melbourne, Felton Bequest, 1923 (1278.779–3)

Fig. 3.2   Jacques de Gheyn II, *Witches at Work in an Arched Vault*, 1604, pen and brush with brown and grey ink, Ashmolean Museum, Oxford

Fig. 3.3   Jacques de Gheyn II, *Witches' Kitchen*, 1604, pen and brush with grey and brown ink on grey paper, Staatliche Museen Berlin, inv. 3205

Fig. 3.4 Jacques de Gheyn II, *Witches Cooking Body Parts*, pen and brown ink, brown wash and black chalk on buff paper. Metropolitan Museum of Art, New York

Fig. 3.5 Jacques de Gheyn II, *Attributes and Creatures of Witchcraft*, *c.*1610, pen and brown ink, black chalk on buff paper. Fondation Custodia, Collection Frits Lugt, Paris

drawn from an album including different kinds of subjects, were clearly drawn as studies for later works and include frogs with exaggerated sexual organs and two examples of a book resting on a skull.[5]

De Gheyn's images stand out in the iconography of witchcraft for the extreme cruelty and violence they display in recording witches' ghoulish and murderous acts. This is further underlined by the harsh appearance of the witches themselves. Almost all de Gheyn's witches bear similar physical features. Their skin is wrinkled, their eyes sunken and steely, their mouths downturned, their noses severe, their chins small and pointed. This gives them a shrunken and mean appearance, and contrasts strongly with younger women with more rounded features that appear in many of de Gheyn's compositions, as well as—much more rarely—in some witchcraft images.[6] I would suggest that the ensemble of figures in *Three Witches in an Archway* (Fig. 3.1) constitutes a kind of counter-Pietà image, in which the cradling of the head of the corpse by the hands of these witches references the intense grief and compassion felt by the Virgin for her dead son in scenes of the *Pièta*, or by all the holy women who weep for Christ after he is brought down from the cross in scenes generally entitled *The Lamentation*. The witches by contrast represent savage cruelty and lack of compassion in the aggressive manner with which they invade and violate the body of their male victim. This designates them as merciless and godless, implacable enemies of the fundamental virtues underpinning a Christian society and order.

The purpose of this chapter is to ask how we might explain this emphasis on the cruelty of witchcraft in de Gheyn's work. The witches' appearance in de Gheyn's drawings has only been approached indirectly by previous scholars. In Linda Hults's fine study, she describes the depiction of de Gheyn's witches as the result of 'a profoundly naturalistic artist paradoxically captivated by the fantastic and the grotesque'.[7] Ultimately, Hults sees these figures as 'melancholic or otherwise deranged', 'a distinct type of woman' that inverts the Calvinist ideal of women in the Northern Netherlands, yet is also 'susceptible to the weaknesses that most afflicted the weaker sex'.[8] Hults's argument is a subtle and complex one, which takes into account the complexity of de Gheyn's whole oeuvre and the range of his styles. But I would argue that there is no paradox in a seventeenth-century artist depicting the natural world he observes around him, and at the same time the imaginative world of witchcraft that is being widely circulated through pamphlet accounts, demonological treatises, medical and judicial works, sermons, and not least, visual imagery.

It is important to stress that these witches are not meant to represent the actual social profile of witchcraft in the later sixteenth-century, older village women marginalized for one reason or another by their neighbours in what is an increasingly competitive and patriarchal society—even if de Gheyn presents them in highly realistic fashion, drawing on the skills he applies to his depictions of the natural world. We can see the same descriptive skills in his depiction of frogs and other animals. But in his images of witches, the whole context—the location, the particular framing of the activities, the paraphernalia and weird monstrous animals or shapes, the witches' bodies in semi-undress as they go about their macabre tasks—makes it quite clear that de Gheyn's brilliant technical skills are being employed not to depict observable physical and social reality, as in his portraits and other images made 'from life', but to render authentic depictions of an imaginative reality. De Gheyn's intellectual and cultural environment in Leiden and later in The Hague was populated with medical and legal men such as Johannes Heurnius, the rector and professor of medicine at the University of Leiden, and Gerard Turning, professor of law at the same university. These men held decidedly sceptical views of the powers of witches, as propagated by Johann Weyer and Reginald Scot a number of decades earlier.[9] To posit that de Gheyn was engaged in a contrary process of stereotyping the cruel violence of witches in order to further their prosecution finds little support in his biography. Rather, he was depicting what was claimed to be the reality of witchcraft in the works of writers like Jean Bodin and Nicolas Rémy.

That leaves open the question as to why de Gheyn's witches embodied a harshness and cruelty that went well beyond that found in witchcraft images created by previous artists. Part of the answer would seem to lie in de Gheyn's understanding of the human imagination and its links to contemporary views about the operation of the humours. As Claudia Swan has argued, de Gheyn's images depended on contemporary demonological theories of the deluded imagination as the source of witchcraft belief; and artists' frequent choice of these subjects was based on their capacity to facilitate the exercise of the imagination. Indeed, she argues further that de Gheyn's images give expression to the pictorial basis of the human imagination and that they represent visual forms of imaginative illusion. We know that a number of lawyers and physicians at the University of Leiden at the turn of the seventeenth century—such as a group of professors of law and medicine who followed the Utrecht jurist Arnoldus Buchelius—believed that *melancholia* was responsible for much of the behaviour associated with witchcraft. In assessing whether witches can float, in a response to the Court of Holland concerning the validity of the water test in witch trials, these professors argued that accused witches who floated did so because the inner organs of melancholics were more hollow than those of others, and they could therefore become more aerated, especially if they held their breath in fear.[10]

The humours also play a key role in the thought of the so-called witch-craft sceptics, such as Johann Weyer, the physician from the Duchy of Cleves, and Reginald Scot, the English country gentleman and MP for New Romney in Kent.[11] The illusory visual hallucinations of witchcraft produced by troubled minds, argued Weyer in *On the Tricks of Demons*, are produced by the Devil tampering with the humours:

> Moreover, we can clearly recognize that the [witches'] pact is illusory and that it is fabricated and confirmed by the deceptive appearance of a phantasm, or a fancy of the mind or the phantastical body of a blinding spirit; it is therefore of no weight. The deception occurs either when an apparition of Satan's choice is cunningly imposed upon the optic or visual nerves by the disturbing of the appropriate humours and spirits, or when a whistling, or whispering, or murmuring, corresponding in form to the corrupt image, is aroused in the organs of hearing by the evil spirit's art.[12]

The analogy of this process is what happens in dreams, according to the *Malleus Maleficarum*.[13] The motion of blood and the humours causes images stored in the memory to be brought to the imagination as mental apparitions and then experienced as dreams. But in the case of people who are awake, the Devil can directly stir up and excite 'the internal spirits and humours', and in that way bring particular images to the imagination, which people then judge to be true. However, this is the work of a distorted imagination. Moreover, what is critical to Weyer's work, as Claudia Swan has clearly shown, is that it specifically links the witchcraft illusions produced by distorted imaginations to the symptoms of melancholy. Whereas the connection between the melancholic imagination and witchcraft had been suggested by others previously, such as by Lucas Cranach in his Melancholy painting series,[14] it was Weyer who argued that melancholy corrupts the imagination, and makes it vulnerable to the intervention of the Devil, who fills 'drousy minds' with the illusions of witchcraft.[15] Reginald Scot took Weyer's claims about melancholy and witchcraft a step further in his *Discoverie of Witchcraft* of 1584. Scot attributed the illusions of witchcraft to nothing other than imaginations distorted by melancholy, produced in turn by the onset of menopause.[16] Whereas belief in the Devil's power to create phantasms in the minds of witches was widespread in the literature of witchcraft from the late fifteenth century, an overt link between witchcraft and a disturbance of the humours, and in particular the influence of the melancholic humour, was very much reliant on the claims of Weyer and Scot.[17]

Key figures in the transmission of Weyer's and Scot's ideas of witchcraft in the Netherlands were Thomas Basson and his son Govert Basson, who translated *The Discoverie of Witchcraft* over the seven years 1602 to 1609, and published it in Leiden in 1609.[18] Thomas Basson was a Leiden printer and owner of a bookshop there, as well as a member of the University from 1595; Govert was de Gheyn's brother-in-law from 1608, when he married de Gheyn's sister, Anna. The work was dedicated to the trustees of the university and the burgomasters of the city, and we know that it was well received. It was precisely in the years that the Bassons were translating Scot that de Gheyn, a close associate of many of the university's members during his residence in Leiden from 1595, was creating his many witchcraft drawings. In *c.*1610 he completed a very large pen, ink and wash drawing, clearly intended to be a representation of witchcraft, that would be widely disseminated as an engraving—the so-called *Preparation for the Sabbath*, probably incised by Andries Stock, and published by Nicolas de Clerck (Fig. 3.6), as were a number of his other drawings at this time.[19] The print and drawing include many of the iconographical details found in the earlier drawings. The two witches turned to the viewer in the centre of the print exhibit similar harsh and shrunken facial features as many of those in his earlier drawings; there is the large book from which the witches read their magical recipes resting on a skull; severed heads, skulls and numerous bones litter the ground; female buttocks and a leg in a ditch are suggestive of a corpse; a monstrous, hybrid winged toad and salamander mounts the rocky crag struck by lightning; smoke billows out from a cauldron, creating heavy thick clouds dripping with dark substances; wild witches ride their brooms, goats, and other monstrous creatures through the dark smoke and vapour in the company of other flying hybrids. It is difficult to imagine that these images by de Gheyn were not influenced by Scot's claims about the fantasies of witchcraft, which were being translated by his in-laws and read, promoted, and discussed by the university circles in which he had moved just a few years earlier.

Fig. 3.6   Andries Stock (?) after Jacques de Gheyn II, *Preparation for a Witches' Sabbath*, *c*.1610, engraving. National Gallery of Victoria, Melbourne, Felton Bequest, 1925 (1658–3)

Nevertheless, to explain the gruesome violence that is at the heart of many of de Gheyn's images of witchcraft simply in terms of distorted imaginations and fantasies seems inadequate. Of all the possible ways to communicate fantasy, such cruelty is hardly required. The reaction to such gruesome images seems more akin to what Reginald Scot wrote with respect to the content of some witches' confessions:

> As touching that horrible part of their confession, in the league which ten-deth to the killing of their own and others children, the seething of them, and the making of their potion or pottage … it is so horrible, unnaturall, unlikelie, and unpossible; that if I should behold such things with mine eies, I should rather thinke myself dreaming, drunken, or some waie deprived of my senses; than give credit to so horrible and filthie matters.[20]

The capacity of de Gheyn's witches to carry out such deeds would seem to be related to another aspect of their humoral and (as we would express it) emotional dysfunction—their hardness, their inability to feel compassion, their inability to cry. As Ulinka Rublack has argued, the proper functioning of the early modern body depended on the 'flow' of the humours.[21] The flow of humours, as well as that of other fluids and juices, it was believed, had to be kept open and not be blocked. It had to be regulated. A lack of flow led to dryness, too much flow to 'anxiety, sorrow, anguish and fear'.[22] Insufficiently warm blood, infected or bad blood, and consequently blood that did not flow adequately, would also produce a heavy and sinking heart, a state of deep melancholy.

Dryness was also the reason witches could not weep, and in some witch trials the absence of tears was even considered one of the sure signs of being a witch. In 1615, for instance, an Anna Gruober of Alpirsbach was accused of weeping without shedding a single tear and this aroused strong suspicion that she was a witch. In 1628, a bailiff claimed that the eyes of the wife of Jacob Küfer had not 'sweated' at her husband's funeral—which showed that she had not a drop of Christian blood, for otherwise 'she would have been moved to tears'.[23] In a case involving a Maria Schramm in Württemberg in 1653, the magistrates noted that the woman never cried, never shed a tear. Together with her evil face, this was a sign of her stubbornness and raised serious suspicions among her interrogators that she was guilty, even if she was ultimately cleared.[24] In a trial in the town of Ebingen in 1622 the magistrates commented on Anna Gebhard, who was accused of stealing Conrad Streich's manhood: 'It has been indicated by the same people that [Anna Gebhard] has a bad reputation ... she defended herself extremely suspiciously with immodest words ... Not a drop of water left her eyes which is an evil sign.'[25] The inability of witches to cry was given a scientific explanation in a medical report prepared for a witch trial in Rothenburg ob der Tauber in 1652.[26] Natural tears come from the water in which the heart swims. The heart sends the water into an artery leading to the head, and from there to the eyes, and in this way 'tears then arise'. But a witch could not be moved to tears—because her heart was dried up, as was the water surrounding it. This hardness and dryness of the heart, a physiological basis for the inability to be moved psychologically and spiritually, closed the heart to the heat that God provided to drive the blood, the flow which created tears.

Similar claims about witches are found in some witchcraft treatises, but by no means in all. The dispute between Reginald Scot and Jean Bodin as to whether the inability to cry in the process of interrogation is a sign that the accused is a witch, drew on the arguments made over a century earlier in the *Malleus maleficarum* [*The Hammer of Witches*] (1487).[27] This work claims, on the basis of 'the accounts of trustworthy men and the teaching of our own experience', that a judge can identify a witch during interrogation if the accused person is urged or even compelled by conjurations to shed tears, but despite this is unable to do so. The text even provides the form of conjuration to be used:

> I conjure you by the loving tears shed on the Cross for the salvation of this world by Our Saviour, the Lord Jesus Christ, and by the most passionate tears of His Mother, the Most Glorious Virgin Mary, which were sprinkled over His wounds at eventide, and by all the tears shed here in this world by all the Saints and the Elect of God, from whose eyes He has now wiped every tear, that you may shed tears to the extent that you are innocent, but not at all if you are guilty.[28]

Heinrich Kramer (Institoris) goes on to claim that experience has shown that the more witches are conjured during interrogation, the less they can cry—even if they cry later in the presence of their guards. For the Grace of Tears is a gift from God to the penitent, that according to St Bernard, can reach heaven and achieve seemingly impossible things.[29] For this reason it is strongly resisted by the Devil. The authors of other witchcraft treatises of the sixteenth century are by no means all of the same view. Nicolas Rémy and Francesco Maria Guazzo, for instance, seem to make no reference to this claim; while such a prominent authority as Martin del Rio explicitly rejects the views of Kramer, Grillando and Bodin.[30] The way weeping could be used by witches to trick their interrogators, and the distinction made between the inability to weep during interrogation, but to weep at other times—both of which points were referred to in the *Malleus*—clearly made it extremely difficult to argue that the inability to weep was an unambiguous proof of witchcraft. Likewise, in King James' *Daemonologie*, tears are referred to as a means by which women can dissemble; yet witches' inability to shed tears is also considered analogous to the 'supernatural sign' by which water refuses to allow their bodies to sink.[31] As many examples from witch trials demonstrate, the inability to weep frequently remained a cause at least for serious suspicion.

The debate about witches' tears was so important because tears were a sign of compassion, and compassion in late medieval Christianity—continuing through to the sixteenth and seventeenth centuries, even if in modified form—was an emotion central to Christian experience and devotion.[32] The most important cultural script for the modelling and exercise of that compassion was the image of the Virgin Mary, filled with sorrow at the foot of the Cross on which her son's body hung, or totally distraught and overwhelmed by grief as his body was lowered, sometimes to be held in her arms, and ultimately to be laid in the tomb. That grief and distraction was primarily expressed, in visual depiction at least, by means of a variety of gestures: by the violent throwing up of arms, by the ringing of hands, by contorted facial features transfixed in sorrow. Such grief also formed the basis of the poignant images of the *Pietà*, the depiction of the sorrowing Virgin supporting the dead body of her son draped across her lap or lying her feet, which gained huge popularity from the fourteenth century onwards. From the second quarter of the fifteenth century, however—just at the time when the witch began to emerge on the discursive and judicial landscape of Europe—this compassion was being more intensely and more frequently expressed through the shedding of tears. Felix Thürlemann and others have explained this appearance of painted tears at the time of Rogier van der Weyden, first as an expression of inner suffering and compassion, and second and most importantly, as a model for Christian viewers to shed their own tears in response. The development achieves a high aesthetic point with the painting of Roger van der Weyden's *Descent from the Cross* in about 1430, in which all but three of the figures are depicted weeping, and the Virgin is shown with tears streaming down her face (Fig. 3.7).[33]

Rogier van der Weyden's *Descent from the Cross* vibrates with deep emotional energy, and, even as it hangs in a secular aesthetic space in the Madrid Prado, it continues to exert an extraordinary impact on its viewers. If we are to believe the great Italian painter Michelangelo Buonarroti, Netherlandish paintings such as this one also drew tears from the eyes of its beholders in the past.[34] While van der Weyden's teacher Robert Campin seems to have been the first to focus on depicting tears in scenes from Christ's Passion, his pupil gave these tears volume and movement as well as a subtle transparency which focused the viewer's attention. The tears that stream down the Virgin's face clearly represent the deep grief of Christ's mother and the intense compassion she feels for the suffering of her son as she passes into unconsciousness. But she is also a model for the feelings of those around her, as well as the external viewers gazing on the scene, exemplifying the compassion that needs to be felt by the true Christian for the suffering Christ. John and the two women above her in the painting, and on the right Mary Magdalen and probably Nicodemus, also exhibit eyes red from weeping, the tears very visible on their faces. Van der Weyden's *Descent from the Cross* is possibly the most powerful of

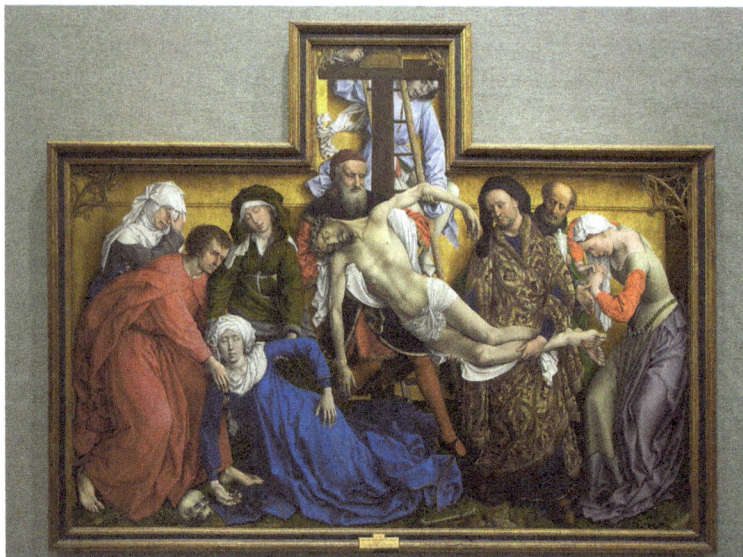

Fig. 3.7   Rogier van der Weyden, *Descent from the Cross*, before 1443, oil on panel. Museo Nacional del Prado, Madrid, Spain. © Peter Barritt/Alamy Stock Photo

numerous paintings and prints, especially produced in the Netherlands, that identified tears—of compassion and of compunction—as emotional scripts to be imitated and performed by devout Christians. 'After 1430', writes Thürlemann, 'it was scarcely possible to dam up the river of tears in Netherlandish painting'.[35]

Susan Karant-Nunn has demonstrated how central the shedding of tears was to late medieval religious culture. In a collection of Holy Week sermons, the *Passionale*, preached by the Passau cleric Paul Wann in 1460, the congregation is encouraged to weep with the tears of Christ, to feel his suffering, to be 'inwardly moved to sympathy', in order that their hearts be softened.[36] Wann urges his hearers to observe Christ's Passion 'with weeping eyes'. And the models for them are those who wept as Christ's body was taken down from the cross—his mother, John, the holy women, Longinus, Joseph of Arimathea, Nicodemus. But not only did they weep: 'The sun and the curtain in the temple mourned and cried, and even the hard cliffs did, and finally the angels in heaven (Isaiah 33:7).' These sermons were clearly meant to exemplify the compassion and compunction which is at the heart of Christianity and to move the faithful to express this physically, emotionally and spiritually through the pouring out of tears and the softening of hearts. Karant-Nunn has also shown how this emotional emphasis on weeping continued well beyond the Reformation in numerous sermons and devotional handbooks, especially those written by members of the new Jesuit and Capuchin orders, such as Peter Canisius, Philipp Kisel and Martin von Cochem. While Lutheran and Reformed preachers and authors tended to moderate the emphasis on Christ's torments and his mother's sorrows as a model for Christian compassion, a significant number of Lutherans such as Johannes Brenz and Cyriakus Spangenberg nevertheless focused on Christ's Passion as a means of instilling inner repentance.[37]

Images of the *Lamentation of Christ* became a common pictorial subject in Netherlandish art during the fifteenth and sixteenth centuries. Numerous artists drew on the strong affective piety of late medieval devotional literature and made it visible by techniques pioneered by Robert Campin and Rogier van der Weyden in the first half of the fifteenth century. As in a later painting by the Leiden workshop of Lucas Leyden's teacher, Cornelis Engebrechtsz (Fig. 3.8), a group comprised of the Virgin, the Apostle John, Mary Magdalen, one or two holy women, and frequently as here, Nicodemus and Joseph of Arimathea, were commonly depicted clustered around the dead body of Christ taken down from the cross, the body extended across the canvas to ensure that devotees could gaze on Christ's five wounds.[38] Christ's head rests in the hands of either one of the holy women or St John; all are overcome by grief and compassion for Christ's suffering and death, their intense emotion made highly visible by the bleary, reddened eyes of his disciples and the tears that stream from their eyes.

We have no evidence that Jacques de Gheyn painted or engraved any such scene. In 1596–98, when he was still in Leiden, he was involved in engraving and printing a Passion series after Karel van Mander, with his apprentice engraver, Zacharias Dolendo.[39] This included a scene of Christ's entombment, which Dolendo engraved and de Gheyn printed. The print includes some of the emotional pull typical of Lamentation images, but its small size (15.3 × 10.6 cm) does not allow one to discern details very clearly. But there is little doubt that de Gheyn would have been very familiar with this subject through the work of his fellow artists, especially in the southern Netherlands. My suggestion is that de Gheyn's

Fig. 3.8   Cornelis Engebrechtsz and Workshop, *Lamentation with Donors & Saints*, *c*.1510–15 (with kind permission of the Archbishop of Southwark, London. Photo credited to Imran Sulemanji)

drawings of witches as cruel and hardened women engaging in extreme and savage violence, and known to be incapable of shedding tears, were figured as the very antithesis of examples of Christian virtue depicted in scenes of *The Lamentation* or *Pièta*. They were godless, unable to shed tears, for they lacked the compassion performed by Christ's selfless sacrifice on Calvary and that of his mother and all Christians in response. De Gheyn's drawing of *Three Witches in an Archway* (Fig. 3.1) represents a counter-Lamentation or counter-*Pièta* image, figuring these tearless witches as women who give vent to their merciless savagery by violating and mutilating Christian bodies rather than feeling compassion for them.

Why so many of the witchcraft scenes created by Jacques de Gheyn II in the first decade of the seventeenth century display levels of cruelty unlike that in the work of any earlier artist, and possibly of any artist through to the nineteenth century, is a complex question. Certainly, as Claudia Swan has argued, de Gheyn's oeuvre oscillates between a scientific naturalism rooted in early modern descriptive science and the fantastic imagery of witchcraft derived from theories of the imagination and creativity. To have and give expression to such interests is by no means contradictory or paradoxical, however, especially in European societies at the turn of the seventeenth century. Indeed, de Gheyn makes use of his technical mastery of representing nature in his witchcraft images, thereby rendering them more physically real and enabling a more powerful impact on viewers. The gruesome activities of de Gheyn's witches, their association with extreme violence and death, their location in dank underground environments, and their harsh physical features communicate their otherness.

From considerations of de Gheyn's social and intellectual environment and networks, however, we can be reasonably certain that these images were not created as descriptions of any kind of social reality. It is most likely that de Gheyn subscribed to a general scepticism about the social reality of witchcraft as propounded in the works of Johann Weyer and Reginald Scot, and therefore these images were pictorial representations of claims made about witchcraft by those concerned to prosecute it and by those accused of witchcraft as well. For it would seem that de Gheyn's images were meant to project the beliefs of witches themselves, whose imaginations had become disordered through compromised humoral and blood flows. Their external physical appearance reflected the internal ravages of melancholy, in turn the result either of natural disposition and practice, or of the direct or indirect intervention by the Devil. But the

Devil finds little place in de Gheyn's witchcraft imagery. The terror lies in the practices of witchcraft and in the bodies of the witches themselves. The argument of this study is that a lack of humoral flow that resulted in a deluded and disordered imagination is necessary yet insufficient to explain de Gheyn's novel focus on the extreme cruelty of witchcraft. The additional element required is the claim that witches not only imagine that they engage in such horrific practices as harvesting body parts and cooking them up for their potions, but that they lack the essentially human and Christian qualities of compassion and empathy that would prevent them from even imagining themselves as engaged in such practices. The inability to weep, to feel the sufferings of others, makes witches heartless and godless; and this is what transforms witchcraft into a terrifying threat both for individuals and the broader community. However, it bears repeating that de Gheyn's works do not describe an actual social threat. His drawings are works of artistic imagination, highly contrived and deliberately wrought artefacts, associative rather than narrative in the way they create meaning. The threat they imagine for witchcraft rests not only on what witches do and do not do, but also on what they feel and do not feel.

NOTES

1. For de Gheyn, see Swan, *Art*; Swan, 'Diagnosing', 60–82; Swan, '*Preparation for the Sabbath*', 327–39; Kok, 'Jacques de Gheyn II', 248–81, 370–96; Kok, Leesberg, and Luijten, eds, *The de Gheyn Family*; van Regteren Altena, *Three Generations*; Hults, *The Witch as Muse*, ch. 5; Meij, ed., *Jacques de Gheyn II*; Löwensteyn, 'Helse hebzucht', 241–61; Judson, *The Drawings of Jacques de Gheyn II*.
2. Swan, *Art*, 125–6, 133–4, 144–8.
3. Hults, *Witch as Muse*, 160–1; Löwensteyn, 'Helse hebzucht', 247–8; van Regteren Altena, *Three Generations*, I, 87–8; II, 86.
4. Swan, *Art*, 144–8; Hults, *Witch as Muse*, 158–60; Löwensteyn, 'Helse hebzucht', 245–6; van Regteren Altena, *Three Generations*, I, 87–8; II, 85–6.
5. Hults, *Witch as Muse*, 162–3; Swan, *Art*, 23, 125; Meij, ed., *Jacques de Gheyn II*, 71; van Hasselt, ed., *Le Héraut*, 46–8.
6. See Fig. 3.3, for instance. Also Löwensteyn, 'A Singular Design', 81–5.
7. Hults, *Witch as Muse*, 148, 160.
8. Ibid., 171–5.

9. Swan, *Art*, 157, 164–8.
10. Swan, *Art*, 165–6. For Buchelius, see also Pollmann, *Religious Choice*, 117–23.
11. For Scot, see Almond, *England's First Demonologist*.
12. Weyer, *Witches, Devils, and Doctors* [1991], 173. The passage is cited in Swan, *Art*, 178.
13. See Kramer, *Malleus maleficarum* [1486], Part I, Q. 7; Kramer, *The Hammer of Witches* [2009], 178. It is significant for the argument of this essay that Montague Summers's translation of this passage omits the role of humours in the dream process, wrongly translating *'propter commotionem sanguinis et humorum'* as 'caused by the flow of blood'; and this translation is reproduced in Swan, *Art*, 177.
14. Zika, *Appearance of Witchcraft*, 99–109, 217–18; Zika, *Exorcising Our Demons*, 333–74.
15. Swan, *Art*, 175–82. On Weyer and Scot, also see Swan, 'Diagnosing'.
16. Scot, *The Discoverie of Witchcraft* [1584], Book III, chs. ix–xi.
17. For the case of the physician Paré, see Paré, *On Monsters and Marvels* [1982], chs. 29–30.
18. Scot, *Ondecking van Toverij* [1609].
19. Here I follow the argument concerning de Gheyn's intention to have the drawing engraved, in Swan, *'Preparation for the Sabbath'*, 331–7. For the print, also see Swan, *Art*, 136–43; Hults, *Witch as Muse*, 160–4; Meij, ed., *Jacques de Gheyn II*, 71–2; van Regteren Altena, *Three Generations*, I, 87–8; II, 84–5.
20. Scot, *Discoverie*, Book III, ch. xii.
21. Rublack, 'Fluxes', 1–3.
22. Ibid., 2, citing a Breslau barber-surgeon in 1582, who attributed this state to bewitchment or a sudden shock in his youth.
23. For these two cases, Rublack, 'Fluxes', 6–7.
24. Kounine, 'Gendering of Witchcraft', 305–6.
25. Ibid., 313.
26. Rublack, 'Fluxes', 7–8.
27. Scot, *Discoverie*, Book II, chs. v–vii; Bodin, *On the Demon-Mania of Witches* [1995], Book 4.1, 4.4; Kramer, *Malleus maleficarum*, Part III, Introduction. Bodin also refers to Paolo Grillando, most likely his *Tractatus de hereticis et sortilegiis* [1536]—written c.1524.
28. Kramer, *The Hammer of Witches*, 549–50.

29. For the Grace of Tears or Gift of Tears, see Nagy, *Le don des larmes*.
30. Del Rio, *Disquisitionum magicarum* [1600]. Del Rio, *Investigations into Magic* [2000], 208–9 (Book 5), just as Bodin before him, refers to Jakob Sprenger as the author of *The Hammer of Witches* (*Malleus maleficarum*); however it is now widely accepted that its sole author was Heinrich Kramer (Institoris).
31. James VI and I, *Daemonologie* [1597], Book III, ch. VI; Normand and Roberts, eds, *Witchcraft in Early Modern Scotland*, 424.
32. See especially McNamer, *Affective Meditation*; Karant-Nunn, *Reformation of Feeling*.
33. Thürlemann, 'Paradoxical Rhetoric', 53–75; Campbell, 'New Pictorial Language', 32–47.
34. De Hollanda, *Diálogos em Roman*, 76–7, cited in Thürlemann, 'Paradoxical Rhetoric', 53–4.
35. Thürlemann, 'Paradoxical Rhetoric', 57.
36. For this and below, Karant-Nunn, *Reformation of Feeling*, 20–6. See also Karant-Nunn's discussion of the *Mirror of the Passion of Our Lord Jesus Christ* by the Nuremberg citizen, Ulrich Pinder, at 220–5.
37. Karant-Nunn, *Reformation of Feeling*, chs. 2, 3, 5. See also the examples of a renewed culture of highly emotional devotion to the Passion among Lutheran noblewomen in the seventeenth century, such as Henrietta Katharina von Gersdorf, at 235–8. For the growing literature on tears and weeping in medieval and early modern Europe, see also Gertsman, 'Introduction' and Christian, 'Provoked Religious Weeping', xi–xx, 3342; Dixon, *Weeping Britannia*, chs. 1–4; Patton and Hawley, eds, *Holy Tears*.
38. Vogelaar et al., *Lucas van Leyden*, 12–17.
39. Filedt Kok, Leesberg and Luijten, *The de Gheyn Family*, Part I, 79–87.

CHAPTER 4

Satanic Fury: Depictions of the Devil's Rage in Nicolas Remy's *Daemonolatria*

Laura Kounine

Witchcraft, women, lust, and envy have been inextricably linked in the history and imagination of early modern witchcraft. Witchcraft was overwhelmingly associated with women both in the contemporary imagination and in our current popular notions about the early modern witch today. Visual representations of witchcraft in the early sixteenth century, such as paradigmatic depictions by Hans Baldung Grien, show witchcraft as female and eroticized (Fig. 4.1). The image of the early modern witch, moreover, was also associated with the figure of Envy (Fig. 4.2) as an old hag, gnawing at her own heart because her envy of others (and in particular, her envy of younger, more fertile, women) was literally consuming her.[1] The witch was shown as lustful and envious: she could be sensuous and eroticized, or dried up and haggard. But she was female, and she was driven by powerful emotions to destroy.

The most famous of early modern demonological treatises, the *Malleus maleficarum* (1486), made the first direct association between witchcraft and women. For its author Heinrich Institoris, most witches were women

L. Kounine
University of Sussex

© The Author(s) 2016
L. Kounine, M. Ostling (eds.), *Emotions in the History of Witchcraft*, DOI 10.1057/978-1-137-52903-9_4

Fig. 4.1 Hans Baldung
Grien, *Three   Witches*
(New Year's Sheet), 1514.
Albertina, Vienna

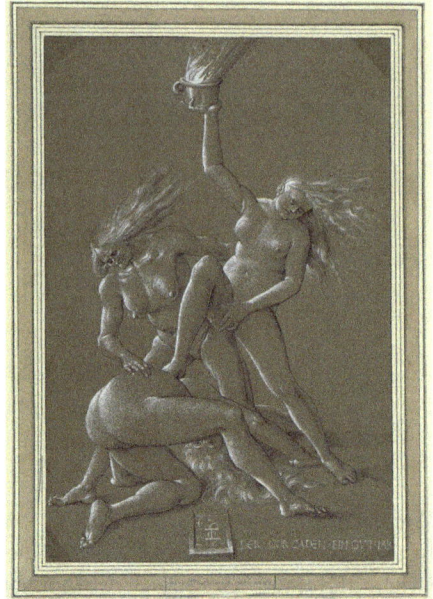

because 'everything is governed by carnal lusting, which is insatiable in
them'.[2] Women, according to Institoris, lacked intelligence, which meant
that they were more likely to renounce the faith; and they were driven by
passions and 'irregular desires' which meant that they inflicted acts of vengeance.[3] According to this argument, witches were female, and this was
due to their unbridled passions.

Stuart Clark, in his magisterial *Thinking with Demons*, further under-
lines the association in intellectual thought between witchcraft and women,
when he writes that it was 'literally unthinkable that witches should be
male'. Clark contends that early modern thinking was premised on a dual
classification system of binary opposites, in which the male–female divide
was hierarchically weighted so that men were correlated with positive values and women with negative values.[4] According to Clark, in this deeply
polarized view of the world, witchcraft was understood as an act of perfect
reciprocity, an act of inversion.[5] Thus, Clark argues, the (female) gender
of the witch is 'precisely what made the crime intelligible as the crime it
was perceived to be—an attack on society in collusion with a Devil who,
because of women's relative sinfulness and weakness, used him as agents'.[6]

Fig. 4.2 Georg Pencz, illustration for Hans Sachs, *Das Feinstselig Laster, der heymlich Neyd* (Nuremberg, 1534). (From *The German Single-Leaf Woodcut, 1500–1500*, 3:965)

In intellectual thought, according to Clark, the witch was always female by default.

This binary classification could only work, of course, when there were clearly defined and understood norms that witchcraft sought to invert. Clark maintains this was the case in the early modern period, and argues that demonology could thus be considered 'a powerful resource of early modern orthodoxy. It had the conservative effect of constructing and maintaining norms by portraying them in their demonic opposites'.[7] In this sense, Clark is firmly underlining the premise that witchcraft was the crime of the female 'other'.

In this chapter, I sketch out three interlinked points. First, I would like to challenge Clark's assertion that male witches, in intellectual thought, were 'literally unthinkable'. Second, in contrast to Clark's assertion that demonology promoted orthodoxy, I suggest that demonological texts were far more contradictory about what the witch was supposed to represent. Third, I probe the ways in which the emotional relationship between the Devil and the witch—if it was not, as I suggest, primarily based on the 'irregular desires' of women—could be understood. Using Nicolas

Remy's *Daemonolatria* as a case study to examine the interplay between the Devil, the witch, and emotions in intellectual thought, I suggest that the relationship between the Devil and the witch *was* primarily conceived of as an emotional relationship, but it was premised on the notion of a violent Devil, driven by jealousy and anger, to explain why people—both men and women—could fall prey to witchcraft. Rethinking the relationship between the Devil and the witch necessitates not only a revised understanding of the gendering of witchcraft—one that cannot be so neatly explained by gendered binaries—but also a reconceptualization of the emotional dynamics that underpinned early modern witchcraft beliefs.

It Was 'Literally Unthinkable that Witches Should Be Male'

Stuart Clark argues that, in elite belief, it was 'literally unthinkable … that witches should be male'.[8] Although Clark consistently and explicitly examines *thought* not reality, and concedes that *in reality* there was a minority of male witches, his argument is nonetheless flawed. Crucially, it is quite simply not true that demonologists did not conceive of male witches, as Rolf Schulte has shown.[9] 'In general', Schulte writes, 'learned discourse was relatively heterogeneous as regards the gender profile of the workers of magic'.[10]

Clark rightly indicates that many commentators have been misled about the misogyny of witchcraft writers by relying solely on extreme passages from Institoris's *Malleus maleficarum*.[11] Indeed, as Clark shows, the connection of witchcraft with women was more actively relied upon by those who were sceptical about the reality of witchcraft and opposed witchcraft persecutions, such as Johann Weyer.[12] But, as I will show, Clark fails to see that the demonological response to Weyer inspired a thorough airing of the possibility of male witches. Weyer's *De praestigiis daemonum*, first published in 1563, represented the first systematic opposition to witchcraft trials.[13] Indeed, where the most well-known demonologists—Martin Del Rio, Jean Bodin, Peter Binsfeld, Nicolas Remy—all discuss the possibility of male witches, Weyer directly associates witchcraft with women. Weyer argued that women's inherent weakness meant that they were prone to melancholia and self-delusion, while men, due to their intelligence, were immune to such delusions. He writes,

Since the so-called lamiae are indeed poor women—usually old women—melancholic by nature, feeble-minded, easily given to despondency, and with little trust in God, the Devil all the more gladly attaches himself to them, as being suitable instruments for him, and he insinuates his way into their bodies all the more easily, in order to confound their minds with various images.[14]

For Weyer, 'witches' were always women: 'sometimes because of the infirmity of age, but always because of the folly and weakness of their sex'.[15] Weyer thus deploys gender stereotypes as virulent as those adduced in the *Malleus*, albeit with the opposite intent—a focus on gender that sets him apart from those against whom he wrote. In contrast, for example, the Suffragen Bishop of Trier and Catholic demonologist Peter Binsfeld was influenced by the local trial of Dr Dietrich Flade, the city of Trier's wealthiest and most influential citizen. In the same year of Flade's execution in 1589, Binsfeld published his demonology, *Tractatus de confessionibus maleficorum et sagarum*, which played a crucial role in spreading ideas about male witches. Binsfeld believed that the sabbat included both men and women, and he emphasized that men were seduced by the Devil through the sins of greed, lust, and drunkenness. Rita Voltmer surmises that Binsfeld here intended to rebut the ideas put forward by Weyer.[16]

It thus comes as some surprise for Clark to argue that most demonological texts largely ignored the issue of gender. Clark does not suggest this is because the gender issue was irrelevant to these writers, but rather that witches should be female was such a self-evident truth they did not see the need to expand on it.[17] I will now turn to a case study of one such text, Nicolas Remy's *Daemonolatria,* to show that the gendering of witchcraft was discussed in ways that complicate the rigid polarizations upon which Clark rests his argument. Indeed, Remy's discourse is plagued with inconsistencies and contradictions which encourage us to view the 'witch' and the gendering of emotions as unstable and fluid categories, not clearly defined constructs. This in turn opens up questions about the unbridled passions that supposedly underpinned the early modern witch-hunts. If the witch was not a clearly defined other, even in demonological thought, then how can we understand the emotional landscape in which a woman or man could fall prey to witchcraft? Put another way, if witchcraft was not simply understood as a female crime in demonologies, then witchcraft cannot be explained simply as women's propensity to temptation, their lasciviousness, or their lack of understanding. Witchcraft was still an

intensely emotional crime in intellectual thought, of course, but historians' understanding of the emotions fuelling people's propensity to Satan's
servitude begs to be reformulated.

NICOLAS REMY'S *DAEMONOLATRIA*

Nicolas Remy and the duchy of Lorraine are almost synonymous, due to
the former's infamous demonological treatise *Daemonolatria*, first published in 1595, in which Remy claimed to have tried over 900 witches
during his tenure as *procureur-général* of the duchy.[18] Like other prominent demonologists of his time, Remy was a trained jurist.[19] Despite his
self-styled reputation as a fearsome witch-hunter, there is little evidence to
back up his claim that he was involved in the conviction of 900 witches.
Moreover, contrary to Remy's claims, as Robin Briggs points out, the
majority of the 144 witch trials directly discussed in the treatise would
not have been personally overseen by Remy himself. While Remy did hold
office for fifteen years, from 1591 to 1606, where he would have overseen
witch persecutions in his role as state prosecutor, the trials discussed by
Remy in his *Daemonolatria* were concentrated in the 1580s, with the last
trial in the treatise taking place in 1591. Remy was most probably reading
the trial records when he compiled his *Daemonolatria*.[20] The trials that he
discusses were thus mediated through the local judges, so that the reader
sees a combination of local understanding of witchcraft and 'intellectual'
analysis. The trials that Remy personally oversaw are especially vivid in his
accounts.[21]

First published in Lyon in 1595 in Latin, Remy's *Daemonolatria* was
issued the following year in Cologne and Frankfurt, again in Frankfurt
in 1597, and a German translation appeared in Frankfurt in 1598.[22] This
makes the *Daemonolatria* one of the most successful demonologies in the
Holy Roman Empire at the turn of the seventeenth century, possibly even
more so than the *Malleus maleficarum*, which, although well known in
intellectual circles, was not published in the vernacular but remained in the
original Latin, with the exception of one Polish edition in 1614.[23] Evidence
of the success of Remy's *Daemonolatria* beyond Lorraine and into the
entire southwest of the Holy Roman Empire can be found in references
of contemporary writings: Hans Jakob Christoph von Grimmelshausen,
the well-known German satirist, refers to Remy as the chief witness of the
witches' sabbat in his descriptions of such occurrences.[24]

The publication of Remy's treatise thus coincided with the height of the witch craze and was part of a plethora of demonological publications at this time, including del Rio, Boguet, Daneau, Binsfeld, and Bodin.[25] Remy's text was part of a growing genre and must be read in this context. Indeed, while these works are heterogeneous in style, they also borrowed heavily from each other, crossing confessional lines and making up a coherent body of work.[26] Like Bodin, for example, Remy's main objective was to refute Weyer through arguments drawn from the trials themselves.[27] He also sought to refute Weyer through the by now standard recourse to biblical texts and classical authors, which all demonologies drew on for proof of the reality of witchcraft. Weyer argued that witches were melancholic victims of the Devil, who, through their own insanity, simplemindedness and 'despondency', were deluded into believing that they were responsible for crimes they had not committed.[28] Remy acknowledged that ignorance may have led people to be duped by the Devil, but contended that this made them no less a threat to the public order and safety. Remy thus called for condemnation and punishment of witches, likening them to 'mad dogs'.[29] Yet we see that as demonologists and witch persecutors engaged with Weyer, they also became influenced by his work. Remy, for example, acknowledged the problem of ignorance in fostering witchcraft accusations, while Binsfeld listed an excess of sorrow as one of the causes for why people fell into witchcraft, a condition 'which is often found amongst women'.[30] Bodin, while condemning the work of Johann Weyer, mined his book for anecdotes and accounts when they could be useful and attempted to refute Weyer by claiming that women could not be afflicted by melancholy for the reason that they were cold and moist: melancholy, Bodin argued, was an illness that afflicted men, particularly learned men.[31]

Remy's text was more than merely a refutation of Weyer, however. Its main focus was on the everyday practices and misdeeds of witches.[32] Remy drew on a large body of witch trials to create a vivid prose.[33] As Briggs points out, Remy's work thus tells us much about popular beliefs based on the trials he presided over, but often falls rather short when it comes to sustained intellectual arguments on the nature of witchcraft.[34] Rather than viewing demonological texts as purely intellectual treatises, then, they can also be read, as Lyndal Roper argues, as part of a genre of entertainment, which inspired drama, art, and literature.[35] Jean Bodin's treatise on witchcraft, for instance, was translated just one year after its first publication in French by the German poet Johannes Fischart of Strasbourg.[36] Pierre de

Lancre used elaborate textual and visual imagery to describe the sabbat.[37] It is important in understanding the success of these works, especially Remy's immediate success in Germany, that we can identify how they may have been written and read.

The *Daemonolatria* thus serves as a problematization of Clark's work, which resists exploring the relationship between demonological writings and cultural practice.[38] Remy's treatise suggests that such a neat demarcation between beliefs and events might not be so simple or, indeed, desirable: while demonological treatises may have been aimed at an educated audience, they also could shed much light on popular beliefs and practices. Further, this text is also useful in challenging some of Clark's assumptions of the binary—and deeply gendered—nature of witchcraft. Remy—crucially—did not follow Clark's mandate that male witches were conceptually impossible. Rather, the first trial with which Remy opens his exposition was that of a man—a man who, in Remy's depiction, reminds us that the emotions motivating witchcraft went beyond the stereotypes of lust and envy.

THE DEVIL AND THE WITCH IN REMY'S *DAEMONOLATRIA*

Remy begins his *Daemonolatria* with the case of Claude Morèle:

> Namely that the evil fiend those / whom he cannot move through good / frequently knows how to bring them into danger and to frighten them. As Claudius Morelius (8 December 1586) [who] was convicted of magic / was asked / what had initially moved him the most / to subject himself to the evil fiend / he answered / how Satan could not have moved him with good words / until he threatened him with the murder of his wife and children / and had thus given him a fright.[39]

Claude Morèle maintained that he had not been seduced by the Devil's tempting words and promises. Rather, it was fear of what the Devil would do to his family that forced him to promise himself to the evil one. It was a chivalrous, if misguided, act on his part. Indeed, Morèle's defence seems to have rested on protecting his (male) honour:[40] he had not been seduced by comely words, and he had acted to defend his family. He was not a weak-minded individual, but instead had made the conscious decision to serve the Devil in order to save those who needed his protection. Of course, by leading his family into spiritual apostasy, Morèle failed in his duties as the patriarch and could thus be construed as a male 'other'. Crucially, however, his was not a feminized account of male seduction; if anything it was a highly masculine defence strategy, grounded in a gendered emotional regime of honour and protectiveness.

This short case study immediately challenges Stuart Clark's hypothesis on the gendering of witchcraft: demonologists *could* conceive of male witches, and even granted male witches precedence in the organization of their works. Moreover, the case challenges Lara Apps's and Andrew Gow's influential argument that male witches, when they were written about in intellectual treatises, were feminized. This raises the question, then: Was there a clearly defined male 'other' in early modern intellectual thought? Who were the male witches, and what did they represent? Did male witches also fall prey to the Devil due to their unbridled passions, and were these passions distinctively gendered? Rolf Schulte highlights this problem of definition and identification in his discussion of male witches in demonological texts. Significantly, Schulte asserts, where concepts of femininity were very clearly described in demonology, the concept of masculinity was founded instead on antonyms of female attributes (that is, their supposed moral, mental, and physical weakness). Thus demonological discourse on the Sabbat could conceive of male witches as having superior roles within this large confederacy.[41] Simultaneously, Schulte suggests, male witches could also be feminized—as Apps and Gow have argued—in that their personality features were considered feminine. Male witches could thus be understood as being both feminized and as performing 'male' roles of power and authority. But Schulte goes on to ask whether the witch-hunts did not 'serve, directly or indirectly, as a means of establishing new norms of gender ideals and asserting and publicizing these norms via the inclusion of men in witch trials?'—thereby suggesting that there were clear gendered codes on how male witches were expected to behave.[42] Although this is a tempting problematization, it seems to contradict Schulte's earlier suggestion that the male witch could fall into a number of different gendered categories. How can these trials then create gender norms when there is also the notion that no clear stereotypes of male witches existed?

The theme of threats of violence from the Devil is reiterated in further male witch trials discussed by Remy. Remy reports,

> Antoine Welch (Guermingen, 19 December 1589) said / the evil fiend threatened to wring his neck / if he did not agree to do that / which was

demanded of him / so that he was also not allowed to refuse him the slightest [request] / indeed he / kept him in fear the whole time / that he would at any moment wring his neck.[43]

The Devil sometimes became even more violent after the pact was made. Remy recounts,

> It was recounted by Kuno Gugnot (Altweiler, 2 January 1585) that he numerous times had been beaten almost to death by him / because he had either too late / or sometimes not even at all appeared at their gathering [Sabbath].[44]

In this way Remy used examples and anecdotes from witchcraft trials to build up drama.[45] His *Daemonolatria* thus came close to the vivid trial narratives that coloured early modern courts. We have already been told that the Devil in Lorraine was a highly violent creature. These details work to pique interest and create a dramatic account. Thus Remy tells us,

> But that he [the demon] had once brought him into the utmost danger and peril / namely that he once carried him through the air / held him over the river Moselle / and threatened to drown him at a dangerous place / if he did not agree / to bewitch and kill / Desiderius Galerius, with whom he was at enmity / which he soon after through constant pressure from the demon / carried out.[46]

Again, we are confronted by an image of a violent Devil; not one who seduces but compels by force. By threatening people's lives, the Devil of Lorraine *forces* witches to make a pact with him. Briggs corroborates this analysis, suggesting 'in Lorraine, therefore, the devil was not leading an alternative religion with an elaborate liturgy, but was an aggressive and punitive master who sought to exercise direct dominion over the followers whom he had cheated and virtually enslaved'.[47] Yet, the defence put forward of violence or threats issued by the Devil was not only the remit of men on trial for witchcraft. Women too used this as a defence. In this vein, Clark's assertion that demonology promoted and reinforced orthodox gendered emotional regimes simply does not hold true.

So Remy tells us of the case of Alexée Driget, who also maintained that the Devil's promises and fair words did not move her to make a pact with him. She only gave in to the Devil when he threatened her livelihood:

When the evil fiend was entirely unable to bring down Alexée Driget (10 November 1586) / he finally threatened her / that he would tear down the wall in her house / as then also shortly thereafter the same wall caved in.[48]

Did this mean that women were reverting to 'masculine' modes of defence by emphasizing their resistance to the Devil's comely words and promises and employing the rhetoric of violence instead? Not necessarily, but it does suggest that we should resist the temptation to characterize witch narratives along binary gendered lines. If Driget's defence did not automatically make her masculinized, then it follows that when men made recourse to the same defence strategies of women, they should not immediately be labelled 'feminized'.

Indeed, the discourse of threat and violence could also be framed in 'typically' gendered ways, with the Devil playing the role of the jealous (male) lover.

Yes / as will elsewhere be told / how they [demons] make a marriage / and hold a wedding / and how they can in no way tolerate / that another courts their lover / or has doings with her / just as it is amongst humans. Nicole Morèle said / as she became suitable for marriage / and so also other demons were around her at that time / she was often for that reason horribly beaten by her demon / namely that she had admitted those same [demons] / [her demon] had also threatened her / that he would treat her worse / if she did not abstain. When they come together at their Sabbat / it is regarded as a great sin / (as they generally all attest) / if the demon of one would touch the spouse of another / or solicit fornication. So maliciously do they know how to play the part of the jealous lover.[49]

This emphasis on the violent passion of the Devil seems significant. Interestingly, in Natalie Zemon Davis's *Fiction in the Archives*, 'jealousy' is a specifically female emotion called upon as a defence for murderous actions against adulterous husbands. Men, Davis contends, did not admit jealousy as an emotion in slaying their adulterous wives or their wives' lovers. Rather, 'honor and obedience were at stake for him, not demeaning jealousy'.[50] Indeed, excessive jealousy could suggest that a man was not fully in control of his emotions and thus irrational, a trait usually assigned to women. In Remy's description of the Devil, however, jealousy is conflated with violence and thus works to create a hyper-masculine, rather than feminized, image of the Devil, suggesting that jealousy can be both a feminizing act and a hypermasculinizing one.[51]

MALE AND FEMALE WITCHES IN REMY'S *DAEMONOLATRIA*

Despite the fact that male witches could clearly be conceived of in the *Daemonolatria*, Remy, like other demonologists, did still believe in and articulate the propensity of witches to be female rather than male. Indeed, the title of ch. 15 in the first book of Remy's *Daemonolatria* was '*That all kinds of people / of high and low standing / male and female persons / arrive at night at the assembly of the witches in large numbers: but the majority are women / for these same are more inclined to evil assaults.*'[52] His discussion of the propensity of witches to be women thus comes relatively late in his treatise; and although he picks up this point again, it is usually with the caveat that men too could be witches.[53]

In line with thinking of the time, Remy perceived women as the weaker sex, physically and intellectually inferior to their male counterparts. It was this feeble-mindedness, Remy surmised, that made women more susceptible to the temptations and deceits of the Devil. While the *Malleus maleficarum*—the most famous yet also least representative of all demonologies—emphasized the lasciviousness of women underlining their pact with the Devil, other demonologists, and significantly the sceptic Johann Weyer, stressed that it was women's simple-mindedness that led them to be duped by the Devil. Refuting Weyer's thesis that women who confessed to witchcraft were weak and delusional on account of their age and gender, Bodin suggested that female witches were, rather, physically strong and cunning, which is why they were able to withstand torture longer than men. However, women also lacked reason, which is why they had smaller heads, and were driven instead by their sexual appetite.[54] Peter Binsfeld, for instance, argued that women were particularly prone to becoming witches because of the weakness of their understanding and the stupidity of their sex.[55] According to Clark, Binsfeld 'offers women's greater despondency in tribulation and more angry desire for revenge'.[56]

Remy too reported that

> Barbelline Rayel (Blainville, 13 January 1587) said / there were far more women than men among them / since Satan can easier beguile women … So I myself find / that more women than men were charged in this. And it is also not without cause / that the wanton supporters are found more often among women / as there are healers / witches / soothsayers / *Vnholden* etc. … Fabius says / it is easier to believe / that a woman carries on with magic. Pliny says / that women have advantage in the art of magic.[57]

Remy argued that women were more likely to be the perpetrators of witch-craft, but this clearly in no way excluded men from the same. In Remy's study, for example, both men and women were ultimately compelled less by their own unbridled passions than by the violent passions of the Devil; indeed around a quarter of the witches mentioned in the *Daemonolatria* were male.[58] Both men and women described the Devil as violent, and attributed their fall to force, not seduction. Remy thus argues:

> Also veritably those that have been accused of magic / are not all female / nor old and decrepit beggars / rather Satan also has men under him / who surrender themselves in his service / even if indeed the same is not quite so common in men / as it is in women. So also several of them were engaged in this / of whom there are a great many / in whom this evil nature has long been inculcated / and they commonly became involved in it in their youth. Be that as it may / whatever they say / everyone knows that neither the female sex nor age can excuse oneself against the given law / ... And no wrongdoing can be excused under the pretext of human weakness. God the Almighty has commanded with emphatic voice and spoken / Be it man or woman among you / who has a familiar spirit by them / should be put to death / Leviticus. 20.[59]

Age, sex, or simply stupidity could thus render a human vulnerable to the Devil. Human weakness made easy prey for the Devil. Indeed, both Remy and Weyer agreed that ignorance was often the cause of witchcraft, the former suggesting that ignorance made easy prey for the Devil, and the latter purporting that ignorance and stupidity allowed for self-delusion. So we find this belief explicitly articulated by Remy:

> That one well knows with what deception / guile / cunning / and lies / he acts when he dares to bring them to fall: so that it is scarcely possible for anybody / to resist and guard himself against his evil deeds / especially / when age / and weakness of the female sex / as well as their country sim-plicity and crassness is added to this.[60]

CONCLUSION

For Remy, witchcraft was not simply deemed to be the domain of 'evil' women, rather it was a crime that could befall any human. There was no one clear representation of the 'witch', even in intellectual thought.

As we can see from this brief discussion of Remy, men could be also quite easily conceived of as witches. Not only could male witches be conceived of and prosecuted, but they could also be remarkably similar to female witches. This is not to say that they were inherently feminized, or took on female characteristics of weakness and feeble-mindedness, but that men and women could often share in the same conceptual framework of human weakness and fallibility. Male witches were not necessarily the negative 'other' to their sex, nor were they feminized. Women, too, could employ the rhetoric of force and violence to explain why they fell prey to the Devil, rejecting the usual seduction trope. These confessions did not make the women 'masculine', or suggest that they were subverting female norms. Rather, these tales highlighted the power and violence of the Devil, and the ease with which he could force or compel humans—both men and women—especially when simplicity, age, poverty, or lust led them to ignorance.

Far from 'promoting orthodoxy', as Clark asserts, these treatises highlight the inconsistency and fragility inherent in the category of the 'witch', the 'feminine' and the 'masculine'. As Remy shows very clearly, 'intellectual' thought could also be plagued with inconsistencies, and demonological works as a whole were not unified on what male and female witches represented. For this reason, we must challenge the idea that demonological literature can be thought to create and sustain norms for 'male' and 'female' behaviour in the real world. While intellectual thought of course contributed to constructing and maintaining gendered emotional regimes, there was far more ambiguity and contradiction in these literary texts on the gendering of witchcraft than Clark's analysis allows. Moreover, by unshackling the ties between witchcraft and women in demonological literature, we are forced to question whether early modern thought was in fact so wedded to the idea of women's unbridled passions—her stereotypically feminine insatiable lust and unappeasable envy—as the cause of their witchcraft. If both women *and* men could be conceived of as witches in demonological literature, this throws open our understanding of the emotional dynamics of fears surrounding witchcraft. Witchcraft was not solely the domain of the female sex; and male witches were not necessarily conceptualized in a feminized paradigm. Rather, men and women could fall prey to the Devil because of human weakness and because of the violence of the Devil.

NOTES

1. Roper, *Witch in the Western Imagination*, ch. 4, 'Envy', 91–100.
2. See Institoris, *Hammer of Witches*, trans. Mackay [2006], 122.
3. Schulte, *Man as Witch*, 99. See also Tamar Herzig's chapter in this volume for an explication and complication of Institoris's thinking about gender.
4. Clark, *Thinking with Demons*, 61, 66–7. See also Clark, 'Gendering of Witchcraft', 426–37.
5. Clark, *Thinking with Demons*, 13.
6. Ibid., 111.
7. Ibid., 29.
8. Ibid., 130.
9. Schulte, *Man as Witch*: see ch. 5, 'Men as potential witches in demonological texts'. On the gendering of witchcraft in Bodin's *De la démonomanie des sorciers* see Opitz-Belakhal, *Das Universum des Jean Bodin*, in particular ch. 5.
10. Schulte, *Man as Witch*, 146.
11. Clark, *Thinking with Demons*, 114–15.
12. Ibid., 117; Schulte agrees: *Man as Witch*, 141. See Weyer's *On Witchcraft*, ed. Kohl and Midelfort, trans. John Shea [1998], bk 6, ch. I, 257–8. Weyer's treatise was highly successful: there were at least six authorized Latin versions printed during Weyer's lifetime, three German translations by Weyer himself, at least six unauthorized German versions, and three unauthorized French versions. See Behringer, *Witches and Witch-Hunts*, 170–2. However, some historians such as Christopher Baxter, Leland Estes, and Sydney Anglo have suggested that Weyer's book was so confused and destabilizing that it may have actually done more to stimulate the renewal of witch trials than to hinder them. See Kohl and Midelfort, 'Introduction', in Weyer, *On Witchcraft*, xv–xxxii.
13. The book provoked a major dispute in several European languages, prompting Weyer to expand his Latin editions of his book (in 1564, 1566, 1568, 1577, and 1583) and to abridge his views for a German-reading public, with German translations published in 1566 and reprinted in 1567 and 1578. At the age of 15, Weyer went to study and work in the household of the mystical sceptic, philosopher, and physician, Heinrich Cornelius Agrippa of Nettesheim (1486–1535), and it is likely that Agrippa exercised a

major influence on Weyer. As early as 1510 in a draft of his highly regarded *De occulta philosophia*, Agrippa had attributed the errors of women accused of witchcraft to senility. See Kohl and Midelfort, 'Introduction', xv–xxxii.

14. Weyer, *On Witchcraft*, bk 6 ch. 8, 268. Weyer recommended for these women 'a sounder instruction in the chief doctrines of our Christian faith'.

15. Ibid., bk 6 ch. 27, 312. However, Opitz-Belakhal points out that Weyer also could conceive of men suffering from melancholia who were deceived by the Devil. See Opitz-Belakhal, *Das Universum des Jean Bodin*, 139.

16. Voltmer, 'Witch-Finders, Witch-Hunters or Kings of the Sabbath?' 82–3. See also Dillinger, *'Evil People'*, on Binsfeld and Flade.

17. Clark, *Thinking with Demons*, 117.

18. The independent duchy of Lorraine, separating the German Empire from the kingdom of France, contained both French- and German-speaking villages and persons.

19. Nicolas Remy (*c*.1528–1612) was *procureur-général* of Lorraine; Jean Bodin (1529–96) was a trained lawyer; the Jesuit Martin Antoine Del Rio (1551–1608) was *procureur-général* of Brabant; Henry Boguet (1550–1619) was grand judge of the lands of the Abbey of St Claude from 1587 and chief judge of Burgundy. For a general overview see Behringer, 'Demonology', 406–24. On Remy and his *Daemonolatria* see also Biesel, *Hexenjustiz*, 89–100.

20. Briggs, *Witches of Lorraine*, 48–50, quote on 48: 'When the *procureur-général* sat down to write his book in the early 1590s he evidently found a very convenient way to collect his material; no doubt by agreement with his friend and colleague Thierry Alix, he must have removed a large collection of trial documents from the archive tower and taken them home. This is the only reasonable conclusion one can draw from the fact that out of the 144 identifiable cases mentioned in his book, just one dossier (for a 1591 trial) can now be found, which may well be a duplicate copy.' See also Biesel, *Hexenjustiz*, 99.

21. I would like to thank Robin Briggs for pointing this out to me. See also Monter and Peters, 'Remy, Nicolas'.

22. Roper, 'Witchcraft and the Western Imagination', 117–41, at 123. See VD16: R1090 (Frankfurt, 1596, Latin edition); R1091 (Cologne, 1596, Latin edition); R1092 (Frankfurt, 1597, Latin

edition); R1093 (Frankfurt, 1598, German edition, German title: *Daemonolatria. Das ist Von Vnholden und Zauber Geistern* ...). The German 1598 edition is the edition used in this analysis.

23. Roper, 'Witchcraft and the Western Imagination', 123. Schulte suggests that the *Malleus* had a greater impact in the sixteenth century before the publication of other demonological works; by the seventeenth century its influence had certainly diminished. Its impact also varied in different regions. See Schulte, *Man as Witch*, pp. 101, 125. On Remy's popularity see also Biesel, *Hexenjustiz*, 96. This is in marked contrast to its apparent lack of influence in Lorraine, where Jean Bodin was more regularly cited rather than the native Remy. There was one vernacular translation into Polish. Stanisław Ząbkowic translated parts II and III of the *Malleus*, skipping part I (*Młot na czarownice*, Cracow 1614), but it is unlikely that this edition had any impact in the Holy Roman Empire. With thanks to Michael Ostling for this reference.

24. Schulte, *Man as Witch*, 125.

25. Roper, 'Witchcraft and the Western Imagination', 122–3. See Schulte, *Man as Witch*, 120–2. See also Behringer, 'Meinungsbildende Befürworter und Gegner der Hexenverfolgung', 219–37, at 223–5; Maxwell-Stuart, *Witchcraft in Europe and the New World*, 56.

26. Roper, 'Witchcraft and the Western Imagination', 122. See also Clark, 'Protestant Demonology', 45–82; Briggs, *Witches and Neighbours*, 21.

27. Behringer, *Witchcraft Persecutions in Bavaria*, 262. On Jean Bodin and his refutations of Weyer, and in particular on how the two authors 'gendered' the witch, see Opitz-Belakhal, *Das Universum des Jean Bodin*, ch. 5.

28. See for instance footnote 14, and see Weyer, *On Witchcraft*, bk 6 ch. 8, 268; Briggs, *Witches of Lorraine*, 21.

29. Briggs, *Witches of Lorraine*, 21.

30. Roper, *Witch Craze*, 93.

31. Pearl, 'Introduction', in Bodin, *On the Demon-Mania of Witches*, 29. On Bodin's arguments regarding melancholy see Opitz-Belakhal, *Das Universum des Jean Bodin*, 140. See also Anglo, 'Melancholia and Witchcraft', 137–56, at 143.

32. Briggs, *Witches of Lorraine*, 121.

33. Ibid., 121. See also Roper, 'Witchcraft and the Western Imagination', 128; Biesel, *Hexenjustiz*, 97–98.
34. Briggs, *Witches of Lorraine*, 121. On Remy's confused arguments see ibid., 121, 149: Remy 'referred to apparitions of the devil to witches in prison, demons which took animal form, and witches who entered houses as cats, mice or even locusts. Where he became less certain was in a long and confused chapter on these transformations, notably into wolves, where he started by suggesting these must be diabolical illusions, then seemed to come round to saying the devil's preternatural powers stretched even to turning humans into animals.' See also Briggs, 'Witchcraft and Popular Mentality in Lorraine', 337–51. See also Maxwell-Stuart, *Witchcraft in Europe and the New World*, p. 58: Maxwell-Stuart suggests that it was out of Remy's experience as an observer and participant in witch trials 'that he produced the somewhat chaotic melange of personal reminiscence, anecdote, court-record and quotation which form his book *Daemonolatreia*'.
35. This is the argument put forward in Roper, 'Witchcraft and the Western Imagination'.
36. Ibid., 120. See Bodin, *De Magorum Daemonomania* [1581].
37. Roper, 'Witchcraft and the Western Imagination'. See Lancre, *Tableau de l'inconstance des mauvais anges et demons* [1613].
38. See Clark, 'Witchcraft and Magic', 97–169, at 136–7: 'Throughout the European scientific community, indeed, witchcraft excited a theoretical interest that bore little relation to the practice of witch-hunting.' See Opitz-Belakhal above for a critique of Clark on this point.
39. Remy, *Daemonolatria. Das ist Von Vnholden und Zauber Geistern* [1598] [VD16 R1093], bk I ch. I, p. 4. Translations of quotations from this edition are my own.
40. For honour as a theme in male witch-trials, see Walinski-Kiehl, 'Males, "Masculine Honour" and Witch-Hunting', 254–71.
41. Schulte, *Man as Witch*, ch. 5, especially 145–51. Interestingly, Remy suggests that social status may have had more importance than gender in his conceptions of the sabbat. See Remy, *Demonolatry*, ed. Summers [2008], bk I ch. XVI, 59, 'Isabella Pardaea, Didier Finance and Alber Magendre said that the more well-to-do witches sat at the top of the tables; and Stephaneta Marchant added that these drank from silver, whereas the poorer

ones drank from earthenware cups, but that in all other respects they were equal partners and participants in all their secret rites.'

42. Schulte, *Man as Witch*, 247. Yet on the same page Schulte notes, in his reference to the widely disseminated work of the theologian Johann Bergmann in 1629, which discussed typical behaviour of men and women, 'historical research has shown that such polarities were not generally existent as social constructs at this time, and the possible spectrum of gender-related attributes and identities was wider than Bergmann allowed ... masculinity was also lived in a way which did not correspond to this classic duality of the sexes'.

43. Remy, *Daemonolatria: Das ist Von Vnholden und Zauber Geistern*, bk I ch. I, p. 4.

44. Ibid., bk I ch. XIII, 96.

45. See Roper, 'Witchcraft and the Western Imagination'. She writes on p. 131, 'The records of witches' trials could themselves become literature. Nicolas Remy packs his text with countless individuals culled from the trial records that had "beaten at his brain" for expression—in his work, demonology comes close to paraphrase of criminal trial records as he summarises scores of individual cases'.

46. Remy, *Daemonolatria: Das ist Von Vnholden und Zauber Geistern*, bk I ch. XIII, 96–7.

47. Briggs, *Witches of Lorraine*, 146. However, one should not treat this image of the punitive devil as a regional peculiarity of Lorraine or a personal idiosyncrasy of Remy. Binsfeld too (for example) espoused an image of the Devil as wielding violent power over his confederates. Schulte, *Man as Witch*, 120; Dillinger, *'Evil People'*, 50; Binsfeld, *Tractat Von Bekantnuß der Zauberer und Hexen* [1590]. On Binsfeld's description of the Devil, see Ibid., fol. 8r.

48. Remy, *Daemonolatria: Das ist Von Vnholden und Zauber Geistern*, bk I ch. I, 4–5.

49. Ibid., 40. On the emphasis on demonic copulation in witchcraft theories, see Stephens, *Demon Lovers*.

50. See Davis, *Fiction in the Archives*, 82–3.

51. Claudia Opitz has suggested that 'the Western connection between the Devil and femininity is unique among the religious cultures of the world', in particular 'because it gave evil a notably "human" and also sexualised form'. Opitz-Belakhal, 'Witchcraft Studies', 94.

52. Remy, *Daemonolatria: Das ist Von Vnholden und Zauber Geistern*, bk I ch. XV, 123.

53. For example Remy, *Demonolatry*, bk III, ch. XII, 184: 'For all those who are infected with this pestilence of witchcraft are women of an advanced and decrepit age; for (though this is certainly rarer) the Demon holds men equally bound by this kind of allegiance.' A similar emphasis is found in Bodin's *Démonomanie*. Although Bodin thought that there were fifty female witches for every man, it is striking that he named more male witches than female ones in his treatise. See Opitz-Belakhal, *Das Universum des Jean Bodin*, 136, 142.

54. See Opitz-Belakhal, *Das Universum des Jean Bodin*, 137. See also Briggs, *Witches and Neighbours*, 259.

55. Schulte, *Man as Witch*, 121. This was very similar to Weyer's argument: women's 'weakness of spirit, mind, and natural disposition'. See for example Weyer, *On Witchcraft*, bk VI, ch. XXII, 289.

56. Clark, *Thinking with Demons*, 116. Durrant also quotes Clark on Binsfeld. See Durrant, *Witchcraft, Gender and Society*, 46.

57. Remy, *Daemonolatria: Das ist Von Vnholden und Zauber Geistern*, bk I, ch. XV, 124.

58. Briggs, *Witches of Lorraine*, 332.

59. Remy, *Daemonolatria: Das ist Von Vnholden und Zauber Geistern*, bk III, ch. XII, 474–5.

60. Ibid., bk III, ch. XII, 481. As Briggs notes, Remy rather erroneously suggests that witches were composed primarily of beggars, although he noticed the apparent contradiction in claims that many rich people were also at the sabbats. See Briggs, *Witches and Neighbours*, 21.

CHAPTER 5

Tyrannical Beasts: Male Witchcraft in Early Modern English Culture

E.J. Kent

If the malevolent mother was a basal stereotype for the early modern English female witch, was there a masculine equivalent?[1] Scholars have shown how ideas of female witchcraft were derived from classical mythology, religious and biblical knowledge, and from literary and oral traditions, to create legal, theological and folkloric stories about the evil female witch and her powers.[2] I am interested in how, in early modern English communities, accusations against male witches were articulations of more generalised ideas about masculine evil, so I am going to locate the early modern English male witch in a cultural landscape beyond that of witchcraft trials. What was the masculinised cultural 'imaginary' that supported a belief that men could be witches?[3]

I follow Diane Purkiss's suggestion that 'masculinities' were 'images and stories that could provide ventilation for rage, fear and anxiety', and that in order understand this properly we need to search the historical record for 'gaps and ... silences were unreason flourishes', rather than just examining 'rational, Cartesian subjects'. Ironically the issue of silence is a

E.J. Kent
Independent Researcher

© The Author(s) 2016
L. Kounine, M. Ostling (eds.), *Emotions in the History of Witchcraft*, DOI 10.1057/978-1-137-52903-9_5

real one for masculinity studies: masculinities are not silenced, but rather 'do not … talk about themselves' so are 'often found in the obliques of texts, not their straight lines'.[4] So taking an oblique look at the masculinities implicated in witchcraft accusations against men, I am going to suggest that the male witch shared significant gendered cultural terrain with the tyrant—a negative, masculine stereotype with a great deal of currency throughout the period of active witchcraft prosecution in early modern English communities. Indeed, I argue that the language of tyranny provided a reservoir of cultural descriptors for masculine evil and that this shaped the ideation of the male witch in both literary and trial representations.

Tyrants and tyranny preoccupied Elizabethan thought in the late sixteenth century, rose to a crescendo during the English Civil Wars, and remained relevant in society and politics right up to the late seventeenth century and beyond. In Elizabethan England citizens could 'scarcely fail to come into contact with some form of literature which brought to their notice the general nature and particular vices of tyranny'.[5] In the first half of the seventeenth century, concerns about absolutism led to anxieties about the nature of government and the prospect of rule by monarchical tyrants. James I, a believer in the absolute powers of the crown, was never called a tyrant. Not so his son Charles I, whom a significant portion of the population believed was a tyrannical monarch, conspiring with Henrietta Maria, his French, Catholic Queen.[6] In the end, Charles I was not merely named a tyrant but executed as one. Royalists staunchly defended Charles, saying that Parliament was the real tyrant because it challenged the divine right of the English monarch. During the Interregnum, Cromwell was labelled tyrannical and 'tyranny' came to describe a ruler not bound by God or man, hence not accountable to any higher authority. At the Restoration, after a brief bout of popularity, Charles II attracted the label of tyrant; in particular his reputation for licentiousness 'suggested the stereotype of the feminised hag-ridden tyrant'.[7] These ideas of the tyrant continued as they had from antiquity—as a means to describe 'one of the most potent antitypes' in political life. The tyrant was a masculine representation of 'absolute transgression'. He was 'the most deformed of all monsters' and 'the most shifting of all shapes'.[8]

The political tyrant is well known to historians, but the figure of the tyrant was not just a device of elite politics.[9] Ordinary English people, since the Elizabethan period, knew the tyrant as a dramatic character who appeared upon many provincial stages, as well as from their preachers who recounted stories of biblical tyrants from pulpits across the country.[10] During the Commonwealth tyrannical behaviour came to be identified with 'the covetous lawyer, and the tithing minister, the rack-renting landlord and the parliamentary grandee': 'tyranny' became the 'catchphrase of discontent'.[11] By the late seventeenth century the language of tyranny used masculine descriptors to represent absolute masculine corruption of diabolic origin. The term 'tyrant' could be applied to any masculine perpetrator and could be used to describe any masculine iniquity.[12] The language of tyranny could contain an entire spectrum of political, religious, economic and social deviance.[13]

*

In 1612 a pamphlet was published in London that described the case of the French Catholic priest, Lewis Gaufredy. Confessing to crimes of witchcraft he had allegedly committed after inheriting books of magic from his uncle, Gaufredy said he was 'possessed' with the 'badde affection … of Ambition, to live in great reputation in the world, but especially amongst honest men'. Reading his magical books, Gaufredy summoned the Devil, making a deal that 'for the space of forty years he might enjoy the full fruition of his detested ambition' by holding the office of 'chief and principal confessor' with all 'place, prerogatives, liberties and honours'. In addition he wanted the 'power … to know carnally women or maids … on whom his pernicious and lustful eyes [fell]', and 'that his charming tongue might flow with eloquence', all while being reputed as 'grave and religious'. The pamphleteer described Gaufredy as a man with a 'worldly excess of prosperity', a 'settled pride raised to a height', who had a 'beastly and strong luxurious appetite … raging within him' and who had become 'merely sensual'. 'Beware', warned the pamphleteer, 'all ye whose souls are luxuriously affected … whose ambition pierces the very heavens, coveting as did those aspiring angels, to be as Gods'.[14]

To say a man accused of witchcraft suffered from the 'badde Affection' of ambition was, in effect, to use the language of tyranny to describe masculine corruption. A long tradition of writers 'discerned the origin of tyranny in "ambition … the lust for power and glory"'.[15] The tyrant was a man in whom the 'mastering passion of ambition' had 'displaced the virtuous rule of reason'. The passion of ambition corrupted a man's will, making him believe that, like Faustus, he could aspire to be 'a mighty God'.[16] The 'disease' of passion made men tyrannical as they lusted after the 'satisfaction of "Ambition, Revenge, Covetousness, or any other irregular Passion"'.[17] In men, tyranny arose because irrational, passionate desires overcame reason.[18]

One of the ways men were believed to use witchcraft was to secure material benefit and/or increase their status: what Willem de Blécourt called the 'male stereotype of the profitable witch'. So it is no surprise that the witchcraft pamphlets of early modern England generally represent male witches as ambitious.[19] Some of these ambitions were relatively modest and predictable. We have already seen the example of Lewis Gaufredy who had ambitions to seduce women, gain wealth and acquire clerical 'prerogatives and honours'. Then there is John Palmer, an accused witch from St Albans, who confessed to practising witchcraft for fifty or sixty years and harboured ambitions for revenge. Palmer allegedly used witchcraft to murder his landlady Goodwife Pearl because she locked him out for failing to pay rent.[20] But the ambitions of other male witches were represented on an entirely different scale. In 1591 the *Newes from Scotland* told the story of John Cunningham, alias Dr Fian, a schoolmaster from Saltpans, who was the 'Registrar' of the North Berwick witches. These witches had reportedly conspired to use weather magic to attack wedding ships bearing Anne of Denmark and James VI of Scotland, trying to kill the king because he was the 'greatest enemy' Satan had. James VI, later James I of England, presided over the interrogations himself and would later produce his *Demonology* (1603) from the experience. Represented as aspiring to kill a king, Cunningham and the other accused witches had, wittingly or not, become involved in the lethal dynastic politics of late sixteenth-century Scotland.[21] Sixteen years later, in England, a pamphlet described the death of the 'wizard' John Lambe. Lambe was certainly personally ambitious, wanting to attract high-status clientele with his magical and other skills. But he was mired in grander ambitions than these. Known as the 'Duke's Devil', Lambe was servant to the increasingly unpopular George Villiers, Duke of Buckingham, royal favourite first of James I, then of Charles I. Lambe's murder by a London mob, and the subsequent pamphlet recounting it, had direct links to the competing, and equally lethal, political ambitions of antebellum England.[22]

It was the tyrannical ambition for knowledge, power and influence that drove men to seek the secret and hidden ways of diabolic witchcraft. As the pamphlet account of John Palmer argued, despite man being 'created with excellent beauty of knowledge in his mind', men were 'impatient to be coop't up within the narrow scantling of his own intellectuals'. This was particularly true of male witches who, as practitioners of the 'curious arts', became 'very busie with the Divel; rather than keep his station, hee will make tryall what the Divel can [do] for his own advancement in knowledge'. Men like these had an 'inordinate desire to know more then his maker has thought fit for him to know'.[23] Like the tyrant, the male witch was uncontained by the 'bounds of Law, Reason or Religion', sinned 'against the law of nature', and used unnatural means to attain unlawful powers.[24]

In early modern English witchcraft pamphlets male witches were invariably associated with actively subversive, anti-social networks, particularly (though unsurprisingly) the Catholic Church. John Walsh, subject of a pamphlet in 1566, was asked if he was taught 'witchcraft and sorcery' by his master, a Catholic priest. In the pamphlet, Walsh's confession is preceded by a history of Catholic Popes and their dealings with Satan.[25] Lewis Gaufredy was a Catholic priest and continued to be so after his deal with the Devil. Indeed his diabolic ambition sought explicit expression within the institution of the Catholic Church.[26] The soldier Giles Fenderlin, subject of a pamphlet in 1652, confessed he consulted a Jesuit to buy magical protection from injury by guns, swords or daggers.[27] John Lowes, a Suffolk clergyman accused of witchcraft several times between 1600 and his execution for witchcraft in 1645, was represented as part of networks of 'popish Recusants', but also those of the Laudian Church, as well as networks of witches and conjurors.[28] John Palmer was thought to know about the 'Conjuring Conclave and Society of Witches in England', and particularly about one 'Marsh of Dunstable ... head of the whole College of Witches'.[29] Male witches were embedded in a multiplicity of overlapping, conspiratorial, anti-Christian and anti-social networks; shadowy, organised groups of God's enemies working to orchestrate the downfall of Christian society.

Tyrants were profoundly allied with conspiratorial networks, and the pamphlets about tyrants and tyranny are thick with dark alliances. To take a single example from the English Civil War, a pamphleteer wrote that Charles I was 'no Saint or Martyr' but a 'great favourer of Papists and an oppressive Tyrant'. The 'worthy Patriots' of 1640 stood against 'inundations of Popery and Arbitrary Power, that King, his Queen, and evil Counsellors were bringing on the three kingdoms'. 'Papists and others that were his favourites, were embarked in the same wicked Designs with him', a king who would 'rather sacrifice a thousand of his good Subjects, than deliver up those evil Counsellors that sought to enslave England'.

King Charles 'admired, encouraged and protected' the 'worst and corrupt sort of Courtiers', the 'ragged Infantry of Stews and Brothels', and the 'spawn and shipwreck of Taverns and Dicing-houses'. In his army Charles had '1000 blaspheming Cavaliers', 'entertained … the most ignorant, profane and vicious Clergy, learned in nothing but their Pride, their Covetousness and Superstition … that from the Press and Pulpit poisoned the People with … enslavements'. The King raised an army of 'English, Scots, Germans and bloody Irish Papists to subject his People to his will and Power'. While such a king governed, how could 'poor England think of being happy or free from Popery, and its natural consequence of Tyranny?'[30]

In the case of both the male witch and the tyrant, the purpose of these networks was to ferment rebellion against lawful secular and sacred authority. The equation of rebellion and witchcraft had a clear, biblical warrant in 1 Samuel 15:23: 'For rebellion is a sinne of witchcraft.'[31] The sin of rebellion associated the tyrant with 'supernatural evil', and tyranny 'with the rule of Hell'.[32] The sin of witchcraft associated the male witch with rebellion. Both the tyrant and the male witch enacted the ur-rebellion of Lucifer, held to be the 'supreme exemplar' of the vice of ambition because of his rebellion against God and his desire to be the king of heaven. Both the male witch and the tyrant were defined by their rebellion against lawful authority—against the lawful authority of men constituted by God to rule, but also against God himself. Both the male witch and the tyrant are masculine stereotypes that represent 'usurpation, treason, [and] political subversion'. The tyrant and the male witch represented individual instances of embodied masculine evil, but also the diabolic legions of evil followers who would rise up to join their rebellion—secret papist traitors, parliamentary usurpers, tyrannical kings, Royalist spies, diabolic witches, or any other of the vast demonic legions believed to beset Christian society. The rebellion of the tyrant and the witch showed the world a 'cacarchy', a prefiguring of Hell where the very worst men ruled society.[33] The tyrant and the witch were the arbiters of rebellion against secular and sacred authority that 'threatens to return men to the brutes'.[34]

In seventeenth-century England, in particular, rebellion was represented as 'a monster … hideous … noisome and destructive to humane kinde … the name of it is rebellion, an ugly beast of many heads'.[35] Rebellious masculinities were monstrous because they were appetitive: the passionate appetites of the ambitious man overthrew the hierarchy of masculine reason, 'converting man into beast'.[36] In the case of tyrannical masculinities, this appetitive, rebellious monstrosity was signified by the treasonous agreement to serve the Devil. Male witches were men who willingly entered a pact with Satan, trading their souls in return for the satisfaction of their ambitions.[37] Likewise the tyrant: in Shakespeare's *Richard the Third*, Richard submitted himself to Satan in order to 'establish … his monstrous rule'. Macbeth, a 'monster whose vices prove him to be the worst of tyrants', admitted his soul belonged to the Devil. The male witch and the tyrant were bestialised by their service to the Devil, which entailed giving over their Christian, human status to become ungoverned monsters. The enormity of their sins—their emulation of Satan, their beastlike passions—all indicated they had ceased to be human.[38] Ambitious, rebellious, allied with anti-social forces, a servant of Satan, corrupt in his lusts, bestial in his passions, the tyrannical male witch betrayed God in return for the power to carry out his will. Male witchcraft could be represented as the 'monstrous rule' of the tyrannical man because the language of tyranny was rich enough, and nuanced enough, to represent men as the 'source of all wickedness'.[39]

In the witchcraft pamphlets, the male witch met his end in much the same way as the stage tyrant: '[a]mbition is their chief motive; they deceive themselves with false arguments, and the realisation of their hopes brings not joy but disillusionment' generally followed by a ghastly death.[40] Dr Fian was repeatedly tortured, then executed. John Lambe was beaten to death by a London mob. John Lowes was hanged during the East Anglian witch-hunt, despite having a charm from the Devil to prevent just that. In the week prior to hanging Giles Fenderlin was haunted by the spirits of bishops and lawyers, warning that his debt to Satan was due. In witchcraft pamphlets the male witch, like the stage tyrant, was 'inevitably punished' and that punishment was 'eminently just'.[41]

Finally the male witch and the tyrant, as deviant masculinities, have had a very similar historiographical treatment with regard to gender. For example, in witchcraft pamphlets, a male witch's ambition could take the form of overweening bodily lusts, signalling masculine sexual evil. This is an aspect of the Gaufredy case when he confessed to using witchcraft to seduce and rape women.[42] The case of John Lambe, particularly, provides a vivid illustration of the moral and physical corruption implicit in the carnally ambitious masculine body. Lambe had previously been prosecuted for witchcraft and conjuration in Worcester. He was moved to a London prison, and there was accused of raping an eleven-year-old serving girl. A neighbour, Mabell Swinnerton, testified to the physical effect of the rape upon the child: 'there was a little specke of the venomous substance …

that stucke upon … her thigh'. When Mabell pulled it away, she saw it had festered, 'so vilde and venomous was the base substance'. Mabell confronted Lambe, accusing him of 'undoing' an honest man's child' asking why, with 'so many strumpets in the towne', he had to 'seeke the ruine of a poor child'. Mabell told him 'you have burnt her, either you have a foule body, or you have dealt with some uncleane persons'.[43] Lambe's moral corruption is signalled by physical corruption.[44] Lambe's soul is foul, corrupted by his many sins, and this debases his flesh: his moral rottenness is manifested in corrosive semen. In these corrupt lusts John Lambe and John Godfrey shared 'one of the commonest vices of tyrants'. Macbeth, particularly, was condemned for lust, as a 'whoore-master' who made his kingdom a 'stewes'.[45] Humanist tragedians also attributed 'unbridled lust' to Herod. The lust of the tyrant was emblematic of his 'lack of self-command' and, when paired with submissiveness to a woman (such has Macbeth to his Lady, Herod to his queen, or Charles I to Henrietta Maria), it marked the 'tyrant's changeling character' which might appear 'quintessentially feminine, or rather effeminate'.[46]

This identification of the lustful tyrant as an effeminised masculinity echoes the way male witches have been described as 'feminised' men. Both masculinities share the common historiographical ground of being aberrant masculinities elided with femaleness. Men so represented are not regarded as fully masculine, thus quarantining patriarchal normativity from deviance. However, while tyranny may have been feminised and, on occasion, tyrants represented as 'womanish', they were generally not female characters. Indeed, to be a tyrant was to harbour inherently masculine aspirations for dominion over people and powers. Like the male witch, the tyrant has an uneasy historiographical relationship to both masculinity and femaleness. Beyond the scope of this essay, this could be resolved by a consideration of the power of negative masculinity, particularly the power of chaotic masculinities—the exercise of masculine power in ways that produced chaos not order. For the seventeenth-century English, living in the shadow of Civil War, this masculine chaos was measured in real terms over a century of political, social and religious upheaval. For them, the idea of the tyrant had immediate psychological, social and cultural power, and so did tyrannical, negative masculinities like the male witch. Rather than being feminised masculine entities, these were evil masculinities aligned with the 'hypersexuality' and 'hypermasculinity' of the Devil and who, like him, were regarded as the agents of a long-anticipated apocalypse.[47]

*

The evidence of male witchcraft I have used so far comes from witchcraft pamphlets published in the first half of the seventeenth century in England. Where some pamphlets contained almost verbatim copies of trial records, others did not. Popular magical tropes and tales augmented some pamphlet accounts. Some were didactic, often serving sectarian and other religious interests. Most pamphlets were produced with an eye to what would sell. So while not entirely fictive, witchcraft pamphlets were not strictly documentary accounts but constructed, literary representations of male witchcraft aimed at the busy London pamphlet market. I want to move now to how male witches were represented in witch trials by looking at the Salem witch trials of 1692. These trials produced the largest body of evidence concerning male witches in any early modern English community; this evidence, albeit like the pamphlets constrained by its narrative form, represents actual accusations of witchcraft made in a legal setting.[48] At least fifty of the 181 accused witches of Salem were male, ranging from boys (the youngest just ten) to senior men (the oldest eighty-three). I am going to use as my examples here the cases of four men—John Proctor, George Jacobs Sr, John Alden and Philip English. I argue that the ideas of tyrannical masculinity—masculine ambition, participation in anti-social networks, and rebelliousness—were all implicated in their identification as witches.

Ambition has long been identified as central to the psychology of the Salem witch trials. In 1974 Paul Boyer and Stephen Nissenbaum noted that one of 'Satan's most insidious guises … in 1692 was that of thriving freeholder and prosperous merchant'. Such witches were accused of using a 'subtle form of wheedling through glittering promises of material gain and economic betterment' to get others to join with the Devil. Boyer and Nissenbaum concluded that the village factionalism that surrounded these trials arose because 'the social order was being profoundly shaken by a superhuman force … We construe this force as emergent mercantile capitalism … Salem Village called it witchcraft.'[49] With this context in mind, the identification of these four men as witches supports the contention that masculine ambition could be diabolised by accusers, just as it was in witchcraft pamphlets.

Proctor, Jacobs Sr, Alden and English could all be readily identified as ambitious men because of their material success. There is considerable evidence that shows John Proctor and George Jacobs Sr were 'thriving freeholders'. John Proctor, aged sixty, was the patriarch of a large family, married to his third wife Elizabeth, and father of eleven children when he was accused early in April 1692. His land holdings were extensive, including inherited property elsewhere in Massachusetts. Proctor and his sons ran a large rented farm, while Elizabeth ran a tavern. The family was 'both prosperous and large'.[50] Proctor's prosperity was the 'conclusion of a successful career built upon the varied economic opportunities available' in the colonial economy. 'A flourishing man of affairs', Proctor had contacts with Boston, Salem Town and Ipswich. George Jacobs Sr was aged eighty-three when accused, the patriarch of a large family, and successful yeoman famer who had lived in Salem Village for thirty-three years, whose daughter had married one of the wealthiest men in Salem.[51] As we shall see, Proctor and Jacobs Sr were forceful characters, with a strong sense of mastery.

John Alden and Philip English were Boyer and Nissenbaum's 'prosperous merchants', who appear to have conducted their business with a keen eye to profit and their own advancement. Philip English was aged forty-one when accused of witchcraft at the end of April 1692.[52] A very wealthy Jerseyan from the Channel Islands, an Anglican, with extensive mercantile holdings in Salem Town, including his own large house and shop, warehouses, real estate, wharves and ships, he had married the daughter of one of the leading colonial families. English had a reputation for being aggressive in his pursuit of business: 'besides his international shipping business and thriving trade in Jersey bond servants, English bought, sold, mortgaged and repossessed many properties in the Salem area ... he was quick to sue for debt [and] many locals distrusted his honesty'. Despite English's wealth the town had significant, ongoing difficulty in getting English's share of the tax collection.[53] John Alden was aged sixty-six in 1692, and was the son of *Mayflower* Pilgrims.[54] Alden was a merchant sea captain who, as commander of the colony's sloop *Mary*, was often about the colony's business between Salem and the French territories to the North. Alden was 'one of the colony's elite, fellow congregant, and business associate' of many colonial leaders. He supplied the colony with 'valuable, even essential services, and if he chose to make some profit ... from certain clandestine voyages undertaken chiefly at the colony's behest', many of the colony's leading men would 'look the other way'; others probably invested in these journeys. Both Alden and English had great confidence in their wealth and social status, and the natural authority this conferred. Proctor, Jacobs Sr, Alden and English all had much in common with de Blécourt's 'male stereotype of the profitable witch', mentioned above, whose ambitions for 'individual gain and achievement' resonated harshly in their communities.[55]

I have argued above that one of the hallmarks of tyrannical masculinities was their anti-social, networked nature. The Salem evidence makes it clear that the accusing community regarded Proctor, Jacobs, Alden and English as having close links to anti-social forces regarded as satanic agents intent on destroying New England. First among these were satanic agents believed to be internal to Christian community. Beginning in March 1692, examinations revealed networks of witch families, first in Salem Village, then in neighbouring Andover. Both John Proctor and George Jacobs Sr were identified as the heads of 'witch families' where wives, sons, daughters and other kin were accused. The narrative that emerged around these families was a story of betrayal at the very heart of godly community—organised networks of families worshipped the Devil, actively working to overthrow the rule of Christ, and establish Satan's kingdom in New England. As household governors and the heads of large families, Proctor and Jacobs Sr were represented as Satan's patriarchs, evil men who would lead their families and community to the Devil. They were central actors in a communal narrative that identified an evil, familial conspiracy at the very centre of village life.[56]

John Alden and Philip English were associated with external networks of demonic agents hell-bent on destroying Christian society in general, and Puritan Massachusetts in particular. The 1692 trials occurred during a significant period of open warfare with the French in Canada, and a series of prolonged 'Indian Wars', both of which were defining features of life in New England for the last two decades of the seventeenth century.[57] In this context John Alden was accused of selling powder and shot to the Indians and the French, an accusation that was very familiar to the people of Salem. The witchcraft accusations against Alden came a mere nine days after yet another report that Alden was delivering supplies to New England's enemies, this time to the French in Arcadia. This was not the first time that official report or colonial gossip had allied Alden to both the French and Native Americans. A ship's crew had refused to sail under his command because he was 'Reported to bee an old Indian trader and was going to trade with the French'. Apparently it was not just sailors who felt this way. When sending him on an official mission, the colonial governors had ordered that he 'did not carry with him any ammunition more than for the Necessary use of the vessell'.[58]

Philip English was also suspect because of his relationships to enemy communities. English was an Anglican from the Channel Island of Jersey. Like all French-speakers, Jerseyans were viewed with suspicion in New England, and Anglicans had been enemies of Puritans since Elizabethan times. Philip English had trading networks that went north to Maine, French Acadia and Newfoundland, south to the Caribbean ports, and back over the Atlantic to Catholic Spain and the Channel Islands. English was undoubtedly in constant contact with many people New Englanders regarded as mortal enemies. There were rumours that Jerseyans in New England conspired with the French and the Native Americans, and acted as French spies. Jerseyans and other French-speakers lived with a 'generalised fear of the French' to the extent that after January 1691 the General Court ruled that no French could take up residence or establish businesses on the frontier or in port towns.[59] John Alden and Philip English were members of the Salem community who dealt with 'threatening outside forces' and appeared to thrive from such contacts.[60]

These diabolic alliances, both internal and external, were regarded as being authored by Satan in order to subvert New England because 'New Englanders are a People of God settled in those, which were once the Devil's Territories' and the Devil was 'exceedingly disturbed'.[61] Participants in these alliances in rebellion against godly New England were therefore in rebellion against God. So it is unsurprising that Proctor, Jacobs, Alden and English should all be characterised by their accusers as men with rebellious attitudes, and their many angry expressions of scorn and disbelief, passionate denials of the witchcraft charges, and challenges to the court's authority, often accompanied by threats of violence, were cited in the evidence against them. John Proctor forcibly expressed his scepticism about the fits of his maid Mary Warren and her role as an accuser to Samuel Sibley, when he met him upon the road. Proctor told Samuel 'if they were let alone so we should all be Devils [and] Witches'. Proctor continued,

> they should rather be had to the Whipping post but he would fetch his jade home & thresh the Devil out of her & more to the like purpose, crying hang them, hang them. And also added that when she was first taken with fits he kept her close to the Wheel & threatened to thresh her, & then she had no more fits till the next day he was gone forth & then she must have her fits again …

Joseph Pope testified that Proctor said to him that if Mr Parris 'would let me have his Indian [he] would soon drive [the] Diuell out of him'. Throughout his imprisonment and trial, Proctor repeatedly, and directly, confronted the men in authority, denying the charges against him, and questioning the legitimacy of the court's process. In July 1692 he wrote a letter to the leading Boston ministers, asking for their intervention because the Salem court, which included some of the colony's most prominent men, was 'inraged and incensed against us', acting on the accusations of self-confessed witches, torturing his sons and others with 'Popish cruelties', and illegally seizing estates.[62]

George Jacobs Sr's belligerent attitude towards the magistrates and his accusers remains palpable three centuries later. When accused of witchcraft by eleven-year-old Abigail Williams, 'he laught', saying he was falsely accused and asking, 'Your Worships, all of you do you think this is true?' Accused by his maidservant Sarah Churchill, Jacobs Sr replied, 'What would you have me say? I never wronged no man in word or deed.' Presented with '3 Evidences' from his young accusers, George replied, 'You tax me for a Wizard, you may as well tax me for a Buzard. I have done no harm.' Accused again by his maidservant of appearing to her and bringing her the Devil's book to sign, George aggressively asserted his innocence, saying finally, 'Well! burn me, or hang me, I will stand in truth of Christ, I know nothing of it.'[63]

John Alden directly confronted his elite peers and erstwhile friends who gathered to hear the charges against him. In an account published five years after the trials, probably given by Alden himself, he calls the young accusers 'juggling wenches'. Alden asked the magistrates why they thought he would come to the village to afflict people he did not know. He 'appealed to all that ever knew him, if they ever suspected him to be such a person, and challenged anyone, that could bring in any thing upon their own knowledge, that give suspicion of he being [a witch]'. Bartholomew Gedney, a leading colonist, replied 'he had … always look'd upon him to be an honest Man, but now did see cause to alter his judgement'. Alden replied, 'he was sorry for that, and added he hoped God would clear up his innocency'. When directed to look at the bewitched accusers in the courtroom, who immediately fell into fits, Alden inquired why the magistrates did not fall into fits when he looked at them? Regarding the accusers he told the court 'there was a lying Spirit in them, for I can assure you that there is not a word of truth in all these say of me'.[64]

John Proctor and George Jacobs Sr were executed, still protesting their innocence. John Alden and Philip English offered further insult to the authority of the Salem court by escaping prison and fleeing its jurisdiction altogether. Later Alden explained that 'observing the manner of the trials, and the Evidence then taken [he] was at length prevailed with to make his Escape'.[65] Returning to a pillaged estate, Philip English bitterly pursued those responsible with court cases for over forty years, until his death in 1734. The story goes that on his deathbed English forgave his enemies but with the caveat, 'But if I get well, I'll be damned if I forgive [them].'[66]

This evidence shows that these accused men these were identified as tyrannical masculinities because they could be characterised as ambitious, subversive, rebellious demonic agents. In the 1692 witch trials tyrannical masculinities were invoked by witchcraft accusers to represent 'images and stories' that 'provid[ed] ventilation for rage, fear and anxiety' about psychologically disturbing men.[67] These men were psychologically disturbing because of their furious assertions of emotive power—anger, belligerence, arrogance, ridicule, scorn, scepticism, disobedience, open challenges to authority, aggression and threats of violence—coupled with the economic, political, religious and social power of adult men, particularly aspirant adult men. This emotionality was evidence that a man had lost the 'civil war being raged between reason and the passions' and raised the question of a man's human status, still a fluid category in the late seventeenth century. English men, like all men, were not human in any 'inevitable, timeless way': there was always the 'capacity to lose one's status' to 'cease to be human', 'to become a beast'.[68] W.A. Armstrong noted that in the 'later tyrant tragedies increasing stress is laid upon the civic disasters' of tyranny. Traces of this are apparent in the Salem witch trial evidence. The accusing communities in 1692 were profoundly traumatised: by frontier war, by the jeremiads of their clergy, by the changes of mercantile capitalism, by the witch trials. Experienced as unprecedented disasters that were evidence that God had abandoned them. The tyrannical masculinities of these men were part of the mosaic of evidence that confirmed God had indeed forsaken them. It showed that male governors were sinners, not saints, and that there was no rule by godly fathers leading the way to salvation, just the tyranny of the Devil as a prelude to eternal damnation.

*

In the pamphlet that describes the life and death of Lewis Graufredy, the pamphleteer wrote that

> Surely Hell it self had placed in the bodie of this tyrant, some ghastlie and uncleane spirit, to bee as an Instrument and guide to this accused Inchanter.[69]

Erica Fudge argues that there were 'two aspects of early modern culture that were ... deeply and imaginatively intertwined ... the colonial rule of the "uncivilised" and reasonable rule over the body'.[70] The pamphleteer's semantic tangle bears out Fudge's assertion. The tyrant is a man who has failed to govern his body and has descended into a monstrous state of masculine tyranny, ruled by his unbridled passions. Such a masculine body is a porous, supernatural body, which invites colonisation by the 'uncleane spirit' of witchcraft, thus creating the masculine 'Inchanter'—doubly diabolic and doubly damned.

Witchcraft accusations were a form of 'anti-tyrannical vocabulary' whereby accusers could 'symbolise the tyranny of their opponents and the threat they posed to rights and masculinities'.[71] The language of tyranny provided early modern English people with a vocabulary that described masculine corruption, specifically the exercise of unlawful power by masculine actors.[72] Such concerns about tyrannical masculine behaviour provide historians with a framework that links the tyranny of plebeian male witches with the tyranny of kings. It suggests that early modern English people on both sides of the Atlantic had significant anxieties about the masculine capacity to succumb to the bestial passions, and the ramifications of this for masculine governance. Accusations of witchcraft against men certainly need to be understood in relation to the history of witchcraft prosecution. But they are also an example of the many dialogues between seventeenth-century English peoples regarding negative assertions of masculine power, all of which have to be understood in terms of the considerable instabilities within patriarchal power in seventeenth-century English communities.

NOTES

1. Willis, *Malevolent Nurture*, 27–81; Purkiss, *Witch in History*, 91–118.
2. For the example see Zika, *Appearance of Witchcraft, passim*.
3. Purkiss, *Literature, Gender and Politics*, 5.

4. Ibid., 1, 4, 5.
5. Armstrong, 'Elizabethan Conception of the Tyrant', 161–81, quotation at 161.
6. Zaller, 'Figure of the Tyrant', 585–619, quotation at 588.
7. Ibid., 598, 604, 607.
8. Ibid., 585, 591–3; Zaller, *Discourse of Legitimacy*, 690.
9. Zaller, 'Figure of the Tyrant', 585.
10. Armstrong, 'Elizabethan Conception of the Tyrant', 163, Zaller, 'Breaking the Vessels', 768.
11. Zaller, 'Figure of the Tyrant', 603–4.
12. Armstrong, 'Influence of Seneca and Machiavelli', 19.
13. Armstrong, 'Elizabethan Conception of the Tyrant', 163.
14. Anon., *The Life and Death of Lewis Gaufredy* [1612], 2, 4. The pagination in this pamphlet is erratic, my pagination with page 1 being the title page.
15. Armstrong citing John of Salisbury, 'Elizabethan Conceptions of the Tyrant', 167.
16. Armstrong, 'Elizabethan Conceptions of the Tyrant', 170, 177, 178; Marlowe, 'Tragicall Historie of D. Faustus' [1990], 4–6.
17. Armstrong, 'Elizabethan Conceptions of the Tyrant', 178; Zaller citing John Locke, 'Figure of the Tyrant', 609.
18. Bushnell, *Tragedy of Tyrants*, 52.
19. Blécourt, 'Making of the Female Witch', 299; Kent, *Cases of Male Witchcraft*, 39–40.
20. Anon., *The Divels Delusions* [1649], 3–4.
21. Carmichael, *Newes from Scotland* [1591], 8–29; Normand and Roberts, *Witchcraft in Early Modern Scotland*, 29–126.
22. Anon., *A Briefe Description of the Notorious of Life of John Lambe* [1628], 1–21; Donaghue, *Fire under the Ashes*, 31–4.
23. Anon., *The Divels Delusion*, 1–3.
24. Armstrong, 'Elizabethan Conceptions of the Tyrant', 177, 178, 179.
25. Anon., *The Examination of John Walsh* [1566], 1–5 (my pagination).
26. Anon., *The Life and Death of Lewis Gaufredy*, 3.
27. Anon., *The Tryall and Examination of Mrs Joan Peterson* [1652], 3–5.
28. Anon., *Magazine of Scandall* [1642], 4–6 (my pagination).
29. Anon., *The Divels Delusion*, 2.

30. D.J., *King Charles I* [1698], 1–4, 14, 17.
31. Berry ed., *Geneva Bible: A Facsimile*.
32. Armstrong, 'Elizabethan Conceptions of the Tyrant', 173, 174.
33. Clark, *Thinking with Demons*, 86–7, David Loewenstein, 'An Ambiguous Monster', 295; Armstrong, 'Elizabethan Conceptions of the Tyrant', 178, 180.
34. Zaller, 'Figure of the Tyrant', 606.
35. Purkiss citing Griffith Williams, *Literature, Gender and Politics*, 177–8.
36. Bushnell, *Tragedy of Tyrants*, 53.
37. Anon., *The Tryall and Examination of Mrs Joan Peterson*, 4.
38. Armstrong, 'Elizabethan Conceptions of the Tyrant', 169, 171–4.
39. Zaller, 'Breaking the Vessels', 768.
40. Armstrong, 'Elizabethan Conceptions of the Tyrant', 171, 179.
41. Armstrong, 'The Influence of Seneca', 19.
42. Anon., *The Life and Death of Lewis Gaufredy*, 4, 12–14.
43. Anon., *A Briefe Description*, 15–20.
44. Purkiss, *Literature, Gender and Politics*, 172.
45. Armstrong, 'Elizabethan Conceptions of the Tyrant', 172.
46. Zaller, 'Figure of the Tyrant', 591.
47. Bushnell, *Tragedies of Tyrants*, 20–5, 120–1; Apps and Gow, *Male Witches*, 126–41; Purkiss, *Literature, Gender and Politics*, 99, 108–9, 134; Timbers, *Magic and Masculinity*, 112, 115.
48. Gibson, *Reading Witchcraft*, 7. I omit William Barker Sr and Samuel Wardwell from this analysis but see Kent, *Setting Up Satan's Kingdom: Male Witchcraft Confessors, Salem 1692*, forthcoming. I have examined George Burroughs elsewhere, see Kent, *Cases of Male Witchcraft*, 135–58.
49. Boyer and Nissenbaum, *Salem Possessed*, 210.
50. Norton, *In The Devil's Snare*, 71; Roach, *Salem Witch Trials*, 34; Rosenthal, *Records*, 173–5.
51. Boyer and Nissenbaum, *Salem Possessed*, 200–2; Rosenthal, *Salem Story*, 120–3; Rosenthal, *Records*, 251–6.
52. Rosenthal, *Records*, 221.
53. Roach, *Salem Witch Trials*, 12, 148.
54. Rosenthal, *Records*, 221.
55. Blécourt, 'Making of the Female Witch', 299; Norton, *In the Devil's Snare*, 107, 181–90.

56. Kent, *Cases of Male Witchcraft*, 148–9.
57. Norton, *In the Devil's Snare*, 187, *passim*.
58. Ibid., 185–91.
59. Ibid., 143–6.
60. Breen, *Transgressing the Bounds*, 200.
61. Mather, *Wonders of the Invisible World* [1693], 5–14.
62. Rosenthal, *Records*, 179, 475, 486, 538, 547, 561–6.
63. Ibid., 250–3.
64. Roach, *Salem Witch Trials*, 246, 364, 387, 399–403, 500, 520, 569–72.
65. Rosenthal, *Records*, 334–5.
66. Roach, *Salem Witch Trials*, 246, 364, 387, 399–403, 500, 520, 569–72.
67. Purkiss, *Literature, Gender and Politics*, 1–5.
68. Fudge, *Brutal Reasoning*, 50, 57, 58.
69. Anon., *Life and Death of Lewis Gaufredy*, 6.
70. Fudge, *Brutal Reasoning*, 50–9.
71. Purkiss, *Literature, Gender and Politics*, 29; Bushnell, *Tragedies of Tyrants*, 147.
72. Zaller, 'Figure of the Tyrant', 609; O'Callaghan, 'Talking Politics', 97–120, quotation at 118.

PART II

On Trial

CHAPTER 6

The Witch in the Courtroom: Torture and the Representations of Emotion

Rita Voltmer

INTRODUCTION

A criminal trial against a suspected witch unfurled itself as a drama of affective performance—a performance that tempts the historian of emotion with its seeming provision of unparalleled records of emotion. Should scholars succumb to this temptation? What specific records or reports have survived to be scrutinized in search of fluid emotions? Thomas Robisheaux has stated enthusiastically that 'trial records are full of reports about the feelings of accusers and the accused'.[1] However, neither the *Encyclopedia of Witchcraft* nor the *Oxford Handbook of Witchcraft* provides an entry on the topic of emotions expressed during the witch trials.[2] This is quite startling since the 'emotional turn', together with both 'the neuronal turn' and the stimulus of gender and body history, has had a significant impact on medieval and early modern history in general. Already in the 1990s, the pioneer in psycho-historical research, Lyndal Roper, had sought to analyse trial records from the southwestern territories of the Holy Roman Empire in search of negotiated narratives, fantasies and emotions about witch-

R. Voltmer
Universität Trier

© The Author(s) 2016
L. Kounine, M. Ostling (eds.), *Emotions in the History of Witchcraft*, DOI 10.1057/978-1-137-52903-9_6

97

craft.[3] However, her psychoanalytical approach to the witches' confessions has attracted well-founded critics, especially amongst German-speaking scholars.[4] Despite others' efforts, a consistent study of witchcraft confessions is still missing, which considers the different legal, confessional, political and social frameworks throughout Europe and its colonies.[5]

Notably, the witchcraft confessions from the Lutheran duchy of Württemberg have been scrutinized thoroughly.[6] The very moderate persecutions in Württemberg, which were strongly supervised by ducal authorities, included single trials imbedded in communal conflicts with charges against so called witches of a long standing dubious reputation. Thomas Robisheaux as well as Laura Kounine have pointed to the fact that in the trial procedures the supposed criminal identity of the witch was the outcome of competition and negotiation, of sometimes contradictory narratives, fantasies and emotions. Alison Rowlands completes the picture with similar findings concerning the Lutheran Imperial city of Rothenburg ob der Tauber.[7] But even in the setting of these southwestern Lutheran courts, which applied torture cautiously and where the accused had a strong agency to defend themselves and get acquitted, the witches' confessions remained an 'exceedingly complex composite constructions which hid their many sources behind the voice of the confessant and which bore the official stamp of the court'.[8]

In extending the perspective developed through studies of these Lutheran regions, my chapter emphasizes the difficulties besetting the attempts in using local witch trial records, stemming from intense, mostly Catholic witch-hunts, to recover the emotions of the persons involved.[9] I argue that we do not find feelings in the records, but *representations of emotions*.[10] Whatever kind of anger, fear, shame, despair, resignation, or depression lingered in the minds and hearts of the persons involved, be it the accusers or the accused, these fluid feelings are lost. In the texts we find labels, stereotypes, norms, narratives of emotions fixed in black and white to be communicated to readers and audiences. Standardized emotions were written down because they were meant to stabilize a legal, and thus a political and religious, truth. They were not written down to satisfy any interest which later-born anthropologists or historians happen to take in the inner personal conditions or conflicts of the witches and their interrogators. Moreover, recent studies on fear, pain and its memory have shown clearly that it is impossible to share the extent of pain, either as reader or as traumatized narrator attempting to convey first-hand experience. Confessions, together with the reported 'emotions' expressed under the threat of pain or during the questioning under torture, are not reliable, but have to be decoded.[11] In 2004, Robisheaux stated rightfully, that 'the history of torture has overshadowed the history of the confession'.[12] Nevertheless, in regard of the hotspots of witch-hunts, it cannot be neglected that torture, interrogation, confession and the respective representations of emotion were intrinsically tied together in a threefold legal, religious and political sense.

THE THREEFOLD IMPORTANCE OF TORTURE

In the continental European states, territories, and lordships (temporal and ecclesiastic), Roman law influenced the legal system and criminal court practice. Up to the middle of the seventeenth century we find a legal system which mixed accusatorial and inquisitorial elements, often based on ducal ordinances (as in Lorraine or Luxembourg) or on the Carolina code established in 1532 for the Holy Roman Empire. Initially, criminal courts were manned with unlearned personnel, but increasingly became staffed with legally trained lay assessors (jurymen), presided over by a judge, who could be a bailiff, a jurist, or a magistrate. Procedural law all over continental Europe defined torture as a legal instrument necessary for extracting the confessions needed to secure a clear verdict. Torture was not only the 'heart of witch trials', but the heart of most of all the early modern trials against capital crimes like sodomy, bestiality, incest, infanticide, high treason, arson, robbery, or theft.

Torture would be applied if highly suspected persons, who were thought to be guilty, refused to confess. The specific form and duration of torture during a criminal procedure remained unregulated in the Carolina code, and was left to the arbitrary judgment of the courts. However, in dubious and difficult to decide cases the Carolina obliged local courts and lay judges to consult the faculty of law at a university or a higher court with learned judges. Only after obtaining the written authorization of a legally trained, superior panel, the local court should continue with the interrogation under torture. The accused could gain an acquittal, if they were able to withstand torture, which was possible in those courtrooms that applied moderate torment according to the *processus ordinarius*. Such 'mild' criminal trials, which were supervised by higher courts or legal faculties, took place in the duchy of Mecklenburg, where at least half of the accused were acquitted, as well as in the duchies of Württemberg and Saxonia.[13] In practice, however, the legal procedure in many courtrooms remained a shady, dubious affair. In 1635 Benedict Carpzov stated that the unlearned judges in most of the German-speaking courts had no idea how to conduct a proper trial according to the Roman Law, either in witch-craft cases or in any other case of capital crime. Moreover, the Carolina included the *clausula salvatoria*, which sanctioned the perpetuation of the old legal customs found in the hundreds of territories, lordships and cities in the Holy Roman Empire. Especially during the witch-hunts, the rules of the *processus ordinarius* were transgressed, ignored or only claimed to be followed. Torture, which was one of the most important instrument to proliferate the intensive witch hunts so characteristic of the Rhine-Meuse region or in Franconia, became relevant in at least three overlapping contexts[14]:

First, in a legal context. According to Roman Law, torture was defined as a judicial instrument to gain a confession from a highly suspected person.[15] The application of torture was allowed only after the intensive examina-tion of incriminating evidence. In dealing with the dark and clouded crime of witchcraft, clear evidence (for instance two eyewitnesses) was hardly ever found. Therefore dubious evidence was allowed: the denunciations of alleged accomplices, ducking (the water ordeal) or pricking in search of the 'Devil's mark' were all treated as sufficient grounds for proceeding to torture. In theory, an innocent person was thought to possess the inner strength and the godly support to withstand torture without any con-fession. Like a fearless martyr, an innocent person fought not for bodily intactness, but for his or her soul's purity. Gallantly and firmly, he or she would endure every harsh torment without giving any false testimony, that is to say, without the deadly sin of lying. In contrast a guilty person, already tormented by his or her bad conscience, was bound to the materiality of the body and to the rebellious (and thus, devilish) resistance against legal, political and religious authority. Such a person could withstand torture only with devilish help or because of hardness of the heart. Moreover, accused persons, coming from the lower ranks of society, were thought to have bodies and minds of greater resistance against pain. Therefore, severe torture had to weaken the body to the point of exhaustion, so that the confession of guilt, which was thought to be buried in the accused body, could be brought to the surface. Recent research has shown clearly: interrogation and torture were not actions with an open end.[16] They were a combat in which the accused person had few to no chances to cling to their own narratives and emotional habits. On their part, interrogations and confessions were not negotiations about plausible stories, but an ill-balanced fight for honour, integrity, and life. On the part of the court and its judges, the confession had to fulfil their expectations and to fit in the already determined legal truth about guilt. In this context, it is noteworthy that recent research in narratology and the law has declared so called voluntary confession as a utopian fantasy.[17]

Second, in a transcendent context. Extracting a confession comprised a sacred ritual act with a deep religious impact, a mixture of torture, exorcism and religious confession. The link between the obligation of every Christian to confess one's sins at least once a year together with the introduction of the inquisitorial criminal system, based on Roman Law (including torture and confession) dates back to the fourth Lateran council in 1215 and the Church's battle against heretics.[18] The English term 'confession', both used for admission of crimes and for the admission of sins, mirrors this explicit ambiguity. Thus, torture prefigured the torments in hell. Where secular courts dealt with the diabolic crime of witchcraft, they appeared to struggle with Satan himself, who had tainted the witch's body, helped it through the torments and obstructed both her material and her spiritual confession. Therefore, bodily pain had to free the accused person from materiality and prepare it for confession as a remedy for the diseased, maculated soul. Theologians argued that free will never could be forced by pain to confess untruth.[19]

Third, in a political context, especially after the introduction of the inquisitorial criminal procedure, torture demonstrated the impressive power of the state. Confessions proved the reality of diabolic witchcraft, witches "eyewitnessed" the reality of a demonic counterworld, which was set against godly (and, consequently, kingly, princely, religious and family) order. Ruling patriarchal authorities felt obliged to cleanse their territory of witches in order to maintain control, peace, order, welfare, and the true religion. Additionally, a political demonology legitimized harsh prosecutions to battle demons and witches. Especially minor principalities followed this doctrine, where the weakness of sovereign legitimacy sought a seigneurial counterbalance in obsessive witchcraft trials. Torture served as an imbedded political instrument to detect the rebellious minions of Satan. The ritual execution at the Final Judgement Day (*Endlicher Rechtstag*) with its read-out or confirmed confessions as well as the symbolic strength of the scaffolds served further political purposes: The seigneurial control was manifested in contesting neighbouring lords as well as the controlling efforts of territorial overlords. In a transcendent perspective, the disrupted godly order was re-established, the corrupted political body healed and saved again.[20]

Torture operated with the invocation of fear, firstly with the fear of being shamed and dishonoured as the torturer's infringing touch transgressed the boundaries of status, gender, age, and bodily integrity. Only secondly did the fear of torture focus on pain. The same has to be said about execution.[21] Torture and its threat had the greatest impact on the accused and their individual emotions. But it was the scribes as constructors of the local witch trial records who shaped felt emotions into representations of emotions.

THE SOURCE MATERIAL: CATEGORIES, PERSPECTIVES, AND PROBLEMS

Massive witch-hunts, for example in the territories of the Rhine-Meuse-Moselle[22] and in the Franconian area, generated different kinds of source material providing us with different perspectives on the lost world of past emotions. Three types of sources with their inherent problems are taken into account:[23]

Trial records from local courts: In recording a local witch trial, many steps in writing were taken, from the original notes and scattered single documents up to a completely new constructed clean copy, which could be presented to supervising courts. Most surviving records, for example the sample of **280** records stemming from the ecclesiastical territory of Saint Maximin, provide not the fully written out original documents, but condensed transcripts. Such abstracts intended to prove that the trial had been conducted in a legal, proper way, that a guilty person had been brought to confession and that the court had acted like an honourable instrument of godly justice. Only a few Maximin records present information about the sequences of the interrogations before and during the physical application of torture. The summaries disguised the torture brutally applied in Saint Maximin, where the accused were brought to confession in a very short time. Similarly, the records of about **340** trials in the Eifel region, coming from the counties of Manderscheid and the small lordships of Neuerburg, Schmidtheim, Wildenburg or Bürresheim are rather monosyllabic when it comes to the description of how the interrogation went on, how mental and corporeal fear, and how emotional suffering was caused in the accused witches.[24] Moreover, the emotions of the inquisitors, of the present priests and torturers are not mentioned at all.

Records from appeal courts. To change the perspective, one has to turn to the records from appeal courts. Nullity suits and petitions brought forward to superior courts such as the Imperial Aulic Court and the Imperial Chamber Court in Germany or the provincial court in Luxembourg, where accused frequently complained about abuse and excessive torture at local criminal courts. Over 1,000 documents addressing the provincial court in Luxembourg have survived: the majority called for the reduction of overestimated trial costs, for nullification of verdicts, rehabilitation and restoration of honour. In these documents, we are given a look behind the curtains of the juridical theatre in the courtroom. These documents reveal another, rather contradictory, perspective to what was going on in prisons, torture chambers and courtrooms.[25] In here, the formally accused so-called witches and their relatives represented themselves as innocent victims, who had been prosecuted by brutal judges. The scribes of the petitions, likewise, worked with legally accepted and expected stereotypes of the humble, innocent applicant and the corrupt judge of bad reputation. Nevertheless the facts about torture and abuse expressed in the petitions could not be strategically posed overstatements, since the circumstances were checked by the supervising court.

Secret letters from the prison. Some accused witches tried to smuggle secret letters out of their prison cells to inform their relatives and to declare their innocence in bitter words. The letters from the Bamberg burgomaster Johannes Junius, from Katharina Henot (Cologne) or from Maria Rampendahl (Lemgo) are well-known.[26] These letters are perhaps the closest thing to come near to individual emotions, but, these texts too present specific narratives of emotions, structured by the so-called witches themselves. Whereas local trial records turned rather quiet when it came to the emotional habits of inquisitors or priests, the respective documents of the appeal courts and the secret letters are more talkative on that topic. They use similar arguments to the strict opponents of witch hunts, for example the Catholics Cornelius Loos and Friedrich Spee or Protestants like Matthäus Meyfarth or Anton Prätorius.[27]

Recent interdisciplinary research on the language, grammar, and narratives of hundreds of German local witch trial records emphasizes that they provide carefully fabricated stories which must be interpreted within the legal framework of their original setting.[28] They served the obvious legal function, to present the relevant legal truth and to depict a lawful trial in which the guilt of the accused witch was proven. During interrogation and under torture, a battle between opposing narratives took place, between the oral stories of the witch, the leading questions of the inquisitor or similar court functionary, and the legal literary standards of the scribe. Thus, during the several levels of interrogation, which led to the final confession, many transformations took place, e.g. from vernacular language into legal language or into Latin. The scribe refined, structured and built up the testimonies of witnesses and the accused. As victors in a disparate battle, the questioner and the scribe usually determined the final story, which unfurled in a retrospective macro-narrative composed of micro-narratives: standard motifs depicting the witches' seduction up to her confession and her remorseful death.[29] Altogether, trial records, however substantial they seem to be, present—even in the testimonies of witnesses and confessions—the specific perspective of the prosecution. Withal, putting testimony into writing was itself an instrument of power and the suppression of the mostly unlearned accused.

In local trial records, it remains very difficult, but not impossible, to carve out individual feelings beyond the structured and stereotyped representations of emotions. Records from appeal courts change the perspective, but nevertheless, this change might bring in not feelings, but opposite stereotypes of emotions. The same has to be said about emotional norms, expressed by the victims themselves in their secret letters. Demonology and the judicial literature of instruction elucidated the normative emotions expected from the witch. In knowing the religious and legal norms of representation, the historian can work out hints of individual expressed emotions. We can assume that in trials which were left unfinished or ended with an acquittal, the macro-narrative and the inherent presented emotions have to be different. Probably records which had not been fabricated under the protocolling rules of the inquisitorial criminal procedure, present different representations of emotion and thus might allow a glimpse of individual emotions.

The Witch: Confrontation, Interrogation, Torture, Execution

According to the cosmological system relating macrocosm to microcosm, mind, soul and body were thought of as co-operating entities, whose outward physical reactions and emotional habits signalled presumed inner conditions, be it obduracy or repentance. Juridical handbooks, based on theological, medical and legal texts from antiquity onwards provided certain presuppositions: the accused person could neither navigate nor fake her or his bodily reactions. Even in telling untruth and lies to the judge, the body must reveal the guilt through certain corporeal signs, like blanching or blushing, trembling or unsteadiness, laughing or staring. Moreover, criminals and the guilty revealed themselves by a certain physiognomic appearance.[30]

Courts with legally trained assessors formed a specific kind of emotional community. Certain semantics determined the norms of the emotional habits of the accused as well as the judges. On both parts, torture acted as a catalyst, which changed the representations of emotion during a witch trial. During the painful process of submitting, repenting and confessing to the patriarchal system of the criminal court, the scribe labelled the habits of the witch with respective stereotypes of emotion:

1. The female body was thought to be of a humid, frigid and weak condition. The female mind could be easily impressed, because women's nature was fluid, volatile, and inconstant. Thus, women were an easy target for the devil.[31]

2. Black bile ruled the bodies of female and male witches, which caused so-called diabolic melancholy. Witches were, indeed, children of the planet demon Saturn, like vagrants, beggars, Jews, thieves, cripples, rebels, outcasts, cannibals or Indians. Their diabolic melancholy caused a predisposition which opened the mind for a pact with the devil. Melancholy and the pact with the devil promoted the witches' addiction to lust, to rebellious behaviour, deadly sins, and the receptivity for devilish visions and illusions.

3. Dark melancholy closed the mouth with concealing silence, it caused hardness of the heart, as well as unrest and false tears of self-pity. Moreover, as deadly sinners to the core, male and female witches were tormented by their bad conscience. Their complexion looked sullen, pale, scarred.

4. The devil himself had entered the body of the witch during coitus and had taken possession of its material and its imagination. With his aerial nature, the demon transformed the witch's body, so that it became lighter to swim (during the ducking) and to fly to the sabbat. Learned debates discussed in which way the evil eye and the foul emanations of the witch could corrupt the judge. Sometimes

on advice of the executioner, in the courtroom several methods were applied to break the devilish power of the witch. These ideas (or better: the fantasies about the polluted body of the witch) shaped both the habitus of the witch and the habitus of the judge in the courtroom.[32]

Texts and images in household books, almanacs, books of astrology, calendars, pamphlets or leaflets spread the knowledge about the *mala physiognomia*, the bad physiognomy of witches, for example as children of Saturn. The labelling worked in both directions: poor, vagrants and other members of the lower ranks could easily be identified as witches, since their outward complexion revealed their addiction to melancholy. For example, during the great Bamberg witch hunts, fear reigned amongst the inhabitants of becoming the next to be seized, since rumours about denunciations were running wild. Ottilia Peßlerin was imprisoned and, since she refused to confess in a first interrogation, her husband was ordered to court to be asked about the behaviour of his wife. According to the scribe's notes, he testified that Peßlerin had shown great anxiety, since two other women of her acquaintance had been seized. Her complexion turned pale, she was driven by unrest and insomnia, by weeping and sadness. She withdrew from human company. Her body flinched between sweating and freezing.[33] This report may be read as a description of fears and feelings; however, the text samples the characteristics of a melancholic witch in the snarl of her bad conscience. Consequently, the document was used as evidence in the witch trial against the Peßlerin.

The witch trials unfolded a stereotyped, monotonous dramaturgy. From the first scene in the courtroom, the witches' emotional habits revealed their guilt. Many trial records describe how the suspected person firstly was confronted with a still living, but already sentenced 'accomplice', who had confessed and had to enact the role of eye witness. In this dramatic confrontation, the newly accused persons confirmed their innocence. Some were shocked in facing their former neighbours, relatives or friends, who had undergone torture and were—so we can assume— not more than a spectre of their former selves. Others remained speechless, others pleaded for mercy and the truth, others expressed insults or laughter; others remarked that only hatred and envy had caused the denunciation, others invoked the Virgin or saints, begging their accusers not to wash their hands in the blood of the innocent.[34] However, scribes and notaries, who were obliged to note the gesture and countenance of the confronted persons, inclined to construe signs of defence and fear as signs of bad conscience and guilt. These attributions clearly show that in practice the theory of torture as an instrument which never could bring the innocent to confession was turned upside down: the accused were already presumed guilty long before torture had been applied. Scribes re-interpreted de facto expressed feelings such as fear or shame in ways that told against the accused. The accused had few means to break this vicious circle of self-affirmative arguments: the protestation of innocence must be falsehood, since the guilt of the witch stood firm. For the same reason, invocations of the Virgin or the saints must be blasphemous. Even the witches' silence during the interrogations, mainly under torture, must be a deafening silence, revealing impenitence and a bad conscience.

Particularly, the witches' incapacity to weep tears of remorse labelled her or him as a minion of Satan.[35] Trial records never tire of narrating the story of witches who only feigned tears with saliva or who moaned without producing any tears at all. Under torture, some witches laughed and cursed, they looked around suspiciously, rolling their eyes and grimacing awfully. Others fell asleep whilst being tortured. These habits and their alleged insensitivity to pain must be due to salves, amulets, or other kinds of evil magic. The witches had to be freed from these diabolic armatures by exorcism, by dressing them in consecrated shirts, by washings and the drinking of holy water, the fumigation with incense.[36] After the witch's conversion to a plausible confession, which matched the juridical expectations of the interrogators and the presumptions of demonology, the emotional habits of the witch changed. A metamorphosis took place: The witch now wept tears of repentance, after having cursed the devil and its machinations. Thus, very often the macro-narrative in a trial record with a conviction to death ends with the emotive narrative of the remorseful, poor sinner. In adopting this image, pressed upon her or him by the authority, the condemned former witch now praised the harsh eradication of witches and demanded even more intense witch hunting. He or she expressed herself as most thankful for being brought to conversion and confession. At this very moment, the witch was treated like a *Blutzeuge*, a kind of a martyr, in whom God's mercy had operated the miracle of conversion.[37]

Comparable narratives unveil a perverted understanding of penitence and repentance, culminating in executions where the delinquents likewise had to show a rueful, contrite behaviour. Peter Binsfeld, the notorious suffragan bishop of Trier, argued that it was a deadly sin to sedate convicts with alcohol in order to quieten their extreme fears of being burned, because thus lulled they could not focus their minds on penitence and on God. He also advised to bestow the Holy communion to the convicts, but early enough so that they would not go into the fire with Christ still in their stomachs.[38] Alleged witches might have taken on the role of a poor, repentant sinner rather voluntarily, because it gave them at least the possibility to stage themselves as martyrs and blood witnesses. However, in the place of execution, many sentenced witches seem to have lost their confidence, and in fear of the burning, they retracted their confession with the consequence of being tortured again. The trial records labelled witches who panicked while being bound to the stake as lost, remorseless sinners. The records of the witches' struggle at the stake, indeed, presents a view of their fearful emotions.

Local trial records tend to paint a whitewashed picture of the applied torture and the bodily reactions of the witches. Accordingly, urinating or defecating during torture or in advance of the burning was labelled as the horrible stench of Evil and not as the signs of pain or deadly fear. Above all, trial records veiled the torture afflicted.

We get a sense of what that torture was really like from other sources. For example, at the end of the sixteenth century a woman named Appolonia served as a witness in an impeachment inquest against the notary Omsdorf who acted as leading figure during the devastating witch hunts in Saint Maximin and in the neighbouring electorate of Trier.[39] Appolonia reported that she had to endure the strappado seven times, once up to several hours, during which the court members went to lunch. Most of the time, she was left alone with the notary and the executioner, because the other assessors of the court, even the bailiff, could not stand the terror of torture. While she was hanging in the strappado, the executioner applied heavy weights at her feet and at her head, so that she feared her neck would break. Because she showed herself impenitent in refusing to answer leading questions, the notary incited the executioner to 'tickle' her more severely by pulling the hanging woman several times by her skirt, applying most painful jerks. But Appolonia refused to confess, which provoked the notary to wrench a pointed stick out of the hands of the executioner and to prick the woman's breasts until blood spurted from them. Her body was shaved all over and in one of the following interrogations on the rack the soles of her feet were burned, her cheeks pierced with a red-hot iron. Finally, the notary had to release her after forcing her to swear an adjuration never to talk about the torment. For nine weeks she was too sick to move her arms; her husband had to nurse her like a little child. Two years after her giving witness in the impeachment inquest, Appolonia was arrested a second time for alleged witchcraft, just as the notary had promised her when he was confronted with her statements. This time, she confessed immediately and was sentenced to death. Appolonia's story was not a solitary case. There are a multitude of detailed descriptions about the cruel, often fanatical, habits of interrogators in the supplications and suits brought before various appellate courts such as the Imperial Chamber Court (*Reichskammergericht*), the Imperial Aulic Council (*Reichshofrat*) in the Holy Roman Empire or similar higher courts in the Spanish Netherlands.[40]

Strikingly, the emotional codes remained the same in local trial records and in the appeal suits, but with the signs reversed: in prisons and torture chambers, the accused witches' cried the bitter tears of the innocent persecuted. With mighty strength they tried to cling to this image of innocence to withstand torture. Some thought themselves to be martyrs, being tortured by tyrants, who acted even worse than heathens and Turks. Their emotional suffering must have been immense, after they were forced to confess falsely.

THE INTERROGATOR AND THE TORTURER

In theory, the interrogator confronted the devil, who had lodged himself in the witches' body. The polluted witches' bodily material had to be destroyed to free the soul, to cause a conversion, and to extract the confession. Demonology, canon law and judicial instructions depicted the interrogators as wise and untouchable by demonic influences. The judge consisted of two different persons and thus, of two bodies: the fallible human body, whose perception, will, suggestion, and finally, emotions could fail, and of the impersonal body of the unerring judge, representing law and power, which never could condemn an innocent.[41]

Judges gained the status of a father confessor with the sacred task to enable contrite penitence in the accused witch and to exhort a full confession of her or his sins. Very often, the local trial records reveal little to nothing about the emotional habits of the members of courts, since the records were focussed on constructing the narrative of overcoming the witch. Likewise, the emotional configuration of the involved ministers and priests is seldom recorded. However, at least some general remarks might be made. Interrogators, judges and notaries tried to frighten the witches with torture as soon as they entered the courtroom, but not all of them could remain in the torture chamber whilst the tormenting took place.[42] The notorious witch commissioner Johannes Möden and his entourage of hangmen and torturers, who together were responsible for more than 300 capital verdicts in the Rhine-Meuse area, always took a good swig of beer and wine before they went off to the witch trials. During the interrogation sessions Möden drank heavily, so that he sometimes fell asleep.[43] Dr. Ernst Vasoldt, too, one of the witch commissioners in Bamberg, several times was denounced as a drunkard. [44] The trial costs leave no doubt of the immense amounts of wine which was consumed during the witch trials in Saint Maximin or the Eifel territories. However, it is hard to decide if these men soothed their emotions during torture with alcohol, if the drunkenness had simply been a common habit, or if the narratives about the judges as drunkards had been an attribution in order to defame them.

In some districts of the Rhine-Meuse area, bailiffs and lords left the task of custody and assisting the torture to members of the local witch hunting committee. In detail and relying on thousand pages of trial records and official correspondence, Walter Rummel has shown how witches were tortured illegally through the hands of their turnkeys and custodians, sometimes to the point of death.[45] The torturers showed no compassion with the suffering delinquent, but ruthlessly invented new torments and whitewashing lies to veil the goings-on in the prison cell. It is hard not to label the habits of the custodian peasants as sadistic. The unbridled passions, clearly, were found with the torturers, who acted out their power over so-called witches, which in their former life had been their neighbours and sometimes their enemies. However, according to demonology and legal standards, the peasant torturers battled against tough-necked enemies of God, whose bodies had to be destroyed to gain confession. Mercy could not be granted. But it seems as if none of the men showed any fear about witches. Maybe they believed that once witches had been arrested by the court, their power was broken. The findings of Jonathan Durrant concerning the witch hunts in Eichstätt support the argument that in fact on the part of the court members and the turnkeys, no fear of witches existed. On the contrary, the imprisoned witches in Eichstätt were sexually abused by their custodians. Sometimes the women sought for sexual intercourse to get pregnant and, thus, be spared from torture or execution.[46]

Witches who denied conversion and confession infuriated their interrogators. For example in Saint Maximin, the notary Omsdorf, in facing the steadfastness of the tortured witch Appolonia, fell into a rage. He insulted her, spat in her mouth and slapped a heavy book around her head.[47] This most remarkable, meaningful reaction revealed that he judged the resistance of the still young woman to be an insubordination and a mere diabolic rebellion against the superiority of his gender, his age and—most of all—his patriarchal authority.

We can presume that the witch trials took a great emotional toll on the judges and torturers. However, the local trial records mostly present us the stereotype of the wise and pious judge. Secret letters, nullity suits and petitions, on the contrary, paint the picture of interrogators and torturers who loosened the reins to their unbridled passions when the witch refused to confess. Frustration led to rage and eventually to the invention of new torture methods. And not fear, but probably disgust, weariness, bad conscience and guilt led some of the men to drink heavily.

THE WITCH IN THE COURTROOM: SOME FINAL QUESTIONS

The setting of the courtroom saw the intersection of the actual emotional community of the judges and interrogators with the imagined emotional community of the witches. Local trial records labelled both sides with a respective emotional code. Even in the records of supervising courts or in secret letters, we find representations and standardizations of emotions. However, this chapter has focussed on witch hunts in the Rhine-Meuse area and in Franconia, and thus, on mostly Catholic persecuting environments where harsh torture dynamized massive witch hunts with hundreds of executions and a very low rate of acquittals or unfinished trials. In looking at other areas with witch trials, many open questions remain:

First, emotional standards shifted where torture was only 'mildly' applied or not applied at all. Differences showed up when professional or non-professional torturers took action. Conditions and backgrounds changed in single cases of witch trials or in the milieu of panics.

Second, emotional standards shifted according to shifting confessional milieus. For example, in Lutheran or Reformed territories with high standards of religious confessions[48] the alleged witches had no ability to free their souls from the deadly sin of false testimony in auricular confession to a priest in secret. The emotional suffering must have been worse for Protestant witches forced to a false confession. According to Mattheus Meyfarth, the Reformed minister and opponent to witch trials, witches who under torture fell into despair and doubts about God's benevolence and justice, were doomed to hell, even if they were totally innocent of the alleged crime.[49] Even Catholic 'witches' could not rely on confessional secrets, since priests were required to denounce those witches who had retracted their confession during confession.

Third, we have to assume gendered emotional standards. Studies in masculinity and femininity have, so far, not taken into account different emotional habits of male and female witches. We know that especially older women were able to withstand torture more frequently than men, especially high ranking men. The trials against burgomasters, Catholic priests, or male elite in general present a clear pattern: The male resistance very often broke away with the humiliating shaving of the beard, the symbol of male honour, with the undressing and with the total subjection to torture. Besides, the male physical condition of greater weight made the strappado much more painful and less durable.[50] Thus, the history of emotions has to be combined with the history of the body, its gendered honour and physical and mental abilities.

Fourth, in every criminal trial where torture was applied, emotional habits were established and written down in records. In comparison, we have to scrutinize records of all kinds of criminal trials *in toto* to evaluate the links between emotionality and witchcraft.

Finally and foremost, we should not only ask why torture brought so many innocent persons to confess, but why so many people withstood the brutal destroying of their body without confession. For example, in juridical environments where certain standards of torturing were maintained, the delinquents were able to endure the pain, because they knew that there was an end to it after a certain amount of time. Some hangmen and executioners who were charged with witchcraft, were able to resist torture, since they knew exactly about the procedure. On the other hand, the accused gave in to confession, after they had lost any confidence in the juridical system, or they had fallen prey to resignation, or they had been talked into confession by their own family members or the father figure of the priest. These changes in perspective would take into consideration emotions other than fear, emphasizing the importance of source material beyond the local witch trial records (like acquittals, petitions or nullity suits). In general, further research into the emotional norms, narratives or labels of alleged witches has to move from appreciating local trial records as 'windows' onto lost emotions of the past. Probably Loos, a theologian working in Trier, gave the most memorable definition of torture: 'The miserable creatures'—meaning the alleged witches—'are compelled by the severity of the torture to confess things which they never have committed. By cruel butchery innocent blood is shed and by a new alchemy gold and silver coined from human blood.'[51] Thus, the historian's research on 'witchcraft and emotions' has just begun.

NOTES

1. Robisheaux, 'German Witch Trials', 197.
2. See Levack, *Oxford Handbook of Witchcraft*, and Golden, *Encyclopedia of Witchcraft*.
3. Roper, *Oedipus and the Devil*, 205–207; Roper, *Witch Craze*, 82–83.
4. Dillinger, 'Annäherung an das Fremde', 64; de Blécourt, 'Sabbath Stories', 88–89; Voltmer, 'Stimmen der Frauen?', 26–27; Zagolla, *Folter und Hexenprozess*, 43; Schild, 'Der gefolterte weibliche Körper', 490–493. Some critiques of Roper's thesis are based on Scarry, *Body in Pain*, 1985.
5. See Robisheaux, 'Queen of Evidence', 178–179; and for example Durrant, *Witchcraft, Gender and Society*, 89.
6. For example Midelfort, *Witchhunting in Southwestern Germany*; Bever, *Realities of Witchcraft*; Kounine, 'Gendering of Witchcraft', 295–317; Kounine, 'Witch on Trial'; Raith, 'Württemberg, Duchy of'. On Bever's neurobiological approach see Voltmer, 'Behind the "Veil of memory"', 96–102.
7. Kounine, 'Gendering of Witchcraft', 306; Kounine, 'Witch on Trial', 233–235; in general see Rowlands, *Witchcraft Narratives in Germany*.
8. Robisheaux, 'Queen of Evidence', 197.
9. Not every Lutheran territory experienced only moderate witch trials; e.g. the duchies of Mecklenburg had 4000 trials, including 2000 executions: Moeller, *Dass Willkür über Recht ginge*. In Reformed Scotland the witch-hunt found about 2,500 victims: Goodare ed., *Scottish Witches and Witch Hunters*.
10. Schnell, *Haben Gefühle eine Geschichte?*, 95–100; Schnell, 'Ansätze und Irrwege historischer Emotionsforschung', 71–113.
11. Touber, 'Articulating Pain'; Silverman, *Tortured Subjects*; Schuster, *Verbrecher, Opfer, Heilige*.
12. Robisheaux, 'Queen of Evidence', 179.

13. Moeller, *Dass Willkür über Recht ginge*; Sauter, *Hexenprozess und Folter*; Wilde, *Die Zauberei- und Hexenprozesse*.

14. See in general Zagolla, *Folter und Hexenprozess*; Schild, 'Der gefolterte weibliche Körper'; Bähr, *Furcht und Furchtlosigkeit*, 314–331; Levack, 'Witchcraft and the Law', 474–477; Clark, *Thinking with Demons*, 591–92.

15. Robisheaux, 'Queen of Evidence', 175–205.

16. See endnotes 20 and 28.

17. Brooks, 'Narrative in and of the Law', 415–426.

18. See in general Robisheaux, 'Queen of Evidence'.

19. Schneider, 'Forum internum—forum externum', 23–41.

20. Scharff, 'Seelenrettung und Machtinszenierung', 151–169; Lembke, 'Folter und gerichtliches Geständnis', 171–199; Voltmer ed., *Hexenverfolgung und Herrschaftspraxis*; Voltmer, 'Hexenpolitik im Saarraum?'; Voltmer, 'Judge's Lore?'; Evans, *Rituals Of Retribution*; Robisheaux, 'Queen of Evidence', 180–181; Motta, 'Evidence, Truth and Sovereignty'.

21. Bähr, *Furcht und Furchtlosigkeit*, 154, 314–340.

22. Electorate of Trier: about 1000 victims; Luxembourg: about 2000 victims; Saint Maximin: about 400–500 victims; Eifel territories (including Imperial counties, dukedoms, and very small entities): in toto about 1500 victims; in Lorraine and the German speaking Saarregion far more than 2000 victims; not including the witch-hunts in the German speaking districts of Lorraine, which yet have not been scrutinized; see Voltmer, 'Hexenpolitik im Saarraum?'; Voltmer, 'Luxembourg, duchy of'; Voltmer, 'St. Maximin, prince abbey'; Voltmer, 'Germany, north and northwest'.

23. Voltmer, 'Witch trials'; Voltmer, 'Stimmen der Frauen?'; Voltmer, 'Judge's Lore?'; Voltmer, 'Witch-Finders, Witch-Hunters or Kings of the Sabbath?'; Briggs, 'Witchcraft and the Local Communities', 199–217.

24. Concerning 'emotional suffering' in the context of torture see Reddy, *Navigation of Feeling*, 123–124.

25. Voltmer and Kobayashi, 'Supplikationen und Hexereiverfahren', 247–269.

26. Topalovic and Hille, 'Perspektivierung von Wirklichkeit(en) im Hexenprozess'; Levack ed., 'The confession of Johannes Junius'. Some of the secret letters never reached their address, but were intercepted by the turnkeys or other people in charge. They were

added to the trial records, probably they have served as further proof for the alleged wickedness of the accused.

27. However, even these contra-narratives about torture and emotions have to be scrutinized more thoroughly in the context of their religious and confessional background; see Bähr, *Furcht und Furchtlosigkeit*, 314–340.

28. See inter alia Macha et al. eds., *Deutsche Kanzleisprache in Hexenverhörprotokollen*; Hille, *Der Teufelspakt in frühneuzeitlichen Verhörprotokollen*.

29. Voltmer, 'Stimmen der Frauen?', 33. Compare the records stemming from the Salem trials, written mostly by scribes who were not legally trained; they likewise, contaminated the protocolling with attributions, norms, and their own inherent interpretations: Doty, 'Telling tales', 25–41.

30. Schneider, 'Die Beobachtung des Zeugen nach Artikel 71 der "Carolina"', 153–182.

31. See Tamar Herzig's chapter, this volume.

32. See in general Zika, *Exorcising our Demons*; Voltmer, 'Von den Kindern des Saturn'; Voltmer, 'Im Bann des Planetendämons Saturn', 115–150; Schild, 'Der gefolterte weibliche Körper'.

33. Gehm, *Die Hexenverfolgung im Hochstift Bamberg*, 165–166.

34. Durrant, *Witchcraft, Gender and Society*, 111–112.

35. Schneider, 'Die Beobachtung des Zeugen nach Artikel 71 der "Carolina"', 167; Schneider, 'Tränen vor Gericht', 57–73.

36. These 'purifying' procedures were applied in Protestant as well as in Catholic territories: Clark, *Thinking with Demons*, 592. However, we do not know exactly how often and in detail these procedures have been used all over Europe.

37. Robisheaux, 'Queen of Evidence', 176–180.

38. Binsfeld, *Tractat von Bekanntnuß der Zauberer und Hexen*, 285–288.

39. Stadtbibliothek Trier Hs. 1534/166, folio 37 passim; Landeshauptarchiv Koblenz, Bestand 56, Nr. 1856, folio 74 recto passim.

40. See Oestmann, *Hexenprozesse am Reichskammergericht*; Voltmer, '...ce tant exécrable et détestable crime de sortilège', 57–92.

41. Motta, 'Evidence, Truth and Sovereignty', 7–8.

42. Levack ed., 'Confession of Niclas Fiedler at Trier, 1591', 175–178.

43. Rummel, *Bauern, Herren und Hexen*, 183–190.

44. Gehm, *Die Hexenverfolgung im Hochstift Bamberg*, 155.
45. Rummel, *Bauern, Herren und Hexen*, 101f.
46. Durrant, *Witchcraft, Gender and Society*, 226–241. The warders's abuses were investigated in Eichstätt separately to the witch trials.
47. See pages 108–109, above.
48. Robisheaux, 'Queen of Evidence', 191–194.
49. Bähr, *Furcht und Furchtlosigkeit*, 325–326.
50. See Voltmer, 'Witch-Finders, Witch-Hunters or Kings of the Sabbath?'; Voltmer, 'Henker, Heiler, Hexenbanner—Hexenmeister?'; Kounine, 'Gendering of Witchcraft'.
51. Burr, 'Witch Persecutions', 15.

CHAPTER 7

'So They Will Love Me and Pine for Me': Intimacy and Distance in Early Modern Russian Magic

Valerie A. Kivelson

In 1965 the American comedian Tom Lehrer worked into his act a little shtick about love and intimacy.

> I know some people feel that marriage as an institution is dying out, but I disagree. And the point was driven home to me rather forcefully not long ago by a letter I received which said: 'Darling, I love you, and I cannot live without you. Marry me, or I will kill myself.' Well, I was a little disturbed at that until I took another look at the envelope, and saw that it was addressed to occupant …[1]

This story generated quite a laugh on the crackly soundtrack of the old LP record. The humor, of course, lies in the preposterous juxtaposition of desperate love and impersonal addressee. A similar odd coupling forms the centerpiece of my exploration of witchcraft and emotion in early modern

V.A. Kivelson
University of Michigan

© The Author(s) 2016
L. Kounine, M. Ostling (eds.), *Emotions in the History of Witchcraft*, DOI 10.1057/978-1-137-52903-9_7

117

Russia, where passionate love magic transferred its intimate efficacy to the most generic targets.

In seventeenth- and eighteenth-century Russia, the harsh hierarchies of family and serf-owning estates generated many of the witchcraft accusations that reached the courts. According to testimony recorded in some 500 secular and religious trials of witches—as well as an assortment of spell books and related texts—love, sex, and power were negotiated within close quarters through the exchange of spells and suspicions. Passions found tangible form in the placement of bewitched objects near the intended target. Spells were recited at crossroads, salt was cast into the winds, bewitched herbs were tucked into bedding. Intimacy and physical contact were essential to the efficacy of enchantment.

Yet Muscovites—particularly Muscovite men—also moved in a broader world populated by strangers who could advance or destroy life-chances at will. Armed with prophylactic spells written out in 'fill-in-the-blank' form, mobile men prepared themselves for any eventuality. Significantly, the spells they hid on their persons deployed the same affective strategies as those unleashed on their intimates. Noblemen, judges, commanding officers, 'powerful people', or the tsar himself were all manipulated by spells that would make them 'love me and pine for me', the spell-caster. In a society reliant on kinship, patronage, and protection, power was negotiated among men through protestations of filial love, childish dependency, and patriarchal obligation. In the realm of magic, passion and desire could upend hierarchies and flip the balance of power. In this context, love magic transferred its passion play into the political sphere, working its emotional enchantments on an expansive, unlimited spatial and social plane. This chapter will explore the translation of love magic from the proximate and intimate to the generic and political.

Magic in Close Quarters

As evident from the reports of witchcraft trials, both the accusers and accused understood the power and vulnerability inherent in physical proximity.[2]

A richly documented case from the town of Dobroe on Russia's southern frontier illustrates the dynamics of witchcraft within an extended household of family and servants, and shows the importance of close spaces in Muscovite ideas about how magic operated. In Russian Orthodox Christianity, priests were expected to marry, so the priest of one of Dobroe's churches, Priest Davyd, headed such a household. In 1676, he filed a complaint in the governor's court against his hired man, Mishka Kireev, and Kireev's wife.

> In past years and in this current year on various dates, roots and dirt appeared in the upper chamber of his house under the ceiling and stuck in the corner. Davyd and his wife also saw those roots in their drinks, in their *braga* (home-brewed beer) and *kvas* (a drink made from fermented grain), and Arinka, the wife of the hired man Mishka, brought those drinks to them. And from those poisonous roots his wife and children are dying. And his suspicion in this matter fell on his hired man Mishka and his wife Arinka.[3]

The placement of these suspicious substances was particularly threatening; they appeared in the rafters of the 'upper chamber', that is directly above the sleeping platform where the family would be its most exposed and helpless. Priest Davyd feared that he would 'perish along with my family and with my little children for no reason'.

The court agreed to pursue the matter and questioned the hired hand about his activities. Mishka blamed his stepfather, Isaika Nekireev, for tucking the roots and dirt in the rafters. Mishka explained that his stepfather intended 'that Priest Davyd and his whole family would wither. And from the withering disease, they sickened.' When the governor ordered Mishka's wife, Arinka, to be questioned, she also pointed her finger at her in-laws. She claimed her mother-in-law had instructed her to bewitch the priest's wife and daughters by administering poisonous roots in their drinks.

The court took these confessions seriously. Both couples were brought in for questioning under torture. Under duress, the suspects elaborated further on the ways that magic exploited physical proximity. Arinka explained that her husband had collected the dirt used in their spells 'from the footsteps where Priest Davyd and his wife walked', thereby taking advantage of the personal aura imprinted in the dirt. Her own role as cook, laundress, and nanny gave her unlimited access to the most intimate objects and spaces of her masters' lives.[4]

> And she, Arinka, stole a headdress [*kokoshnik*] and headscarf [*podubrusnik*] from the priest's wife, and her mother-in-law told her to put that headdress and headscarf under a post with a spell and to say: 'As heavy as this post, so may it be heavy on the priest's wife.'[5]

Like footprints, items of clothing carried a tactile trace of their wearers. Moving from headdress to more intimate undergarments, Arinka described how she tore a bit of cloth 'from the blouse of the priest's wife, right at the heart, and she brought the rag to her mother-in-law to use in bewitchment'. Food also provided an easy vehicle for bewitchment. Arinka admitted that 'she gave the priest's wife and daughters roots mixed into their drinks on the instruction of her mother-in-law'.[6]

If Arinka's testimony focused on food and clothing, her husband's stepfather dwelled more on the placement of enchantments within the most vulnerable domestic spaces.

> Isaika was tortured, given ten blows, and with the first shaking and with ten blows he said: … he told his stepson to take dirt from the footprints where they had walked and to bring that dirt to him so that he could say a spell on it, and then he stuck it in the chamber under the ceiling so that Priest Davyd and his wife would wither and from that disease would die. And he told his stepson to put roots in the stove in the main chamber to work bewitchment as well.[7]

The Russian stove was far more than a source of heat. It was the warm, protective center of the household. The nook behind the stove was the warmest sleeping spot, granted to newlyweds, grandparents, or heads of household. This same nook was a productive site of folklore, the favorite hiding place both for the household spirit (*domovoi*) and for the lazy youngest sons of fairytales. Baba Yaga, the canonical witch of Russian folklore, enjoyed nothing better than roasting stray humans in her oven; an oven with fairly explicit sexual as well as maternal innuendo.[8] Isaiko's placement of bewitched roots in the stove subverted the very heart of the household and, like his assault on the sleeping chamber, took advantage of the family's trust and vulnerability. Betrayal of trust figured even more blatantly in Isaiko's confession of slipping a root into the cradle where the priest's grandson lay exposed and utterly defenseless, 'so that he would die'.[9]

Precisely what these transcriptions signal about the actual practices of any of the actors is impossible to say, given the distorting effects of court performance and the violence of torture. What they do reveal clearly, however, is that all involved parties understood magic to take place in close quarters. Those accused of inflicting that harm, whether confessing their actual actions or scrambling to put together some story that would satisfy their torturers, drew on the ideas about witchcraft that circulated in their society. Accusers, accused, witnesses, and court officials all converged on an understanding of where and how magic worked, and they all found plausible the idea that physical contact and spatial immediacy lent efficacy to charms and curses. When Muscovites looked for the people most likely to wish them harm, they looked first to the denizens of their own homes. When they sought physical evidence of that harm, they peered into the nooks and crannies of their houses or examined their headscarves and intimate underclothing.

In his recent comparative exploration of African witchcraft, Peter Geschiere draws out the contributions of intimacy and proximity to fostering witchcraft anxiety. 'Almost everywhere', he writes, witches 'are believed to strike from close by: witchcraft is a form of aggression that is most dangerous because it comes from inside'.[10] It operates most potently within a sphere of intimacy, in which daily interactions require a fundamental level of trust. At the same time, that very intimacy creates vulnerability to all sorts of threats, occult and otherwise, making trust difficult to maintain. Only an irrational leap of faith, a suspension of suspicion, Geschiere argues, allows people to retain a sense of trust in the face of ever-present danger. As the conflict between the priest and his servants demonstrates, that leap of faith could be tenuous, and when doubts crept in, accusations could fly.

WITCHCRAFT AND EMOTION

Muscovite sources rarely expose the inner recesses of the heart. A largely illiterate society, not much given to secular or even religious introspection, early modern Russia is notoriously silent on questions of sentiment. And yet witchcraft trials prove exceptionally expressive on the topic. A townswoman in Murom, for instance, confessed to bewitching a number of other people, including 'the woman Ulitka, out of jealousy'. In her testimony, she described living unhappily in the home of her in-laws and 'admitted that she put a stake in her father-in-law's bed to cause illness of the heart … She bewitched her father-in-law because he acts unkindly toward her.' Her goal, she explained was 'to make him love her'.[11]

Love or its absence lay at the heart of many confession narratives. For example, in 1647 a jilted peasant woman confessed to cursing her former lover out of jealousy. Holding a hair stolen from a corpse, she recited, 'As a dead body does not stand up, so may he, Fedor, not stand [perish].'[12]

Love was the essence in a well-known case that unfolded in Moscow in 1638–39, a case that involved magical tampering with the tsar and tsaritsa themselves. Dar'ia Lamanova, a gold-embroiderer employed in the tsaritsa's embroidery workshop, confessed under torture that she had sprinkled ashes in the tsaritsa's footsteps on the advice of an old fortune-teller named Nast'ka. She hoped to make the tsar and tsaritsa 'love her and treat her kindly'. Dar'ia added that the old woman also helped wives avoid mistreatment by their husbands. She 'works love spells, and she can take away the anger [*serdtse*, lit. heart] and jealousy of men toward women'. 'She says spells over salt and soap, and then [women] can give the salt to men in their food and drink, and wash themselves with the soap.' The interrogators soon discovered that other women in the workshop also relied on spells to pacify abusive spouses, an all too frequent issue for Muscovite wives. Dar'ia's friend Avdot'ia 'used [the enchanted salt] on her own husband too, and she made his anger and criticism [*serdtse i um*, lit. heart and mind] go away'. Spells could encourage kindness not only to wives but to others as well. 'That same old woman gave something enchanted to [another needleworker from the tsaritsa's workshop], so that her husband … would be kind to her … children.'[13]

Arrested and questioned, the old, blind Nast'ka initially denied everything. In a court-ordered confrontation between the two women, Dar'ia called on her to confess. She enumerated the old woman's specific rituals, some of which duplicate those already encountered in cases described above, and she reiterated the goal of the procedure: to win the love of her superiors.

> Remember, she said to her, how Mistress Avdot'ia Iaryshkina told me about you, and I came to you on her advice and, having ripped off the collar of my black blouse, I brought it to you, and with that same collar I brought you salt and soap. And you asked me if Avdot'ia was my real name, and I told you that it was, and you burned the collar of my blouse at the stove, and you said spells over the salt and soap, and when you were done with the spells, you told me to sprinkle that in the sovereign's footprints, where the tsar and tsaritsa and their children and people close to them walked; and you said that then I would have no harsh treatment from the tsar and tsaritsa and the people close to them would love me.[14]

When 'tortured severely and burned with fire', the blind woman dropped her denials and confessed that she had instructed her clients to sprinkle the enchanted ashes in the tsaritsa's footprints, but not with any evil intent, but rather so that when the tsar and tsaritsa stepped over that ash, whoever had cases pending before the tsar, they would succeed in their suits, and then they would receive the tsar's kindness and the people close to him would be good to them.

She even recited some of her spells for turning wrath to love, the central agenda of her magic, whether aimed at the highest authorities or at domestic tyrants. One spell, much in demand from her female customers, aimed to turn a husband's anger to love through the power of analogy: 'As quickly as soap washes away, so quickly may the husband fall in love with his wife. As a blouse is light on the body, so may the husband be to his wife.' The spell exploits the power of self-love to encourage conjugal affection: 'As people gaze at themselves in a mirror, so may the husband look at his wife and never tire of looking.'[15] Once again, from the point of view of the accused practitioner and consumer, magic was imagined as a tool employed to mitigate harshness and engender love.

A similar goal appears in the testimony of a male shepherd accused of witchcraft in 1673. He explained to his interrogators that he engaged in 'no heresy or witchcraft or any kind of evil at all'. Rather, he endeavored to mend human relations, to cure the sick and to improve marital relations. For couples afflicted with sexual dysfunction, he prescribed sending to the 'person of the female sex' a cup of river water. It was critical to the success of the procedure that it come from the river and from no other source. Before he gave the river water to the woman, he would recite a beautiful, prayer-like spell over it:

> Have mercy, Most Blessed Mother of God. Intercede for us sinners. Be merciful. Cover the sinful souls of your male slave So-and-So and your female slave So-and-So with your incorruptible mantle. In the whole world, protect them. Give them, Mother of God, love between them and [allow them] to live in congress as of old, in love, so that they now and forever will live in congress together. And when they comb their hair with that river water three times in the night, so may the woman So-and-So keep combing her husband, your slave, So-and-So, day and night and in the hours when the river flows. Eternal glory to you, and to those aforenamed people, husband and wife, eternal life.[16]

The recipients of the spell, the 'male slave' and 'female slave', were not necessarily enslaved people, although slavery was widespread and legal in Russia until its abolition in 1723 and the majority of the peasant population was enserfed after 1649. The form of address derives from an Orthodox Christian convention of speaking of 'slaves of God' and 'slaves of the tsar'. More sinister spells, as we will see below, omit the divine referent, leaving simply a 'slave', but commonly the full formula was used. This was magic that derived its efficacy from the affective threads, both destructive and loving, that bound families, households, masters and serfs, lovers and even members of the heavenly hierarchy in oppressively close intimacy.

'MISERY OVERTOOK HER': EMOTIONS AS VEHICLES OF POWER

It is not surprising that strong feelings produced in close quarters led to the use of magic. Envy, desire, discontent, and anger are all closely associated with witchcraft in many parts of the globe. More noteworthy is the way that Russian magic deployed emotions themselves as the engines animating curses and spells.

Two emotions in particular moved about and did things in the world. Love and Misery were explicitly deployed and evoked by spell-casters and manipulated in their subjects. In the spells of the blind witch Nast'ka, we have already seen the magical force of redirecting narcissistic self-love (gazing in a mirror) outward toward another. Love spells and incantations also addressed the emotional state of Misery directly, as a sentient being. Spell-casters engaged Misery to travel the world and to bring about the desired transformations. The following love spell, taken from the spell book of a small landholder in 1688/89, exemplifies this pattern:

> Oh, you, Satan with [your] devils,
> With little ones and great ones,
> Fly out from the Ocean-Sea,
> Take my fiery Misery,
> Go around the white world,
> Do not set fire to stump, log, or moist tree,
> Not earth, [nor] grass,
> But set afire the soul of that slave for me.
> On the Sea-Ocean, On the island of Buian,[17]
> There stands a bathhouse,
> And in that bathhouse lies a board,
> And on that board lies Misery.
> I, the slave So-and-So, came along,
> What's with you, Misery,

That you grieve and are sad?
Don't grieve, Misery,
Don't be sad, Misery,
Come, Misery,
Come to female slave So-and-So, Misery;
So she will grieve and be sad.

'Misery' transfers its own woeful essence to the anonymous, fill-in-the-blanks love object, 'female slave So-and-So'.

'Misery' or *toska*, the primary actor and addressee of the spell, refers to a complex emotional state, claimed by Russians in the nineteenth and twentieth centuries as their natural state of being, their exclusive cultural patrimony. Vladimir Nabokov observed that 'no single word in English renders all the shades of *toska*':

At its deepest and most painful, it is a sensation of great spiritual anguish, often without any specific cause. At less morbid levels, it is a dull ache of the soul, a longing with nothing to long for, a sick pining, a vague restlessness, mental throes, yearning … a feeling of physical or metaphysical dissatisfaction. In particular cases it may be the desire for somebody or something specific, nostalgia, lovesickness. At the lowest level it grades into ennui, boredom, *skuka*.[18]

This is a lot to load into a single emotional term. How many of these subtle tones of anguish layered the term in early modern usage is hard to determine. At some level, with characteristic early modern Russian bluntness, 'misery' meant physical pain. It was sometimes paired with the term *lomota*, aches. For instance in 1692 a monastic peasant named Matiushka confessed in court that he had learned 'to say a spell over salt and over water and to bewitch people and send misery [*toska*] and aching pains [*lomota*] to them'.[19] Similarly, witnesses in possession investigations testified that '*toska* overtook her', attributing corporeal power to a metaphor, which in turn produces physical consequences.[20]

More frequently, however, the pain associated with *toska* was decidedly emotional. Another love spell from the 1688/89 spellbook reads,

May she pine and long for me, for the slave So-and-So. As a fire burns for a year and half a year and a day and half a day and an hour and half an hour, so may that slave burn for me, with her white body, her ardent heart, her black liver, her stormy head and brains, her clear eyes, black brows, and sugary lips. May she suffer as much misery [*toska*] and bitterness as a fish without water. May that slave So-and-So suffer as much bitterness for me for a day and half a day, for an hour and half an hour, for a year and half a year, for a week and half a week, ... may that beautiful girl cleave to that youth for all the years and thus let it be.[21]

Even when spells did not address Misery directly as an active force, they regularly aimed to inflict *toska* and its various forms of suffering. They relied on the somatic expression of *toska* as the driving, activating force of their magic. Misery and its sister emotions—pain, longing, grief, delight, desire—work their magic, transcending distance and effecting change in the world.

As the cuckoo bird grieves for her nestlings and cries for them, so may that female slave of God grieve and cry for me. And as the stars delight in the moon, so may that female slave of God delight when she sees me. And as a mare grieves for her foal, so may female slave of God grieve for me every hour of every day. I go, male slave of God, to the Ocean-Sea, and on the Ocean-Sea lies a burning white rock. On that rock stands a dry tree, and as that tree withers away, so may that female slave of God dry and wither away for me, slave of God. On that tree sits an iron man. He beats with his iron staff on the burning white rock, and as the rock catches fire, so may that female slave of God catch fire for me, carnally and fiercely and with all her flesh and being. And when she doesn't see me, male slave of God, may she grieve and cry and may she leave her father and mother and for all eternity, Amen. For all eternity, Amen. For all eternity, Amen.

So-and-So goes to the Ocean-Sea; there on an island stands a hut, and in it is a bird without wings. As miserable as the bird is without wings, so may it be for the female slave So-and-So. As miserable as a fish without water, so may it be also for female slave So-and-So. As one millstone grinds over another, so may the heart of female slave So-and-So. [22]

These incantations move from one layer of emotion to another, drawing them all together into a binding knot. Burning, withering, pounding, suffocating, grinding, catching fire, the spell's target must suffer the fierce pain of longing bodily and in her 'being', and must abjure all other society for the company of her would-be lover.[23]

MAGIC ON THE MOVE: ANONYMOUS TARGETS AND AUTHORITIES IN LOVE

Love spells would seem to belong to precisely the kind of personal relations and to operate in just the kinds of tight domestic spaces that characterized so much of Russian magic. Love and sex, after all, must involve two particular individuals locked in emotional and carnal connection. Yet, the texts themselves call attention to a profound problem with this analysis: The spells are handy catchalls, conveniently addressed to a generic, to-be-announced love object, the equivalent of Tom Lehrer's 'occupant'. The standard formula, *imiarek*, translated here as So-and-So, means literally 'say name'. Instead of plying particular individuals with enchanted roots and herbs, or identifying specific individuals, these handy aphrodisiacs were directed at So-and-So. The men who stocked up on 'love spells' kept them on hand (like a pack of condoms) in case the need arose. The 'intimacy' of their magic was impersonal and portable.

Muscovite men found plenty of call for adaptable spells when they were out in the world, facing unforeseen circumstances. People did not always stay crammed in the stifling spaces of the household; they also moved in a broader terrain. Despite the efforts to tie people to the land and limit mobility (an effort most evident in the increasingly strict conditions of serfdom through the seventeenth and eighteenth centuries), men of all types, from tsarist officials to serfs and slaves, were constantly on the move. Whether out and about in the world, or stuck at home and wondering about developments in the world beyond the village limits, practitioners of witchcraft developed a variety of techniques for deploying their enchantments at long range. This is a complicated problem for magic more generally. If intimacy and proximity are critical to witchcraft, how does it succeed in playing on a wider stage? If normally one would sneak into the master's sleeping chamber and slip roots into his bedding, how would one work spells remotely?

Russian witchcraft developed several approaches to resolving this conundrum of distance. The 'evil eye [*sglaz*]', for instance, could project ill-wishes beyond the limits of physical touch, but this still did not reach very far into the world. A Tatar woman read palms in 1630 to provide a couple in Elets Province with news about their son, off serving in the distant Don region.[24] Another option was to deploy spirits or devils to carry out tasks. In 1629 a peasant accused a fellow villager, Fedka Rebrov, of bewitching his son. The denunciation expanded on Fedka's magical practices:

And that Fedka knows all about herbs and much sorcery [*volkhovstvo*]. He looks in water and calls devils [*besy*], and they tell him what's going on a hundred versts away, and what illnesses people suffer from and who bewitches them; and he recognises people without seeing them [*za ochi*] and knows what kind of hair and marks [they have] and [their] height. And he looks in the water in a trough and says who will die and who will live and by whom they are bewitched [*isporchen*].[25]

E.B. Smilianskaia describes another case where devils helped people keep track of their distant loved ones. According to testimony from her 1764 trial, Katerina Ivanovna came to the aid of her neighbors who were desperate to know if their absent sons and husbands were alive or dead. She sent her two domesticated devils to investigate, and they obligingly returned, one 'in the guise of a man and wearing a kaftan', to report that the missing men were alive. Indeed the son of one would soon send a letter to his parents.[26] The use of devils or spirits was fairly unusual, though, and other techniques came into play more frequently. As evident in the love magic and spells to win the hearts of the powerful, emotions set loose in the world could transport as well as activate magical forces.

For men on the move spells offered a comforting sense that they were ready to face whatever obstacles they encountered. Prophylactic spells written out in 'fill-in-the-blank' form were found in men's pouches, tucked in their belts, tied on their crosses, and hidden under their hats. One man admitted he had lost a spell that had fallen out of his sock. Suspects were prosecuted for carrying incantations meant to ease interactions with authorities: 'a spell book for when you go to trial'; 'a spell to protect from torture (or to withstand torture)'; a spell 'to be unconvictable'.[27]

Over one hundred such 'spells to power' survive from the seventeenth and eighteenth centuries. According to Smilianskaia 'spells to power' comprised 20% of all those recorded in the 240 eighteenth-century trials she studied. They ranked just behind the front-runner, healing spells (30%) and ahead of both love magic (16%) and curses (15%). Spells addressed to the powerful never address specific goals but instead aim to sway hearts and minds: 'As King David made the Hebrew kings and princes meek and peaceful, so may the hearts of the judges of slave of God So-and-So become meek toward me, slave of God So-and-So.'[28] Their format, in other words, is precisely analogous to that of love spells.

A spell from a notebook dated to 1688–89 protected the bearer against 'boyars' (that is, noble landholders and officials): 'As Orthodox Christians bow to Christ, so may princes and boyars bow to So-and-So. Let Christ protect, cover with his mantle, erect an iron fence to protect from … enemies.'[29] A trial in 1745 turned up a 'little paper' with a spell written in 'small letters' that said, 'I do not fear the tsar, and I do not obey the tsar. And as the heart of a dead man does not grow enraged and he does not raise his hands, so from no court on earth let there be judges whose hearts would grow enraged or who would raise a hand against me, slave of God So-and-So.'[30] The need for protection from boyars, princes, and judges indicates the kind of mistreatment that ordinary people expected from their superiors. A specific term, *sil'nye liudi* or 'strong people' circulated widely to denote those who abused their positions through extortion and coercion. The prevalence of such spells indicates that abuse was the norm not only within marriages but also throughout society. Fortifying oneself through any means possible was a necessary and wise precaution, and winning the love of the powerful was seen as an effective form of protection.

A 'spell against evil-doers and to power' from the end of the eighteenth century starts off with a fear-inducing incantation:

> As your terrifying divine visage and the unfathomable divine power of the Life-Giving Cross strikes fear in the devil, so may my opponent fear me, slave of God So-and-So.

It then changes tone entirely, flipping from terror to delight as the operative emotion:

> As the day delights in the sun, the night the moon and the bright dawn and the many stars, so may my opponent delight in me, slave of God So-and-So.[31]

This evocation of delight, already familiar from the love spells, characterizes many of these 'spells to power'. They bestow on the caster entrancing, irresistible beauty and bind the authorities in a haze of delight or a trap of love. Men were brought to trial for carrying 'a spell so people will delight in you'; 'a spell so that people would love you'; 'a spell so that people would love and fear one. … 2 spells so that princes and boyars should love you. 3 spells so that people should love you and say nothing against you'; 'a letter, and in it was written a spell to change the hearts of angry people'; 'a spell so people would love you and fear you'. 'As the powerful cannot live without bread and salt, so may they be unable to live without So-and-So.'[32] This is the language of love spells, repurposed toward protection against the abuses or manipulation of the emotions of 'strong people'. Open-ended spells translated love magic from the proximate and intimate to the generic and political. They aimed to *create* intimacy not for its own sake but to soften the hard edges of Muscovite hierarchy. With the open-endedness of other fill-in-the blank formulas, they were generally directed to types of people in the plural: not the tsar, but generic tsars;[33] not a government functionary but all government functionaries. The spells directed at people in power deployed the same affective strategies as those unleashed on their intimates, but the targets were completely anonymous.

An ambitious spell from the end of the eighteenth century sets itself a broad agenda:

> May all mankind living on the earth take joy in me: old and young, male and female, all princes, judges, authorities, all those empowered over me in any place, in any of my affairs.

This opening gambit is hard to beat, but to do so, the spell calls on the protective love of parents for their children:

> And like father and mother love their children, so may princes and judges and authorities and all those empowered over me, and all mankind living on earth ... Love me, your slave, Lord, with the kindness and prayers of all of your saints. Henceforth and for all eternity ...[34]

Smilianskaia writes,

> The relationship between the subject of the spell and the authorities sometimes is conceived of as love, and the description of [this love] reaches a high degree of emotionality. Judges and bosses should twist around So-and-So like hops around a tree and like a swallow around her nest and her nestlings; they should be unable to live without him, as one is unable to live without bread, salt, and drink, without father and mother; they should marvel at him as at red poppies, and cherish [him] like the soul in their bodies; they should flock to him as the birds of paradise flock to the voice of the heavenly

Sirin bird; once they have set eyes on So-and-So, they should never be able to forget him.[35]

As Geschiere argues, witches most often threaten from within, but they can also operate at 'the ambiguous position at the interface of the in- and the outside'. [36] This ambiguous grey zone is precisely where Muscovite 'spells to power' and fill-in-the-blanks love spells operated, using their analogic power to transform outside into inside, anonymity into intimacy, remote targets into adoring lovers.

EMOTION AND MUSCOVITE SOCIOPOLITICAL ORDER

In her call to historians to start 'worrying about emotions in history', Barbara Rosenwein writes that 'emotions are among the tools with which we manage social life as a whole'.[37] In early modern Russia, emotion was explicitly identified as a tool for social organization, even for survival. Emotions occupied a publicly recognized role in shaping all human inter-actions. Society was structured as a web of kinship and patronage; power relations were negotiated through a language of love, dependency, and obligation. No categorical divide separated personal, religious, and politi-cal spheres; language developed no distinctive emotional and 'rational' registers. The standard mode of address to authorities was the humble, often tearful petition. Whether a request was addressed to state officials, serf-owners, or one's own parents, at least through the seventeenth cen-tury the humble supplication was the sole genre of expression, and the more self-abasing, the better. Petitioners identified themselves using demeaning, infantilizing diminutives of their names: Andriushka or Vanka or Kostka for Andrei, Ivan, or Kostiantin. Men and women alike articu-lated their despair in stark terms: their miserable little houses had been destroyed by bandits; their little wives and families or little fatherless chil-dren were going hungry; they were desperate and destitute, homeless, wandering between houses without food or comfort; caught in the hands of corrupt officials, they were languishing in jail, dying hungry deaths for no reason.

Delighting, loving, weeping whether from grief or piety: these were gender-neutral virtues, manifested by tsars and saints as well as by com-mon men and women. The model of parental love, with its unconditional, protective commitment as well as its stern guidance, served as a constitu-tive metaphor for the Muscovite imagination of ideal communities. Stern, protective parental love and its corollary, pious, obedient filial love, provided the ideal model of interaction. The eighteenth century introduced new political forms and values, and, by mid-century elite culture melded traditional emotional expression with new, imported sensibilities and sentimentalism, but the reliance on devices that would inspire love or pity—and hence patronage and protection—continued both in ordinary affairs and in the terrain of magic.[38]

Without other means to grease palms or win the support of earthly authorities, men on the road attempted to defend themselves by erecting a force field of love, a rather surprising choice of weapon. The emotional manipulation and charged affective formulas developed in the close confines of house and hearth translated smoothly into the necessary tools of survival in the courts, the regiment, and the hierarchies of power.

'EMOTIONS DO THINGS TO THE WORLD'

In the literature on the history of emotions, the notion that expressions of emotion can wield transformative power in the world apparently came as big news. In an important book and series of articles, William M. Reddy announced that 'emotives', that is, emotions and their expression, 'do things to the world'.[39] This eureka moment comes as no surprise to anyone who studies witchcraft. One of the central premises of magic is that hostile sentiments—envy, anger, hatred—are not mere interior dispositions but rather agents, powers that reach out and act in the exterior world. Their malevolent force can be released by an evil look, delivered through a muttered curse, or simply projected by malicious thoughts. In a world of magic, where words, glances, and gestures pose real and immediate danger, emotions can be deadly. Their toxins can poison those within the close confines of intimacy, and their narcotic power can take effect in the wide, anonymous world, where human relations and bonds of love and longing must be conjured and secured as a fundamental requisite of survival.

Rosenwein urges us to study 'emotional communities' to

> uncover systems of feeling: what these communities (and the individuals within them) define and assess as valuable or harmful to them; the evaluations that they make about others' emotions; the nature of the affective bonds between people that they recognize; and the modes of emotional expression that they expect, encourage, tolerate, and deplore.[40]

Early modern Russia might well be characterized as a community of pathos and protection. Misery and love served as the official currency of exchange, and emotional bonds provided the frail conceptual support that held society together. The logic of this emotional community in turn endowed the personification of Misery and the power of Love with the ability to stalk the world and to redirect hearts. Navigating the spaces between intimacy and distance where witchcraft tends to occur, Russian magical practices drew on widely held ideas about the agency of emotion as a transformative force in the world.

NOTES

1. Tom Lehrer, *That Was the Year That Was* (Reprise/Warner Brothers Records, 1965).
2. Approximately 230 reports of trials of witchcraft and magic survive in the archives of the tsar's secular courts from the seventeenth century and nearly the same number from various secular and ecclesiastical courts from the eighteenth century. The archives preserve the exchange of orders from the central administrative agencies and responses from the local courts. Some cases survive only as brief entries, while others preserve hundreds of manuscript pages of detailed correspondence.
3. This case is preserved in two archival documents at the Russian State Archive of Ancient Documents in Moscow: Rossiiskii Gosudarstvennyi Arkhiv Drevnikh Aktov (RGADA) f. 210, Belgorodskii stol, stlb. 826, ll. 81–96; and Ibid., Prikaznyi stol, stlb. 721, ll. 121–5, 154–5. It is partially published in Novombergskii, *Koldovstvo*, no. 26, 99–106, quotation at 99. All of the following quotes come from these sources.
4. Women's roles in the household made them particularly vulnerable to witchcraft allegations in western Europe as well. See Purkiss, *Witch in History*, 91–144; Martin, 'Devil and the Domestic', 73–89.
5. Novombergskii, *Koldovstvo*, 101–2.
6. Ibid.
7. Ibid., 103.
8. Johns, *Baba Iaga*. Note, however, that Baba Yaga is hard to trace in Russian sources before the eighteenth century.
9. Novombergskii, *Koldovstvo*, 103.

10. Geschiere, *Witchcraft, Intimacy, and Trust*, xviii; Geschiere, this volume.
11. RGADA, f. 210, Prikaznyi stol, stlb. 861, ll. 1–28.
12. Ibid., Belgorodskii stol, stlb. 284, ll. 391–418; Novombergskii, *Koldovstvo*, no. 11, 63–73.
13. Kotkov, Oreshnikov and Filippova, eds, *Moskovskaia delovaia i bytovaia pis'mennost'*, 238, 243. On this case, see also Perrie, 'Tsaritsa', 297–314; and Kantorovich, *Srednevekovye protsessy o ved'makh*, 170–175.
14. Kotkov, Oreshnikov and Filippova, eds, *Moskovskaia delovaia i bytovaia pis'mennost'*, 239–40.
15. Ibid., 240.
16. RGADA f. 210, Belgorodskii stol, stlb. 768, ll. 135–7; Novombergskii, *Koldovstvo*, no. 25, 94–9.
17. The island of Buian figures in Slavic mythology in various guises. In folktales recorded later, it is the home of the winds, it appears and disappears mysteriously, and it is the place where the wizard Koshchei the Deathless hides his 'death' in material form.
18. Quoted in Steinberg, 'Melancholy and Modernity', 819.
19. RGADA f. 159, Prikaznye dela starykh let, op. 1, no. 326, ll. 1–5, quote on l. 1.
20. Ibid., Prikaznyi stol, stlb. 300, ll. 16–25, 32, 160; stlb. 314, ll. 159–67, 192–3.
21. Ibid., stlb. 1133, stolpik 2, l. 177.
22. Ibid., ll. 184–5; Toporkov, Zagovory v russkoi, 366.
23. Ibid. See also interesting parallels in Frick, 'Witches of Wilno', 887–9; and the classic account of the emotional force of love charms and their relation to misery and pain: Winkler, 'Constraints of Desire', 71–100.
24. RGADA, f. 210, Moskovskii stol, stlb. 54, ll. 244–63, 327 (Novombergskii, *Koldovstvo*, 28).
25. RGADA, f. 210, Moskovskii stol, stlb. 54, ll. 32–42, 196–213; Novombergskii, *Koldovstvo*, 14–25. In the seventeenth century a verst was about 1.5 km. It was shortened to just over 1 km in the early eighteenth century.
26. Smilianskaia, *Volshebniki,bogokhul'niki,eretiki*, 93.
27. RGADA, f. 159, Prikaznye dela starykh let, op. 1, no. 326, l. 1 (sock); Prikaznyi stol, stlb. 434, ll. 4–200; stlb. 564, ll. 696–705; stlb. 734, ll. 115–203; RGADA, f. 210, Prikaznyi stol, stlb. 749;

and stlb. 734, ll. 117–18 (torture); Toporkov, ed., *Russkie zagovory*, 105, 106, 389; Smilianskaia, *Volshebniki, bogokhul'niki, eretiki*, 110 (for going to court), 146 (inconvictable).

28. Toporkov, *Russkie zagovory*, 105 (2nd quarter of the seventeenth century).

29. Ibid., 391. The spell actually protects against boyars and *witches*, an interesting example of anti-witchcraft magic.

30. Smilianskaia, *Volshebniki, bogokhul'niki, eretiki*, 152.

31. Toporkov, *Russkie zagovory*, 527.

32. RGADA, f. 159, Prikaznye dela starykh let, op. 1, no. 326, l. 1. RGADA, f. 210, Prikaznyi stol, stlb. 434, ll. 4–200; stlb. 734, ll. 115–203; Toporkov, *Zagovory v russkoi*, 389; Maikov, *Velikorusskie zaklinaniia*, no. 351, 151–2. On 'social spells' or 'spells to power', see Ippolitova, *Russkie rukopisnye travniki*, 326–64; Smililianskaia, *Volshebniki, bogokhul'niki, eretiki*, 142–86; Toporkov, 'Verbal Charms', 532–9.

33. There are exceptions, such as a spell directed against Peter the Great: Smilianskaia, 'Zagovory i gadaniia', 105.

34. Toporkov, *Russkie zagovory*, 532.

35. Smilianskaia, *Volshebniki, bogokhul'niki, eretiki*, 197.

36. Geschiere, *Witchcraft, Intimacy, and Trust*, xviii–xix.

37. Rosenwein, 'Worrying about Emotions in History', 842.

38. Ransel, 'Character and Style', 212–31; on patronage; Marker and May, *Lives of a Russian Noblewoman*; Smilianskaia, *Volshebniki, bogokhul'niki, eretiki*; Wirtschafter, *Play of Ideas*.

39. Reddy, 'Emotional Liberty', 270; see also his *Navigation of Feeling*.

40. Rosenwein, 'Worrying about Emotions in History', 842.

CHAPTER 8

Emotion and Affect in Lorraine Witchcraft Trials

Robin Briggs

In early modern Europe witchcraft accusations provide some striking demonstrations of the management of emotions, even though witchcraft was naturally and strongly linked to the red mist of anger. In the Lorraine cases that provide the evidence for this chapter, the accused routinely confessed that the Devil had urged them to seek vengeance on their enemies, and whispered encouragement to attack those with whom they were quarrelling; if they did not provide a motivation of this type the judges tended to ask for it. Regret after bewitching their adversary often induced them to provide a cure once their temper had cooled, although sometimes the Devil obstructed these attempts. In Lorraine this idea was given additional force because numerous witches explained how the Devil supplied them with a powder to cure their victims. On the face of it this was an extraordinary facility for the Devil to provide, but there was an internal logic behind these stories: they fitted with the widespread belief that illnesses inflicted by witches could only be cured when the witch removed the curse. This was fundamental to the everyday conduct of people in this

R. Briggs
All Souls College, Oxford

© The Author(s) 2016
L. Kounine, M. Ostling (Eds.), *Emotions in the History of
Witchcraft*, DOI 10.1057/978-1-137-52903-9_8

137

environment, where witchcraft was readily invoked to explain a wide range of afflictions, with the corollary that the suspect might be induced to make gestures of good will that were expected to bring about a cure. So while witchcraft was about anger, this was balanced by techniques for managing it and restoring good relations.

In the imaginary symbolic world of transactions with the Devil these everyday practices found expression in the red and black powders that induced sickness or death, and in the white powder that could remove the original spell. Moreover for those making the confessions the secret master who gave his servants the ability to harm and to heal was empowering them to turn their emotions of the moment into actions, aligning their psychic life with a version of external reality. One crippled beggar-woman found a wonderful way of expressing this when she identified her personal devil, not by the routine local names of Persin or Napnel, but as Pensée de Femme, a personification of her own thoughts. This obliging gentleman told Mengeotte Gascon

> that he gave her power over all those who did her harm, and towards whom she bore any hatred, so that by striking them with her hand she could make them die or sicken as she wished, while she could heal them if she wished, that she should have no worry about this, giving her some powder to use if she wished or the power simply to touch them with her hand.[1]

A similar logic would explain why a few of those who tried to insist on their innocence were prepared to admit they would have liked to be a real witch just for an hour or a day, in order to avenge themselves on their enemies.

Anger was unsurprisingly one of the three routine explanations witches offered for their original surrender to the Devil; the others were despair at their poverty or hunger, and the Devil's corollary emotional promises to make them rich, or at least ensure they did not want. The judges at Neufchâteau made their expectations about such a package plain when they asked Jeanne Magnien 'whether when she was angry and furious someone did not appear offering to console her, suggesting that she should give herself to him and he would help her'.[2] Many female witches claimed to have been angry with husbands who beat them or spent money drinking and failed to provide for their families. Another common reason was being upset because other villagers alleged one was a witch. Nicole Nigal was angry because a visiting German 'doctor' (probably just as unqualified a healer as herself) had called her a witch, and the same day she went to collect wood, muttering to herself 'the thief, the coward, may the great Devil confound him, continuing her curses and talk of the Devil in this fashion'. Then a man in black with a circle round his hat appeared to give her powder to use on those who insulted or harmed her.[3] Men, who made up 28% of those tried in Lorraine, were on the whole less forthcoming than women about their emotional state at the moment of seduction. Many simply reported the deceitful promises to supply them with money, while those who went beyond this cited debts, the loss of animals, and disputes over inheritances among the reasons for their vulnerability. An exceptional case was that of Jean Perrin, who returned home for dinner in the woodcutting season to be criticised by his wife for not working hard enough. This was apparently normal behaviour from a wife he described as 'rioteuse', who had beaten his son from his first marriage until he sent him away from home. When Jean went out again that evening he met a man with long black hair and a beard, Parsin, who said that if he would serve him he would no longer have to fear his wife.[4] That was an unusual kind of family trouble for a man to admit, whereas women were frequently maltreated by their husbands. Few can have experienced a greater panic than La Grande Lucye, whose story was that her husband had come home drunk as she was preparing to bake bread and went to beat her. After fleeing into the garden she suddenly thought that he might throw the baby into the heated oven; at this moment of terror the enemy appeared to her and seduced her.[5]

Several others among the accused reported fear for children, with Mongeatte Tendon actually offering two different stories. At first she placed her seduction two years earlier, when one of her sons had been imprisoned on charges of sodomy and making a cousin pregnant; a hideous figure in black with claws appeared and offered to get her son out of prison if she would believe in him. Then she admitted to having become a witch thirty years before, when her young daughter had been lost one night when looking for their animals. She was still searching for her after noon the next day when her husband returned from St Dié to say he heard a girl had been eaten by animals, leaving only her head. Mongeatte was in despair when Persin appeared, promising to find her daughter if she would give herself to him; after accepting the bargain she had to keep it when he found the girl sleeping under a bush.[6] Sadly this daughter, Marguitte Thierry, was herself to be convicted nineteen years later, when one witness recalled the story of her childhood escapade, and she explained that she had been afraid to return home because she had lost her father's cows.[7] Barbelline le Jalley told a rather different story about her yearning for children, rather than fears for those she already had. The Devil had first approached her after a great quarrel with another woman, offering to teach her the means to have her revenge. He then disappeared, only to return the next day and tell her 'that she had been to great pains to make pilgrimages so that she could bear children. But if she would believe in him and renounce God, he would give her good instruction in how to have children.' She accepted the offer, commenting that she had indeed made many pilgrimages for this reason, and since God had not helped her she was ready to renounce him.[8]

Persin made another kind of wish-fulfilling promise to Marguitte Lairain, as a young woman living with her father and distressed because he was in prison accused of witchcraft; he would find her 'a handsome young man to marry her, then give her every kind of assistance so that she would never want'.[9] In a similar vein he pretended to sympathise with an older woman, Catherine la Rondelatte, who was passing through the woods 'all dreaming and thoughtful' about her long widowhood, her lack of children, and the fact that her family did not want her to remarry; after raping her he falsely promised, 'I will make you a lady and give you great wealth.'[10] A more visceral type of misery featured in several confessions, like that of Jaulne Curien, who placed her seduction sixteen years earlier, when

> the soldiers were around everywhere, and there was such poverty in the land that they had a great dearth, during which she suffered greatly because she had not eaten for three days and nights, while she was burdened with children whom she had no means to feed or maintain, except by roots they went out to find.[11]

This was the devastation inflicted on large areas of Lorraine by the great mercenary army of the Duke of Bouillon in 1587, an episode recalled by a significant number of people. Another story of hunger came from Marion Arnoulx, orphaned by the time she was five or six and seduced as a half-starving young woman guarding animals out in the fields.[12] A small range of further reasons for anger and vulnerability could be added, ranging from the deaths of husbands or children to such seeming trivialities as children staying out too late in the fields, or hens damaging a garden. What made Lorrainers miserable and angry enough to yield to the Devil can be summed up as bereavements, economic misfortunes, empty stomachs, and selfish or brutal husbands.

The witchcraft suspects mostly lived in small rural communities, where everyone knew everyone else, and gossip played an enormous part, shaping and reshaping individual reputations. Historians of early modern European societies have generally agreed that they placed a premium on standing one's ground when challenged in any way; those who backed off showed weakness that diminished their standing and laid them open to further attacks. A high proportion of recorded cases of violence began with insults by word or gesture, with taverns as far the most common location.[13] Fights between men normally generated legal action only when a death ensued, although there are odd references to fines paid by aggressors for assaults resulting in injury. Worthy people were supposed to respond to public insults by seeking reparation, including a rather nominal fine; despite poor record survival the limited evidence suggests that most insults were either ignored or dealt with by informal reconciliations. In one archive for which we have a count, 97% of the defendants in slander cases were men, so the world of feminine gossip, immensely powerful though it was, simply fell through the net untouched.[14]

Witnesses and judges frequently suggested that the accused had failed to respond when accused of witchcraft, to which the standard responses were that they had no witnesses, were so poor they dared not risk the costs if they failed, or could not get their husbands to act. In a situation where most accusations took many years to mature there was clearly a great deal of local interaction, building up pressure on the suspects. Jean le Clerc, mayor at Sainte-Marguerite, told George Jolbay

> that people had great ideas and suspicions about his wife, on account of various bewitchments she was alleged to have committed, and that he would do well to put this in order, otherwise they would be obliged to arrest her and put her on trial, which words only moved her husband to say that he wished she was already burned if she were such, without ever demanding reparation.[15]

Several other husbands are recorded as taking a similar line, perhaps trying to detach themselves from any suspicion of complicity; their apparently craven behaviour may not have been so unwise, because a vigorous defence sometimes became the catalyst for a formal charge.

The accused needed to measure their words carefully, as Babillon Girard found when she said she would have taken those who implied she was a witch to court if she had had witnesses. When she added that she would have wished to be revenged on them the judges quickly asked whether in this case she had felt ill will, 'or wished she had the power to harm them by killing them or causing their deaths'. With rash honesty she replied 'that she would willingly have had the power to do this, because she had great difficulty in enduring talk implying such insults and she would have been very pleased if people had accused her openly and in public so that she would have had more chance of avenging herself'. Babillon then agreed to the suggestion that after quarrels she had wished harm to other people or their property; to the question whether such results had followed she said they had not, then added that after her dispute with Nicolas Biche he had become impotent and died some time later, although she did not know how this had happened.[16] In a similar fashion one witness reported that Mengeatte Grand Jacques had told her years earlier that 'she wished she could be a witch for two hours to do as she wanted', then replied to protests that it was just to harm those who called her witch. Stories of this kind, which Mengeatte admitted to be true in her case, were told about several others.[17]

If the trial records provide a reliable guide, then violence against suspected witches more commonly took the form of insults than of physical assaults, but angry confrontations could spill over into blows. Jacquemin Gerard thought Claudon Bregeat had given him the sickness that had kept him in bed for three weeks, so struggled out with the help of his wife to confront her in the street. He threatened to kill her with an arquebus if she did not heal him, then his wife struck Claudon with a stick amidst more threats to kill her. The response was that they wronged her, because the illness came from God, but she would soon cure him. On getting home he lay as if dead for an hour and a half, then recovered completely within two more days.[18] How far such scenes can have triggered a version of the placebo effect we can never tell, when most illnesses run their course naturally, but something of their intensity still comes across. Jean Grainel said he was surprised that Catherine la Rondelatte had not died from the blows he gave her, notably on an occasion when he met her alone outside the village. By his account when she saw him approaching in a fury she cried, 'Jean Grainel, God help you, you are very angry', to which he replied 'Witch, I am coming this moment to kill you, you have caused the deaths of my horses and my animals, now you too will die by my hands.' He then beat her until she begged him for mercy, saying, 'I will never cause you or anything to do with you any harm or trouble.' After a further beating she complained to the local *prévôt*, who fined Grainel and made him promise not to molest her again, although he failed to pay the fine.[19] In the most extreme cases the suspect was injured so badly that she died (all the known instances involved women), which led the perpetrator to flee and then seek remission from the duke. Sixteen killings of witches are recorded leading to pardons between 1564 and 1627, in seven of which the violence related to an attempt to force the woman to heal one or more supposed victims.[20] In a 1593 case François Thiébault, the mayor of Huillecourt, was helped by a number of others to tie up an itinerant beggar-woman over the fire, with an axle under her knees, and roast her until the small boy she was thought to have bewitched began to walk again.[21] Another death resulted from the use of the swimming test (quite exceptional in the Lorraine of the period), although here the motive given was merely general fear and suspicion.[22] It was a disastrous frost damaging the vines that led to the arrest of four women at Stainville in 1601; when they were only banished by the local court they were stoned by a crowd and two of them were killed, after which at least 60 people sought a pardon.[23] No other direct communal action of similar kinds is known for the duchies of Lorraine and Bar in the decades of the major persecution between the 1560s and the 1630s. There are a few instances where the trials suggest some kind of prior organisation in the village, but this implies a much less violent emotional response to witchcraft; we may reasonably suspect that discussions about taking suspects to court were quite common, since witnesses would have preferred to keep them secret.

As historians have always realised, letters of remission are sources that need careful handling, because the supplicants used the services of scribes who knew the correct formulae.[24] It was essential to show that the killing had not been premeditated, and it was almost a routine to claim that the victim would have survived had they obtained proper care. Toussaint Alexandre provided a rationale for beating up witches when he explained how he had met Cunisse Daniel on the road, and thought of her bad reputation and the two horses for whose loss his father blamed her, while he had also heard that witches had no power over those whom they feared and who had beaten them. He had been drinking, so after accusing her and striking her with his fists he 'could not contain himself' from striking her across the back with his sword. Toussaint did not get off quite so easily as most others, having to serve a year's banishment to obtain his pardon.[25] Trials occasionally reflected the fear that those who were tried for witchcraft only to be released might avenge themselves on those who had testified against them, but this did not normally take such direct form as was reported by Pierre Roussel, who had been ordered by the *prévôt* to help with the arrest of François Foissard. When Foissard was freed he went around saying that Roussel and another man who had taken part would die by no other hands than his own, often lying in wait for them with gun, sword, and dagger. He had succeeded in injuring Roussel's hand with a sword, then one day the latter saw him waiting in ambush with his gun and got his shot in first. Four years later he obtained his pardon, after he had been to Rome to obtain a papal dispensation for his crime.[26] Although there was a stylised element in these attempts to make violence or loss of emotional control sound reasonable, they do fit with the broader pattern of emotional overflow and management seen in witchcraft cases generally.

What the letters of remission also allow is some attempt to quantify violence in early modern Lorraine, although this must inevitably be a very inexact business. Homicide rates are just about the only long series with any plausibility as a guide to past behaviour, with the best-known estimate for Western Europe showing a remarkable decline over time. According to these calculations, annual rates per hundred thousand of population, which had stood at a perhaps rather dubious 41 in the fifteenth century, went down to 19 in the sixteenth and 11 in the seventeenth, before dropping to 1.4 in the twentieth.[27] One standard caution is that the failings of medical care in the past must have affected the outcomes; it would seem quite plausible to at least halve the figures for the seventeenth century against those for the twentieth. In this light some elementary counting for the reign of Duke Henry II of Lorraine (1608–24) is surprisingly suggestive.[28] Omitting a number of cases of wholly accidental homicides, these seventeen years saw 377 remissions for homicide, roughly twenty-two per year in a region whose population was not much above 500,000. From an excellent local study of the *prévôté* of Bruyères we know that around half of those found guilty of homicides gained remission, while there will have been the usual 'dark figure' of unsolved or unreported cases, so fifty per year would be a reasonable estimate for the whole region. The upshot is that the European figure of 11 per 100,000 looks very close to that for Lorraine around 1620. Among the 377 known individuals (all but seven of them males), around 250 look to have come from a typical cross-section of the rural populations. At that rate only a small minority of villages—20% at the most—would have seen a homicide of any kind over the seventeen years. While minor violence was evidently commonplace, heavily concentrated in and around the taverns, the informal social structures that imposed restraint must have worked remarkably well. By a curious statistical quirk the numbers tried for witchcraft were also running at about fifty per year over the half-century between 1580 and 1630, with the difference that this led to an average of forty executions per year for a crime that was never pardoned once a death sentence had been passed.[29] One might add that on average Lorraine witches were accused of causing around 2.6 human fatalities each; they were certainly seen as murderous, but not on an epic scale when the powers attributed to them are considered. It is surprising, given the very high levels of infant and child mortality, and the propensity to blame such losses on witchcraft, that the average female suspect was only accused of causing 1.3 such deaths (for men it was naturally much lower at 0.35).[30] So even accusations of *maléfice*, which could have seen fantasy run wild, were strikingly cautious in practice. This reinforces the very important point that in Lorraine at least the notion of an emotionally frenetic witch-craze is implausible; both emotional and legal responses to witchcraft were unexpectedly constrained, although the statistics show that the inhabitants of the duchy were less reluctant than most Europeans to bring formal accusations.

This pattern of limited violence also shows up in the inner structure of the trials, where most cases show a very slow process, with reputations building over long periods, often extending to decades. Here even the most basic calculations are hardly possible, because too many past incidents are undated, but it is evident that only a minority of suspects ever came before a court, while many villages never saw a single trial. Lorraine had one of the highest rates of persecution in Europe, when measured against population, so this is an important point about the limitations still visible on close inspection. Village witchcraft was of course primarily an idiom for explaining sickness and misfortune, which morphed into a form of therapy. At this everyday level one went to the *devin* (a local witch-finder) to be sure that you had identified the witch correctly, then tried to put them under pressure to provide a cure. Although it might have been expected that serious trouble would follow when a sick person died, this does not seem to have been remotely predictable. Attempts to stir up action might fail or lead to legal action, as they did for a young man named Claudon Mathieu, who said before a large group outside the church of Leintrey that if everyone subscribed a small amount of money he would have the greatest witch in the village taken. Another man reckoned that the unnamed witch was Mathieu Margeron, and said he would contribute, only for someone else to tell Margeron in his presence, 'Here is Jean Courtier, who says he will give ten francs to help have you burned.' The suspect made no comment, 'nevertheless since then, while the said Margeron showed him a perfectly good face, he could not believe within himself that he did not bear him a grudge'.[31] It looks to have been hard to get a prosecution going, partly because individuals did not like exposing themselves, partly because annoyance rather than panic was the typical reaction to suspicions. In theory witches were the deadly enemies of everyone around them, committed as they were to repeated attacks on fertility and well-being, and equipped with powers to turn their ill will into damaging action. Yet this terrifying potential apparently remained a rather distant abstraction, which neither the people nor the judges took very seriously most of the time. One sign of this was the relative lack of interest in the details of the sabbat. With the partial exception of the German-speaking fringe of the duchy, the diabolical conspiracy hardly extended beyond some relatively marginal storm-raising, which the majority of poor witches did their best to resist.[32] The witchcraft of the trials is mostly a strikingly domesticated affair, based on very ancient notions about *maléfice*, and open to negotiation at the personal and local level. People feared witches, but many of them also seem to have believed that resolute action could keep them in their place.

Nevertheless we must suppose that intense fear could be generated for those who believed that they or their families were under attack, and that sufficiently large groups might develop shared feelings that drove communal action against particular suspects. Accusers and accused frequently agreed about the difficult relationships behind specific charges, even if they interpreted them very differently. Situations where people felt guilt about their own aggressive and hostile behaviour operated on both sides. The accusers could readily project their own anger onto the witch, anticipating some covert form of revenge, while the witch could be persuaded of his or her own evil power under the stress of isolation and torture. The instinctive feeling that there is a link between ill will and real harm to others runs very deep, somewhere beyond rational assessment or control. In their confessions witches did not always confine themselves to the script provided for them by the witnesses; they were liable to add further misdeeds beyond those of which they were accused. These supplementary admissions are probably best explained as emerging from the inner worlds of the accused, as a statement of the things they would have liked to do to enemies, and of the deep animosities their unhappy situation had generated. No less than 22% of the Lorraine accused confessed their guilt before they were subjected to the torture. Fear of the ordeal must have been operating here (as some admitted), but it seems clear that some of these unfortunates had accepted the roles in which they were cast, to the extent of seeing themselves as bad people who deserved to be punished. A rather different explanation is needed for the handful of children who told vivid stories about the Devil and the sabbat, with fatal consequences for adult members of their families. There is nothing to suggest that the children positively wished to implicate their parents; where motives can be detected these related to a desire to impress other members of their age group, even to establish a kind of domination over them. The sabbat must have been widely discussed in neighbourhood and family gatherings, not least because confessions were read out in public at the time of executions, putting new materials into circulation. The Lorraine sabbat did not much resemble Michelet's fantasy of a counter-culture of the oppressed, when nearly all accounts described it in terms of servitude to a brutal master, who provided disgusting food and was quick to beat the recalcitrant. Even so, the idea of a nocturnal anti-world where people got up to unspeakable things had its own perverse excitement, very well conveyed in one or two of these children's accounts.[33]

Far more commonly infants and children were thought to be the targets for bewitchment; there is nothing in this material to suggest that parents were indifferent to such misfortunes, which normally led them to confront the supposed witch, whatever the risks, and do everything they could to ensure they inspected and touched the sick child. The high frequency of deaths in the early years presumably did induce greater emotional resignation than in recent times, once the worst had happened, but people were reported as crying and lamenting at their children's suffering, as they begged older women for help. A frequent story was that the witch had admired and petted the child immediately before the illness began, implying that it was normal to behave in this way. Françoise Bourguignon was accused on rather different grounds, because when she saw Jean Charton with his six-month-old son in his arms she said 'that he was making a great fuss of him, when it was a son and they had one already, while they would have plenty of children yet, so they should not make such a fuss of the first ones'.[34] This and other evidence strongly implies that children were valued and treated affectionately, however hard some aspects of their lives may have been. The accused (men as well as women) were liable to express concern for their own children's fate if they were convicted, and there are some signs that those with dependent children were more likely to resist the torture. This material seems quite incompatible with some of the strange claims that have been made about virtual indifference to children in the past.[35]

Where affect between older family members is concerned, the picture is a mixed one, but it is not surprising that negative attitudes to the suspects on the part of relatives should crop up in this material, when a conviction for witchcraft was likely to have grave repercussions on the whole family. Some husbands made real efforts to defend their wives, others tried to distance themselves, while tensions over property might also complicate matters with the broader kinship network. Nevertheless the family context provides one major reason for the caution with which formal accusations were made. If any family member had even a modest reputation for witchcraft, then they were at risk of being denounced as an accomplice seen at the sabbat when a neighbour was convicted; elsewhere I have cited numerous threats made by suspects, who shrewdly reckoned to frighten off potential accusers in this way.[36] Of course the other risk was that the witch might resist the torture and return to the village, complete with strong motives to take revenge on those who had been involved or had testified. In some cases where a second trial took place there were witnesses alleging that just this kind of hatred had brought retribution on them or their kin. Bearing witness could be dangerous in other ways, as Claudon de Benamenil found out after testifying against Noel Purel, because Noel named him as an accomplice, while other people were claiming that Claudon had said a lot of things beforehand that he had not included in his deposition. Soon Claudon found himself on trial, and had to resist the torture to secure his release.[37]

While we would hardly expect to find a great deal of information about love and sexual relations in these grim documents, they are not completely absent. Two men, who denied to the last that they were witches, admitted sexual misconduct and assault on such a scale that they were put to death for this alone.[38] One of them, Jean Aulbry, was ultimately denounced by his wife, to whom he had put an extraordinary set of demands that she allow him to keep a whore, have an abortion if she became pregnant again, and renounce God to take the Devil as her master. Aulbry admitted much of this, suggesting that some wicked person must have cast a spell on him, and also confessed that when he was in his rages he felt that he ought to do everything that he thought or that came into his head, even when he sometimes thought that he should kill his wife, then when he had recovered his senses he repented of having done and said the things he had.

He sounds like a genuinely sick man, whose behaviour evidently horrified the judges, and was seen as falling outside any normal range.[39] At a more sympathetic level George du Hault added to his conventional witchcraft confessions that before his marriage he had fallen in love with his brother's young wife, then they had carried on a secret affair for some eight years.[40] Another extramarital relationship emerged during the trial of Jeanne Martin, when the widow of Jacques Valentin Finance alleged she had killed him by blowing in his face at the *poisle* or winter evening gathering. According to Jeanne herself she had blown powder into his mouth when he came up to kiss her, at the instigation of another witch with whom he had quarrelled, despite the fact that he 'was her best friend and loved her alone'. She had also tried to kill his wife, who was jealous of 'some familiar dealings between them', with a poisoned pear.[41] Chretienne Parmentier had got to know a young man called Jean Heckstein when pasturing her master's horses, then he realised she was in love with him, and tried to take his distance, only to become 'troubled in his mind'.[42] Another young woman with a dubious reputation was Georgeatte Pelisson, accused of harming other members of her age group because of jealousies arising from village dances.[43] Pierron Voignier had been in the service of the widow Françatte Jardel for five years, when

> she had made him so much in love with her and abused him by some unknown means so that he was determined to marry her, and he could not be anywhere where he could not see her, but finally the urgings of his closest friends, who reminded him of her reputation for witchcraft, led him to extricate himself as best he could.[44]

More than forty years on her teenaged promiscuity was remembered against Jeanne Bigenel, said to have at that stage 'become active in matters of love. When she was pregnant several young men who had been associated with her each tried to pass this off on one of their companions.'[45] These are faint yet telling echoes of a world in which passionate love, although deeply mistrusted for its disruptive power, was certainly not unknown.

No one should be surprised to find ample evidence within these witchcraft trials for fear, anger, and hatred; the enforced intimacy of small poverty-stricken rural communities provided an ideal breeding ground for negative emotions. In Lorraine these feelings drove one of the highest rates of prosecution in Europe. Yet close analysis of the trials also exposes the multiple ways in which people managed the resulting tensions; at the local level caution and restraint often seem more evident than unreasoning fury. There were a few suspects who took a bold line, threatening legal action and encouraging belief in their powers of secret revenge. Relatives and others blamed another small group for their quarrelsomeness. Much more typical were those who offered conciliatory gestures, made efforts to provide remedies, and were thought to have removed the spells cast at a moment when they had briefly lost control (usually under provocation). This was the attitude implied by Mongeatte de Luce when she said 'that one would have to live very well to avoid having quarrels with a few people, but for all that she bore none any hatred'.[46] Some of the comments reported by witnesses combined the idea of self-control with that of hidden malevolence. Mongeotte Lausson had said at the *poisle* 'that when someone angered her she remembered it for another seven years, without giving any sign of this', while Jehenne la Moictresse was described as 'extremely crafty and cunning' because she told a young woman 'that when she was angry with someone she never gave the least sign of this, and she should do likewise'.[47] Mengeon Clement Thiriat told a younger neighbour 'that she did not yet know what it was to live in the world, and that it was necessary to put on the best and finest appearances with those one hated the most'.[48] Complex attitudes and an instinct for self-preservation were evident here, on the part of people whose world was essentially that of a small community, within which reputations were under constant review. Most of those who have figured in this chapter played their part in the therapeutic system linked to witchcraft, which relied largely on the physical effects linked to emotions. Supposed victims might well be feeling a great deal worse because they thought themselves bewitched, while modern understanding of the placebo effect explains how even genuine illnesses could be relieved by what were essentially emotional transactions. Witchcraft may be a work of the imagination, but mind–body relationships are very complex, so that beliefs can cause sickness and even death, and they can also help healing and stimulate the immune system. For those who believe in it there is good evidence that it works, within certain limits.[49]

This was one of those frontiers where the sweeping constructs of demonology matched up rather poorly with attitudes on the ground. Villagers knew that people often had good reasons for feeling angry, while those who felt guilty about their own part in disputes were likely to worry that ill-will might have noxious effects. Yet we must ask whether witchcraft suspects could possibly have survived so long, if the seemingly inexorable mechanism of scapegoating had operated in a mechanical fashion. Ordinary people could tell stories about the Devil and the sabbat without buying into the theory of a great diabolical conspiracy, with most harmful acts being attributed to individuals or occasionally to married couples. Witchcraft was so much a part of everyday life for the mass of the population that it became relatively domesticated, as just one of the dangers one faced; there were ways of dealing with it, and it was part of the magical universe that was largely taken for granted. Precisely because accusations were normally formed at moments of great emotional tension, passions could ebb away again once the crisis had passed, and the categorisation of neighbours as witches often remained tentative. Although some witnesses in the trials claimed to be certain about instances of bewitchment, many others preferred to juxtapose disputes and misfortunes without making any specific claim about the causal links between them. All these hesitations suggest what common sense would also indicate, that ultimately passions had to be bridled for the vast majority of the time if social order was to be maintained, and that restraint only gave way when the pressure became too intense. Just how that happened in specific cases remains largely mysterious, but for many of the witches arrest and trial must surely have resulted from a surge of emotions at the group level, bringing a good number of people together in that cathartic moment when they sought openly to compass a neighbour's death.

NOTES

1. Summaries of all the trials cited, with long citations, are available online at http://witchcraft.history.ox.ac.uk/. My reference number for each trial is given in the endnote, with the archival reference for the departmental archives of the Meurthe-et-Moselle at Nancy. This case is [317], B 8941 no. 1. Where the case is also discussed at more length in Briggs, *Witches of Lorraine*, page references are given in the form *Lorraine*, 298–302 (the section on this case).

2. [089], B 4576; *Lorraine*, 95–7, 182–3.
3. [319], B 8945; *Lorraine*, 303–6.
4. [294], B 8721 no. 2.
5. [074], B 4094 no. 2.
6. [175], B 8680 no. 5.
7. [285], B 8717 no. 2; *Lorraine*, 276–7.
8. [179], B 8682 no. 1.
9. [250], B 8702 no. 11.
10. [073], B 4094 no. 1. A full translation of her statement is in Briggs, *Witches and Neighbours*, 21.
11. [225], B 8691 no. 14; *Lorraine*, 289–90.
12. [189], B 8684 no. 2; *Lorraine*, 127–8.
13. Muchembled, *Violence au village*; idem, *History of Violence*; Ruff, *Violence in Early Modern Europe*.
14. Marchal, *Prévôté de Bruyères*, 217–21.
15. [147], B 8667 no. 9.
16. [106], B 5769.
17. [109], B 6760.
18. [003], B 2192 no. 2; *Lorraine*, 193.
19. [073], B 4094 no. 1.
20. These cases are taken from the departmental archives of the Meurthe-et-Moselle, in B36, B47, B50, B51, B55, B64, B65, B66, B70, B72, B73, B78, B86, B89, B92, B99, B100.
21. B64, B66.
22. B66.
23. B72.
24. For discussions of these problems see Davis, *Fiction in the Archives* and Gauvard, *'De grace especial'*.
25. B51.
26. B73.
27. Eisner, 'Long-Term Historical Trends', 83–142.
28. These letters are in B94–117.
29. *Lorraine*, 44–58 has a discussion of these statistics.
30. These calculations are based on my own sampling of the trial records.
31. [029], B 3323 no. 5; *Lorraine*, 231–2.
32. For the sabbat see *Lorraine*, 135–52; and Briggs, *Witches and Neighbours*, 32–43.

33. Michelet, *La sorcière*. For these topics see the very subtle discussion in Roper, *Witch in the Western Imagination*, 132–55, 'Witches' Children'.
34. [006], B 2199 no. 2; *Lorraine*,105–6.
35. This comment is directed less towards Philippe Ariès, although his implausible views do not fit with the material either, than against such historians as Lloyd de Mause and Lawrence Stone.
36. Briggs, *Witches and Neighbours*, 315.
37. [034], B 3325 no. 1; *Lorraine*, 236–7.
38. The first was Jean Gerardin, [063], B 3792 no. 2; *Lorraine*, 64.
39. [231], B8693 no. 2; *Lorraine*, 350–3.
40. [156], B 8677 no. 2; *Lorraine*, 356–9.
41. [164], B 8677 no. 10; *Lorraine*, 117–18.
42. [015], B 2583 no. 1.
43. [182], B 8682 no. 4; *Lorraine*, 110–11.
44. [190], B 8684 no. 3; *Lorraine*, 264–6.
45. [131], B 8281 no. 1; *Lorraine*, 163–4.
46. [223], B 8691 no. 12; *Lorraine*, 113–14.
47. [068], B 3804 no. 3 and [050], B 3358; *Lorraine*, 158 and 335–6.
48. [068A], B3813; *Lorraine*, 88–90, 353–5.
49. Bever, *Realities of Witchcraft*, provides a wide-ranging discussion of the medical literature on these points.

CHAPTER 9

Speaking of Love in the Polish Witch Trials

Michael Ostling

INTRODUCTION

In this chapter I attempt to treat the records of witch trials as windows into the feeling hearts of accused witches—to remain unsatisfied with 'emotional regimes', 'emotional representations', and even 'emotional dispositions', seeking instead to apprehend emotions themselves: passing and ephemeral 'occurrent emotions' frozen like mayflies in the amber of recorded history.[1] I take up this task in trepidation but without despair, convinced that such an attempt has some chance of success insofar as one is willing to rethink the prevailing metaphor for the 'space' of emotions from Pascal (or even from Augustine) to Freud: of the heart as an unknowable interior place.[2] Like the mind, the (metaphorical) heart is 'not the name of another person, working or frolicking [or loving or hating, burning or aching] behind an impenetrable screen'; instead it names the actions and words and blushes, the behaviours and expressions and bodily reactions, through which we experience our own emotions and imperfectly infer the emotions of others.[3] To be sure emotional expression can be dissimulated and representations of it can be distorted—as Rita Voltmer so powerfully

M. Ostling
Arizona State University

© The Author(s) 2016
L. Kounine, M. Ostling (eds.), *Emotions in the History of Witchcraft*, DOI 10.1057/978-1-137-52903-9_9

reminds us, this is especially true of the emotional representations assembled by court records to script witch trials as 'dramas of affective performance'.[4] And yet there is no prima facie reason to assume historians must be less adept at discerning emotions through the distorting filters of the documents available than we are at inferring other stocks of our trade: motivations, intentions, reasons, interests. I hope here to probe the limits and the possibilities entailed by a history of emotions grounded in the witch trials: asking whether we can use the trials to go beyond representations (or rather, to blur overdrawn divisions between representation and reality). This methodological inquiry is coupled to a substantive one: I seek to discover whether we can find in the trials emotions other than those most obviously germane to witchcraft—envy, wrath, fear, hate. Perhaps looking for love in all the wrong places, I hope to find affection and even romance in the records of early modern Polish witch trials. My strategy will be to tack between these overlapping concerns, moving substantively from aggression towards affection, and methodologically from the outside inward—from strategic, ritual, or frankly 'insincere' emotional expression to expressions arguably more representative of actual emotional states. Ending with a case study of an accused witch in love, I hope to show that the witch trials, treated with care, can provide a window into the hearts of accused witches—and by extension into the hearts of those two overlapping silent majorities, women and the illiterate, from which the accused were so commonly drawn.

The study of early modern affection is the study of unsatisfactory sources. In her excellent monograph on the Christian family in early modern Poland, Elżbieta Wróbel bewails the impossibility of knowing anything about peasant and commoner love-relationships, for lack of sources.[5] For the literate elite we have diaries, letters, manuals of comportment. For certain sorts of special people such as mystics or demoniacs, we can turn to hagiography and exorcism records.[6] In contrast, the unlettered (and the unpossessed) leave few such traces. Marriage contracts and wills are reticent and formulaic, written by clerical scribes and notaries with little interest in the 'actual' emotions of their customers.[7] Sermons and satires help us to reconstruct emotional regimes—the emotions people ought to feel—but this tells us more about the concerns of their authors (and, often enough, about the transmission of tropes from classical antiquity into the sixteenth and seventeenth centuries) than it does about anyone's actual emotional habitus.[8] Typically the ephemera of everyday emotion is captured, frozen into recorded form for our perusal centuries later, only when extreme emotions and their lamentable effects come to the attention of criminal courts—jealousy and rage in cases of homicide and assault, infatuation and lust in prosecutions for seduction or infanticide.[9] Witch trials provide a rich trove for the exploration of such extreme (and nearly always negatively valued) emotion, but I will argue below that they also provide occasional glimpses of gentler emotions. If we dare to heed Malcolm Gaskill's call to 'turn up the volume on the voices of the past'[10] we might hear, among the cries of burning passion, fainter whispers of affection, loyalty, and love.[11]

WITCHES, WIVES, AND WHORES

By definition, witchcraft involves the use of 'apparently supernatural means to cause uncanny misfortune or injury to others ... not for straightforward material gain but from envy or malice'.[12] Edward Bever has argued forcefully that at least sometimes the experience of bewitchment and its attendant ills derives from the somatoform and psychophysical disorders caused by a 'witch's' emotional aggression.[13] Other scholars locate the 'real' aggression on the side of the accuser, who projects or displaces his hatred and fear onto the witch-figure—a position classically developed in the 'denial of charity' model of Keith Thomas and Alan Macfarlane.[14] Małgorzata Pilaszek has recently argued for a model setting 'witch' and 'victim', curse and accusation, on an equal footing. Drawing on the cognitive linguistics of George Lakoff and Mark Johnson, Pilaszek adduces parallels at several levels of formality: the spells and curses of a quarrelsome woman generate suspicions of witchcraft (and possibly its real experience through psychosomatic mechanisms); the malicious gossip and slander of neighbours generate accusations and counter-accusations; and the formal indictments, denunciations, and confessions of witch trials generate convictions. All three levels share the character of verbal attack with consequences both psychological and objective, all are permutations of a single master metaphor: 'argument as war'. As Katarzyna Mączarka, an accused witch before the Poznań court, declared, 'nie byłyby czary bez gwary'— 'there would be no witchcraft without squabbling'.[15] The records of witchcraft accusation and confession give us evidence for emotions—but only emotions of a certain kind.

The town court records of early modern Poland are replete with accounts of such 'squabbling', especially in defamation suits arising from public accusations of witchcraft. Witnesses to these street quarrels delightedly reported a wealth of early modern invective. Here is a sampling, in approximate chronological order, from the towns of Kraków, Lublin, and Nieszawa between 1637 and 1790:

> You whore, you witch, you went out to peasant women to buy witchcraft in the villages [to which the other responded] You're the same, you're more a whore than I am! ... You witch, you bewitched my cow and my horse! ... Whore! You eat with devils, I eat with the apostles of God! ... What is that to you, you village woman, you witch! ... Whore! Witch! Hag! ... You witch, you sent my son to the gibbet to collect the noose. You whore, you witch! ... Whore! Witch! ... You whore! You witch! ... That thief, that sorcerer, that drunk, with his whore of a wife! ... Whore, thief, witch![16]

Or as one witness summarized one public scene—and with it this whole genre of discourse:

> They called each other witches, they called each other whores, they called each other peasants.[17]

The slander suits brought to court to defend honour which had been publicly defamed could sometimes backfire on the plaintiff, as in Nowy Sącz in 1670, when Elżbieta Stepkowicowa demanded an apology from a neighbour-woman who had 'bewhored me and called me a witch'; instead she found herself answering charges for witchcraft that led her eventually to the stake.[18] More often, the ritual of the court allowed potential witch trials to find a bloodless conclusion through stilted expressions of public reconciliation, as in Lublin in 1690:

> If I should have offended you with disparaging words, I did so out of the hastiness of my tongue, overcome with rancour. Please, for the love of God, I ask that you might desire to forgive me, for I consider you virtuous and I revoke those words of mine.[19]

The problem seems clear: the insults yelled aggressively in the streets emanate a whiff of immediacy, a feeling that one has been vouchsafed a taste of real occurrent emotion (although in passing one might note the conventionality of these insults—their sincerity conveyed in clichés). In contrast, the more peaceful 'emotion' of the apology seems obviously rehearsed and ritualistic (though one might want here briefly to query the impulse—a relic of Reformed and Enlightened critique of 'mere ritual'—to equate ceremony with insincerity).[20] Such apologies tell us much about the public play of emotional regimes—the use of the courts as arenas for the expression and resolution of conflict—but they vouchsafe no glimpse into private feelings of genuine reconciliation or amity.

Nevertheless, we do catch what seem to be occasional genuine glimpses of the friendlier emotions in the testimony of accused witches and the witnesses who testified on their behalf. In the records of the witch trials in western Ukraine, Kateryna Dysa has found narratives of neighbours who came to the defence of neighbours; or husbands who testified about the kindness and decency of their wives.[21] In the Polish trials, one finds occasional testimony of a similar kind, though the diffident caution with which some husbands defended their accused wives' honour is unlikely to set many hearts aflutter. Bartłomiej Lewczyk testified only that 'he doesn't know his wife [Regina] to have bewitched Wojciech Koziełek, and for the whole time they have lived together, for quite a few years, he has never noticed her doing anything like witchcraft'.[22] The husband of Jadwiga Talarzyna testified somewhat ruefully that his wife could not possibly be a witch, since after all, 'I have nine cows, but I don't have even a drop of milk, and my wife always used to say, "they call me a witch, even though I have to buy cheese".'[23] In a much later trial, the husband of an accused witch testified, 'We've lived together for fifty years, we've lived among our neighbours, conceived children, but we know no enchantments, I've earned my crust of bread by the work of my hands, and my wife knows nothing about [how to charm] cows.'[24] Such testimonials hardly measure up to the devotion displayed by the husband of an accused Württemberg witch, who testified that 'he loves her deeply, and would give his body and life and everything he owns for her, and added that she is not that kind of person'.[25] Nevertheless, these husbands attest quietly, and at some risk, to long-successful marriages.

It would be anachronistic to demand of early modern emotions that they count as authentic only insofar as they ring personal and sincere to our modern ears. Nevertheless, most of the emotions encountered so far, with the possible exception of the insults shouted in the streets of Lublin, have seemed decidedly muted, formal, even instrumental. From this distance in time one simply cannot say whether Jadwiga Talarzyna's husband's defence of his wife arose from affection, or long use, or loyalty, or simply a desire to have her around to cook his porridge.

However, perhaps the emotional deficiency is our own: we may want to re-examine historiographical assumptions that set us up for disappointment when the emotions displayed on trial prove insufficiently passionate. A history of emotions that rules out of court those emotional expressions which might have ulterior motivation is probably a discipline without a subject, while a history programmatically preferring strong emotion runs the risk of becoming the history of histrionics. Indeed, as we shall see, the poetic power of emotional expression bears no necessary relation to its expression of authentic feeling—a problem illustrated with especial clarity when we turn to the subject of love magic.

'So That You Cannot Live Without Me'

As elsewhere in Europe, male Polish literary culture attributed to the female gender an unbridled, insatiable lust that could motivate a turn toward the dark arts. Drawing on the biblical image of the evil Queen Jezebel, who performed 'countless harlotries and sorceries' (2 Kings 9:22), the polemicist-priest Stanisław Orzechowski described the unpopular Queen Barbara Radziwiłłówna as having been raised by 'shameless women, all poisoners and witches'.[26] A parallel tradition, derived more from Greco-Roman than from biblical traditions, depicted women as overcome with lust and jealousy. Here we can adduce examples from the witch trials themselves, while also worrying whether such examples tell us anything beyond conventional tropes. Consider the arsenal brought to bear by Zofia Philipowicowa, housekeeper in the manor of Sir Jan Podlodowski, to regain the affection of her noble master:

> The late Mrs Zawadzka (it would be ten years ago) taught me to get the heart of a pigeon, dry it, powder it, and give it to his late honour Sir Jan in a drink, so that he would be friendly toward me; I gave that pigeon's heart to his honour to drink, and his house servants and I myself ate the boiled [heart] and drank it, sharing it half and half with his honour, and saying the following words: 'Just as a male pigeon cannot live without his female pigeon, so let it be that you, christened and called Jan, cannot live without me, christened and called Zofia.'
> *Also* that same late Mrs Zawadzka taught me to let a drop of blood fall from my heart-finger [i.e. ring-finger] into a drink, and give it to his honour to drink, saying the following words: 'Just as I cannot live without my blood, so you christened and called Jan, cannot live without me.'
> *Thirdly she testified:* That same Anuska [Zawadzka] taught me to tie a stick of aspen wood in the fireplace on a string from [my] underclothing so that he would have a yearning toward me.[27]

The emotions here expressed differ hardly at all from the love spells (both literary and actual) familiar to us from classical antiquity, from sources such as Apuleius' *Golden Ass* or the corpus of Greek Magical Papyri.[28] Indeed, Zofia's ritual of placing aspen wood in the fireplace to generate a burning 'yearning toward me' closely resembles a literary spell from Szymon Szymonowic's contemporaneous *Sielanki*—

Here I burn dried ash-tree leaves.
Just as they burn, and leave no ash,
So let his heart burn within him!

—a poem-cycle itself modelled closely on Theocritus' *Idylls*.[29] The language of this and Zofia's other spells represents love as a passion, a *passio*—a suffering, burning up, an invasion of overpowering desire rendering the intended love-object as necessary as life itself. Love-magic spells from other Polish witch trials paint a similar picture, as when the Poznań cunning woman Dorota Gnieczkowa described a charm she had prepared for a client:

Welcome, dawn. Go for me to this Filip, tear his heart apart, so that he can neither drink, nor eat, without her, and so that he might desire neither maiden, nor widow, nor any other creature, except only Łucja. In Nomine Patris.[30]

John Winkler has taught us to read such spells in terms of displacement and externalization: the spell-caster imagines their object of desire suffering the same pangs of lust they feel themselves.[31] And yet in the Polish trials one detects a disjunction between the powerful emotions expressed in the spells and the rather more prosaic situations of the spell-casters. Except in the spells themselves, Zofia Philipowicowa does not express any indication that she 'cannot live' without Jan Podłodowski. Rather, she seems worried that the termination of their affair might threaten her comfortable position as housekeeper; the passionate poetry of her spells is directed toward a more practical goal: 'that he would be friendly toward me'. Indeed, she uses a similar spell to curry the favour of Sir Jan's brother Paweł, who seems to have disapproved of their affair:

That same Anuska [Zawadzka] taught me to yank the horseshoe from his horse, or the earth from under its feet, when his honour sir Paweł rode to visit us in Koszyce, so that he would be friendly toward me, and Jagnieszka the cook buried that earth in the fireplace and as she stuck it there I spoke these words: 'Just as you, christened and called Paweł, cannot be without this soil, so also don't be without myself, christened and called Zofia.'[32]

Here we find the same poetry of strong yearning, with no suggestion outside the spell itself that Zofia loved sir Paweł or wanted him to love her—she simply sought his approval.

Similarly elsewhere: it is tempting to suspect that the house-servant Zośka Janowska's gentler spell to gain the love of her master, a well-off widower of Rzeszów, might give us access to her own warm feelings of affection. At the advice of a cunning woman, she mixed a stolen eucharistic host with her spittle, added it to Mr Szastak's food, and recited, 'Just as a crowd gathers around the communion, so let him gather around me, christened and called Zośka.'[33] In vain: Zośka's master ignored her entirely except when he chose to beat her. A friend's testimony from her trial in 1718 recalls Zośka's dissatisfaction with this result:

> I gave [the cunning woman] a *tynf*, and it doesn't help at all. Szastak doesn't speak to me or think about me, as wrathful as he was before, so he remains. She assured me: if you give him [the potion] in his food or drink, he will love nobody but you, until he takes you as his wife, but he beat me yesterday with a staff, and I paid a *tynf* for nothing.[34]

The spells speak of burning desire or the adoration inspired by the Body of Christ; in contrast, the spell-casters hope for some kindness, some consideration, a more benign master–servant relationship, an amelioration of abuse.[35] The distance between the language of the spell and the spell-caster's apparent intent provides a warning against drawing too straight a line between ritual texts and the emotions of their consumers or users.

'BECAUSE I LOVED THAT HUSBAND OF MINE'

I'd like to end this chapter with the story of Zofia Baranowa of Lublin: a drunk, a part-time prostitute, a purveyor of snakeskins (for luck), snake venom (as a poison?), and the herb *pokrzyk* (probably an amulet made from its root, possibly for use as a love charm).[36] Charged with witchcraft for unclear reasons in 1643 and interrogated without torture, Baranowa recounted a story of sex and love and loss and yearning—a story that in its directness and power, its departure from the lukewarm affection or the passionate but formulaic love-charms explored above—both tempts the historian of emotions and presents us with knotty methodological problems. Zofia's case is fascinating in that she seems to have treated her confession as an opportunity to express and explore her life-story not in resistance to, but rather through and by, the stereotypes of the demon-loving witch. Most accused witches both in Poland and elsewhere sought to downplay allegations of sexual relations with demon lovers, confessing to such erotic encounters only after excruciating torture: as Lyndal Roper has noted, 'even when conviction was a certainty, these accused witches tried to minimize the extent of their sexual involvement with the devil'.[37] In contrast, Zofia embraced the demon-lover motif; in doing so, she gives us a portrait of an early modern woman in love.

Zofia was asked the standard questions—how she learned her witch-craft, what other witches she knew, whom she had harmed. Abruptly, however, and without any apparent provocation, Zofia's testimony took a strange turn. I quote at length:

> I've had relations for a few years without my husband, with someone else I myself don't know who, and this man with whom I've had relations is cold like a corpse, and smells. And this was after the death of my [first] husband, and he doesn't speak to me, and I don't have relations with my [current] husband, only with him, and he is warm only on the surface, and at any time he knocks me into the mud, and I didn't make confession to the priest about this, because he forbade me to.
>
> *She also testified*, that I drink vodka, and when I'm with him among people I see him and he sees me, but others don't see him. And he walks like my late husband, and he told me to call him Paweł because I had a brother named Paweł. And he's had relations with me for a long time, as if he were my husband.
>
> *She also testified*, that I've done my business with him on the road and in the grove, and I lay down myself, and he was in the shape of Szydłowski, my dead husband, he has hideous hands and ugly horns, and curly hair.
>
> *She also testified*, that before he started coming to me, he appeared to me in dreams, that Paweł in the shape of Stanisław Szydłowski, my husband, and he said to me: move over, I said to him, but you died! He said: Tsk, don't worry, I am still alive to you, and he appeared to me in the shape of my husband, because I loved that husband of mine.
>
> *She also testified*, that he was with me during the [last] month about two times, on Tuesday, on Thursday and now this last Thursday, before I was in

the brothel, he visited me and had carnal relations with me, that Paweł, and he told me to go to the executioner [in the brothel], because my husband had been beating me. And that Paweł never gives me anything.

She also testified, that I had relations with that Paweł because I married my current husband against my will, and he wasn't to my taste.

At this point, the interrogators seem to have attempted to take some control over Zofia's idiosyncratic narrative. Subsequent testimony cleaved more closely to the standard demonological line. 'Paweł, in the shape of Stanisław Szydłowski' is now called 'this devil'—and Zofia confesses that she renounced God and the Virgin and her baptism, that she took communion without confessing her diabolical liaisons to her priest, and that she had been to a witches' dance. Nevertheless, she continued to shape her testimony into a story about marriage and love:

Asked where she met with this devil she answered: I met with him in the grove, sometimes twice in one day. And he was there on Tuesdays, Thursdays and Wednesdays, that is at the new moon and the full moon, and for his sake I lived in disagreement with my husband, who liked to beat me, however I had strength, for that devil gave me strength.

She also testified, that when I was in the house of ill repute, at the executioner's, that devil was with me during that time, in the shape of my late husband.

The court, evidently unsure what to make of all this, ultimately chose to sentence Zofia only for her trade in snakes and herbs. The sentence, of flogging, is one of the mildest known to me for any town-court witch trial in Poland, and has suggested to at least one scholar that the court assumed Zofia to have been insane.[38]

Confronted with such a narrative, by turns intimate and bizarre, what options are open to us as readers and interpreters, and what responsibilities? First, I think we must listen carefully—a choice not without ethical ramifications. Walter Stephens has traced the elite theological origins and motivations for the motif of diabolical sex, and has argued that accused witches were forced to confess erotic encounters to assuage demonological doubts about the interaction of body with spirit.[39] Scholars as various as Sigrid Brauner, Charles Zika, and Lyndal Roper have discussed the demon-sex motif as pornography intended to titillate, repulse, and reinforce gender norms.[40] And Rita Voltmer reminds us forcefully that witch trials were affective dramas, but that these dramas were scripted, directed, and produced by the magistrates, notaries, and torturers.[41] To treat the voices of the coerced actresses as records of their own inner lives is to add insult to injury, slandering the tortured and the dead. And yet we must listen anyway—the only thing worse than misconstruing the voices of accused witches would be to ignore them in light of the methodological problems they raise. As I have argued in a different context elsewhere, the horror of the witch trials imposes upon us an ethics of remembering, a responsibility to recover as much as we can about the lives of the accused.[42]

Second, one must note the close correspondence of Zofia's account, both as a whole and in many details, with both the demonological motif of demonic sex and with more folkloric accounts of devil pacts. Consider, for example, parallels between Zofia's testimony and that of her exact contemporary Abigail Briggs, in Suffolk in 1645. Just as he did to Zofia Baranowa, the Devil appeared to Abigail, shortly after the death of her husband, in the shape and appearance of that husband, and lay with her, promising in her late husband's voice that 'I will be a loueinge husband to you.' She consented to his attentions, and he promised to help her gain revenge on her enemies, but 'she found Satan a liar'.[43] It would not be too difficult to provide examples of similar confessions from all over Europe. Zofia's narrative, then, though heartfelt and seemingly sincere, is a more than twice-told tale.

Seen from this perspective, there is almost nothing original or, one might want therefore to say, individual or inward or 'authentic', about Zofia's testimony. Moreover, what *is* original seems entirely opaque to analysis, as when she mentions having 'lived for a while on Szpitalna street, in the hut of Zabłocka, and only frogs go into that hut'. Nearly everything can be found elsewhere, either in the elite demonological discourse, in Slavic or Polish folklore, or both. Zofia's narrative, both in overall structure and in many details, follows standard motifs: almost none of the story originates with her. But it would be a great mistake to assume, thereby, that she had nothing *of* herself to say.

For Zofia Baranowa's testimony is, above all, a love story—a story she tells to herself as much as to her judges. Too much attention to the folkloric details of demonic sex—the missing nostrils, the horns, the body cold like a corpse—should not distract one from the singular fact that this testimony of a possibly insane herbalist contains one of the very few first-hand expressions of marital or romantic love from an early modern Polish common-woman.

'[A]nd he appeared to me in the shape of my husband, because I loved that husband of mine.' In its pathos and naiveté, this simple statement demands of the reader, as I have suggested above, a commitment to an ethics of remembering. It requires an acknowledgement: that whatever else Zofia Baranowa's testimony might represent and whatever uses we may put it to, it is, first, an extremely personal statement, by a particular person, trying to make sense of her own life. Although her Paweł is violent, rough, and in many ways disappointing—as, perhaps, her husband Stanisław Szydłowski had been—he is above all a reminder of that husband. For his sake she 'lives in disagreement' with her current, abusive husband Wojciech Baran. Paweł helped Zofia to withstand Wojciech's beatings: 'however I had strength, for that devil gave me strength'. At Paweł's urging she made the momentous decision to leave her abusive marital home and take up residence at the brothel (perhaps, permanently, as an employee—however, this is not clear). Through Paweł's urging she refused to have sex with Wojciech: 'and I don't have relations with my husband, only with him'. In contrast to most narratives of diabolical sex (and despite Paweł's coldness, smell, and horrid appearance) she had sex with him willingly and often: 'I've had business with him on the road and in the grove, and I lay down myself. And he was in the shape of Szydłowski, my dead husband, he has hideous hands and ugly horns, and curly hair…'. It is impossible, and misguided, to try to separate the diabolical elements in this narrative from the personal elements: they run together seamlessly. Zofia's narrative is not a diabolical script peppered with personal reflections, nor a personal introspection diverted unwillingly into demonological channels. The narrative forms a whole, at once scripted and deeply personal.

This chapter has hinted that witch trials provide many such voices, many such narratives: junctures where the subject and ideology meet, where people learn to feel, and to understand, both the emotions ascribed to them by society (or culture, or patriarchy), and also to express emotions less obviously connected to the conflictual context of a trial for malefice. If we listen closely, we can sometimes hear words of love in the most unlikely of places.

RANKEAN REFLECTIONS

Historians have traditionally found it sufficiently difficult to establish 'what actually happened', in Ranke's famous phrase. 'What was actually felt'—especially if we confine emotion to the sincere, unaffected, interior disposition of a sensitive subject—is a question the answer to which is permanently withheld from our prying eyes.

But perhaps it is this definition of 'actual' authentic emotions which sets us up for failure. Emotions are not hidden in the heart: insofar as they exist accessibly at all, either to ourselves or to others, they are acted and enacted, bodily and therefore public documents of expressive culture. One is reminded of Umberto Eco's famous account of the 'postmodern attitude', as one in which one cannot unironically declare 'I love you madly', and yet one can 'succeed, once again, in speaking of love' by the ironic-yet-sincere declaration, 'as Barbara Cartland would put it, I love you madly'.[44] The attitude may be postmodern, but the tendency to speak one's deepest emotions through timeworn tropes is old and universal. As Lyndal Roper has noted of a witchcraft confession itself simultaneously intimate and standardized:

> narratives in which people try to make sense of their psychic conflicts usually involve borrowing from a language which is not at first the individual's own. We might say that coming to understand oneself can involve learning to recognize one's feelings in the terms of a theory, psychoanalytic or diabolic, which one might not originally have applied to oneself.[45]

The anthropologist Michael Jackson makes a similar point in relation to the witchcraft confessions of Kuranko women in Sierra Leone and Guinea:

> [T]he self-confessed witch does more than passively submit to the succession of misfortunes that have overwhelmed her. Nor does she blindly recapitulate the stereotypes men promulgate; rather, she actively uses them to give voice to long-suppressed grievances and to cope with her suffering by declaring herself the author of it. Thus, she determines how she will play out the role which circumstance has thrust upon her. She dies deciding her own identity, sealing her own fate.[46]

Both Roper and Jackson help us to extricate ourselves from the quandary with which this chapter began, and which the case of Zofia Baranowa rendered exquisite: how (and whether) to look for 'real' emotions in the courtroom dramas of the witch trials. Both answer, in slightly different ways: one does not discover the individual by subtracting discourse and examining whatever is left over, nor by peeling away convention and motif to reveal an authentic core. People express their subjectivity, to themselves as to others, *through* the motifs and structures available. This is as true of witchcraft confessions as it is, for example, of the sonnet form in poetry, where both a rigid structure and a time-worn collection of metaphors do not prevent new poets from expressing new, individual, and sincere protestations of love.

NOTES

1. For the distinction between 'emotional dispositions' and 'occurrent emotions' see Elster, *Strong Feelings*, 26. I borrow the image of emotions caught in amber from Mark Seymour, '"Emotional Arenas": A New Concept for Historicizing Emotions?' Public lecture, Centre for the History of European Discourses, University of Queensland, 16 October 2014.
2. Pascal, *Pensées*, Brunschvicg edition, 277. On the historical development of modern conceptions of interiority and inwardness, see Taylor, *Sources of the Self*, 111–210. For a critique of ahistorical historiographies that treat emotions as interior, see Scheer, 'Are Emotions a Kind of Practice?', 195–204.
3. Ryle, *Concept of Mind*, 51; cf. Ryle, 'Thinking of Thoughts'. My appreciation of Ryle is filtered through the work of Clifford Geertz: especially his 'Thick Description', which develops Ryle's thought in directions useful to a history of emotions as public, interpretable 'acted documents' (ibid., 10). On the shortcomings of Ryle's own treatment of emotion (shortcomings overcome, to my satisfaction, by Geertz), see Stout, 'Ryle's Conceptions of Emotional Behaviour'. See also Scheer, 'Are Emotions a Kind of Practice?', 220: the 'feeling subject is not prior to but emerges in the doing of emotion'.
4. See Voltmer's chapter, this volume.
5. Wróbel, *Chrześcijańska rodzina w Polsce*.
6. E.g. the affective piety typified in the life of the Carmelite mystic Anna Maria Marchocka, or anecdotes expressive of the sexual yearnings and traumas of young women acting out their frustrations in the drama of possession. Marchocka, *Autobiografia*

mistyczna; Marcin Kałowski, *Informacya o początkach y dalszym progressie Cudownego Mieysca Łagiewnickiego* [1723], briefly discussed in Ostling, *Between the Devil and the Host*, 179.

7. For a discussion of this sort of source and its limitations, together with an attempt to reconstruct some hint of the inner lives of peasants from such sources, see Wiślicz, *Zarobić na duszne zbawienie*; cf. Wróbel, *Chrześcijańska rodzina*.

8. See e.g. Wiśniewska, *Świat płci żeńskiej*. Several chapters in the present volume (e.g. those of Tamar Herzig, Laura Kounine, and E.J. Kent) highlight the promise of such sources for a history of emotional regimes or emotional norms while also signalling their limitations as a source for occurrent emotions.

9. For a model of what can (and what cannot) be learned about love from such sources, see Wiślicz, *Upodobanie*.

10. Gaskill, 'Witchcraft, Emotions, and Imagination', 174.

11. I am hardly the first to have searched the witch trials for love. Already in the nineteenth century, Jules Michelet was all too willing to invert demonological fantasies of diabolical sex to construct his own fantasy of sexually liberated pagan sorceresses; while more recently G.R. Quaife treated demon lovers as expressions of the sexual frustrations of early modern peasant women: Michelet, *Satanism and Witchcraft*; Quaife, *Godly Zeal and Furious Rage*, 101–5. The clumsiness of such approaches inspired much-needed critique (e.g. Brauner, *Fearless Wives and Frightened Shrews*, 20–4; Stephens, 'Incredible Sex'). For exemplary attempts to find love and affection in witch-trial records while remaining aware of the dangers involved, see Roper, *Oedipus and the Devil*; Durrant, *Witchcraft, Gender and Society*.

12. Hutton, 'Global Context of the Scottish Witch-hunt', 19.

13. Bever, 'Witchcraft Fears'; *Realities of Witchcraft*. See also Bever's chapter in this volume.

14. Macfarlane, *Witchcraft in Tudor and Stuart England*, 205–6; Keith Thomas, *Religion and the Decline of Magic*, 560–7; for critique, see Barry, 'Keith Thomas and the Problem of Witchcraft'.

15. Pilaszek, *Procesy*, 57–61; Lakoff and Johnson, *Metaphors We Live By*.

16. I take most of these outbursts from the Lublin archives: Archiwum Państwowe w Lublinie (APL), Acta Miasta Lubelskiego (AML),

sig. 210 f. 445, sig. 211 f. 288, sig. 226 ff. 57v, 477v; the remainder are quoted after Wiśniewska, *Świat płci żeńskiej*, 114; Pilaszek, *Procesy*, 328, 54, 71. For a similar public outburst in seventeenth-century Rylsk (Muscovy), where a marketwoman called her rival a 'whore', 'potion-maker', and 'concoctor of root-magic', see Kivelson, *Desperate Magic*, 99.

17. APL, AML sig. 61 f. 120 (Lublin 1738). On the conflation of 'witch' and 'whore' as 'the twin images of evil femininity', see Roper, *Witch in the Western Imagination*, 80; Ostling, *Devil and the Host*, 219–20.

18. Uruszczak, 'Proces czarownicy w Nowym Sączu'.

19. APL, AML sig. 116 f. 271v.

20. Muir, *Ritual in Early Modern Europe*, 166–90, 294–302; Bell, 'Ritual'.

21. Dysa, 'Witchcraft Trials', 89–102. Cf. Briggs, *Witches and Neighbours*, 225–31.

22. This lukewarm (or merely cautious) testimony, together with similar characterizations from her brother and a neighbour ('You never hear about this woman being mixed up with any kind of witchcraft'; 'nobody complains of her') sufficed to clear Regina of the charge of sending a devil to possess the local tax-collector. APL, AML sig. 144 ff. 379–81, 391–4; cf. Zakrzewska-Dubasowa, ed., *Procesy o czary w Lublinie*, 66–72.

23. Kaczmarczyk, 'Proces o czarostwo', 309–12.

24. Trembowla 1763; quoted after Z. Pazdro, 'Proces o "perepiczkę"', 273.

25. Kounine, 'Gendering of Witchcraft', 306.

26. Orzechowski's *Oratio* [...] *contra matrimonium secundum Sigismundi Augusti regis Poloniae*, quoted after Anna Brzezińska, 'Accusations of Love Magic' 123. Orzechowski and others argued that Barbara had won Zygmunt August's hand through love magic, and hinted that she may have poisoned his first wife Elizabeth. For discussion of the Jezebel trope, see Lesses, 'Most Worthy of Women', 72–4.

27. APL, AML sig. 38 ff. 113–16; cf. Zakrzewska-Dubasowa, ed., *Procesy o czary w Lublinie*, 13–20. The trial took place in the small town of Skrzynno in 1639, but the records were written into the *acta* of Lublin at the request of sir Paweł Podlodowski.

28. Faraone, *Ancient Greek Love Magic*.

29. Szymonowic, *Sielanki* [1614], no. 15. For commentary, see Szyszkowski, 'Pierwiastek ludowy (I)', 128–9.
30. Woronczak, 'Procesy o czary', 50–5.
31. Winkler, 'Constraints of Desire'.
32. APL, AML sig. 38 ff. 113–16. The spell proved ineffective: Sir Paweł brought Zofia to trial for witchcraft after his brother's suspicious death; she avoided capital punishment but was banished from Skrzynno and its environs.
33. Dydek, 'Czary w procesie inkwizycyjnym'.
34. Ibid. A *tynf* was a coin struck from inferior metal, with the nominal value of a golden *złoty*. Largely because Zośka's witchcraft involved the Eucharist, she was sentenced to especially horrific punishment: her hand was cut off and nailed to the city gates, and she was burnt alive at the stake.
35. For a much fuller explication of this dynamic, see Kivelson, *Desperate Magic*, and her contribution to this volume. For a somewhat analogous reinterpretation of ancient erotic charms and spells, see Frankfurter, 'Social Context of Women's Erotic Magic'.
36. *Pokrzyk* [lit. 'the screamer'] is today a common name for mandrake (*Mandragora officinarum* L.), used throughout Europe for magic, especially love and fertility magic. However, in early modern Poland *pokrzyk* usually denoted deadly nightshade (*Atropa belladonna* L.) or an amulet made from a mandrake substitute such as bryony (*Bryonia alba* L.). See Ostling, 'Witches' Herbs on Trial', 194–5.
37. Roper, *Oedipus and the Devil*, 216; cf. Ostling, *Devil and the Host*, 214–21.
38. Karpiński, *Kobieta w mieście polskim*, 322.
39. Stephens, 'Incredible Sex'; *Demon Lovers*.
40. Brauner, *Fearless Wives*; Zika, 'Fears of Flying'; Roper, *The Witch*.
41. See Voltmer's chapter, this volume.
42. Ostling, *Devil and the Host*, 191–2; cf. Wyschogrod, *Ethics of Remembering*.
43. Ewen, ed., *Witch Hunting and Witch Trials*, 300.
44. Eco, *Reflections on The Name of the Rose*, 67–8.
45. Roper, *Oedipus and the Devil*, 206; cf. Jackson, 'Witches, Wives and Mothers'.
46. Jackson, 'Witch as a Category', 326.

CHAPTER 10

Over-Familiar Spirits: The Bonds between English Witches and Their Devils

Charlotte-Rose Millar

In early modern England witches were viewed as malicious, dangerous men and women who failed to properly regulate their emotions. Accused witches were often portrayed in popular pamphlets as impoverished, once-powerless men and women who, through their pact with the Devil, were able to draw on diabolical power to act out their desires. In English witchcraft narratives, the Devil most commonly appeared as a small domestic animal known as a familiar spirit. Familiars performed a dual role, a duality related to their two origins: they were devils from hell sent *to* the witch to tempt her, and they were external embodiments of witches' internal thoughts and desires, sent *from* her to act out those desires and thoughts in the world. Through forming a personal bond with this creature in the form of a demonic pact, witches were able to act upon their overwhelming hatred, envy, malice and greed to maim or kill their neighbours, destroy livestock and kill children. In most of the historiography to date English witchcraft has been seen as a predominantly malefic crime, one not overly

C.-R. Millar
The University of Queensland

© The Author(s) 2016
L. Kounine, M. Ostling (eds.), *Emotions in the History of Witchcraft*, DOI 10.1057/978-1-137-52903-9_10

concerned with the role of the Devil. This view is beginning to change but there are still elements of the diabolical in English witchcraft that are not fully understood. Focusing on the crucial role of the familiar, a devil in animal form, in witchcraft narratives encourages us to re-evaluate the importance of diabolical ideas in English witchcraft beliefs.[1] This chapter will explore the different ways in which the bond between familiar and witch was represented in witchcraft pamphlets. It has three main aims: first, to reconsider the prevalence of diabolical ideas in English witchcraft narratives; second, to explore how early modern English witches used their bond with the Devil to act upon their desires; and, third, to demonstrate how familiar spirits can be understood as physical manifestations of a witch's hatred, desire and fear.

English witchcraft was portrayed in popular pamphlets as a diabolical crime motivated and sustained by emotion. Of the fifty-five witchcraft pamphlets published throughout the sixteenth and seventeenth centuries, only two fail to mention witches' reliance on the Devil to help them inflict *maleficium*.[2] In all but five of these pamphlets the Devil is represented as a familiar spirit.[3] This representation is usually explicit through the description of animalistic creatures acting as the Devil but, in a handful of pamphlets, becomes more implicit through references to hidden teats found on the body of the witch. The familiar is a staple of English witchcraft literature. The high percentage of familiars visible in pamphlet narratives appears to be significantly higher than those in trial records.[4] This suggests that pamphlet authors chose to publish cases in which the role of the Devil was a key concern, either as a warning against the trappings of Satan (as is clear in many epistles) or out of the belief that stories of demonic animals would sell. The preference given to diabolical narratives would have created a very specific understanding of witchcraft amongst English readers and positions pamphlets as a key source for understanding the connection between witchcraft and diabolism in early modern England.

Since the beginnings of modern witchcraft scholarship, popular pamphlets have been viewed as a crucial source for understanding witchcraft beliefs. Alan Macfarlane has argued convincingly for the importance of pamphlets in studying witchcraft, claiming that they are 'a vital and reliable source providing otherwise inaccessible material and correcting the somewhat narrow impression of witchcraft prosecutions given by indictments'.[5] More recently, scholars such as James Sharpe, Marion Gibson, Barbara Rosen, Emma Wilby and Frances Dolan have all added their voices to this earlier analysis and emphasized the importance of pamphlets in understanding English witchcraft beliefs.[6] Witchcraft narratives allow witnesses, accused witches and victims to 'give voice to their interests and suspicions, their feelings and desires, all within the formal setting of persuasive legal storytelling'.[7] These stories are, of course, mediated through legal clerks and magistrates, and pamphlets, as opposed to depositions, add another level of complexity through the addition of another male mediator: the (usually anonymous) author. Like many historians of witchcraft, I am cautious of reading pamphlets as evidence of "historical truth"; rather I focus on what these sources can tell us about what people believed to have occurred.[8] Although it is difficult to 'distinguish cleanly between how cases actually unfolded and how witnesses or pamphleteers chose to tell that story',[9] pamphlets remain one of the most valuable sources for the study of English witchcraft.

Through their reliance on pre-trial documents (particularly strong in pamphlets from before the 1590s) and their integration of statements from witnesses, accused witches, and supposed victims, pamphlet stories allow us an insight into how witchcraft narratives were constructed by a number of different voices and how the combination of these voices presented a clear depiction of English witchcraft as a diabolical crime. These narratives highlight how early modern people understood the demonic pact, how they conceptualized witchcraft and what level of importance they gave to the role of emotion in a witch's decision to perform acts of witchcraft. In these documents the role of the Devil and a witch's relationship to him is crucial. Pamphlets circulated widely throughout England and recent studies of literacy demonstrate that they would have been accessible to far more than the 10 to 20% of people whom we know were able to sign their name.[10] Witchcraft pamphlets were a genre accessible to a large stratum of the early modern populace. Their importance in creating and sustaining specific beliefs about witchcraft cannot be underestimated. As Keith Thomas has argued, 'contemporaries ... were dependent for their knowledge of the subject [of witchcraft] upon the chance appearance of a pamphlet account of a notable trial'.[11] Although English witchcraft has historically been viewed as a non-diabolical crime, my focus on pamphlets allows us to see that the concept of the diabolical witch was circulating strongly throughout England.

Writing about emotion in witchcraft narratives is not new. Already in 1970, Alan Macfarlane proposed his now well-known theory of the 'charity-refused' or revenge model of English witchcraft.[12] Macfarlane argued that early modern English witches were thought of as malicious, ill-natured people who had a wicked disposition and were full of desire for revenge.[13] Coupled with the work of Keith Thomas, Macfarlane's 'revenge-model' of witchcraft still remains the most common way to interpret English witchcraft narratives, although it has been qualified and its scope circumscribed by more recent research.[14] Robin Briggs and Malcolm Gaskill have furthered the work of Thomas and Macfarlane through emphasizing the importance of neighbourhood relationships and interpersonal conflicts in witchcraft.[15] For Briggs, witches were those who 'had done no more than find themselves at odds with their neighbours'.[16] Gaskill also explored the significance of neighbourly conflicts and argued that 'an appreciation of fear and anger is vital for understanding witchcraft'.[17] This chapter builds on the work of Macfarlane, Thomas, Briggs and Gaskill but has a particular focus on how witches were believed to form emotional bonds with their familiar spirit. I will be focusing on female witches as, although male witches (approximately 10% of the accused in England) were also believed to engage in intimate interactions with familiar spirits, there are very few examples in pamphlets of male witches using their familiar spirits to act upon their desires; those that we do have are very brief.[18] For this reason, this chapter focuses on the more developed stories from female narratives. Deborah Willis, Diane Purkiss and Lyndal Roper have already explored the (anti-)maternal overtones of the bond between female witch and devil in great depth and my own work has explored the sexualized elements of these relationships.[19] It is only through the familiar, a devil in animal form, that the witch is able to act on her emotional desires. By viewing the familiar in this way, this chapter sympathizes with the interpretations of both Roper and Purkiss as women's tales of witchcraft as fantasies. For Purkiss, these fantasies 'enabled village women to negotiate the fears and anxieties of housekeeping and motherhood'.[20] Rather than confining myself to these issues which centre on the mother–child relationship, I ask what happens if we attempt to understand witchcraft narratives as stories that reflect accused witches' overwhelming emotions and, more specifically, how the familiar can be seen to represent these emotions. For Roper, witchcraft trials provide a genre that allowed women to "speak" and to transform their own life experience into the 'language of the diabolic'.[21] As she has eloquently explained, witches 'used elements of their culture to create narratives which made sense of their lives: of their unbearable hatreds, agonies, jealousies'.[22] Applying this reading of witchcraft narratives to an English context has implications for our understanding of the use of emotion within witchcraft stories and, importantly, also asserts the importance of diabolical ideas to English witchcraft narratives in an attempt to counter the traditional view of English witchcraft as an almost entirely non-diabolical crime. In the following narratives, we see women's anxieties and emotions given diabolical power through the familiar spirit. We then see these women's confessions printed and circulated as evidence of the growing danger of the Devil in the world. To understand witchcraft narratives, we must try to understand the mind of the witch as well as the motivations of the pamphleteer, the judge, the witnesses and the victims. My analysis below attempts to unpick how accused witches may have understood their own diabolical narratives.

I have chosen to look at pamphlet narratives about three different groups of witches: Joan Prentice, described in print in 1589; Joan Flower and her daughters Margaret and Phillipa (sometimes known as the Belvoir witches), described in pamphlets from 1619 and 1635; and Temperance Lloyd, Susanna Edwards, and Mary Trembles (also described as the Bideford witches), described in two pamphlets from 1682 and a third from 1687. All seven of these women were accused of, and confessed to, making a pact with the Devil in the shape of a familiar spirit.[23] I will analyse the first moments at which they met the Devil, why they chose to join with him, how their relationship with their demonic companion developed and, finally, how they used the Devil to act upon their desires and attempted to blame the Devil for their own malice. As noted above, pamphlets include a multiplicity of voices and it is often hard to distinguish what comes from the magistrate, the clerk, the witnesses, the accused witch, the alleged victim, or the pamphleteer. As Gibson has highlighted, pamphlets from before the 1590s were heavily based on pre-trial records and, as such, allow the voice of the witch to come through strongly.[24] Pamphlets after this time show more signs of interference from the pamphleteer. The below analysis is based both on attempting to understand how accused women chose to construct their diabolical narratives and also on how pamphlets represented these narratives and, in doing so, created an understanding of English witchcraft as an activity based on an emotional relationship with the Devil.[25]

My first narrative, from 1589, demonstrates the changing bond between witch and devil and also explains how familiars made pacts with witches.[26] The pamphlet begins by explaining how accused witch Joan Prentice first met the Devil. At about ten o'clock at night, Bidd, a 'dunnish culloured ferret, having fiery eyes, approached accused witch Joan Prentice in her home'.[27] Bidd tells Joan that he is Satan and that she must give him her soul.[28] Joan hesitates and asks how she can give away her soul when 'her soule is appertained onely unto Jesus Christ, by whose precious blood shedding it was bought'.[29] Unfazed, Bidd explains that if Joan gives him some of her blood this will override Christ's claim. Apparently satisfied, Joan agrees, and after Bidd sucks blood from Joan's finger, the pact is complete. In this narrative, and in the vast majority of English witchcraft pamphlets, the demonic pact acts as a transformative moment, one in which Joan becomes a witch in league with the Devil. The familiar, as an agent of the Devil, performs the Devil's role and convinces Joan to stray away from Christ and give her soul to Satan. It is only through her agreement with a demonic agent that Joan is able to access supernatural powers. In pamphlets, the pact was nearly always made at the first meeting between witch and devil and was viewed as a necessary prerequisite for becoming a witch.

Unusually for witchcraft narratives, this pamphlet does not provide a reason for Joan's decision to join with the Devil. Despite this, it is possible to analyse the emotional overtones present in the narrative. Bidd appears to Joan at night when she is getting ready for bed. He tells her not to be afraid and reassures her that he will not hurt her. The next time Bidd appears is also at night. On this second occasion, Bidd leaps into Joan's lap and then onto her bosom where, laying his feet upon her left shoulder, he sucks blood from her cheek (Fig. 10.1).[30] This melding of the cosy and demonic reminds us of James Serpell's suggestion that we can view familiar spirits as demonic pets, and provides a formula for how we might imagine that witches may have interacted with their familiars.[31] It seems clear that many sightings of familiar spirits were based on real animals which accused witches may have treated as pets. Thomas has argued that the unusual animal forms that many familiars took could be an example of the early modern belief that pet-keeping was morally suspect as, like bestiality, it blurred the lines between the animal and the human.[32] To view familiars as mere pets is to ignore their demonic characteristics, their links with medieval demons, with fairies and with premodern associations of the links between certain animals and devils.[33] However, the idea that pet keeping was morally suspect does add another layer to how associations with animals may have been viewed by a witch's neighbours, as well as providing a clue for how witch and familiar may have interacted.

After sucking Joan's blood, Bidd declares, 'Joan, if thou will have me doo anything for thee, I am and wilbe always ready at thy commandement.'[34] At this prompting, Joan 'beeing a little before fallen out with

Fig. 10.1 Accused witch Joan Prentice engaging in a blood pact with her familiar, Bidd. Anon., *The apprehension and confession of three notorious witches* (1589), title page and sig. B1v

[the wife of] William Adams ... willed the ferret to spoile her drinke ... which he did accordingly'.[35] Joan only becomes able to act on her desire for revenge with the help of her demonic spirit. Bidd continues to appear to Joan, always before bed, and continues to suck blood from her left cheek. The relationship ends, however, just weeks before this pamphlet was written. Joan has attempted to beg for alms at the home of Maister Glascock but a servant has sent her away saying that Maister Glascock and his wife are away from home so she must 'be contented for that time' until they return.[36] Joan 'departed greatlye discontented' and that night, after feeding Bidd blood from her left shoulder, Joan asks him to 'goe unto Maister Glascocks house, and nippe one of his Children a little, named Sara, but hurt it not'.[37] The next night Bidd returns and says that he has done what Joan asked, 'namely, that he had nipt Sara Glascock, and that she should dye therof'.[38] Joan is appalled and yells at Bidd 'thou villaine what hast thou doon?'[39] At this outburst, Bidd vanishes away, never to appear again.[40] At this point in the narrative, Joan has lost control of her dangerous desires and is horrified by what they have wrought. There are many ways to read Bidd's disappearance. Perhaps the most orthodox is if we remind ourselves that Bidd is a devil, a trickster, and cannot be trusted.[41] This may have been the position taken by the pamphleteer who has portrayed Bidd as a demonic, untrustworthy trickster who disappears forever after having deceived Joan, acquired her soul and killed a child. This would not be a surprising portrayal given the widespread contemporary circulation in popular print and biblical texts of the Devil as the Father of Lies.[42] Indeed, this very pamphlet begins by warning its readers of the 'illusions of Sathan'.[43] However, we must remember that pamphlet narratives do not represent just one voice. As noted above, and explained most fully by Marion Gibson, pamphlet narratives represent an amalgam of voices from the accused witch, the pamphleteer, the witnesses, the judges and the supposed victims.[44] It is possible that, for Joan Prentice, Bidd disappears because Joan is completely horrified by the death of Sara Glascock, an innocent child. By giving in to her anger and malice, Joan has killed a child. As a result of this horror, Joan rejects the creature that allowed her to act upon her emotional desires.

Until this tragedy, Joan and Bidd have had an amicable relationship. The emotional undertones of their relationship are perhaps best seen in Fig. 10.1. This frontispiece image (repeated inside the pamphlet) depicts Joan cupping her breast and stomach, while Bidd sucks blood from her cheek. Bidd's continual night-time sucking, his words of reassurance and the image's highlighting of Joan's breasts and stomach are all evocative of a close relationship with maternal undertones. But the relationship cannot just be defined as one of a mother and surrogate child. Bidd's role in hurting Joan's neighbours gives him a much stronger role—he is not just an affectionate pet or surrogate child. He is a creature who represents an external embodiment of Joan's malice. This mutually beneficial relationship is only made possible through the making of the pact, a key moment in witchcraft narratives. Through forming a pact with a small, animalistic creature, witches were able to form personal relationships with the Devil.

In 1618 Margaret Flower, a servant working for the Earl of Rutland, fell under suspicion of theft.[45] Margaret was well known for her laziness, her malice and her association with base characters. Even more seriously, she was suspected of working with her mother, Joane Flower, a suspected witch, for unknown but undoubtedly evil purposes. Joane Flower was a 'monstrous malicious woman, full of oaths, curses, and imprecations irreligious' who had eyes which were 'fiery and hollow … speech fell and envious [and a] demeanour strange and exoticke', all of which 'gave great suspition that she was a notorious Witch … who dealt with familiar spirits'.

Unsurprisingly, Joane's neighbours were terrified of her, particularly by her 'curses and threatening of revenge'.[46] Margaret Flower's base lifestyle and the suspicion that she was a thief who was plotting unnamed evil with her mother, Joane Flower, led to her dismissal from the Earl's household.

Margaret's dismissal infuriated both herself and her mother. Joane lost complete control of her emotions and cursed the Earl's family.[47] At this exact moment, the Devil 'perceived the inficious disposition of this wretch, and that she and her Daughters might easily bee made instruments to enlarge his Kingdome'.[48] The Devil appeared and offered the Flower family his service in exchange for their souls. Joane and Margaret agreed and entered into the Devil's service as witches. The pact is cemented through an exchange of blood and 'abominable kisses', a phrase suggesting both deviant sexuality and affection.[49] These kisses, combined with embraces, become an ongoing feature of the relationship between these accused witches and their familiars. In this narrative, Joane and Margaret have been targeted by the Devil at a time when they are particularly angry and have lost control of their emotions. The two women lose little time in using their newfound powers to act upon their malicious desires. From this time on, the Earl and the Countess are 'many times subject to sicknesse and extraordinary convulsions'.[50] The eldest son, Henry, 'sickened very strangely' and died, the next eldest son Francis was 'most barbarously and inhumanely tortured by a strange sicknesse' and, not long after, their daughter Katherine 'was set upon by their dangerous and divellish practises, and many times [was] in great danger of life, through extreame maladies and unusuall fits'.[51] Joane and Margaret's familiar, a cat called Rutterkin, played an active role in these attacks. Joane's other daughter, Phillipa, confessed that

> by the commandement of her mother [she] brought from the Castle the right hand glove of the Lord *Henry Rosse* ... who presently rubd it on the backe of her Spirit *Rutterkin*, and then put it into hot boyling water, afterward shee pricked it often, and buried it in the yard, wishing the Lord *Rosse* might never thrive.[52]

In this narrative, Joane has only been able to realize her desires through the use of Rutterkin, her demonic cat. Although Joane does not physically send Rutterkin to hurt the children (as Joan Prentice does with her demonic ferret, Bidd), this cat is instrumental to Joane's ability to act upon her emotions.

For Margaret and Joane, devilish familiars allow action on their overwhelming anger and desire for revenge. Phillipa Flower has different motives for joining with the Devil: she is madly in love with local man Thomas Simpson. Rather than appealing to her desire for malice, in Phillipa's case the Devil offers her love. Phillipa confesses that when her familiar (which takes the shape of a white rat) first appeared to her, she gave it her soul because it promised to do her good and to cause Thomas Simpson to love her.[53] This familiar continually sucks at Phillipa's left breast—an act that can perhaps be viewed as a substitute for the love Phillipa would like to share with Thomas. Thomas does fall in love with Phillipa but unfortunately this is not a long-lasting romance. The man eventually comes to his senses and testifies that he must have been bewitched because 'hee had no power to leave her'.[54]

The story of the Flower family was published in 1619 and again in 1635.[55] Within these narratives we see a range of emotional interactions between witches, devils and victims. In the case of all three witches, their emotions are crucial to their decision to enter into a pact with the Devil. Margaret and Joane are recruited while they are particularly angry and hungry for revenge. Phillipa, on the other hand, is seduced by promises of love. The Devil's promises are not based on material gain but on emotional desire. As well as the promises themselves, the way in which the three accused interact with their devils has emotional undertones. Margaret and Joane kiss and hug their familiars and Phillipa suckles hers at her breast. Through their familiar spirits, these witches forge personal relationships with the Devil which allow them to act upon their desires. For Margaret and Joane, Rutterkin allows them to take the revenge that they so desire and, for Phillipa, her white rat causes Thomas to love her and, also, perhaps acts as a substitute for love from its continued suckling at an intimate part of her body. These familiars do not simply provide witches with magical powers—they are deeply in tune with their innermost desires and are fundamental in allowing them to be expressed.

Temperance Lloyd, Mary Trembles, and Susanna Edwards, commonly known as the Bideford witches, are the subject of three pamphlet accounts, all published in the 1680s.[56] The main source of information is the 44-page 1682 pamphlet which is made up almost entirely of witness statements and confessions given before magistrates.[57] The other two pamphlets, from 1682 and 1687, add very little information, focus predominantly on Temperance, are sensationalized and moralizing, and sometimes even contradict the longer pamphlet. As Jonathan Barry has pointed out, however, they still may contain elements of truth.[58] It is possible that the second two pamphlets were based on evidence from the assizes, whereas the first is based on evidence taken from Bideford.[59] These three accounts paint a detailed picture of different aspects of the trial proceedings, and, through their detailed depictions of witches' confessions (particularly in the longest pamphlet), they allow us to speculate on how the Bideford witches told their demonic tales.

Temperance, Mary and Susanna were all executed.[60] Although another woman, Alice Mollard, was sentenced to death in 1685, these three executions are the last that we are sure to have taken place for witchcraft in England.[61] Unlike the Flower witches, all of whom have strong emotional motivations for joining with the Devil, the Bideford witches initially appear to enter into pragmatic arrangements. In 1670, Temperance recounts, 'she was tempted by the Devil to be instrumental of the death of *William Herbert* ... and that the Devil did promise her that she should live well, and do well'.[62] Temperance gives into temptation and kills William. Susanna Edwards enters into a pact for similar reasons. The Devil, after establishing that Susanna is poor, says that 'if [she] would grant him one request, that she should neither want for Meat, Drink, nor Clothes'.[63] Susanna very willingly agrees and, afterwards, 'a little Boy, which she thinks to be the Devil, came to her house and did lie with her, and that he did suck her at her breast'.[64] It is this promise of a comfortable life that Susanna uses to seduce Mary Trembles, after which time, 'the Devil in the shape of a Lyon' appeared to her.[65] The three women's 'oppressing Poverty' makes it clear why the Devil's claims are appealing.[66]

The relationship between witch and devil differs in this pamphlet from the descriptions given in earlier narratives. The tale of witchcraft, however, remains very familiar. For Susanna and Mary, their first use of diabolical power is out of a desire for revenge. One day Susanna and Mary beg at the house of John Barnes but his wife, Grace, refuses them alms. The two women wander off but return a short while later and ask for 'a Farthings worth of Tobacco'.[67] Grace once again refuses, in response to which Susanna tells Mary that 'it should be better for ... *Grace* if she had let [her] have some'.[68] Using their diabolical powers, Susanna and Mary return invisibly to the house 'where they did pinch and prick the said *Grace Barnes* almost unto death'.[69]

In this narrative, Susanna and Mary have drawn on their diabolical power to seek revenge—however, rather than sending familiars in their stead, or using them to help take revenge, they are seemingly able to act alone. Under examination though, Susanna claims that the Devil, who appeared in a shape of a lion, had 'intice[d] her to make an end' of Grace Barnes. All three witches blame their murderous desires on the Devil, sometimes claiming that they were beaten if they refused to act. Mary claims that even though the Devil did not threaten her with physical violence, he did frighten her.[70] By blaming the Devil, all three women are able to separate themselves from their murderous desires. In the same way that Joan Prentice was horrified by what her malice had wrought, Susanna and Mary blame the Devil for their desire to hurt Grace.

Susanna and Mary admit to making their own way to Grace's house to attack her, but claim that the Devil tempted them to do it. Rather than this being a mere expression, Susanna is explicitly referring to a devil in the shape of a lion who enticed her to vengeance. Like Susanna and Mary, Temperance also claims that the Devil forced her to 'that the Devil forced her to hurt Grace against her will'.[71] Temperance testifies that the Devil carried her to the door of Mrs Grace Thomas, which was open, and told her to kill. Unlike Susanna and Mary, however, Temperance claims that she bore no malice to Grace and that the Devil forced her to hurt Grace against her will.[72] At the Devil's prompting, Temperance claims that she bruised' Grace but refused to kill her, for which the 'Devil beat [her] about the Head grievously'.[73] Here Temperance seems to be attempting to blame the Devil for her own aggressive desires.

Susanna, Mary and Temperance's aggressive attacks (or their desire to aggressively attack) are more easily understood if we remember the extreme poverty of all three accused. Much of the narrative describes their daily begging from door to door and, in one telling examination, Mary confesses that she would have killed Grace Barnes if she had not 'split some of the Meat she was then carrying'.[74] The accused's extreme desperation and hatred of those who refuse to help them speaks to their uncontrolled emotional state as well as anxieties about charity and neighbourliness that circulated during the seventeenth century.[75] For these women, the Devil is a powerful way of explaining their own fearful desires. It is only with the Devil's encouragement and assistance that they are able to act on their emotional impulses.

These pamphlets simultaneously conjure an image of women who are completely terrified by their demonic master and offer a way of explaining how women made sense of their uncontrolled desires. In all of the above narratives, Lyndal Roper's words ring true: 'the Devil whom witches encountered was not an abstract force or a symbolic figure of evil … he was, first and foremost ... a character with whom one had a relationship'.[76] The confessions of Temperance, Susanna and Mary demonstrate the complex nature of belief surrounding witch and devil relationships. For these witches the Devil becomes a source of fear and danger after their initial agreements. He gives them the power to hurt their neighbours and tempts them to do so. In one case, he even forces Temperance to hurt a woman she claims that she did not want to injure.

The Devil does not just give power to Temperance, Susanna, and Mary; he also gives them a way to explain their malicious and murderous actions. It is clear that Susanna and Mary were furious with Grace Barnes for her refusal to give them alms. Rather than admit this, however, the two women are able to claim that they were tempted by the Devil. As well as demonstrating the links between a witch's internal desires and her pact with the Devil, the story of the Bideford witches also highlights the complex nature of the bond between witch and devil. When we compare these three witches to Joan Prentice and the Flower family we see an even broader range of emotional experience. These witchcraft narratives were characterized by a strong bond between witch and devil. The relationship between witch and devil was complicated: it could begin either as a purely pragmatic arrangement or as a way of fuelling one's anger or desire for love. Common to all of these narratives is the importance of emotion, the diabolical, and the way in which contemporaries understood English witches as men and women who had made a personal connection with the Devil. For early modern women accused of witchcraft, the Devil acted as a conduit for their internal desires, as a way to both act upon and then explain their overwhelming emotions.

NOTES

1. For a fuller discussion of the importance of diabolical ideas in English witchcraft pamphlets see Millar, *The Devil is in the Pamphlets* (forthcoming).
2. The two seventeenth-century pamphlets that fail to link witchcraft with the Devil are: Anon., *Magazine of Scandall* [1642] and Anon., *Strange and wonderful news from Yowel* [1681].
3. Pamphlets that mention the Devil but do not mention the presence of a familiar spirit are: Anon., *A Most Certain, Strange and True Discovery of a Witch* [1643]; Anon., *Signes and Wonders from Heaven* [1645]; Anon., *The Power of Witchcraft* [1662]; Anon.,

Strange and Wonderful News from Yowel [1681]; and Anon., *Great News from the West of England* [1689].

4. It is extremely difficult to calculate the percentage of trials in which familiars featured given the loss of records. See Ewen, *Witchcraft and Demonianism*; Macfarlane, *Witchcraft in Tudor and Stuart England*, 2nd edn, 25; and Sharpe, *Instruments of Darkness*, 107–19.

5. Macfarlane, *Witchcraft in Tudor and Stuart England*, 2nd edn, 86. See also the earlier work of C.L. Ewen for his emphasis on the importance of pamphlets to the study of witchcraft: Ewen, *Witchcraft and Demonianism*, 7. This is partly the case because of the limited number of depositions surviving from England and, also, the brief nature of many of these records. In contrast to countries that had an inquisitorial system, English depositions were often brief and not routinely recorded. See Gaskill, 'Witches and Witnesses in Old and New England', 55–6.

6. Gibson, *Reading Witchcraft*, 6; Sharpe, *Instruments of Darkness*, 105; Rosen, *Witchcraft in England*, 20; Dolan, *True Relations*, ch. 2; and Wilby, *Cunning Folk and Familiar Spirits*, 46.

7. Clark, ed., *Languages of Witchcraft*, 12.

8. See Clark, ed., *Languages of Witchcraft*, particularly the chapters by Peter Rushton, Marion Gibson and Malcolm Gaskill; and also Dolan, *True Relations*, 55. For a detailed study of representations of truth in English witchcraft pamphlets see Gibson, *Reading Witchcraft*.

9. Dolan, *True Relations*, 61.

10. We now know that judging people's ability to read by their ability to sign their name is inaccurate: this method ignores the fact that reading was taught before writing and that writing (but not reading) was often omitted from girls' education. We also now know that it was common for early modern people to read aloud and that most people experience reading primarily aurally rather than visually. For the original estimates see Cressy, *Literacy and the Social Order*, 176. For newer studies see Thomas, 'The Meaning of Literacy', 103; Spufford, *Small Books and Pleasant Histories*, 22; and Brayman Hackel, *Reading Material in Early Modern England*, 58.

11. Thomas, *Religion and the Decline of Magic*, 2nd edn, 537.

12. Macfarlane, *Witchcraft in Tudor and Stuart England*.

13. Ibid., 158.
14. See Barry, Hester and Roberts, eds, *Witchcraft in Early Modern Europe*, particularly the introduction.
15. Briggs, *Witches and Neighbours*; Gaskill, *Crime and Mentalities*.
16. Briggs, *Witches and Neighbours*, 3.
17. Gaskill, *Crime and Mentalities*, 65.
18. See, for example, Misoda ... [name is obscured], *The Divels Delusions* [1649], 3; or Anon., *The Witches of Northamptonshire* [1612], C3v.
19. Purkiss, 'Women's Stories of Witchcraft', 408–32; Willis, *Malevolent Nurture*; Roper, *Oedipus and the Devil*; and Millar, 'Sleeping with Devils', 207–32.
20. Purkiss, 'Women's Stories', 410.
21. Roper, *Oedipus and the Devil*, 20.
22. Ibid., 20.
23. A note on terminology: The familiar is a devil in animal form. However, man-like devils can also be referred to as familiar spirits. Pamphlet narratives generally did not distinguish between 'the Devil' and 'a devil' or a familiar spirit. Sometimes the familiar spirit is referred to as 'the Devil', 'the devil', 'a devil' or one of many 'devils'. Other names include 'imps', 'sprites' or 'spirits'. In the pamphlets studied, the Devil is described interchangeably as 'the Devil' and as a familiar spirit. Both of these names demonstrate the demonic nature of the creature. Although this may seem confusing, it is not possible to separate these terms and in pamphlets and trial records these terms are, in the words of Darren Oldridge, 'blurred': see Oldridge, *The Devil in Early Modern England*, 138.
24. Gibson, 'Accusers Stories in Print', 41–54.
25. For an example of how to read 'veiled female voices' that have been mediated by clerical and legal processes see Cressy, 'Agnes Bowker's Cat', 9–28.
26. Anon., *The apprehension and confession of three notorious witches* [1589].
27. Ibid., sig. B1r.
28. Ibid., sig. B1v.
29. Ibid.
30. Ibid., sig. B2r.
31. Serpell, 'Guardian Spirits or Demonic Pets', 157–90.

32. Thomas, *Man and the Natural World*, 39–40.
33. See Millar, 'Familiar Spirits' (forthcoming); Purkiss, 'Fairies', 346; Wilby, *Cunning Folk and Familiar Spirits*, 17–25; Sharpe, 'Familiars', 349; and Oldridge, *Devil in Early Modern England*, 138.
34. Anon., *The apprehension and confession of three notorious witches* [1589], sig. B2r.
35. Ibid.
36. Ibid., sig. B2v
37. Ibid., sigs B2v and B2r.
38. Ibid., sig. B2r.
39. Ibid.
40. Ibid.
41. For more on the Devil as trickster see Johnstone, *The Devil and Demonism*, 60–141, 170–5.
42. For familiars tricking their mistresses see, for example Phillips, *The Examination and Confession of certaine Wytches* [1566], sig. A7r, 2A4v; W.W., *A true and just recorde* [1582], sig. A4v.
43. Anon., *The apprehension and confession of three notorious witches* [1589], sig. A2v.
44. Gibson, *Reading Witchcraft*.
45. Anon., *The Wonderful Discoverie of the Witchcrafts* [1619]. For two recent books on this case see Borman, *Witches*; Honeybone, *Wicked Practise & Sorcerye*.
46. Anon., *The Wonderful Discoverie of the Witchcrafts* [1619], C3 r–v.
47. Ibid., C4v.
48. Ibid. D1r.
49. Ibid.
50. Ibid., D1v.
51. Ibid., D2r. As Gibson has explained, there is much confusion over the dates of these deaths. Henry died in 1613, years before this pamphlet was printed; but the pamphlet does not accurately depict this. There is also confusion about whether or not Francis was alive or dead at the time of the witches' arrest (Christmas 1618), as we know that Francis did not die until March 1620. The many contradictions and loss of legal records make it difficult to accurately date the events of this pamphlet. Gibson, *Early Modern Witches*, 276–8.
52. Anon., *The Wonderful Discoverie of the Witchcrafts* [1619], F3r.

53. Ibid.
54. Ibid. C3v.
55. Anon., *The Wonderful Discoverie of the Witchcrafts* [1619]; Anon., *Witchcrafts Strange and Wonderful* [1635].
56. Anon., *A true and impartial relation of the informations* [1682]; Anon., *The tryal, condemnation, and execution of three witches* [1682]; and Anon., *The life and conversation of Temperance Floyd* [1687]. The story of the Bideford witches was also retold in a ballad of 1682: 'Witchcraft Discovered and Punished'. Temperance Lloyd was also known as Temperance Floyd and Mary Trembles was also known as Mary Floyd. For an in-depth study of this case and a survey of recent literature see Barry, *Witchcraft and Demonology*, 58–102.
57. Jonathan Barry has analysed the reliability of these pamphlets; see Barry, *Witchcraft and Demonology*, 76–81.
58. Ibid., 96.
59. Ibid., 98.
60. Sharpe, *Instruments of Darkness*, 121.
61. Ibid., 226.
62. Anon., *The life and conversation of Temperance Floyd* [1687], 7; Anon., *A true and impartial relation* [1682], 18.
63. Anon., *A true and impartial relation* [1682], 36.
64. Ibid. For a study that discusses the sexual dynamics of these pamphlets (and of English witchcraft pamphlets more broadly) see Millar, 'Sleeping with Devils', 207–31.
65. Anon., *A true and impartial relation* [1682], 34.
66. Anon., *The life and conversation of Temperance Floyd* [1687], 7.
67. Anon., *A true and impartial relation* [1682], 35.
68. Ibid.
69. Ibid.
70. Ibid., 38.
71. Ibid., 35.
72. Ibid., 35.
73. Ibid.
74. Ibid., 35.
75. See Macfarlane, *Witchcraft in Tudor and Stuart England* for a fuller exploration of these anxieties.
76. Roper, *Oedipus and the Devil*, 234.

PART III

In the Mind

Bullying, the Neurobiology of Emotional Aggression, and the Experience of Witchcraft

Edward Bever

In 1562 an old woman from Cannstatt in the Duchy of Württemberg named Magdelena Horn confessed that she had 'recently so ill-treated ... a child that ... it died from it'.[1] In 1611, a young woman named Agatha Sacher from Dornstetten appeared uninvited at the wedding of a man who had jilted her, which caused the bride such distress that she became 'crazed', threatened suicide, and had to be taken to a doctor.[2] Ten years later in the village of Metzingen, Katharina Masten, who was more than seventy years old, berated and hit a servant girl who refused to let her take food from her master's larder in repayment of a loan so forcefully that the girl collapsed 'and could only crawl away'.[3] A few years after that a swineherd's wife in Sindelfingen named Catharina Ada barged in on an annual ritual during which the cow herders' wives divided up a gift of bread from the farmers whose cattle their husbands tended. Anna Rueff,

E. Bever
State University of New York College at Old Westbury

© The Author(s) 2016
L. Kounine, M. Ostling (eds.), *Emotions in the History of Witchcraft*, DOI 10.1057/978-1-137-52903-9_11

a cow herder's wife whom Catharina took a place next to, developed a headache, 'became lame on her right side' the next day, and 'her suffering increased day by day … so that the following Thursday evening she became crazed, would not eat, talk, or listen, but shouted and bellowed, until she died'.[4] To the end she 'insisted that the swineherd's wife had inflicted' her ailments.

In all of these cases there was evidence that the women had committed the acts attributed to them. The mother of the boy whom Magdelena said she hit reported that he had complained of her abuse before he died. A witness testified that Agatha Sacher had said she wanted to 'hurt Ziegler's fiancé' and had earlier claimed to be able to work magic. Similarly, Katharina Masten was reported to have said 'she gave the girl what she deserved', and there was no dispute that Catharina Ada had barged into the cow herders' wives' gathering and stood next to Anna Rueff, although no specific threat was attributed to her.

All of these cases formed part of a sample of small witch trials that I discussed in my book *The Realities of Witchcraft and Popular Magic*. In it, I argued that in a small but significant fraction of witchcraft trials, the accusations were based, in two ways, on real *maleficium*, or occult injury.[5] First, as indicated above, the evidence in these cases suggests that the accused did do things related to the injuries attributed to them. Second, in some cases the things they did could have caused the misfortunes ascribed to them. Some involved surreptitious physical violence, while in others the magical influences attributed to the suspects really could, through a combination of overt or subliminal communication of hostility and psychophysical influences on disease, have caused or contributed to the victim's malady.

Given that the source materials are four-hundred-year-old judicial records, the degree of certainty we can have about what people intended and did and what consequences their actions may have had varies widely and can never be absolute, but we can gauge the plausibility of the attributions and the probability that they were valid. Of the cases mentioned above, Magdelena Horn appears strongly to have deliberately caused injury to the boy surreptitiously through physical means. Agatha Sacher appears strongly to have wished her ex-boyfriend and his bride ill and may or may not have consciously employed magic against them; either way, aggressively intruding on their space and possibly showing her hostility in other ways almost certainly caused the bride's distress. Katharina Masten clearly meant harm but seems to have acted spontaneously; and if her assault affected the girl more strongly than a septuagenarian woman's blows could be expected to through physical force alone, whatever additional impact it had does not appear to have involved deliberate use of magic. Catharina Ada appears not to have set out to inflict harm, yet could well have through her aggressive behavior. Overall, I estimate in the book that about 15% of suspects consciously engaged in practices or unconsciously manifested behaviors associated with *maleficium*, and conclude that their behaviors could in some cases have posed a genuine threat to the health and well-being of their neighbors.[6]

The Realities has provoked considerable debate about our ability to discern what really happened in witchcraft cases.[7] However, while using documents from witch trials clearly presents special challenges, these are problems of degree rather than kind; in the end all we can hope for from any historical source in particular cases is to judge the plausibility and probability that what is reported is true. More general conclusions then reflect the cumulative weight of evidence about what could plausibly have happened and what is probably true.

In order to reinforce the plausibility of my conclusions, this chapter will begin by exploring research relevant to the issue of actual behaviors that I became aware of too late to use in the book: modern adult bullying, which has significant parallels to early modern witchcraft. It also provides evidence of the power of interpersonal emotional aggression on a victim's health, which the second part of the chapter will explore further by reviewing recent work in social neuroscience that makes it possible to trace in much more detail the connection between the emotions of one person and the physiological responses of another than was possible when I wrote *The Realities*.[8]

WITCHCRAFT AND BULLYING

Ever since the Enlightenment educated Westerners have been skeptical of allegations of witchcraft, rejecting not only the purported diabolic conspiracy, but also claims that harmful magic could have effects, or was even practiced to any significant extent. Research into modern adult bullying provides evidence, though, that interpersonal aggression can be a more common and more distressing feature of daily life than we may like to think. Its existence does not prove that malefic magic was practiced in early modern Europe, of course, but it can affect our estimation of its plausibility in general and its possibility in any particular case. Bullying is part 'of a wide range of behaviors loosely labeled "human aggression"'.[9] Intra-group aggression is so basic that there are 'obvious similarities between human and non-human' forms and 'when individuals fail to use culturally appropriate methods of anger management, cultures have specific labels to describe' them. It therefore seems worth taking a closer look at the phenomenon of modern adult bullying and contrasting it with the *maleficium* ascribed to early modern witches.

The word 'bullying' may bring to mind trivial school-yard harassment, but bullying in schools is actually 'a significant public health concern world-wide', while adult bullying such as workplace bullying, spousal abuse, and child abuse have severe consequences for their victims and society at large.[10] While rates of bullying vary, spousal and child abuse are common problems, and 'the incidence of workplace bullying is far greater than was ever thought'.[11] In Norway and Finland about 10% of workers reported having experienced it within the past six months, while in the UK 50% said they had. Overall rates of bullying in different contexts vary from 1–5% to 90%.[12]

Bullying takes many forms, from physical violence through verbal assaults, 'glaring, ignoring' and hostile gestures, to social undermining via gossip, betrayal, and ostracism.[13] Indeed, 'one of the most startling impressions … is the ingenuity that perpetrators have shown in finding ways of inflicting misery on their victims', and their 'enthusiasm … for doing so'.[14] Not surprisingly, bullies are 'high in anger'.[15] Some bullies are psychopaths, and '26 percent of [workplace] bullying is accounted for by one percent of the employee population', but that leaves almost 75% of cases attributable to a wider range of people who are not clinically disturbed but who 'just do not care' about 'the pain they cause'.[16] Bullies can actually be quite emotionally sensitive, but they use 'their understanding … to better hone their weapons'.[17] In some cases, bullying can actually be 'unintentional', for 'many of the behaviors of bullying are only a little removed from everyday living experience'.[18] In fact, 'the nature of bullying is often ambiguous. The bully may deliberately (and effectively) confuse the victim by appearing nice one moment and nasty the next.'[19] Bullies often display 'Machiavellian talents … bringing pain to their victims without discredit to themselves'.[20] Whether intentional or unintentional, overt or covert, though, bullying flourishes because it works, bringing not just psychological satisfaction to the bully but also power in the social world. Bullying is 'a tactic' to 'intimidate others … victims and competitors are rendered emotional and ineffective' and potential rivals deterred.[21]

There are clearly some parallels between modern adult bullying and the behaviors ascribed to early modern witches. Some of the interpersonal displays are similar, like verbal assaults, glaring, and hostile gestures. In both, the tactics employed tend to divide by gender: women usually bully using indirect social manipulations while men are more likely to use direct forms of physical and verbal violence; witchcraft was strongly identified with women, while early modern men were thought more prone to open physical violence.[22] Bullying, like witchcraft as anthropologically defined, can be unintentional as well as intentional, and can be perpetrated in ambiguous ways that mix positive and negative social signals. The emotions behind the two—anger, aggression, and a pleasure in, or at least lack of remorse for, causing suffering—are also similar. So too is the fact that while in theory witches were motivated by pure malice, in practice accusations often connected witchcraft to some concrete dispute; bullying, too, can be gratuitous but also serves practical ends.

There are some important differences as well. In modern society, bullying generally happens within workplaces, schools, and families, whereas witchcraft accusations were most often made by neighbors. Witchcraft involved women employing verbal violence, curses, and threats, more typically than modern female bullies. Bullying can involve a variety of behaviors not associated with witchcraft, like throwing tantrums and engineering ostracism. On the other hand, witchcraft, unlike bullying, was identified with the use of magic, and accusations frequently involved poison. More generally, witchcraft was thought to involve a mortal animus that bullying does not. On balance, while many aspects of witchcraft can be seen as forms of bullying, and witchcraft and bullying share similar motives and purposes, witchcraft was not just a form of bullying. Bullying can cause illness and even drive its victim to suicide, but normally it aims to merely humiliate and dominate the victim. In contrast, while witchcraft too was used to assert power over other people, its focus on the infliction of physical injury up to and including death set it apart.

Despite the differences between modern adult bullying and early modern *maleficium*, the unquestionable reality of the former makes allegations of the latter seem more plausible, particularly when combined with a recognition of the high levels of interpersonal conflict, bitter enmities, and violence that were endemic to many early modern communities.[23] Should we dismiss out of hand Magdelena Horn's un-coerced and corroborated confession that she surreptitiously hit a child just because it occurred in the context of a witch trial? What if there had been no concern about whether

Magdelena did this in the service of the Devil, and the trial had simply been for child abuse? Similarly, should we categorically reject the possibility that Agatha Sacher intended to cause distress when she went uninvited to the wedding of the young man who had jilted her? Is it implausible that Katharina Masten berated and hit the servant girl who refused to let her take food from her master's larder in repayment of a loan? Diabolic witchcraft may have been an imaginary crime, but *maleficium* involved a variety of forms of interpersonal aggression that were possible, plausible, or even probable. In some cases, given what we know about some peoples' readiness to inflict harm on others, they seem almost certain. While most witch accusations were certainly baseless, generated by neighborly scapegoating or judicial coercion, some were undoubtedly true, and the evidence in each case needs to be judged on its merits: its internal characteristics, its congruence with other evidence, and its general plausibility.

Research on modern adult bullying reinforces the plausibility of another aspect of early modern *maleficium*: the ability of interpersonal aggression to cause harm. Schoolyard bullying is 'a significant public health concern world-wide' because it causes physiological as well as psychological problems.[24] Bullying is responsible for one third to one half of stress-related absences from work.[25] The psychological consequences of workplace bullying include anxiety, depression, post-traumatic stress, and suicidal impulses.[26] Furthermore, victims of bullying are at significantly higher risk for physical ailments.[27] Symptoms include psychophysical problems like headache, high blood pressure, nausea, chest pains, neck aches, muscular pain, gastric upsets, and impotence, and stress-related 'biological alterations ... to cortisol levels' associated with 'lowered immunity to infectious disease' and other cortisol-related disorders.[28]

In the decade since I wrote *The Realities* significant advances have been made in social neuroscience that make it possible to understand in much greater detail how such influences might be projected and received. The balance of this chapter will therefore turn to recent research on, first, anger and fear, the two emotions most centrally implicated in the process, and, thereafter, on intersubjectivity, the visceral connections between people that mediate the communication of emotion and precipitation of psychophysical distress.

THE NEUROBIOLOGY OF ANGER AND FEAR

Our understanding of the emotions has gone through a series of changes in the past few decades. Since time immemorial they were considered to be fixed aspects of the human condition, natural reactions of human beings to events and relationships varying mainly by individual temperament, with some channeling influences by cultural conventions. In the late twentieth century, however, social-constructionist understandings that emphasized the variety of emotional regimes across cultures and the power of enculturation over the psyche came to dominate the social sciences and history.[29] Yet in the same period, cognitive scientists discovered evidence that at least six emotions—anger, fear, disgust, sadness, surprise, and happiness—are 'universal in their performance and in their perception'.[30] Meanwhile, neuroscientists were exploring the modularity of the mind, the fact that specific areas of the brain handle specific aspects of cognition, including complex and even conscious activities like recognizing faces, understanding physical processes, and feeling fear.[31] Neuroscientists have also been investigating the role of specific chemicals in experience and behavior, and this converging evidence that there are basic emotions hardwired into the human nervous system has challenged social-constructionism in turn.[32]

Social constructionists have pointed out that the ability to recognize the basic facial expressions varies from culture to culture, and even basic emotionalists have to recognize that there are many other emotions which differ significantly across cultures and over time.[33] Human emotions clearly have both biological and social dimensions, and involve an interplay between different parts of the brain that conduct low-level processing and higher-order cognition. Among neuroscientists the social-constructionist v. basic emotionalist debate has evolved into a disagreement over whether the 'basic emotions' are standard packages or if they are combinations of more elemental cognitive processes like approach and avoidance or pleasant–unpleasant that are more subject to cultural influences than basic emotionalism suggests.[34]

Both of the most prominent emotional elements of the witchcraft interaction, anger and fear, are among the 'basic' emotions. Fear is the simpler, for it is one of two basic emotions for which a specific neural substrate has been identified (the other is disgust).[35] While recent research has cast doubt on characterizations of the amygdala as the 'fear center' of the brain, it is connected by relatively direct, fast links to the perceptual system; triggers the 'fight or flight' response; directs attention of higher brain centers to the source of the fear-inducing stimulus; and has a 'well-established' role in learning and storing 'the conditioned fear response' to stimuli, including social stimuli.[36] Fear is related to another, but evolutionarily newer and 'cortically controlled', emotion, anxiety, which is characterized by intermittent arousal stimulated by cogitations about potential dangers, and is associated with activity in the left prefrontal cortex.[37] Fear and anxiety are closely associated with extreme and chronic stress, which can cause a wide variety of health problems that will be discussed below.

Interestingly, anxiety is complemented in the right prefrontal cortex by another evolutionarily more recent emotion, anger, which has a relationship to aggression similar in ways to anxiety's relationship to fear, although aggression is not an emotion but a behavior.[38] Nevertheless, most forms of aggression involve a subjectively perceived impulse to eliminate the stimulus that triggers them. These forms, which are collectively characterized as reactive aggression, are quite distinct from the other form, predatory, which is planned, purposeful, and proactive.[39] In contrast, reactive aggression lacks planning, shifts readily from one target to another, and shows little 'cortical involvement'.[40]

The cortex's main relationship with reactive aggression is actually inhibitory. About half of a propensity toward violence is attributed to the regulatory influence of cortical processes, in particular those anticipating reprisal (the other half is genetic).[41] Children's beliefs about the acceptability of aggression are fluid up to six to eight years old, and they learn to moderate their aggression according to their individual experiences and their culture's scripts.[42] Societies therefore range widely in the levels of aggression that characterize them.

Anticipated reprisal can also modify aggression's expression, driving it from overt to covert forms.[43] More generally, aggression's onset and expression are strongly shaped by culture through both punishment and scripts conveying when and how to manifest it.[44] However, regulation of aggression does not depend just on complex but short-term calculations of immediate interest plus cultural norms that have to be transmitted from generation to generation and are only imperfectly adopted during individual development. Instead, the human brain has a built-in propensity to modulate aggression thorough the emotion anger.

There is clearly a 'unique relationship between anger and aggression', but the two do not always occur together.[45] There is therefore some dispute whether anger causes aggression or just accompanies it.[46] In any case, though, there's no question that 'anger entails a disposition to aggressive action', and this disposition is what gives it its moderating role.[47]

Anger is a complex emotion involving multiple, and somewhat variable, parts of the brain, but it is 'part of the basic biology of the human species, spontaneously appearing in infancy, effectively universal, and manifesting a "species-typical neural basis"'.[48] Anger activates a set of specific physiological processes which are 'preparation for verbal and physical aggression'.[49] Many of these can be observed by others, and may therefore induce them to cease whatever activity has triggered the anger rather than engage in a physical fight.

Anger is thus a social emotion in which aggression is threatened as a warning, a way of acting out interpersonal conflicts that is less damaging than physical combat.[50] It is most frequently directed toward other people, and its triggers are often conceptualized as retribution for violations of social bonds. In general, it is induced by the appraisal that someone voluntarily acted in a way that is either intentionally harmful or whose negative outcome was predictable.[51] However, blameworthiness is not always necessary to trigger anger, and the extent to which anger focuses on acquaintances or strangers varies considerably across cultures.[52] More generally, what constitutes a negative event; whether it can be presumed to be under another person's control; and whether that person is causing it maliciously or with culpable negligence are typically defined by social structures and symbolic meanings. In the end, however, the important thing is that another person's negative behavior be deterred.

Threat displays are just one of a variety of emotional presentations that communicate peoples' beliefs and intentions and thereby play a 'critical' role in 'the formation and maintenance of social relationships'.[53] Emotional displays involve a range of bodily systems including facial expression, prosody, and body movements.[54] Bodily movements manifesting anger include commanding or combative postures, fist-clenching, arm-waving, intrusion into personal space and similar preparations for or simulations of aggressive acts. Prosody includes the sonic qualities of speech, which convey the 'underlying emotion' of the speaker and can reinforce or contradict the words' semantic meaning.[55] Similarly, anger produces a characteristic facial expression that communicates rapidly and effectively.[56] Facial expression, like other anger displays, is influenced by culture, in particular often inhibited, but the characteristic features of an angry face are innate, made and recognized across cultures.[57]

On the receiving side, people are 'biologically prepared' to process angry faces 'as threatening stimuli'. Facial expression recognition is handled by a separate neural system from identity recognition to speed up 'activation of the arousal system'.[58] Facial expression recognition is not done holistically, but 'by analyzing component information (eyes, nose, mouth, etc.)'.[59] The eyes are a particularly 'salient feature' emotionally, and have been termed 'the diagnostic region for recognizing anger expressions'.[60] This is particularly interesting in relation to evil-eye beliefs, given their connection to witchcraft beliefs. Gaze detection is a primal ability, used by predators and prey alike; primates engage in 'gaze following' in order to detect 'intentions and goals', and they 'are clearly sensitive to ... eye contact'.[61] This threat signal is processed along with others by the amygdala, which exhibits a particular sensitivity to social emotional stimuli.[62] While higher cortical centers are involved in the processing of anger recognition, including activation of the areas that 'suppress current behavior' (the objective of the anger display), there is evidence that the amygdala 'plays a key role' in the process of comprehending anger by translating perceptions into visceral experience.[63] In other words, 'facial expressions ... can induce congruent emotional responses' as people unconsciously 'mimic [the] subliminal facial expression' of a person they are observing.[64]

Intersubjectivity and Psychosocial Factors in Disease

The idea that people understand anger displays at least in part by unconsciously mimicking them and thereby triggering their own aggressive impulses and experiencing their own anger is an application of a recent key discovery of social neuroscience, mirror neurons. Mirror neurons were discovered when researchers noticed that when one monkey observes another act, some of the motor neurons involved in that act in their own brains fire.[65] Imaging studies have established a similar effect in humans, and mirroring has been found to involve not just visual impressions of motor actions, but other experiences like hearing an action, being touched, feeling pain, and feeling disgust, so that now mirror neurons 'are thought to encompass a broad set of complex behaviors and cognitive capacities'.[66] Called 'shared-substrate' processes because the same neural circuitry that controls actions and generates emotions is used to understand them, the importance of mirror neurons 'as a mechanism for understanding others' by conducting 'embodied simulations' has 'been established' as an 'intuitive and powerful form of communication', which 'transmits the experience of doing and feeling from one brain to another'.[67] Mirror neurons appear to be the basis for the 'low-level mechanism … for copying' that is present at birth, and play a vital role in peoples' ability to understand the actions and feelings of others.[68]

Mirror neurons have even been found to play a role in linguistic communication.[69] However, some critics argue that too many issues in social cognition have been ascribed to them, even questioning their role in monkeys' cognition and their very existence in humans.[70] Nevertheless, while some of the more extreme claims for mirror neurons will likely be discredited, their existence and a significant role for 'shared substrate' processes will almost certainly be upheld. A more consequential criticism therefore concerns their limits. In particular, recent research into empathy indicates that 'empathizing' is not 'purely an index of mirroring', but instead involves both mirroring and perspective-taking.[71] The chief alternative or, more likely, complement to the mirror neuron system is Theory of Mind, our ability not only to understand that other sentient beings have minds that think to further their own goals, but also to integrate context and history with visceral input from the mirror neuron system to infer their inner thoughts and feelings.[72]

Interestingly from the point of view of animism and magic, 'the shared circuit for actions responds to complex, meaningful actions regardless of whether they are performed by humans', animals, or robots, an 'overgeneralization' that can be explained by game theory: 'in a dangerous world it is safer to treat something as smart that is not than vice versa'.[73] Also, mirror neurons may have helped convey the optimism of cunning folk to their patients during magical healing rituals, thus contributing to their ability to offer efficacious help with medical problems in a way that was not dependent on (although undoubtedly reinforced by) the patient's beliefs.[74]

What role mirror neurons might have played in malefic witchcraft is less clear. If the amygdala does mediate understanding of anger by mirroring it, then mirroring plays a key role in the process by which one person's anger can cause another's malady. However, it is not necessary for this specific mechanism to work for the effects of anger to be felt viscerally. Threats 'need to be registered and handled swiftly', but 'consciousness is limited and slow', so, whatever the precise mechanism, the brain 'can process incoming stimuli before they reach conscious awareness', creating non-conscious influences on cognition and behavior.[75] The nervous system is quite sensitive 'to emotion-specific cues', so even 'without strong emotional feelings', such cues 'have the capacity to activate both cognitive responses' and autonomic reactions.[76]

Emotionally significant stimuli come from both the natural and the social environments, but when considering the internal processing triggered by them the distinction loses importance, for at this level the social is part of the natural. 'Humans are ... social animals adapted to living in groups, descended from a long line of species that were also adapted to groups'; the 'phylogenetic development of the human brain is integrally tied to the social environment, such that the brain is inextricably social'.[77] Recent work in social neuroscience has revealed 'the social nature of the self, its inherent intersubjectivity', on a neurological level.[78] The mind is social and embodied not metaphorically or incidentally, but fundamentally.[79] Its capacity to understand and many of its forms of understanding are direct manifestations of the complex, evolutionarily kludgy way the nervous system works. Human understanding involves not just symbolic references to reality, but direct expressions of reality. Furthermore, it is informed not only by the immediate sensations of mirror neurons and other shared neural substructures, but also by genetically programmed neurocognitive modules that react to and process stimuli in evolutionarily shaped, pre-programmed ways. This means that while 'social relations are so fundamental for humans that nonsocial stimuli or events are often anthropomorphized, or infused with social meaning',[80] the reverse is also true: social meaning and relations are infused with the direct influence of physical and biological structures and processes. And those physical and biological processes can have somatic effects regardless of their current social meaning, by channels that immediately connect low-level systems in one nervous system with those of another.

In the case of witchcraft, the innate sociability of the nervous system makes people vulnerable to other peoples' hostility. We have focused on anger displays here because witchcraft suspicions are commonly connected to interpersonal conflicts among people who have routine face-to-face contact, but displays of other hostile emotions like envy or disdain can also have a physiological impact when they threaten harm. The medical understanding of psychological influences on health has evolved from the psychodynamic rechanneling of repressed feelings posited by Freudian psychology to a much broader range of psychophysical interactions largely connected to the impact of the stress response.[81] The stress response mobilizes the body to fight or flee, but this can cause problems if it is particularly intense or protracted.[82] Relatively superficial complaints like muscle-, stomach-, and headaches can result from exaggerated bodily manifestations of these processes, but these can cause considerable discomfort and even become debilitating. In addition, stress can have deeper and more severe somatic effects as well: 'suppression of cellular immune function … chronic increases in blood pressure … abnormal heart rhythms … increased susceptibility to infectious disorders … [and] the development of hypertension, cardiovascular disease, and … diabetes'.[83] The wide range of maladies that can be caused or contributed to by these effects seems significant in light of the common perception that witches could cause a wide, relatively open range of disorders.[84]

Stress becomes chronic when the stressor recurs frequently, particularly if it is unpredictable or uncontrollable, and 'social stress is one of the most taxing threats that humans experience'.[85] Social stress can take many forms, and among the most powerful are aggressive treatment and displays of anger. 'The negative effects of poor interpersonal relations are widespread and include a host of mental and physical health problems.'[86] The 'relation of aggressive treatment and stress' has been 'well demonstrated', and 'alterations in biological and neurological functioning' have been shown to result … from 'the stress of victimization'.[87]

CONCLUSION

Just as the reality of modern adult bullying enhances the plausibility of allegations of witch-like behaviors, an understanding of the intersubjective connections between peoples' nervous systems enhances the plausibility of attributions of harm. Given the inherent difficulty of diagnosing psychosocial influences on health and the limitations of historical records, it is impossible to say whether a specific attribution was valid with certainty, but an appreciation of the intersubjective connections between human nervous systems should inform our understanding of early modern witchcraft in two ways. First, in any particular case, while an attribution may have been made maliciously or mistakenly, it was not necessarily invalid; as with allegations of interpersonal aggression, each case must be evaluated on its own merits rather than categorically dismissed. Second, in general, historians should proceed from the assumption that such influences are not only possible, but, beyond playing a role in some individual cases, they could also make important contributions to the larger belief system.

To begin with, it seems probable that the idea of witchcraft, that people could project their hostility to cause others harm, reflected the fact that people can project their hostility to cause others harm. Belief in this possibility may intensify its effects, but it is not necessary for them to occur, so it seems reasonable to give the physiological process priority over the cultural construct in this case. Moreover, linked to other physiological processes by which bodily actions, facial expressions, rumination, and deliberate channeling of thoughts can induce emotions and cause them to be displayed, it helps understand sorcery as anthropologically defined— the use of rituals to achieve harmful magical effects—as a way of artificially generating the emotional displays responsible for witchcraft.[88] On the beneficent side of magic, the effects of mirror neurons and shared substrates in communicating optimism would seem likely to have contributed to the efficacy of magical healing, and research into the physiology of social support suggests that it, and particularly the effects of the hormone oxytocin that is connected to social bonding and counteracts the effects of cortisol, a primary stress hormone, plays an important role in healing as well.[89] More broadly, our growing understanding of the neurophysiology of intersubjectivity should heighten our appreciation of how much magic involves the manipulation of the nervous system in both its practitioners and its targets.

Peter Stearns has written that 'the analytical goals' of the history of the emotions 'center on change, either in emotions themselves or in the environments in which they operate', but that 'examining change involves establishing baselines, so that new trends can be carefully evaluated against real, rather than assumed or imagined, past standards'.[90] Understanding the neuropsychological bases of witchcraft, sorcery, and beneficent magic is critical to establishing the real baseline for these phenomena, and provides the foundation for a realistic appreciation of both the changes and the continuities in the transition to modernity.

NOTES

1. Hauptstaatsarchiv Stuttgart, A209/719(1565), fol. 3-5-1565; see also Edward Bever, *Realities of Witchcraft*, 9–10, 38, 40, 73–5, 76, 411.
2. Bever, *Realities of Witchcraft*, 12, 14, 23, 28, 49, 56, 222.
3. Ibid., 10, 14, 22, 61, 307.
4. Ibid., 13, 17–18.

5. Ibid., xiv–xvi, 3–39, 433.
6. Ibid., 56–7.
7. For the debate, see the contributions to 'Forum: Contending Realities', 81–121.
8. Harmon-Jones and Winkielman, 'Brief Overview of Social Neuroscience', 3–4; Iacoboni, 'Quiet Revolution', 439; Bert Uchino et al., 'Social Neuroscience of Relationships', 475.
9. Randall, *Bullying in Adulthood*, 32–3, 8, 14; Tanaka-Matsumi, 'Cross-Cultural Perspectives on Anger', 81.
10. Rossi, 'Effects of Bullying Victimization', 129; Coyne and Monk, 'Overview of Bullying and Abuse', 231.
11. Rossi, 'Effects of Bullying Victimization', 130; Coyne and Monk, 'Overview of Bullying and Abuse', 238; Randall, *Bullying in Adulthood*, 17.
12. Coyne and Monk, 'Overview of Bullying and Abuse', 238.
13. Randall, *Bullying in Adulthood*, 12.
14. Ibid., 7.
15. Coyne and Monk, 'Overview of Bullying and Abuse', 247.
16. Boddy, *Corporate Psychopaths*, 44; Randall, *Bullying in Adulthood*, 7.
17. Ibid.
18. Coyne and Monk, 'Overview of Bullying and Abuse', 235; Randal, *Bullying in Adulthood*, 16.
19. Rigby, *New Perspectives on Bullying*, 123.
20. Randall, *Bullying in Adulthood*, 7.
21. Boddy, *Corporate Psychopaths*, 45–6; Randall, *Bullying in Adulthood*, 34; Rigby, *New Perspectives on Bullying*, 124.
22. Robbins, *Anger, Aggression, and Violence*, 32–3, 35; Coyne and Monk, 'Overview of Bullying and Abuse', 239; Chakrabarti and Baron-Cohen, 'Empathizing', 408–9.
23. Bever, *Realities of Witchcraft*, 43–5.
24. Rossi, 'Effects of Bullying Victimization', 129, 141.
25. Randall, *Bullying in Adulthood*, 20.
26. Rigby, *New Perspectives on Bullying*, 120, 116; Randall, *Bullying in Adulthood*, 13, 19; Rossi, 'Effects of Bullying Victimization', 129, 141; Boddy, *Corporate Psychopaths*, 45.
27. Rossi, 'Effects of Bullying Victimization', 141.

28. Randall, *Bullying in Adulthood*, 19–20, 147; Knack and Vaillancourt, 'Evidence of Altered Cortisol Levels', 205; Rigby, *New Perspectives on Bullying*, 124.
29. Kassinove and Sukhodolsky, 'Anger Disorders', 22–3; Stearns, 'History of Emotions', 18–19, 21–2, 26–7, 28; Hayward, 'Enduring Emotions', 830.
30. Hennenlotter and Schroeder, 'Partially Dissociable Neural Substrates', 443; Ward, *Student's Guide to Cognitive Neuroscience*, 377–8.
31. Bever, 'Current Trends' 5–6; Schwaninger et al., 'Processing of Facial Identity and Expression', 321; Ward, *Student's Guide to Cognitive Neuroscience*, 396, 405.
32. Van Honk and Schutter, 'Vigilant and Avoidant Responses', 216–17; Taylor and Gonzaga, 'Affiliative Response to Stress', 469.
33. Social constructionists: Tanaka-Matsumi, 'Cross-Cultural Perspectives on Anger', 85–6; basic emotionalists: Ward, *Student's Guide to Cognitive Neuroscience*, 380.
34. Harmon-Jones, 'Asymmetrical Frontal Cortical Activity', 137, 151; Ward, *Student's Guide to Cognitive Neuroscience*, 177–80.
35. Hennenlotter and Schroeder, 'Partially Dissociable Neural Substrates', 443; Heberlein and Adolphs, 'Neurobiology of Emotion Recognition', 32.
36. Ward, *Student's Guide to Cognitive Neuroscience*, 382–6; Adolphs and Spezio, 'Role of the Amygdala', 374.
37. Van Honk and Schutter, 'Vigilant and Avoidant Responses', 197–8.
38. Robbins, *Anger, Aggression, and Violence*, 19.
39. Siegel and Victoroff, 'Understanding Human Aggression', 210–14.
40. Ibid., 213; Randall, *Bullying in Adulthood*, 38; Carré, Murphy, and Hariri, 'What Lies Beneath the Face of Aggression?' 224.
41. Robbins, *Anger, Aggression, and Violence*, 30–1; Siegel and Victoroff, 'Understanding Human Aggression', 214; Siever, 'Neurobiology of Aggression and Violence', 429–30; Alia-Klein et al., 'Neural Mechanisms of Anger Regulation', 385; Reiman and Zimbardo, 'Dark Side of Social Encounters', 176; Randall, *Bullying in Adulthood*, 37, 41.
42. Siegel and Victoroff, 'Understanding Human Aggression', 214; Robbins, *Anger, Aggression, and Violence*, 65.

43. Randall, *Bullying in Adulthood*, 41; Siegel and Victoroff, 'Understanding Human Aggression', 109; Siever, 'Neurobiology of Aggression and Violence', 430.

44. Kassinove and Sukhodolsky, 'Anger Disorders', 7, 11, 18–20; Tanaka-Matsumi, 'Cross-Cultural Perspectives on Anger', 81; Park et al., 'Social Status and Anger Expression', 1122.

45. Holbrook et al., 'If Looks Could Kill', 455; Berkowitz, 'A Different View of Anger', 322; Robbins, *Anger, Aggression, and Violence*, 19.

46. Cause: Siever, 'Neurobiology of Aggression and Violence', 437; Randall, *Bullying in Adulthood*, 38; Holbrook et al., 'If Looks Could Kill', 455. Accompany: Kassinove and Sukhodolsky, 'Anger Disorders', 12.

47. Van Honk and Schutter, 'Vigilant and Avoidant Responses', 201.

48. Caveats: Reiman and Zimbardo, 'Dark Side of Social Encounters', 174; Kassinove and Sukhodolsky, 'Anger Disorders', 3; Hennenlotter and Schroeder, 'Partially Dissociable Neural Substrates', 446. Basic biology: Sell et al., 'Formidability and the Logic of Human Anger', 15073; Kassinove and Sukhodolsky, 'Anger Disorders', 17; Robbins, *Anger, Aggression, and Violence*, 12.

49. Reiman and Zimbardo, 'Dark Side of Social Encounters', 175; Kassinove and Sukhodolsky, 'Anger Disorders', 11.

50. Sell et al., 'Formidability and the Logic of Human Anger', 15073; van Honk and Schutter, 'Vigilant and Avoidant Responses', 201; Holbrook et al., 'If Looks Could Kill', 455; Sincaceur et al. 'Hot or Cold', 1019.

51. Tanaka-Matsumi, 'Cross-Cultural Perspectives on Anger', 87, 84; Kassinove and Sukhodolsky, 'Anger Disorders', 24; Randall, *Bullying in Adulthood*, 35; Royzman et al., 'CAD or MAD?' 892–4; Berkowitz, 'A Different View of Anger', 322.

52. Berkowitz, 'A Different View of Anger', 323; Robbins, *Anger, Aggression, and Violence*, 9.

53. Van Dijk et al., 'A Social Functional Approach to Emotions in Bargaining', 600; van Honk and Schutter, 'Vigilant and Avoidant Responses', 216; Norris, 'I Know How You Feel', 85.

54. Heberlein and Adolphs, 'Neurobiology of Emotion Recognition', 38.

55. Grandjean, Bänziger, and Scherer, 'Intonation as an Interface between Language and Affect', 235, 237–8; Wildgruber et al., 'Cerebral Processing of Linguistic and Emotional Prosody', 249; Kotz et al., 'Lateralization of Emotional Prosody', 285–6.

56. Yang and Tong, 'Effects of Subliminal Anger', 916; Schwaninger et al., 'Processing of Facial Identity and Expression', 321; Hennenlotter and Schroeder, 'Partially Dissociable Neural Substrates', 443.

57. Culture: Norris, 'I Know How You Feel', 98; Tanaka-Matsumi, 'Cross-Cultural Perspectives on Anger', 87. Biology: Robbins, *Anger, Aggression, and Violence*, 6; van Honk and Schutter, 'Vigilant and Avoidant Responses', 200.

58. Van Honk and Schutter, 'Vigilant and Avoidant Responses', 200; Schwaninger et al., 'Processing of Facial Identity and Expression', 321; Hennenlotter and Schroeder, 'Partially Dissociable Neural Substrates', 447; Gallese, 'Before and Below "Theory of Mind"', 659; Kassinove and Sukhodolsky, 'Anger Disorders', 16.

59. Schwaninger et al., 'Processing of Facial Identity and Expression', 321.

60. Adolphs, 'Neurobiology of Emotion Recognition', 374; Hennenlotter and Schroeder, 'Partially Dissociable Neural Substrates', 447.

61. Stone, 'Evolutionary Perspective on Domain Specificity', 323, 341, 325.

62. Norris, 'I Know How You Feel', 91.

63. Hennenlotter and Schroeder, 'Partially Dissociable Neural Substrates', 447–8; Chakrabarti and Baron-Cohen, 'Empathizing', 412–13; Carré, Murphy, and Hariri, 'What Lies Beneath the Face of Aggression?' 224.

64. Yang and Tong, 'Effects of Subliminal Anger', 916; Carré, Murphy, and Hariri, 'What Lies Beneath the Face of Aggression?' 224.

65. Cowdell, 'Hard Evidence for Gerardian Mimetic Theory?' 221.

66. Keysers and Gazzola, 'Toward a Unifying Neural Theory', 383, 379, 384, 386; Firat and Hitlin, 'Neuroscience and the Difficult Art', 781.

67. Heberlein and Adolphs, 'Neurobiology of Emotion Recognition', 31; Keysers and Gazzola, 'Toward a Unifying Neural Theory', 379, 391, 394; Eshuis, Coventry, and Vulchanova, 'Predictive Eye

Movements', 438; Gallese, 'Before and Below "Theory of Mind"', 662; Iacoboni, 'Quiet Revolution', 446.

68. Neiworth, 'Thinking about Me' 144; Keysers and Gazzola, 'Toward a Unifying Neural Theory', 379; Decety, 'A Social Cognitive Neuroscience Model', 263; Gallese, 'Before and Below "Theory of Mind"', 661, 666.

69. Jackson and Crosson, 'Emotional Connotation of Words', 213–14; Keysers and Gazzola, 'Toward a Unifying Neural Theory', 396.

70. Hickok, *Myth of Mirror Neurons*.

71. Keysers and Gazzola, 'Toward a Unifying Neural Theory', 395; Chakrabarti and Baron-Cohen, 'Empathizing', 412; Norris, 'I Know How You Feel', 96; Leiberg and Andes, 'Multiple Facets of Empathy', 434–5.

72. Bever, 'Current Trends', 8–9; Norris, 'I Know How You Feel', 95–8; Keysers and Gazzola, 'Toward a Unifying Neural Theory', 396.

73. Keysers and Gazzola, 'Toward a Unifying Neural Theory', 394–5; Bever, 'Magic and Religion', 697.

74. Bever, *Realities of Witchcraft*, 293–4.

75. Wiens, 'Subliminal Emotion Perception', 105; Jensen et al., 'Nonconscious Activation of Placebo', 15959; Yang and Tong, 'Effects of Subliminal Anger', 920.

76. Yang and Tong, 'Effects of Subliminal Anger', 915, 920.

77. Stone, 'Evolutionary Perspective on Domain Specificity', 316; Firat and Hitlin, 'Neuroscience and the Difficult Art', 781

78. Decety, 'A Social Cognitive Neuroscience Model', 346.

79. Harmon-Jones and Winkielman, 'Brief Overview of Social Neuroscience', 9.

80. Norris, 'I Know How You Feel', 87–8.

81. Bever, 'Witchcraft Fears', 576–81; Robbins, *Anger, Aggression, and Violence*, 86.

82. Decety, 'A Social Cognitive Neuroscience Model', 455; Kudielka, Hellhammer, and Kirschbaum, 'Ten Years of Research', 56–7; Knack and Vaillancourt, 'Evidence of Altered Cortisol Levels', 205; Carter, 'Neuropeptides', 431; Hayward, 'Enduring Emotions', 833.

83. Decety, 'A Social Cognitive Neuroscience Model', 456; also Uchino et al., 'Social Neuroscience of Relationships', 478.

84. Bever, 'Disease', 283.

85. Bartolomucci, 'Chronic Psychosocial Stress', 57; Rigby, *New Perspectives on Bullying*, 123; Kudielka, Hellhammer, and Kirschbaum, 'Ten Years of Research', 57; Knack and Vaillancourt, 'Evidence of Altered Cortisol Levels', 206; Decety, 'A Social Cognitive Neuroscience Model', 467; van Honk and Schutter, 'Vigilant and Avoidant Responses', 208, 216; also Uchino et al., 'Social Neuroscience of Relationships', 474.
86. Knack and Vaillancourt, 'Evidence of Altered Cortisol Levels', 205.
87. Randall, *Bullying in Adulthood*, 148; van Honk and Schutter, 'Vigilant and Avoidant Responses', 197; Knack and Vaillancourt, 'Evidence of Altered Cortisol Levels', 205.
88. Berkowitz, 'A Different View of Anger', 325; Kassinove and Sukhodolsky, 'Anger Disorders', 15; Ray, 'All in the Mind's Eye?' 133; Ochsner, 'How Thinking Controls Feeling', 107.
89. Decety, 'A Social Cognitive Neuroscience Model', 456–7, 463, 467–9; Carter, 'Neuropeptides', 427, 429.
90. Stearns, 'History of Emotions', 18.

CHAPTER 12

Witchcraft and the Dangers of Intimacy: Africa and Europe

Peter Geschiere

For anthropologists who have personally encountered 'witchcraft' in the field, the topic is saturated with emotion. Is this different when one mainly works with written sources, as is the case for many historians?

Many anthropologists give the impression that in the field they risked being overwhelmed by the emotions triggered by 'witchcraft' (or whatever term they use for occult aggression). This applies not only to anthropologists working in Africa or Melanesia, always considered to be hotspots for such topics. One of the most emotional ethnographies of witchcraft is Jeanne Favret-Saada's now classic monograph on the Bocage in French Normandy, a study which movingly and perceptively reports on the author's struggle to remain in control while getting more and more involved in the dark intrigues of aggression and counter-aggression between farms.[1] Similarly, during my own research among the Maka in the forest area of Cameroon, witchcraft became one of the most emotional topics I had to deal with. In this society there seemed to be no problem

P. Geschiere
University of Amsterdam

© The Author(s) 2016
L. Kounine, M. Ostling (eds.), *Emotions in the History of Witchcraft*, DOI 10.1057/978-1-137-52903-9_12

at all to 'look into people's hearts and minds'—the challenge mentioned in Chapter 1 of this volume. Since both accusers and the accused would literally shout out in public the most horrible suspicions and confessions, adding gruesome details about supposed nocturnal activities and confrontations, even the most stoic researcher might be carried away by this dramatic show of emotions. Of course, one cannot generalize. Such topics were and are dealt with in more subdued ways in neighbouring societies in Cameroon and elsewhere in Africa. But despite such differences it is clear that most anthropologists are forced—at least in the field—to face the deep passions the witchcraft imaginary can mobilize.

This may be different for historians. Some time ago Diane Purkiss (herself an interloper into history from literary studies) reproached historians of early modern European witchcraft for indulging in 'rituals of distanciation':

> Rather than trying to understand how witch-beliefs were structured for and by the believers, historians have often bent their energies towards explaining witch-beliefs away. Assuming witch beliefs were an abnormality and a pathology, they sought to explain how such ideas could have arisen, rather than what those ideas were … The only serious question to be asked about witchcraft, it seems, is still 'why, oh why?'[2]

Since then, things seemed to have changed. Laura Kounine notes a shift in focus 'away from persecution to the "witch" herself'—a shift that brings historians closer to the upsurge of emotions from the cases they are analysing.[3] Still, it is a valid question how one can do justice to the emotional force unleashed by these images and practices, despite the distance imposed by working with documents. On the other hand, the overabundance of emotions with which anthropologists have to struggle in the field raises its own problems. A general anthropological problem—how to be sure one is not projecting one's own feelings onto the dramatic scenes under study—presents itself most strongly with witchcraft because of both the force and the elusiveness of these emotions. I will come back to this.

One relation that is especially conducive to explore the different ways in which researchers deal with emotion is the link between witchcraft and intimacy, a topic on which I recently published a comparative study.[4] Indeed, it is striking that historians who do write a great deal about emotions are often those who work on witchcraft in the intimate spheres of life.[5] For an anthropologist working in Africa this is hardly surprising; in

Africa, witchcraft seems to be in many contexts the dark side of kinship: witches are thought to have a special hold over their relatives and the worst attacks are invariably supposed to come from inside 'the house'. In my recent book I tried to show that this link can be generalized: in other parts of the world as well witchcraft seems to be about the terrible realization that precisely the inner sphere, where solidarity and trust should reign, is a hotbed of jealousy and aggression. Witchcraft is so frightening because it strikes from close by.

In this chapter I want to focus on this link between witchcraft and intimacy, not only because it is especially on this sensitive point that the researcher is confronted with an upsurge of emotions, but also because it allows for interesting comparisons between anthropological studies on Africa and work, by historians but also by others, on Europe. As noted, this link may be general, but there seem to be different regional implications. In the following I propose to focus on these differences—notably between Africa and Europe—because they seem to offer a good entry point to explore how researchers can deal with emotions. Important in this respect is that in the cases below there seems to be a crucial turning point. In each case, the intimate sphere reveals itself to be full of dangers, but this does not necessarily lead to suspicions of witchcraft. It is only at a particular moment that suspicions seem to condense and people start to refer to witchcraft, with dramatic consequences. The question is when this turning point is reached—under what circumstances and what pressures? It seems that such a turning point is a particularly apt moment to try and grasp the emotions involved. The question is how differences in the sources available to researchers affect their interpretations of such crucial moments.

Too Many Witches in One Compound

A first case study from my own research in the 1970s in a Maka village in the Cameroonian forest area can serve to introduce these themes of intimacy, emotions, and the turning point when people turn to assertions about and accusations of witchcraft:

> The compound of old Tsjume (pseudonym) was struck by a rapid series of misfortunes. First one of the kitchens collapsed. Then Tsjume became ill: he had long suffered from rheumatism, but the symptoms suddenly became much worse. Then his third wife—his favourite who was still young—died

abruptly. People whispered it was witchcraft, and sought the witch as usual within the compound itself. Rumours mostly pointed at Nanga, the first wife of Tsjume, who had always been jealous of his other wives and who, moreover, had quarrelled with her husband because he was very severe with their only son, Kangbud. It was said that she was so angry that she had given her co-wife over to the witches of her band so that they could eat her.

However, after a few days, Nanga became sick too. She quickly became emaciated and no longer got up from her bed. This was generally inter-preted as a new sign of her guilt. According to some, she was tortured by her conscience. Others said that she had fallen ill for fear of being attacked herself by her acolytes, because that is how things work in the nocturnal world of the *djambe* (witchcraft). Two days later, Nanga's son transported her to her native village. She died a few hours after arriving there. After this, the roles were reversed. The brothers of Nanga openly accused Tsjume of giving his wives over to the witches, and refused to cede their sister's corpse for funeral rites. They wanted her to be buried in her own village, and not in her husband's compound since he had treated her so badly. Nanga's burial in her native village ended with a violent brawl between her brothers and Tsjume's family.

But even after the burial, Tsjume's problems did not end. A few weeks later, his second wife, who had already been ill for some time, also died. Furthermore, Tsjume's own state of health continued to be of concern. Finally, Tsjume began accusing Meguya, another woman who lived in his compound. Until then Meguya had remained untouched by the rumours because she had an outstanding reputation. She was very active in the church (Presbyterian) and had come to live with Tsjume after refusing to stay with her husband (of the same family as Tsjume) who drank too much and squandered the money Meguya earned with the sale of food-crops. Moreover, Meguya displayed exemplary behaviour during the whole affair. She cared for all of Tsjume's wives and even tried as much as possible to maintain their farms. Nonetheless, Tsjume appeared one day in front of the catechist's house and declared loudly, so that everyone could hear him: 'This woman Meguya, is crazy with fear. She already gave my three wives to the witches. Now she is desperately seeking other victims for fear of being eaten herself by her nightly companions.' The sole reaction I heard from Meguya, a stoic woman, was a brief but effective comment: 'People who know so well what the witches do are the first to leave their bodies in the night.' She thus accused Tsjume of dabbling himself in witchcraft, but in a manner suf-ficiently implicit so that he could hardly respond.

After several days, Tsjume's health recovered little by little. Kangbud, his son still refused to move or speak to anyone. He sat on a chair in front of the house, his eyes wide as if in a trance. From time to time he murmured that he would go to Bertoua (the capital of the province) to consult a great *nganga* (healer). This *nganga* would help him to avenge his mother. But one week later, he participated in a large work party and I noticed that he was happily drinking and bantering with his friends. After several weeks, people hardly spoke about all that had happened. And my neighbour concluded, 'Apparently the witches have settled the whole affair among themselves.'

Some background is no doubt required here.[6] The setting of this case is a relatively small Maka village of about 600 people. Like most of the villages in the forest area it consists of several *grandes familles*—patrilineages— who claim a common descent but who, after colonial conquest (1905/10) were forcefully brought together by the colonial authorities (first the Germans, after 1915 the French) to live along the new road in one larger village in order to facilitate the levying of taxes and forced labour. Prior to this the Maka (nowadays still a small group of about 100,000 people) lived in small autonomous family-hamlets, dispersed in the forest and without any form of central authority. The imposition of colonial rule came as a shock: when I started my research in the 1970s old men still remembered seeing the Germans enter the village and recollected their families' amazement that a complete stranger could have the presumption of ordering people around. Moreover, colonial rule was quite violent in the forest area because of the desperate efforts of the new authorities to levy labour and surplus products for the *mise en valeur* of the area.

Cameroon became independent in 1960, but this part of the country remained quite inaccessible and backward in many respects. Still, the villagers themselves often proudly insist that *le développement* is all around. Nearly all people have been to school for at least a few years. Already in the 1970s people regularly commuted to the urban centres in the east and to the country's big cities, Yaounde and Douala. Moreover, everyday life in the villages had been deeply affected by Christian missions—in the village in this case especially by the Presbyterian church, founded by American missionaries already in the 1920s, but now increasingly surpassed by the Catholics, who arrived later (in the 1930s).

What does this case illustrate about the intersection between witchcraft and intimacy, and about the torrent of emotions triggered by it: fear, anger, indignation, and the feeling of being trapped? The link between intimacy and aggression is given already with the imaginary around the *djambe* to which all persons in this case refer. Nowadays people will invariably translate this term as *sorcellerie* (witchcraft). However, this translation poses serious problems; as elsewhere in Africa, it distorts a local notion that has a much more general scope. Yet, we have to take such a translation seriously: it is the term that people use nowadays and as such it produces new meanings. Ideas about occult aggression ('witchcraft') are especially prone to constant innovations, borrowings, and hybridization. So, the search for an 'authentic' core is particularly misleading in this field: the very idea of authenticity denies the ongoing dynamics of these notions.[7] Elsewhere I have extensively described the Maka imaginary around *djambe*, so a short sketch must suffice here.[8]

> People describe the *djambe* as a nasty creature living in someone's belly which gives its owner (*djindjamb*—a person who took the trouble to develop his or her *djambe*) special powers. The main power is the capacity to transform oneself into an animal or a spirit. Especially at night when the owl calls, the *djindjamb* will leave his or her body and fly off into the night—'along the cobwebs of the *djambe*'—to the *sjumbu*, the nightly meeting of witches. There terrible cannibalistic banquets are staged.[9] Each *djindjamb* has to offer a relative to be devoured by the other witches. Basic to Maka discourse on the *djambe* is that it is about the betrayal of one's kin to outsiders. All my informants agreed: the witchcraft of the house (*djambe le ndjaw*) is the worst. In many respects *djambe* is positioned between the intimate world of the house, on the one hand, and on the other the outer world and its fascinating opportunities for self-enhancement. Witches are supposed to have a special hold over their relatives, but they use this in order to hand over their victims to outsiders.
>
> However, this is only the dark core of the *djambe* notion. Apparently it can be used in many other ways as well. A particularly noteworthy example is that *nganga* (healers) are also supposed to have an overdeveloped *djambe*—this is why they can 'see' the witches, 'fall upon them', and force them to deliver their victims. To my surprise, I myself turned out to have a *djambe* that permitted me to drive my modest Citroen 2CV without causing an accident. *Djambe* can be channelled for constructive purposes: to heal, to accumulate wealth and power. However, there is always the danger that the basic instinct—that of betraying and cannibalizing one's relatives—will break through. For this reason the *nganga* remains a dangerous and potentially suspect person. *Nganga* will always insist that their 'professor' has bound them with heavy interdictions to use their *djambe* powers only to heal and not to kill; but people are not altogether sure about this—as said, there is always the risk that the basic instinct of the *djambe* will manifest itself.

Another surprise for me was how deeply the *djambe* notion turned out to be affected by modern technologies. Rumours about the nightly escapades of the *mindjindjamb* (witches) refer to their use of planes and airstrips, and the *miedou* (medicines) that were most sought after were those bought from mail-order firms in Europe. Moreover, *djambe* was not at all limited to the village. On the contrary, it was constantly referred to in more modern settings—in the city, in education, healthcare, and sport, and most of all in national politics and new forms of entrepreneurship. *Djambe* in fact offered a seductive discourse to address the riddles of modern development: the rapid emergence of outrageous new inequalities, the enigmatic enrichment of a happy few, and the ongoing poverty of the many. This capacity of the discourse to graft itself onto new developments might be the secret of its surprising resilience despite deep changes, in Africa as elsewhere.

Yet all this innovation notwithstanding, the *djambe* remains closely linked to the familiar realities of village and family. This capacity of a local discourse to graft itself onto modern changes is certainly not special to the Maka area. On the contrary, everywhere in Africa local notions that people now generally translate with terms like *witchcraft* or *sorcellerie* seem to provide tempting discourses to interpret modern developments that are baffling to many. It is this ambiguity that I tried to catch in the perhaps too adventurous title of my 1997 book, *The Modernity of Witchcraft*.

In Tsjume's story there were certainly such modern elements (the key role of the church, rumours about nocturnal planes) but the key theme was no doubt that witchcraft is working from the inside. Tsjume's torrent of accusations, swerving from one target to the next, never went outside his compound. Clearly he was pushed by a nagging fear of being attacked from inside. It is precisely because of this feeling of betrayal and a danger lurking close by that such witchcraft crises are so full of emotions.

But what about emotions in this particular case? I was especially moved by the sight of Kangbud, Tsume's son, sitting in silent sadness in front of the house, not talking to anyone and not reacting to anything. I had grown quite fond of this young man, his quiet but dignified bearing and the earnest look in his big eyes. But now his eyes seemed to radiate an unbearable sadness. I interpreted this as a deep mourning about his mother and the shameful way she had been treated by his father. This seemed to me a normal reaction. But later on, after having read more about the many cases in present-day Africa where fathers are accused—or at least suspected—to have 'sold' their sons in order to protect their own relative wealth,[10] I had to face that I might have been projecting what I would

have felt myself onto Kangbud's sorrow. It could very well be that he took
Meguya's implicit accusation of Tsjume being a witch most seriously, and
that it was not sorrow but rather fear—fear of being his father's next victim– that put him in such a state of depression. But how can one find out
about this? I did not dare break through Kangbud's silence with questions
about what he felt. And even if I would have been tactless enough to do
so, what would have been the value of his answers?

One solution that helped me in my research was to try and leave the
level of discourse—of questions and answers—and to look for occasions
where emotions were acted out or acted upon. Here the notion of a turning point—a threshold when suddenly witchcraft becomes an obvious reference—can be useful. In Tsjume's case the compound had been always
full of tensions, especially when he returned from his farms, drunk from
palm-wine. But it had never been rocked by a spasm of witchcraft accusations as in the story above. It is clear that, as usual, a rapid succession of
mishaps formed a fertile soil for witchcraft rumours. But the real turning
point was Nanga's burial in her own village and not in Tsjume's compound. Funerals are dramatic events all over Africa, but this one had been
particularly tense. Among the Maka, a married woman should be buried in
the village of her husband, especially when she has sons in that village, as
Nanga had. Funerals in Maka land are always full of mock fights—it is the
moment for the acting out of what anthropologists call 'joking relationships'—but Nanga's funeral turned into a real fight over the body. In the
end Tsjume had to accept defeat and leave Nanga's body with her brothers. During the funeral (two days and a night), I was overwhelmed by the
torrent of emotions—anger, furious accusations, and calls for revenge, all
mixed with grief about Nanga's death

JEALOUSY, RECIPROCITY, AND WITCHCRAFT: A PRECARIOUS BALANCE

In another case—one that I could follow over forty years—the explosion
of witchcraft rumours and accusations came even more unexpectedly. The
leitmotif of this case—recurrent in cases elsewhere in Africa and beyond—
is the problem how to strike a balance between jealousy and just redistribution. Jealousy within the family is an emotion that is an obvious cause
for witchcraft. Everybody will agree also that the way to deal with it is fair
redistribution. But what is fair when inequalities become ever larger?

A sad example of such struggles—showing how difficult it is to keep out of witchcraft's vicious circles—is offered by a Maka family I have known since 1971. I came to know the family after it was cited to me as one of the last examples of a *ndjaw boud* (extended family, lit. 'people of one house') that had retained its cohesion. In 1971, the family lived in a sprawling compound with a constantly growing array of houses and kitchens inhabited by seventeen adults and a much larger number of children. I knew other families of a similar size, but over time they all split up for various reasons. This family seemed to keep its cohesion—at least until quite recently.

My main contact in the family was Franklin (pseudonym), who was exceptionally conscious of the need to share. Indeed, to me he seemed a living incarnation of what anthropologists like to call *reciprocity*. Traveling with him was a time-consuming affair, since in each and every village he seemed to have a relative or a friend at whose home we should stop, offer a small present, and chat a little. For Franklin, it was unthinkable to pass through a region without paying his respects to even very distant or indirect relations, lest people might think he wished them harm.

However, over time the solidarity within this family bulwark came under stress, and Franklin began to speak of threatening witchcraft attacks. In the beginning he was very vague about where such attacks were coming from, but over time it became clear that he thought the danger was coming from inside. More recently a switch took place, when Franklin and his wife became themselves the target of witchcraft rumours.[11] The main focus for such rumours was the success of two of Franklin's sons at the university. Expatriate friends had paid for their schooling. The rumours started when the two boys had almost finished university, so that they might gain access to lucrative positions. Their father and his brothers had also done quite well for their generation, holding lower-salaried jobs; however, the boys' success at the university would introduce a new kind of inequality within the family.

The witchcraft rumours took shape only gradually. It all started when Franklin's wife planted 'medicine' around their house, trying to block out bad influences. Then Franklin invited a *nganga* (a healer who was passing through the area) to purify the place. In 2005 his wife insisted that they build a new house at a little distance from the family compound, and another *nganga* was invited to come and 'seal' this place. Apparently they still saw themselves as potential victims of others' jealousy. But subsequently Franklin was accused of using witchcraft himself to block the progress of children from other branches of the family.[12] Franklin's two boys were said to be enjoying such success because they were fortified by Franklin's powers. Of course everybody knew that the money for the boys' schooling had come from Franklin's expatriate friends. Moreover, he himself—ever insisting on the need to share—had gone to great lengths to let others profit from this boon: for example, his sons lived with their cousins in the city so that the latter could study as well. Yet his continued drive toward reciprocity seemed of little avail against the jealousy raised by the young men's success.

As is typical in such cases, the accusations were not directed against the sons—everybody continued to praise them as the hope for the whole family—but against Franklin, who was by now an ageing man. The main accusations came from his brother who had worked as a bookkeeper for the government and had returned to the village after he was pensioned. He brought along his own son: a handsome boy, quite well dressed, who was clearly out of place in the village, yet seemed to be trapped there. The contrast with Franklin's sons, who came for short visits and then returned to the city, was glaring.

Some three years ago the rumours became very insistent and Franklin got really worried and also angry that apparently his unfailing insistence on sharing was no longer effective against the threat of jealousy. Once he complained bitterly that 'people become too jealous these days'. Although subsequently the rumours died down and Franklin seemed to become more relaxed, it is quite clear that the suspicion is still there and can flare up any moment again.

In this case, the relation to intimacy is as clear as in that of Tsjume. There is also an event—be it less dramatic than the funeral of Tsjume's wife—that triggered assertions of witchcraft: the confrontation between Franklin's successful sons and their nephew who had to face a definitive return to the village. Again, this offered a concrete setting for the expression of suspicions—themselves acted out in concrete measures, like 'sealing' one's compound—and equally frantic denials. It is at such turning points that emotions are expressed in most tangible ways.

EUROPE: NEIGHBOURS, NOT KIN?

The intersection between intimacy and witchcraft, a hotspot for emotions, is also strategic for exploring regional differences in their framing. As already suggested, this intersection is certainly not exclusive to Africa, but returns all over the world. Focusing on this intersection can help, for instance, to explore different trends in Africa and Europe, trends that are of direct interest for bringing emotions into our studies.

For Europe as well, many researchers—both in historical studies of early modern times and in anthropological studies of more recent developments—link witchcraft and proximity. But they mostly emphasize a basic contrast: in Europe witches are neighbours, not kin. I hope to show that the two cannot be so easily opposed and that deeper differences might play a role here; this might also have considerable consequences for the emotions involved.

Recently several historians of Europe have undertaken to study witch-craft in a global perspective. In their global comparisons, Europe emerges as a special case where witches are neighbours. For instance, in Ronald Hutton's very ambitious 'global definition' of witchcraft, this is a basic contrast with Africa, India, and America where witches are often kin.[13] A powerful case for this is made also by Robin Briggs in his overview of European witchcraft studies under the programmatic title *Witches and Neighbours*. Briggs includes a whole chapter titled 'Love and Hatred: Spouses and Kin', but it presents an image strikingly different from the notion of the house as a hotbed of accusations in the African examples above. Briggs does recognize that 'if ties of blood bind people together, it is often with a special intensity of mutual hatred' and he does cite cases in which internal accusations and fears tear a family apart. Yet the chap-ter is mainly about whether a woman who is denounced as a witch by a neighbour would be defended by her own folk. And Briggs concludes that 'family members normally rallied to defend one another in a crisis'.[14] Clearly for him as well, accusations and rumours come mainly from out-side the home; they may even stimulate people from one home to make a common front.[15]

A similar contrast emerges from Jeanne-Favret-Saada's fascinating study, already quoted, of the vicious circles of accusations, *sorcellerie* and *contre-sorcellerie*, in the French countryside in the 1970s.[16] The author, an anthropologist herself, is also categorical: occult aggression comes from neighbouring farms, not from inside the house. Her ethnography offers, indeed, a mesmerizing image of peasants' fear that their farm is being drained of its life force by evil practices by a neighbour and of desper-ate efforts to seal their own farm against these bad influences. The *sor-cier* is the neighbour outside the house and not the relative inside. But precisely because Favret-Saada's ethnography is so rich and detailed it is worthwhile to follow in more detail the distinctions she makes; in fact, her ethnography seems to allow for another reading which blurs the contrast between the European witch as a neighbour and the African one as kin.

In the book's case studies people look for the witch close by. In France as elsewhere, bewitching is supposed to require regular physical contact. But the *désorceleur* (the healer) always discourages people from looking among their close kin and rather diverts attention to one of the neighbours. Initially victims do suspect, for instance, their own brothers—and in view of unequal sharing of inheritances there is ample reason for this—but the *désorceleur* always redirects their attention. Favret-Saada is clear: the people identified as witches are neighbours, maybe even one's best friend, but never kin.

Indeed, the complex therapy the *désorceleurs* are prescribing expresses a fervent effort to close the house against outsiders. The whole farm has to be fenced, and all entry points have to be protected with bags holding special powders. Moreover, strict avoidance is required in everyday life: one has to shun all contact with the *sorcier*, never visit his house, refuse to shake hands, never look into his eyes; if he speaks to you, just repeat the last word; if he enters your compound despite all this, quickly throw blessed salt at his ass (*il faut lui saler le cul*). The *désorceleur*'s main ritual only crowns this long-term operation of closure: after all these therapeutic preparations, the healer will stage the big act, often a real struggle ('ugh, this one is really powerful') for breaking the spell. This ritual can take different forms, but if things go well, it will bring the witch running to the place in great agony: cooking an oxen heart and piercing it with pins will make him feel as if he were being stabbed all over; roasting salt in a baking pan so that it jumps and cracks will make him dance and jerk.[17] This is a sure sign that the *désorceleur* has succeeded in gaining the upper hand—that he managed to return evil for evil. From now on the bewitched will eagerly look for any sign of decay in the neighbouring farm, for all their own complaints—fatigue and illness, loss of livestock, cows that give no milk, fields that do not produce—should now haunt the neighbours.

For Favret-Saada, the therapy against a witch attack is a drastic closure of the house against outsiders, not a reconciling of the people within the house as in the preceding cases on Africa.

Yet, in her last book Favret-Saada complicates this radical dichotomy, placing her insights in a longer historical perspective by comparing contemporary practices with a very detailed folklore study from the late nineteenth century, *Esquisses du Bocage normand* by Jules Lecoeur.[18] Lecoeur's descriptions of popular ideas on occult attacks differ in crucial respects from the patterns Favret-Saada was confronted with in the 1970s. She relates this difference to the further crystallization of the small family farm as the dominant socio-economic form in the area in the twentieth century. In many respects the imaginary of *la sorcellerie* as she studied it in the 1970s corresponded to a closure of the house as the unit of production, management, and consumption. This socio-economic closure seems to be reflected in the farmers' speculations about occult aggression.

Some examples from Lecoeur's descriptions suggest that in his days tensions among kin may have been more important in witchcraft accusations.[19] In general, Favret-Saada's reckoning of who is kin and who is not seems to be influenced by the narrow definitions of the house that were apparently used by her informants. In some cases the perceived witch is a cousin or an affine,[20] but she does not see this as an exception; apparently since they lived outside the victim's house, they did not count as kin. The general trend toward closing the house may relate to Favret-Saada's emphasis on neighbourly witchcraft; it may also influence people's imaginary on *la sorcellerie* in specific ways. In Europe as well, then, the conceptual knot of proximity and occult aggression is too complicated to be undone by the simple opposition of neighbours versus kin. Rather, more complex differences between what is and is not seen as 'the house' may play a role.

In this respect there are striking differences with the African examples above. Favret-Saada's insistence on the closure of the house seems to correspond also to the historical examples from sixteenth- and seventeenth-century Europe. In these contexts as well, struggles over witchcraft tended to oppose houses against each other, thus imposing a closure of each house. This is very different from the image of the house as in the Maka conception of the *djambe le ndjaw* (the witchcraft of the house) that was central in the preceding cases. There, as in many other African examples, the origin of witchcraft was, indeed, primarily looked for within the house. But it is crucial to note that the limits of the house are highly relative in those African contexts. The Maka term *ndjaw boud*—literary 'the men of one house', now mostly translated as 'family'—can have narrower or wider dimensions depending on the context: it can refer to the people living in one compound, but it can also include related groups living close by in separate compounds, or even migrants, who are still seen as members of 'the house' no matter how far away they live. From the literature on Europe—both Favret-Saada's ethnography and the historical studies—a conception of the house emerges that is more fixed and determined by the spatial limits of the house or compound. The differences between what is counted as intimacy cannot be grasped by a radical conceptual contrast as the one between neighbour versus kin, but rather refer to varying ways of delimiting what is seen as 'the house'.[21]

CONCLUSIONS

To return to the central theme of this volume, To what extent can a focus on intimacy and the idea of a turning point in the crystallization of witchcraft suggest an approach for trying to grasp emotions and their often chaotic role in the denouement of witchcraft affairs? One suggestion emerges quite clearly from the above: it is vital to try and grasp situations in their totality. This may sound like self-evident advice, but it is worthwhile to insist on it in view of the general tendency to try and reduce witchcraft imaginaries to something else (to what would be 'really' behind all these mesmerizing fantasies). Such a reductive attitude is not very helpful if one wants to understand, for instance, the depth of Kangbud's despair as Tsjume's compound was shaken by an avalanche of witches. The first step might rather be to try and take people's experiences as seriously as possible and not ignore them as rationalizations of some sort of 'real' issue. Focusing on a specific element in what often is a most chaotic cascade of events might serve academic clarity but it does not help to understand how a given situation makes certain interpretations seem inevitable. Or, to put it more bluntly, I now have much more difficulty in understanding the weight of the *djambe* imaginary on people's minds than when I lived in a ramshackle hut, time and again overtaken by torrents of alarming events. One way or another, the full weight of the context has to be taken into account if we want to understand people's obsessions and anxieties. I hope to have shown also that following the different ways in which such emotions are framed can inspire fruitful comparisons, helping us to surpass the current but simplistic contrast between the witch as neighbour (Europe) or relative (Africa). Such a comparison can help to highlight instead structural differences in the conceptions of 'the house' as more open (Africa) and more closed (Europe)—differences that are of direct significance to present-day issues.

Promising concepts for a more totalizing view come from new beginnings in the anthropology of the senses. In my last book I was especially inspired by Birgit Meyer's work on religion, and notably on her focus on 'aesthetic persuasion'.[22] She uses 'aesthetic' in the Aristotelian sense of a *condensation* of the senses. Her fieldwork in Ghana on Pentecostal churches in the 1990s—when these churches quite suddenly started to expand in an unprecedented way: huge gatherings, sophisticated use of new techniques of communication—clearly impressed her by the power of such a condensation. In trying to reach believers, Pentecostal pastors do not rely on the message only, rather they strive to give their services an ecstatic quality in which sound, touch, movement, smell—deafening music, enchanted singing, speaking in tongues, dancing with abandon, and so on—create a total experience. This is a very simplistic rendering of a very complex argument. But the strength of Meyer's approach is that precisely by focusing on such key moments as these services she analyses why certain images grasp the audiences—or when they fail to do so. Focusing on the condensation of experience—rather than trying to dissect its elements—helps to understand the intensity of feelings.

Of course, such an approach is very suitable for anthropological fieldwork that allows researchers to immerse themselves in the excitement of the moment (if they dare to do so). However, an example like Thomas Robisheaux's recent study, quoted before, of one of the last witchcraft trials in southwestern Germany (1672), shows that such a totalizing view can also emerge from an archive-based (micro-)historical study.[23] Grasping the cogency of the drama in its unfolding—with all its ambiguities and uncertainties—he shows how historians can recover from their sources the emotional turmoil from which accusations of witchcraft arise.

NOTES

1. Favret-Saada, *Les mots, la mort, les sorts*; English translation: *Deadly Words*.
2. Purkiss, *Witch in History*, 61.
3. Kounine, 'Gendering of Witchcraft', 296. Pioneering studies in this respect include Sabean, *Power in the Blood*; Roper, *Oedipus and the Devil*; among more recent work see Di Simplicio, 'Witchcraft and Infanticide', 411–42; and Ostling, *Between the Devil and the Host*.
4. Geschiere, *Witchcraft, Intimacy, and Trust*.
5. See note 3.
6. For more detail see Geschiere, *Village Communities and the State*.
7. Meyer, *Translating the Devil*.
8. Geschiere, *Modernity of Witchcraft*.
9. It is striking how much this imaginary resembles European stereotypes: leaving one's body at night, transforming oneself and flying away to a nightly meeting with fellow witches. In the beginning I was worried by such resemblances (borrowings? influence of missionaries?) but later I learned that this complex of transformation,

going out, flying through the night to secret meetings is present in the most different corners of the globe. See Geschiere, *Witchcraft, Intimacy and Trust.*

10. See Niehaus, *Witchcraft and a Life in the New South Africa.*

11. Such spectacular reversals are stock in trade in witchcraft cases. The Maka have a saying that people who talk too much about witchcraft are like the owl who calls the witches: they are the first to go out at night themselves. Hence accusing someone of witchcraft can be very dangerous—like a boomerang the accusation can fly back to the one who uttered it.

12. Specifically, Franklin was suspected of *kong*, a new form of witchcraft that turns its victims into zombie slave-labourers and helps to explain (and to criticize) sudden and widening disparities of wealth. See Geschiere, *Modernity of Witchcraft.*

13. Hutton, 'Anthropological and Historical Approaches to Witchcraft', 422. Compare also Behringer, *Witches and Witch-Hunts.*

14. Briggs, *Witches and Neighbours,* 226, 252.

15. Compare also David Sabean's subtle analysis of the long-term transformations of a peasant community in Württemberg in its interaction with changing forms of *Herrschaft* (domination) from 1580 to 1800. He also opposes neighbourhood to kinship, but he immediately complicates this distinction by adding another one, between affines and blood relatives: Sabean, *Power in the Blood.* See also Thomas Robisheaux's more recent case study on present-day Baden-Württemberg, where accusations shift from neighbours to kin: Robisheaux, *The Last Witch of Langenburg.*

16. Favret-Saada, *Les mots, la mort et les sors.*

17. Favret-Saada, *Désorceler,* 34, 46; see also Favret-Saada, *Les mots, la mort et les sors,* 250–97.

18. Favret-Saada, *Désorceler,* 55–76.

19. For instance, there is an intriguing contrast with how Lecoeur described the culminating ritual in the *désorceleur*'s therapy in the nineteenth century. He mentions also the cooking and piercing of an oxen heart, but in those days only the *désorceleur* and the bewitched person would lock themselves up in the house—the rest of the family had to wait outside (as possible suspects?). See Favret-Saada, *Désorceler,* 63.

20. Favret-Saada, *Les mots, la mort et les sors,* 322.
21. This often amazing elasticity of African conceptions of kinship and the house is becoming an urgent topic with the greater mobility of African migrants, now even transcontinentally. One can hardly understand the dilemmas of these migrants if one does not take into account that even though they 'crossed the water', they are still seen as part of 'the house' and, therefore, still in reach of the *djambe le ndjaw* (witchcraft of the house). Elsewhere I have tried to relate this phenomenal—and ongoing—elasticity of kinship in Africa to a quite special historical relation between people and resources (not land but labour being the main bottleneck in increasing the production) that in African studies is often summarized as 'wealth-in-people' (in contrast to the 'wealth-in things' characteristic of many parts of Europe and Asia). Of course such contrasts have to be nuanced and relativized, but they point to special traits that have considerable effects. See Geschiere, *Witchcraft, Intimacy and Trust,* 208.
22. Geschiere, *Witchcraft, Intimacy and Trust*; Meyer, 'Aesthetics of Persuasion', 741–63.
23. Robisheaux, *The Last Witch of Langenburg.*

CHAPTER 13

Psychotic Reactions? Witchcraft, the Devil and Mental Illness

Sarah Ferber

Writing the history of emotions is part of an apparent trend over recent decades in which the study of individuals, social groups and institutions has been supplanted by the history of discourses and selected aspects of human identity and dealings, such as sexuality, the body and, more recently, the senses. Peter Stearns and Carol Stearns, in a pioneering 1985 article on 'emotionology' in *American Historical Studies*, sought to systematise the study of the history of emotions, writing that 'Such a study will, we hope, illuminate how and why social agencies and institutions either promote or prohibit some kinds of emotions, while remaining neutral or indifferent to others.'[1] Early work in the history of emotions did not constitute a revolution, however, possibly because of the often low and always contested standing of psychohistory, or because many attempts at writing the history of emotions seemed to be something of a disappointment. But now, the history of emotions is setting the agenda for much research in medieval and early modern studies. In relation to witchcraft in particular, the pro-

S. Ferber
University of Wollongong

© The Author(s) 2016
L. Kounine, M. Ostling (eds.), *Emotions in the History of
Witchcraft*, DOI 10.1057/978-1-137-52903-9_13

231

posal of Stearns and Stearns remains of great value, in that it sought to de-individuate emotions, projecting them onto a wider social canvas, where emotion and its categorisation are necessarily related to the workings of power and authority. For Stearns and Stearns, agencies and institutions give specific forms to the historical expression of human emotion, as forces which the pathways of emotions (as they gradually deepen or become overgrown) themselves in turn reshape and recreate.

Since the middle ages, in Western Europe and its colonies, views from within institutions—notably but not exclusively law, theology and medicine—have investigated the authenticity, moral foundations and pathologies of human emotion in relation to witchcraft and demonology. These perspectives have served inter alia to entrench a persistent notion that belief in magic, witches and demons has a natural affinity with mental illness or emotional instability, in a manner distinct from the beliefs of the religious mainstream. The present chapter will challenge this notion. It begins with a consideration of a basic organising structure for knowledge about witches and demons, the Dewey Decimal System of library cataloguing, and its categorical assumption that witchcraft belongs close to 'mental derangement' and at some distance from 'religion'. Examples of research from the late twentieth century show in turn that such an assumption remained powerful even in some recent historiography. Next, the chapter will turn to the present day, to consider psychiatric and legal interpretations of the actions of people who have killed in the belief that they were performing an exorcism. Through these examples the chapter will derive support for the claim of Stearns and Stearns that studying agencies and institutions in the history of emotions is worthwhile, and specifically will address historical assumptions that belief in magic, demons and witchcraft can exclusively be identified with ignorance, mental illness and extreme emotion.

To consider past and present phenomena in light of the study of categories might seem somewhat passé, bearing the hallmarks of the recently critiqued 'linguistic turn'.[2] But I will argue that such a reading facilitates the process of historicising emotions by drawing attention to the ways in which different institutions, by making normative or categorical statements, sanction certain behaviours while marginalising others. If the interpretation of emotions within institutional and disciplinary contexts affects such important 'real-world' classificatory choices as sane or insane, guilty or not guilty, there remains ample room for the linguistic approach to have historiographic value. And indeed, if emotions are ignored in such a context, this, too, can be significant. The argument here is that both historically and in the present day the choices of agencies and institutions, as they interpret beliefs about magic, witches and demons, bear with them a politics of emotion that warrants our attention.

THE DEWEY DECIMAL SYSTEM

American librarian Melvil Dewey designed his cataloguing system in 1876 on the widely accepted presumption that all categories of knowledge can be isolated and set logically alongside others. Many major libraries still use the system which is revised periodically to reflect disciplinary changes. In the original Dewey system, under the major section entitled 'Philosophy' (100–199), the 130s subheading of 'Anthropology' leads to sub-subheadings of 'Mental physiology and hygiene' (131) and 'Mental derangements' (132) and then 'Delusions, witchcraft, magic' (133). Thus beliefs in magic and witchcraft (and implicitly in demons) are directly aligned with delusion, but are also proximate to mental illness. The positions of 131–133 under 'anthropology' also evoked something of a link with primitivism, while beyond 133 lay what might be called the secularist replacements of 'Delusions, witchcraft and magic': 'Mesmerism' (134), 'Sleep, dreams, somnambulism' (135), 'Temperaments' (meaning the humours, 137), physiognomy (138) and phrenology (139). 'Sexes' (136) fits well here in these early years of the scientific study of another irrational field, before Freud.[3] The Dewey system, then, provides a neat historical register of an assumption that witchcraft in some way lies naturally adjacent to the world of extremes and 'mental derangement', and that witchcraft and belief in it are both irrational and marginal. But why should witchcraft be included automatically in the history of the unconscious and irrationality? And what might such an assumption exclude from our sightline? The first question can be addressed here by reference to the second, for principally what is eclipsed is religion, which in the history of Christianity has sought institutionally to delimit its practices from both magic and witchcraft.[4] Religion is nowhere in the vicinity of witchcraft in the Dewey system. The 130s section is a full 130-plus places apart from 270 Ecclesiastical History, which contains:

271 Religious orders
272 Persecutions
273 Doctrine

In the current updated Dewey system, 132, formerly 'Mental derangements', is listed as 'unassigned'.[5] 'Witchcraft, delusions and magic' as a category disappeared altogether and 133 is now the more anodyne 'Specific topics in parapsychology & occultism'. In practice, however, most history of European witchcraft remains classified under 133.4. Thus it remains under the 100 heading, now of 'Philosophy and Psychology', while religion, including the history of religion, is still under 200. Psychology, meanwhile, has become Freudianised, with new categories such as (127) 'The Unconscious and the subconscious'.[6]

FRENCH HISTORIANS OF POPULAR CULTURE

Dewey reflected and helped to perpetuate the attitudes of his times, but a similar view of belief in magic, witches and demons in European history remained evident in otherwise innovative twentieth-century research into the history of popular *mentalités*. Already in 1983 Stuart Clark critiqued this view as it had emerged among leading French historians of *mentalités*, such as Jean Delumeau, Robert Mandrou and Robert Muchembled. (Interestingly Stearns and Stearns praised the same writers as early exponents of the history of emotions. These historians, they observed, 'tried to explain rituals, beliefs, and institutions in terms of the emotional climate of medieval and early modern Europe'.[7]) In an enduring article, Clark challenged the view of these historians that acute negative emotion and even mental frailty were the reasons behind practices of magic and ideas about witchcraft. He argued that these scholars were mistaken to interpret early modern belief in magic and witchcraft as reflecting ignorance and emotional vulnerability, the natural consequence of which was a belief system that was, in effect, inherently mad.

The French historians shared with Dewey, from a century before, a view of witchcraft as naturally associated with the primitive, for which read: unsophisticated, unruly and too much subject to feelings. Clark's insights into the difficulties of such an approach are worth quoting at length. He demonstrates that in the view of these scholars,

> Men were subject to terrors of fantasy about nature, their own bodies and the actions of spirit agents. Psychological traits grew out of their obsessive fears—they were brutal, aggressive, a prey to their passions, insensitive and morbid, and they lacked self-control. Mandrou also derives the collective psychological instability of the peasants from their environmental difficul-

ties. The fact that their grasp of things lacked precision was especially worrying. The struggle to subsist brought about an 'anxiety psychosis' while malnutrition led to 'the mentality of the hunted with its superstitions, its sudden outbursts of anger and its hypersensitivity'. For Jean Delumeau the causes and incidence of the collective trauma of 'fear in the west' are again wider than the sphere of the peasants alone. But the most enduring and most widely held were the fears identified with technical inadequacy and its corresponding mentality—involving fear of the sea, of the stars and of portents and ghosts: 'The men of the past, especially those of the rural world, lived encircled by a hostile environment in which the threat of sorceries appeared at every moment'.[8]

Clark challenges any presumption that if a person used magic it could only be in order to defeat an irrational fear with an equally irrational appeal to ineffectual practices within an implausible cosmology.

Against the idea that despair was the prime mover behind action, Clark suggests that a proactive attitude in relation to the efficacy of particular actions implies, by contrast, a degree of optimism. Referring to exorcism rites for example, he suggests that they 'could not have been practised at all if men and women were always deemed to be the losers; whereas winning the contest warranted other emotions than fear'.[9] Thus Clark works to undermine the 'positivist and teleological'[10] assumptions of the influential French school by severing the link they presumed between excessive emotionality, even psychosis, and the material conditions of life. Clark develops his argument further to show the deep and defining link between the marginal and mainstream of early modern Catholicism. He refers to the importance of one of the emotions imputed to the divinity Himself, wrath, as a structuring component of the early modern worldview. Thus Clark makes clear that the behaviours of rural people in European history are as readily understood by reference to ideas from theology as they are to emotional responses to the material conditions of life.[11] He concludes,

We cannot, then, with Muchembled, trace a notion such as the wrath of the divinity to the misfortunes of popular experience because it was precisely this notion which gave life to the language concerned with fortune and misfortune. ... Nor ... can we regard the relevant rituals as a reflection of technological or emotional shortcomings when by performing them men and women were able to effect practical intentions and arrive at affective states.[12]

Considering witchcraft and demonology automatically in the light of the history of emotions could potentially be a regressive step if doing so positions as extreme a set of social phenomena that many witchcraft historians—Clark chief among them—have now shown was in a deep sense mainstream, or at least located within the complex dynamics of mainstream and marginal; legitimacy and pretension; falsehood and authenticity. To locate witchcraft and belief in demons in a special place that keeps it safely away from religion and rationality, by means of a focus on emotions, can distort understandings of witchcraft and detract from the overall value of studying emotions in history. A focus on emotions is suitable for the subject of witchcraft as an interpersonal issue, because an alleged act of witchcraft is often by definition one of harm, but to assume that witchcraft is therefore always about emotion can detract from attention to its place in the history of ideology.

Some examples from present-day law and psychotherapy show this issue to be not only a historiographical one, but of contemporary relevance in the public sphere. The examples to be considered here show a persistent tendency among the educated to presume that emotions to do with belief in demons are atavistic. These cases show that a medical diagnosis of individual psychopathology for widely held, culturally sanctioned beliefs in demons can still be valid for the purposes of law. Such categorisations by educated people can serve to embed, whether intentionally or not, the precepts of theology within the rationalising discourses of medicine and law. This paradoxical process shores up the credibility of the religious mainstream from association with the violence that can accompany as central a Christian tenet as its demonology.

PSYCHIATRY IN THE COURTROOM

Our focus turns to two instances of exorcism killing, among numerous such contemporary cases.[13] How attorneys have defended the perpetrators of these deaths and injuries varies widely, ranging from a version of an insanity defence to an argument that the defendants were acting rationally as responsible, ersatz (if failed) therapists.[14] One tragic 1999 case of Christian lay exorcism in Sydney led to the death of a child, Samani Amete. In this case, the boy's mother killed three-year-old Samani, whom she believed to be possessed by demons. Others assisted her, including some family members. The mother was diagnosed as not guilty of manslaughter on the grounds of mental illness, while two others who assisted her were found guilty of manslaughter. Thus within the bounds of accepted legal protocol, a group activity was divided into a series of separate individual activities. We can appreciate, of course, that legally the defence of an individual member of a group must be able to make an individual case; it is also quite possible that Ms Amete was suffering from a mental illness, while those around her merely shared her views about demons. But here we might consider the implications of Clark's analysis of the idea of mental illness as a basis of belief within a community of shared belief. Clark refers in this observation to neurosis, but the analogy is relevant: 'what is meant by the description "neurotic" is logically dependent on a conception of some contrasting state of normality; it could never be intelligible therefore to say of a whole society that it was "neurotic"'.[15] Thus, while not being defective at law, the decision to declare the principal perpetrator in a manslaughter trial not guilty on the grounds of mental illness follows a distinctive legal logic, while avoiding a cultural logic that would suggest the same beliefs were either consistent and therefore uniformly culpable or the product of a mental illness suffered equally by all defendants.

Moreover, harking back to Dewey and using the kind of thinking to which Clark addressed himself, one of the formal catchwords for the New South Wales Supreme Court's hearing into the death of Samani Amete is 'Primitive Religious Beliefs'. The choice of heading seems to derive, as it were, naturally from the fact that those involved were from the Pacific Islands. Yet they were Christian, belonging to the Samoan Assembly of God Church.[16] The Assembly of God is a branch of Protestantism which sets particular store by its ministry of 'deliverance' (either explicitly or implicitly from demons). However, this does not make it 'primitive', if this problematic term from a modern legal case can be taken to mean pre-Christian or pre-colonial. The Assembly of God is a large church with international links. Nor are beliefs about demons by definition syncretic, 'primitive' aspects blending dangerously with otherwise harmless Christian beliefs, as belief in demons in contemporary Christianity is unremarkable and entirely orthodox. Such are some of the preconceptions which too readily categorise such a case as culturally alien.

Another late twentieth-century case, this time involving a Catholic family in Italy, provides a basis for further reflection on the same problem: What are the implications for mainstream belief in demons when it is assumed that belief in demons is an individual pathology? Does the routine assumption of a link between derangement and belief in demons, an idea traceable back to Dewey and beyond, have implications for understanding the religious mainstream? The case from Italy involved a 45-year-old man, Mr A., who claimed that he was channelling the spirit of a saintly personage named Padre Pio when he killed the six-month-old daughter of his brother-in-law, in the belief the child was demon-possessed. The events leading up to the case took place in a village near Rome in the mid-1990s and provided the basis for an article by two psychotherapists (Maria Civita DeMarco, a psychologist, and Stefano Ferracuti, a psychiatrist).[17] It is their article rather than the case itself which is the basis of my investigation here, but the fate of the child remains, nonetheless, my core concern.

Some background will be of value in relation to one of the authors, Stefano Ferracuti. In 1996, Ferracuti and two other researchers published an article which described the condition of ten people experiencing what they self-diagnosed to be demonic possession. Taken as proof of this was that their emotional distress reached a peak in the presence of an exorcist.[18] The person in question was none other than the famous Vatican exorcist, Dom Gabriele Amorth (d. 2016), whose promotion of a cult of exorcism traversed three papacies and continues to grow. (Disturbance in the presence of an exorcist, of course, recalls one of the chief historical criteria for clerical or medical diagnosis of possession, which is the reaction attributed to the demon in the presence of holy persons or objects.) Ferracuti identifies himself in this article as less a psychiatric researcher than a participant observer, clearly signalling to the people he diagnoses with Dissociative Trance Disorder (DTD) that he believes in the reality of their self-diagnosis of demonic possession. The article ends as an apologia in defence of the therapeutic benefit of the rite of Catholic exorcism for people with the possession trance form of DTD, while having proposed that the condition only appears when the exorcist is near. Thus a psychiatrist continues the tradition of nineteenth-century alienists, in exploring belief in demons as implicitly related to mental health. But unlike most nineteenth-century writers (such as J.-M. Charcot and his colleagues, including Freud), Ferracuti is not writing in a secularist tradition. Rather he supports the view that these people's condition is a medical one, even though the only signs of their experience of demon possession tended to arise in the presence of an exorcist and the best way to treat them was by engaging the services of the very source of their torment. (If the same thing occurred in relation to the presence of a psychiatrist the illness would be called iatrogenic.) To state that the alleged demoniacs are mentally ill while noting that source and cure are identical blurs any sense of a boundary between religion and science and becomes in effect a form of medical apologism for mainstream religious doctrine.

The 1996 article, then, provides the context for that of 2004, in which Ferracuti and DeMarco describe the circumstances which led the man, Mr A., to kill a six-month-old girl. The series of events leading to the death of the infant began when Mr A.'s father-in-law was suffering from what proved to be a terminal illness. The family thought that the cause of the elderly man's illness and subsequent death might have been an occult force, the presence of which was indicated also by unusual occurrences in the house. They called in several non-medical healers, including a priest, a 'santoni' (male healer), and 'a practicing sorceress from Rome'.[19] The sorceress said that 'someone had... bewitched the house and the family' and began to perform ceremonies.[20] Mr A. the account states, became 'anxious and sceptical about what was happening'. The family and the witch fell out over money matters and the witch left. Mr A. 'became increasingly restless' and 'withdrew into the family house'.[21] Then he began to manifest, among other symptoms, olfactory hallucinations, unresponsiveness and a stiff neck.[22] He also stared at a picture of a holy man, the Capuchin Padre Pio, a southern Italian priest who died in 1968, was beatified in 1999 and canonised in 2002.[23] One of the women in the family said Mr A. was experiencing a positive possession by Padre Pio, which the man and the rest of the family accepted, the family now addressing him as 'blessed'.[24] In several later episodes, the man had 'frequent, uncontrolled, possession trance' experiences, and said he felt the 'presence of the devil in the house whenever his brother-in-law, who was a nonbeliever, came to visit the family with his newborn daughter'.[25] He 'declared the baby had to be exorcised because she was possessed by the devil. The whole family agreed, and during the exorcism the baby died from a cerebral hemorrhage caused by shaking the head. Mr A. claimed that he was completely amnesic of the episode.'[26]

In the homicide case that followed, the defence offered a diagnosis of 'histrionic personality disorder' which the court accepted; the authors note that a 'diagnosis of DTD [dissociative trance disorder] was also proposed' in the particular form of a 'possession trance'.[27] The possession in this case was not by demons, but by Padre Pio. Key features of a diagnosis of Dissociative Trance Disorder include:

(2) Possession trance, a single or episodic alteration in the state of consciousness characterized by the replacement of customary sense of personal iden-

tity by a new identity. This is attributed to the influence of a spirit, power, deity, or other person, as evidenced by one (or more) of the following:

>   a.   Stereotyped and culturally determined behaviors or move-
> ments that are experienced as being controlled by the possessing agent
>   b.   Full or partial amnesia for the event.

Moreover, 'The trance or possession trance state causes clinically significant distress or impairment in social, occupational, or other important areas of functioning.'[28]

The account which Ferracuti and DeMarco provide is a tick-box itemisation of all the key diagnostic features of the claimed condition, implicitly a retrospective medical statement in defence of the man whom the court convicted of murder. The authors acknowledge that the man was influenced by his religious beliefs and acted in keeping with the beliefs of his family and indeed with their encouragement. Nonetheless, the DTD diagnosis had formed part of an attempt by the defence in the case to mitigate or minimise the offence.

In publishing a research article based on prison visits to the man, which found him to have had DTD but effectively to be in remission, the two psychotherapists were able to insist on the validity of a potentially exculpatory diagnosis.

Notwithstanding the defence's provision of evidence to support a claim of mental illness, the court found the man guilty and sent him to jail for 18 years. Neither psychiatric diagnosis proposed to the court appears to have affected sentencing. However, in relation to DTD, the court reasoned that

> even if Mr. A had DTD, one body and one person alone performed the
> exorcism. In addition, even if the exorcism was practised by an identity
> claiming to be Padre Pio, this identity was not psychotic and had performed
> acts that could be considered logical and coherent in that mental state (and
> in that familiar situation).[29]

Thus the Italian court found a way to recognise the legitimacy of the Catholic belief system at work in this case, while finding the accused guilty and avoiding scandal in relation to the growing cult of Padre Pio. This seems an elegant quasi-secular solution. However, it is not clear if the family was held legally accountable for their endorsement of Mr A.'s motivations or his actions. It is on this point that the diagnosis of DTD takes an unusual turn. As in the Amete case, how is it possible to square the claim of an individual pathology with the evidence that others shared the same reality?

Over several years after Mr A.'s imprisonment, the authors observed his behaviour 'longitudinally' finding that he had 'had no further episodes of dissociation and no other psychopathological symptoms'.[30] They refer to the man's actions as evidence that his psychological state was 'anthropogenic', meaning culturally derived, but interacting with specific aspects of his own personality. 'Hence', the therapists conclude, 'rather than being irrational, Mr. A's behaviour was coherent with the role of Padre Pio as this religious figure was conceptualised by the group'.[31] The diagnosis of DTD which had been intended to exculpate the man also implicitly defended the belief system which had underpinned his actions.[32] Seemingly, in the view of these medical experts, Mr A. was less guilty because he was sick, even though the sickness itself was culturally derived. Thus their article was able to maintain that although since he had been in jail the man was no longer saying he was Padre Pio, the diagnosis of DTD—rejected by the court—had nonetheless been correct.

In the legal setting, many kinds of psychiatric diagnosis, even paradoxically an 'anthropogenic' one, can provide the potential for a legal defence against the requirement in a murder trial for *mens rea* (intention to carry out the act) and grounds for release into the community. Ironically, a 'not guilty' verdict could have meant release into a community in which the exact beliefs which were said to justify the crime enjoy credence. In this case at least, for the author-therapists, psychiatric diagnosis has come full circle, reversing the secularist narrative, subtly functioning as a medium for the defence of theological truths. Mental illness in the DTD 'possession trance' case is thus able to stand in as religion's double when the specific effects of religious sentiment are socially unpalatable, leading to homicide.

DISCUSSION

This essay has considered agencies and institutions which have established the means to understand emotions and behaviours related to magic, witchcraft and demonology. It has sought to defend the view that historians might still profitably turn to the history of agencies and institutions to study the historicity of emotions. The emotions under study here are not primarily emotions as experienced by individuals but as classified by authorities.

We have seen that, from the first Dewey system, through to late twentieth-century French historians and into the late twentieth-century legal system of New South Wales and legal psychiatry in Italy, there persists a common assumption of a natural affinity between mental illness and belief in demonic power. Yet the existence of belief in the reality and power of demons as part of mainstream religion is in all these instances set aside. At its best, this approach can serve to perpetuate clichés about the uneducated as the repository of extreme emotions. At worst, such assumptions can shore up the view that there is a distance between cases of violence and mainstream religion, with violence being attributed to the uneducated, who are presumed to be less able to control strong emotions. This need not happen in any conspiratorial way; rather, power comes from what is 'safely assumed'. That is the reason for interrogating categories of emotions, as they can so readily become invisible.

Christianity is a religion which cool-headed 'reasonable' people can practise but its less palatable manifestations can be too readily assigned to the province of the deranged or the primitive. Modern cases of exorcism killing have highlighted the persistence of assumptions which permit the professions to distance the marginal from the mainstream, but also the emergence of new ways to legitimise the margin as pathological in a way that preserves the legitimacy of the central belief system. In the case from Italy, the psychotherapist scholars erected an effective bulwark in defence of mainstream Catholicism by setting aside as extreme the behaviour of a man whose religious beliefs underpinned his killing of an infant.

The examination here of several nineteenth- to twenty-first century moments has sought to illustrate and give weight to a concern that an emotionological approach to beliefs in demons and witchcraft might underwrite outdated tendencies both to situate emotions outside of time, and to quarantine belief in demons and witchcraft from considerations of rationality and mainstream religion. Two final observations remain. First, a rereading of the two legal cases considered here can provide a further dimension to our theme, as, in neither case did the legal forum consider the emotions of the case relevant to its deliberations. Rather, questions of sanity and insanity were in the foreground as the basis of a legal determination. But both the deceased children were family members of the perpetrators. Was something lost from the legal forum in its incapacity to speak of anything other than a question of reason? Emotions here are perhaps more significant for their absence. And finally, on the question of historical method, it could be observed that one of the arguments made against the linguistic turn in historiography is that in studying systems of meanings interlinked in time, there is little space to address change. However, considering the history of the disciplines and the professions is one way to pursue the study of change which sets one discourse alongside another in a particular historical moment. In the cases considered here, we have seen how traditions of truth-seeking internal to medicine and law have mediated understandings of emotions, in keeping both with their specific disciplines and agendas, and with the temper of the times.

NOTES

1. Stearns and Stearns, 'Emotionology', 813.
2. Bever, 'Popular Witch Beliefs and Magical Practices', 65.
3. Dewey, *A Classification and Subject Index*.
4. See Zwissler's chapter, this volume.
5. According to the current copyright holders of the system this change occurred in 1962. Thanks are due to Kristina Truthan at OCLC (Online Computer Library Center) for this advice.
6. See Online Computer Library Center, 'DDC 23 Summaries'.
7. Stearns and Stearns, 'Emotionology', 816.
8. Clark, 'French Historians', 70, citing Jean Delumeau.
9. Ibid., 93.
10. Ibid., 72.
11. The divine emotion of jealousy, as expressed in the early commandments of the decalogue, pertaining to the worship due to God, could equally be adduced here.
12. Clark, 'French Historians', 94. Clark's early insistence on drawing imagined extremes of demonic belief back towards the centre pointed to the framework of his master work of 1997, *Thinking with Demons*.
13. More than thirty exorcism deaths have occurred since the 1970s. In the majority of these cases, women and children have been the victims. These figures are the findings of the ongoing research of the legal scholar Dr Adrian Howe and myself.
14. In the 1993 case of *R. v. Vollmer*, two people were convicted of the manslaughter of Joan Vollmer. The defence argued that belief in demonic possession was 'reasonable' and that Joan Vollmer's assail-

ants (who included her husband, Ralph Vollmer) had acted on the basis of this reasonable belief. See Ferber and Howe, 'The Man Who Mistook His Wife for a Devil'; and Howe and Ferber, 'Delivering Demons, Punishing Wives', 123–46.

15. Clark, 'French Historians', 89.
16. Catchwords: Criminal Law and Procedure; Manslaughter; Primitive Religious Beliefs; Exorcism. Supporting Roles of Offenders. New South Wales Supreme Court (2000), *Regina v. Penetito Mika*; *Regina v. Siniue Sagato*, NSWSC 852 (11 August 2000).
17. Ferracuti and Civita DeMarco, 'Ritual Homicide', 59–64.
18. Ferracuti, Sacco and Lazzari, 'Dissociative Trance Disorder', 525–39.
19. Ferracuti and Civita DeMarco, 'Ritual Homicide', 61.
20. Ibid.
21. Ibid.
22. Ibid.
23. Padre Pio (1887–1968) was a controversial figure even in his own lifetime. Born in Pietrelcina, Italy, Pio was said to bear stigmata, have visions and effect healing. A cult grew up around him as a 'folk saint' and for many decades before his death, the church hierarchy disputed his legitimacy and how to respond to the cult he inspired. See Christian Jr, 'Holy People in Peasant Europe', 110–11. Padre Pio's modern cult extends worldwide, embodying, it could be argued, the triumph of pre- and counter-Vatican II devotional enthusiasm, just as the Catholic resurgent endorsement of exorcism now does. On Dom Gabriel Amorth, the Vatican exorcist, see, e.g., *Daily Mail Reporter*, 28 May 2013: '"I've rid the world of 160,000 demons"'.
24. Ferracuti and Civita DeMarco, 'Ritual Homicide', 61.
25. Ibid., 63, 61.
26. Ibid., 61.
27. Ibid., 62. See also Ferracuti, Sacco and Lazzari, 'Dissociative Trance Disorder', where the authors specifically refer to the 'further study' signalled in the DSM IV, 525.
28. Cited in During et al., 'Critical Review of Dissociative Trance and Possession Disorders', 237. The use of this psychiatric condition as grounds for defence came at a crucial time in the history of the psychiatric category. In 1994 the *Diagnostic and Statistical Manual*

of Mental Disorders (DSM) proposed this syndrome as a new category of diagnosis in need of 'further study': see Kingsbury, 'What is Dissociative Trance Disorder?' 8. The description of criteria for DTD provided here comes from the one in use in the 1990s, DSM IV-TR. In the current (2013) DSM V, the 'possession trance' element of the disorder, which was the basis for the defence, has been removed and the symptoms of DTD have been reduced overall significantly. American Psychiatric Association, 'Dissociative Disorders', section 300.15 (F44.89).

29. Ferracuti and Civita DeMarco, 'Ritual Homicide', 62.
30. Ibid.
31. Ibid.
32. It is not clear if either of the authors had served as expert witnesses at the trial, although it is possible they did.

PART IV

In History

CHAPTER 14

In Memorium Maleficarum: Feminist and Pagan Mobilizations of the Burning Times

Laurel Zwissler

The moment when a feeling enters the body is political.

—Adrienne Rich, as remembered by Alison Bechdel.

… they were killed for living the same sort of life I live right now but with longer skirts and fewer cable channels.

—Sarah Vowell.

In this chapter I consider the popular afterlife within feminist circles of the academically discredited thesis of 'the Burning Times'—the early modern witch-hunts as an explicit and intentional gendercide. Through its adoption as a 'useful past' within feminist and contemporary Pagan

L. Zwissler
Central Michigan University

© The Author(s) 2016
L. Kounine, M. Ostling (eds.), *Emotions in the History of Witchcraft*, DOI 10.1057/978-1-137-52903-9_14

communities, this version of history provides an intimate martyrology which both explains emotional dissatisfaction with present conditions and motivates political action for future change. This chapter analyses the emotions of history, the emotions stimulated and sustained through the recollection and memorialization of imagined pasts. Putting ethnography and textual analysis in dialogue with work on religion and emotions,[1] I ask what the narrative of the stubborn survival of the Old Religion through centuries of persecution and sacrifice does for feminists and Pagans today.

Personal responses, triggered by reflecting on the tragedies of witch persecutions from emotionally invested perspectives, serve to place current individual and political struggles into meaningful historical and cosmological contexts: a process resembling that by which the early modern diabolical witchcraft complex folds unconnected misfortunes into a larger paradigm of satanic evil overrunning God's world.[2] My project here is to explore the social and rhetorical mechanisms that construct such emotions and to analyse the practical results for communities today of these perceived relationships with 'witches' in the past. Drawing on historically significant sacred literature within contemporary Paganism and feminist spirituality, and on ethnographic fieldwork among North American feminist activists who identify with Witchcraft as a religion, this chapter explores some of the discourses contemporary Witches mobilize in the name of the victims of historical witch-hunts.[3]

This project is informed by foundational authors of the feminist spirituality movement, which first began at the intersection of the women's movement and the alternative spirituality movement of the 1960s and 1970s.[4] Mary Daly, Zsuzsanna Budapest and Starhawk clearly articulate a set of themes relating to women and religious Witchcraft, and their impact on feminist spirituality and Pagan Witchcraft endures.[5] Their views are further popularized by Donna Read's film *The Burning Times*, on which Starhawk was a consultant and in which many prominent leaders in feminist spirituality participated.[6] The *Goddess Trilogy*, of which this film is a part, has in turn affected Witchcraft communities profoundly. I supplement this textual and media analysis with ethnographic fieldwork within a Reclaiming-influenced Pagan collective and a focus-group discussion conducted with Reclaiming, Alexandrian, Unitarian and Dianic-trained Witches.[7]

SORTING WITCHES

The distinction between the witch in the historical imaginations of feminist activist communities and the Witch celebrated by feminist religious Witchcraft is very uncertain. Feminist activists and feminist Witches belong to overlapping communities, and both groups agree that the women who were accused and killed as 'witches' were victims of patriarchy.[8] However, they don't necessarily agree wholeheartedly on the reasons these 'witches' were targeted. Were these women mainly victims of gender oppression or religious persecution? Even if one were to focus on the contemporary Pagan community exclusively, it is itself incredibly diverse: moreover, many Pagans are invested in their religious identities as forms of alterity and counter-cultural resistance in ways similar to feminist identities founded on a stance of political opposition to perceived mainstream culture.[9] Challenges of definition are compounded by the presence of Pagan Witchcraft and related ritual actions in activist environments, such as anti-globalization demonstrations and environmental protests. Paganism's emphasis on action over belief is one reason for broader activist tolerance of ritual practices, such as spiral dances and chants, in environments otherwise implicitly suspicious of 'religion', contributing to Paganism's status as a de facto 'civil religion' within progressive circles.[10]

Given all this, the historical witch of political feminist narrative and the Witch of religious Witchcraft are difficult to definitively separate because they are often both represented within the same communities and mutually influence one another. Moreover, as I explain below, the narrative of witch-hunting as gender-cleansing[11] comes to Paganism from the first wave of American political feminism. Therefore, communities of feminist witches, Pagan Witches, and feminist Witchcraft practitioners have been bubbling and boiling together in the same cultural cauldron for generations.

HERSTORY: YOU KNOW THIS STORY

It has many variations, but here is one.

Despite efforts of a dour, missionizing Christian church, the common people of Europe continued to practise the religion they inherited from humanity's peaceful, nature-loving origins. Women, honoured for their role as life-creators, led joyful ceremonies under the moon, in harmony with the plants and animals that made up their living world. Meanwhile, male priests conducted body-hating, guilt-inducing liturgies in cold, grey-stone cathedrals. During the early modern period, the tension between these religions, gynocentric Paganism and misogynist Christianity, exploded in the form of Christian persecution of members of the Old Religion, under the guise of hunts for Satan-worshiping, baby-eating witches. Millions of women were snatched up, tortured and executed in hideous ways, traumatizing Western culture for centuries and erasing the memory that there was once a different way to be, other than sexist, violent and sad.

Until now: now that you know, you can remember.

The story that those tried as witches in early modern Europe were practitioners of a woman-friendly, matriarchal religion stretching back to humanity's dawn is a familiar one. Over the last century or so the story's bards have come clothed in both academic and ritual magician robes. Jules Michelet, Charles Leland and Margaret Murray appropriated those killed during the witch-hunts to their academic projects;[12] Gerald Gardner and Doreen Valiente gathered them into their religious visions.[13]

Yet, those women were Christian. We can know this: they called out to Jesus and Mary under torture.[14] To claim them as Witches is to silence them further, to plunge them back under after they barely surface into our view, wavering behind documents transmitted by others: names on lists, archived transcripts, broadsheets. Witch, as religious martyr, comes into being only at the moment of a Christian woman's death.[15]

Memorializers handle this contradiction in different ways, if they address it at all. Even dedicated Witches accede that not *all* the people persecuted for Witchcraft actually were practitioners like themselves.[16] In Read's film *The Burning Times*, the narrator voices over the continuing Spanish dialogue of a *curandera*, Marguerite Despuedes, who has just told the camera that she is 'appointed by the Eternal Father with the work of God, our Lord, the child Jesus'. Over this unequivocal declaration of Christian piety, the film's narrator glosses, 'Like Marguerite, many European healers who were burned relied on Christian faith when performing their cures, but their healing arts were rooted in the traditions of their ancestors'—implying that those traditions are not Christian.[17] Feminist Witches may thus ignore the explicit Christianity of both the women persecuted in historical witch-hunts and women today, often women of colour, who practise traditional healing arts. This rhetorical strategy leaves the feminist Witchcraft community open to charges of appropriating the experiences of marginalized women transhistorically and cross-culturally.[18]

It is, however, important to remember that *all* religions are engaged in intense processes of cultural and historical translation. For example, contemporary Christians project their current ethical values and life-choices back in time and across the world to find reflections of themselves in the early Jewish followers of Jesus. Nonetheless, there are two important differences between the projection of Witchcraft onto communities who would not or do not claim the label themselves, and the efforts of more mainstream religions to find continuity with the past. The first is that contemporary Christians can find people in the past who did consciously identify with their religion, even if their orientations, practices and lives were very different from those of practitioners today. Second, people seem much more eager to charge feminist Witchcraft with appropriation than more established religions. The charge is not unwarranted, but it may apply as easily far beyond this particular community.[19] Impassioned critiques of feminist Witchcraft as appropriating the past may thus have more to do with gut-level reactions to the larger messages of feminism and culture-change that the movement represents;[20] these critiques also strengthen, rather than disrupt, the internal worldview of feminist Witchcraft as marginalized. While the language has changed, there is nonetheless still a group of women, called witches, being denounced for their lack of participation in male-dominated learning and for their stubborn maintenance of a subversive, alternative culture. This dynamic is not identical to the early modern persecutions by any stretch, but it helps fuel a role-play that reinforces notions of emotionality, logic and gender for all participants, both within the religion and within the academy.

Despite decades of scholarly work debunking the myth that 'witches' were Witches, the story remains popular, not only within feminist and Pagan circles, but within broader culture. It has become established as routine fact through the same mechanisms by which demonological fantasy established itself as fact in early modern Europe: through generic retellings; through learned print; and through popular entertainment.[21] It sounds right to people because they have heard it many times before: 'Oh, yes, I've heard/read/seen something about that.'

CRONE GAGE

There are also reasons why this story resonates so effectively within contemporary feminist communities: it is a distinctly *American* invention and export borne out of the early phase of political feminism. The first claim of executed witches for the cause of the women's movement came from Matilda Joslyn Gage, part of the US suffragist triumvirate with Elizabeth Cady Stanton and Susan B. Anthony at the end of the nineteenth century.[22] Her *Woman, Church and State*, originally published in 1893, serves as a denunciation of Christianity's role in oppressing women and includes chapters cataloguing stages in the development of this oppression, including: the fall of the 'Matriarchate' to the 'Patriarchate'; the sexual subjection of women to feudal lords, Catholic priests and husbands; and the witchcraft trials.[23]

The idea that there is political power in strong emotions, even in suffering, also comes to contemporary feminism through the first wave. Progressive-era suffragists built their platform on the idea that women are morally *superior* to men because they are closer to emotions and nature.[24] They insisted on sentimentalism, in explicit contrast to rationality.[25] Theirs is a political argument based on ideas of the virtue of strong emotions: men and women inherently experience emotions differently; women feel more deeply; rather than proving that women are less capable of participating in the hard decisions of politics, women's stronger emotionality makes them more authentic, wise and positioned to govern justly. It is within this cosmology of emotion that *Woman, Church and State*, as a horror-show compendium, a random pastiche of tragic anecdotes, comes to make sense. The prose is meant to be evocative, to raise the emotions that ultimately will inspire the righteous to act for social change.

THE ENEMY OF MY ENEMY IS ME

Driven underground by conservative social forces of the post-Second World War 1950s, the American movement for women's equality began to resurge in the 1960s, peaking in the 1970s.[26] The image of the Witch emerged during this time as a popular symbol of the movement. An example of a feminist activist group that mobilized the imagery of witchcraft was WITCH, founded in 1968. Members of WITCH produced a manifesto proclaiming the links between current feminist struggles and the witch-hunts and, in one of their most publicized actions, dressed in stereotypical 'witch' costumes and hexed Wall Street on Halloween.[27] In 1974, radical feminist Andrea Dworkin declared the witch-hunts a culturally specific form of 'gynocide'.[28]

The outline of the Pagan Witchcraft story connects assumptions about prehistorical goddess religion to the witch persecutions and serves as a meta-narrative about the fall of peaceful, matriarchal cultures to patriarchal invaders at the dawn of history.[29] This is an important reason for the levels of investment contemporary feminist communities have in the Pagan Witch theory; it is seen as proving the survival of goddess religion from ancient times and provides legitimacy to assertions of prehistorical matriarchy, to political feminism and to contemporary Pagan practices. This connection is not always consciously articulated, but implicitly structures stories of the early modern period.

In some ways, feminist Witches are absolutely right: witchcraft discourse is a culture war. 'Witch', as a permutation of 'heretic' before it, is a stereotype that morphs and shifts with circumstance and context. It is an empty category seeking specific bodies to instantiate it, an externally assigned possession. In my focus group with self-identifying Witches, Alana said, 'If you look at the ways that the victims were presented— Pagans and Jews and Witches and anybody else—it was a stamp. They were created as Other and destroyed as Other and when that Other was gone, a new Other was more or less found.'[30]

While historians have long recognized this ascriptive character of the witch-label in the early modern period, contemporary Witches go further through self-identifying with the labelled victims. As discussion-participant Lavender said,

> I'm seeing the persecution now with the government and the growing fascism, the ways they depict environmentalists as 'foreign funded'. Now, with all the spying on everybody, it feels like we are back in The Burning Times, but now the people being burned are people who care about the planet, who care about other people, social justice, environmental justice, you know, saving the planet.[31]

River said, 'It's corporate.' For her, both the witch-hunts and current problems are about 'the history of stuff. "I want more stuff, I need lots of stuff. I want *your* stuff."'[32] For these Witches, there is a direct correlation between persecutions in the past and government repression in the present.

While the immediacy of Lavender's identification throws the process into relief, feeling back into the past is a common practice. Witch trials, like other atrocities, are a rupture in the smooth flow of assumed progress. For people today, the trials create problems in envisioning a sensical universe, even as they helped solve parallel problems for participants in their original social contexts. Ever since historians began looking back at the early modern trials, they have been engaging in similar projects to Lavender's above, with varying degrees of self-reflection.

The history of early modern European 'witchcraft' is rife with emotions, as skilfully displayed in the preceding chapters: fear, envy, lust, guilt, greed, trauma, despair, self-righteousness and relief. However, scholars have tended to relegate those emotions to the past: *those* people could not deal with their emotions, so they used 'witches' as emotional crutches, as scapegoats, as catharsis.[33] Nonetheless, the idea of demonic witchcraft has always invoked emotional responses in later observers. No matter what else they might be, responses by historians are *always also* emotional.

First, some of the fish in the barrel: Murray fantasizes joy, sex and resistance into her historical work; Michelet finds an outlet for his pity and political disgust; Montague Summers proclaims his fear of Satan and women.[34] However, the personal inflections go beyond these usual suspects. Purkiss explicates the androcentric, Enlightenment smugness that generally permeated witch-trial scholarship for much of the twentieth century. Although historians needed the strangeness of early modern beliefs to prove their own rationality, they also looked for intellectual allies in the past. This caused over-identification with early modern witchcraft sceptics, such as Reginald Scot (who in fact objected to witchcraft on theological, rather than scientific grounds), and an outsized backlash against Murray, as too emotionally caught up in her subject, unlike proper (male) historians.[35] Historians have perhaps made feminist Witches' point for them, that all this ostentatious 'objectivity' really is sometimes just a ruse.

Forbidden Knowledge, Widely Published

Suspicion of androcentrism sheds further light on the seemingly contradictory way Witches approach the work of historians. Witches rely on academic historians for reliable information about the persecution of their foremothers. Yet because, in their perspective, everyone is just telling a *version* of the truth that supports their partisan interests, it is imperative for personal authenticity and for the health of our culture that feminist

Witches tell their own. As in Alison Bechdel's recollection of second-wave feminist icon Adrienne Rich (see the epigraph to this chapter), emotions are not separate from, but integral to, political power.[36] Emotional truth is the most important factor in determining the validity of a historical narrative.

In feminist Witchcraft, personal truth reveals the cosmic truth of the Goddess; facts are only useful in so far as they reaffirm this transcendent reality.[37] This is best demonstrated through Zsuzsanna Budapest's narrative of a pesky heckler who appeared regularly at her presentations on ancient goddesses. She writes that this critic's 'favourite way of goading me was by relentlessly asking about the exact date of the statues in my slides and where they were found. I had never been able to convince her that my primary purpose in these talks was to get across their meaning, not their dates.'[38] These two women speak at cross-purposes: one in the language of history; the other in the language of thealogy.

The women's spirituality movement emerged out of the consciousness-raising practices of second-wave feminism.[39] Practitioners embraced Monique Wittig's mandate to transcend patriarchal culture through memorialization of what came before:

> There was a time when you were not a slave, remember that. You walked alone, full of laughter, you bathed bare bellied. You say you have lost all recollection of it, remember! You say there are not words to describe it; you say it does not exist. But remember! Make an effort to remember! or failing that, invent.[40]

Wittig's formula is key to understanding the seemingly contradictory undertow of anti-intellectualism behind a movement which nonetheless relies on the painstaking recovery of lost knowledge through research and analysis.

The feminist Witchcraft community is rather notorious among historians for investment in and perpetuation of the unsupportable number of nine million women killed.[41] This number comes from Gage. Without reference to calculations or source literature, she writes, 'It is computed from historical records that nine million persons were put to death for witchcraft after 1484, or during a period of 300 years'.[42] In *Gyn/Ecology* Mary Daly repeats Gage's number, citing her and noting that there is disagreement on this point, but, by her next book, *Pure Lust*, she presents it as given.[43] Largely through Daly, the nine-million number was taken up by second-wave feminism, though many later authors simply give the number without citation or cite other authors who give no citation.[44]

A two-tack strategy, accepting or rejecting historical scholarship based on compatibility with the preselected narrative, is especially obvious in these discussions of numbers. One method is to ground high numbers in historical fact, or at least to advocate higher numbers as more responsible estimates through the use of academically accepted criticism.[45] However, in the end, Witches reaffirm the importance of emotional truth over factual argument. Starhawk and Hilary Valentine write in their initiation manual, *Twelve Wild Swans*,

> Estimates have ranged from 100,000 to 9 million, but today most historians tend toward lower figures. In a way, it doesn't really matter, because even if a single woman were tortured and then burned alive in front of her agonized friends and family for the crime of honouring the Goddess, it would create terror and horror that would long outlast her cries.[46]

What matters to these Witches is the overall effects of persecution on culture generally and on women in particular, repercussions that have remained obscured and unexamined because misogynist powers triumphed and erased the history of their atrocities: 'History is written by the winners.'[47] Traditional academic history is accepted as valid when it provides useful stories to shore up accounts of witch-hunts as misogynist, horrifying and above all Christian persecutions of Paganism, but historians are suckers, at best, or patriarchal henchmen, at worst, when they produce work that throws these theories into question or directly contradicts them.[48]

On the other hand, we have the proponents of this narrative performing their authority by using products of this very same knowledge system as represented by the academy and professional historians. For example, a revealing practice among feminist Witches is the copious use of footnotes in their discussion of the Burning Times. While the same sources tend to recur—sources that academic witchcraft historians have deconstructed and dismissed, such as Michelet, Murray and Gardner, or seriously reinterpreted, such as the *Malleus maleficarum*[49]—they are nonetheless presented in the texts as academic, normative and authoritative. Feminist Witches inhabit an awkward position in relation to historical evidence. Feminists are meant to use these histories as containing shards that can be lenses through which to glimpse the truth of women's history.[50] Yet, official histories are distorted lies told by misogynists to mislead women.

Feminist Witches mint their own history, but where does it spend? Largely, historical research as practised by feminist Witches is valued as currency not in academe, but in popular culture and religious subcultures. In a very post-structuralist turn, feminist Witches play both sides.[51] When the history 'works', it is solid proof. Where it does not, it is counterfeit and must be dismissed as a trick that draws us away from the truth. And yet, ultimately, this epistemology is not post-structuralist at all: the Truth is out there to be discovered; it is knowable. You will know when you've found it because it will *feel* true in your heart and 'work' in your life.[52]

TURNING INTO A WITCH

Early modern trial procedures required the accused to participate in the process of producing individual narratives explaining how they, personally, fulfilled the stereotype of a diabolical witch.[53] Witchcraft beliefs and stories, both learned and popular, conveyed to all members of society that witches were usually women.[54] Moreover, these beliefs implied that all women were potential witches. For women who were painfully aware of their inability to live up to impossible, because competing, gendered ideals—of selflessness and contentment, for example, or of fecundity and chastity—witchcraft provided a language for them to describe this perceived failure.[55] In other words, witchcraft discourse encouraged both men and women to suspect the women in their lives, but for women that included scrutinizing their own thoughts and feelings.[56] Witchcraft trial procedures provided systematic structures through which women were disciplined into *turning themselves* into witches.

The process required people accused of witchcraft to 'remember' their fall, to think back to when they had first met and consummated their pacts with the Devil, to recall and recount what they had witnessed and done at the sabbat, and to recite what *maleficium* they had committed. Neither historians nor contemporary Witches argue for the face value of these confessions, though, following Michelet and Murray, Pagans may argue that they are inverted code for actual events.[57] These tales are inventions of the process. People under duress were *forced* to 'remember and, failing that, invent'.

For Witches today, the process of 'remembering' the Witches of the past is similar, in that it is a process of emotional discipline that results in a new or reinforced identification with historical witches. The process is not entirely a pleasant or comfortable one, either, though it is hardly reasonable to equate it with physical torture. Nonetheless, through dwelling on specific trial procedures, or through the recounting of generic, non-specific stories about trials and executions, contemporary feminists turn themselves into Witches and turn accused witches into reflections of themselves.

Identification with women tried and executed for witchcraft is a discipline; it involves suffering, mentally imposed. What would it feel like to be tortured, burned? Such total identification requires a blurring of boundaries between the past and the present, the self and other. The process only works if you commit your imagination. Read's *Burning Times* exemplifies the effort contemporary Witchcraft communities put into this exercise of historical projection. The film includes: historical re-enactments of women in cloaks scurrying furtively down narrow, stone alleys; close-ups of woodcuts of execution scenes overlaid with a soundtrack of gruff male crowds, women's sobs and crackling flames; and museum displays of torture implements, such as the iron maiden, thumbscrews and the mouth pear, with narration describing their use.[58]

Contemporary Pagan communities have taken different approaches to the challenge of whether to take the Burning Times narrative literally, especially as it relates to stories of The Craft's rediscovery in the mid-twentieth century. As Pagan and feminist spirituality communities become more integrated with academic scholarship, some practitioners have denounced such integration on religious grounds. Recently Sabina Magliocco has highlighted historical literalism as part of the minority trend she identifies as 'Pagan Fundamentalism', 'centred around two hot-button topics: the historicity of Wiccan foundational narratives, and the nature of the gods'.[59] Margot Adler also urged fellow Pagans away from investing so deeply in specific foundational narratives that their communities cannot accommodate new academic discoveries, many of which suggest that Craft origin stories are creative history.[60]

One of the ways around these conflicts has been to treat Burning Times history metaphorically, as leaders such as Starhawk and Adler have done. However, such caveats are usually not offered explicitly in oral tradition. For example, in the focus-group discussion, participants spoke very literally about the persecutions of witches as persecution of people like themselves, if not religiously, then politically, much as Sara Vowell identified with uppity Salem women in the second epigraph above.[61] Only when asked specifically about whether they thought that early modern witches did the same things that they do today did they become more qualifying.

This reflects a practice through which internal conversations within a community repeat historically suspect assertions, but members may qualify them as a kind of shorthand for more complicated views when questioned about their accuracy.

For newer members of the community, or for outsiders, the implicit caveats may not be as well understood as they are by more experienced members. For example, while the women in the focus group took misogyny as an obvious contributor to early modern persecutions, Charlie, the lone man in the circle, felt that they had not addressed it: 'The power of patriarchy is something that no one has touched on.'[62] The other participants assured him that feminist consciousness structured their previous comments so profoundly that it need not be said, 'It's implicit.' These types of rhetorical practices, taking agreed background information as given, mean that informal community discourse may represent the least academically compatible versions of history.

Pain Is Already Political

Feminist Burning Times horror stories are meant to reveal the often subtle but real violence that underpins male-dominated culture today and occasionally erupts into view through some of the other phenomena often discussed in combination with witch-hunts, such as domestic violence, sexual violence, genital cutting and prostitution.[63] It provides historical context for present feelings by linking contemporary struggles to the past. To invert the feminist rallying cry, it makes the political personal.

This function contributes to the creation and maintenance of what William Reddy calls an 'emotional refuge', a space within which individuals can express non-alignment with dominant 'emotional regimes' and the cultural values they underpin.[64] For feminist Witches, their practice provides an emotional refuge from patriarchy and capitalist modernity: as Lavender said in the focus group, 'You know, those people confiscating the witches' property to make themselves rich? The same thing is happening here. We're going to take away their jobs and their unions and their pensions, so that the 1% gets richer.'

Witch-trial narratives contribute effectively to emotional refuge in part because they give justification for the emotions of discontent, sadness and fear that many women may already experience in male-dominated culture. For women who do not feel satisfied with traditional gendered roles such as mother, home-maker, and sexually available lover of men, these narratives provide an explanation for not feeling the way they are 'supposed to'. In combination with the myth of matriarchal prehistory, their constructions of historical alterity and solidarity among Witches provide a reframing, an analysis of contemporary culture, not as normal, natural or ideal, but as violent and tragically coercive.

At the same time that they allow for the expression of these negative emotions, the placement of witch trials within the larger frame of the repression and re-emergence of the religion of the Goddess also provides a possible resolution for those feelings. It suggests that witch-martyr stories do not bring needless pain, but rather provide motivation necessary to power a restructuring of the world into one in which pain and fear are no longer the dominant emotions that women and other marginalized people are forced to feel. Starhawk is the author most conscious of using the narratives in this therapeutic way. In the beginning of *Truth or Dare*, she ends a poem:

> When we are afraid, when it hurts too much
> We like to tell ourselves
>   stories of power
>   how we lost it
>   how we can reclaim it
> We tell ourselves
>   the cries we hear may be those of labour
>   the pain we feel may yet be that of birth.[65]

The horror stories also exemplify Reddy's point that emotional refuges are neither unequivocally safety valves nor subversions of the emotional regimes that undergird political power.[66] Visions of change are partly earned through stories of broken female bodies, enforcing 'the witch's place as ultimate victim'.[67] The Burning Times myth represents alterity, but it can also be subsumed within torture fantasies that are sometimes difficult to discern from the misogynist narratives of demonologists themselves. Both end in women's corpses. It is the purposes to which their dying pain is ascribed, the defeat of Satan or the survival of the Goddess, that result in support for different cosmologies.

Despite its complicated relationship with theatres of torture, the myth of the feminist Witch does practical work. It is a story of shared terror and suffering, but it is also a story of hope. In the end, what makes a more emotionally satisfying story: (1) Those poor women died screaming and sobbing for nothing; or, (2) Those brave women died for an eternal truth that survived to be rediscovered and honoured by those who have come after them? It is hope that sets this narrative apart from 'just the facts' of empirical history.

CONCLUSION

Contemporary feminist identification with women persecuted as witches during the early modern period tacitly accepts stereotypes of women as emotional, but draws different conclusions from those that insist emotionality disqualifies women from public discourse. As Ahmed has noted, 'Feminists who speak out against established "truths" are often constructed as emotional, as failing the very standards of reason and impartiality that are assumed to form the basis of "good judgment"', even though historians prove repeatedly that all political discourse is rife with emotional judgments and appeals.[68] Feminist Witches use the persuasive power of stories of Burning Times martyrs to explain women's emotional discontent under patriarchal oppression and to alchemize these negative emotions into hope, which fuels action for social change.

After surveying my main textual and film sources, my head was full of torture and mourning, but my conversation with the focus group reminded me how important qualitative work is, especially in relation to textual analysis. All of the Witches in the circle are familiar with the authors I discuss here, appreciate them, and are inspired by them. All of them feel personally connected to Donna Read's films. In their conversations with me, however, they did not stress the horror stories, but rather solidarity. Together, they analysed the destructiveness of othering discourse as a way to separate communities and keep people from sticking up for one another. Ina said, 'Is this a pendulum thing? Are we always going to come back to oppressing the other? As Witches we have to believe that we are evolving beyond it, that we don't see people in terms of other.'[69]

Perhaps this emphasis on social change is unique to the Reclaiming-influenced community with which I work, but, even if this were the case, it is a good reminder that, just as feminist and Pagan communities are incredibly diverse, so are the attitudes towards and stories about women who were persecuted in the early modern period. There is no single version of 'feminist Witch', or even of 'The Burning Times'. It can be unsettling for historians and other academics to find our work evaluated on religious grounds by contemporary Witches, some like the ones who spoke with me, some very different. A little magic, 'the art of changing consciousness at will',[70] may transform such discomfort into wonder that, sometimes, strangers put as much of their hearts into our work as we do.

NOTES

1. For an overview, see Corrigan, 'Religion and Emotions'.
2. Broedel, *The Malleus Maleficarum and the Construction of Witchcraft*; Clark, *Thinking with Demons*.
3. A note on capitalization: when discussing historical victims of witch persecutions, I do not capitalize words such as 'witch' or 'pagan', because, from the perspective of accepted academic history, those accused of witchcraft did not identify themselves with those terms. In contrast, when discussing contemporary practitioners of Witchcraft as a religion and their perceptions of people in the past with whom they identify, I do capitalize such terms to acknowledge the legitimacy of Witchcraft and Paganism as religious communities.
4. Eller, *Living in the Lap of the Goddess*.
5. Hutton, *Triumph of the Moon*, 340–68.
6. Read, dir., *The Goddess Trilogy*. This collects *Goddess Remembered* (1989), *The Burning Times* (1990) and *Full Circle* (1993). Participants include, for example, Carol Christ, Merlin Stone and Luisah Teish.
7. Fieldwork conducted 2001–04, 2010; focus group conducted 7 June 2014; all in Toronto, Canada. I have deep gratitude for the Witches who have shared their time and worlds with me. While I am conscious that this analysis will not reflect their views in all the ways they might wish, it is the result of my sincere engagement with our conversations; my method is always motivated by respect and frequently by affection.
8. Ethnographies of contemporary communities that religiously identify with women persecuted as witches include Luhrmann, *Persuasions of the Witches' Craft*; Eller, *Living in the Lap of the Goddess*; Salomonsen, *Enchanted Feminism*; and Fedele, *Looking for Mary Magdalene*.
9. Pike, *Earthly Bodies, Magical Selves*; Pike, *New Age and Neopagan Religions in America*; Davy, *Introduction to Pagan Studies*; Salomonsen, *Enchanted Feminism*; and Magliocco, *Witching Culture*. On feminist identities, see Ahmed, *The Cultural Politics of Emotion*, 172–8.

10. Zwissler, 'Second Nature', 16–23; Zwissler, 'Spiritual, but Religious', 51–69.

11. On the Burning Times narrative appropriation of the Jewish Holocaust, see Purkiss, *Witch in History*, 15–18.

12. Michelet, *La Sorciere*; for discussion, see Hutton, *Triumph of the Moon*, 137–42; Leland, *Aradia*; Murray, *Witch-Cult*; Murray, *Divine King of England*.

13. E.g. Gardner, *Witchcraft Today*; Gardner, *Meaning of Witchcraft*; Valiente, *ABC of Witchcraft*.

14. See for example Ostling, *Between the Devil and the Host*, 192.

15. Finding 'Witch' in the body of the executed is reminiscent of finding the 'subaltern' in the body of 'the sati', as Gayatri Spivak famously does. As Ania Loomba critiques, 'Such a figure is in fact the most perfect instance of subaltern silence, since she is a conceptual and social category that comes into being only when the subject dies. The to-be-sati is merely a widow, the sati is by definition a silenced subject.' Spivak, 'Can the Subaltern Speak?' 271–313; Loomba, *Colonialism/Postcolonialism*, 196.

16. Starhawk, *Spiral Dance*, 20; Dworkin, *Woman Hating*, 141; Budapest, *Holy Book of Women's Mysteries*, 3.

17. *Burning Times*.

18. Peskowitz, 'Unweaving', 137–43; Klassen, 'Colonial Mythology of Feminist Witchcraft'.

19. Zwissler, 'Second Nature'.

20. Purkiss (*Witch in History*) notes that scholars seem especially eager to denounce Margaret Murray, as opposed to other scholars who offer equally unlikely interpretations of the witch-hunts, and suggests that at least some of the motivation for targeting her is unconscious sexism. Male scholars not taken so to task include, for example, Quaife, *Godly Zeal and Furious Rage*; and Harris, *Cows, Pigs and Witches*.

21. Clark, *Thinking with Demons*; Roper, *Witch in the Western Imagination*.

22. Bammer, *Excluded from Suffrage History*.

23. Gage, *Woman, Church and State*.

24. For an overview, see Eller, *Gentlemen and Amazons*, 122–32.

25. For historical context on sentimentalism and its relationship to the French Revolution, see Reddy, *Navigation of Feeling*; Scott, 'Sexularism'. For an overview of the connections between emotions and politics in modernity, see Eustace, 'Emotion and Political Change'.

26. Evans, *Personal Politics*.
27. Echols, *Daring to Be Bad*, 96–8, 116; Adler, *Drawing Down the Moon*, 179, 206–7; Rountree, *Embracing the Witch and the Goddess*, 33–5.
28. Dworkin, *Woman Hating*.
29. Eller, *Living in the Lap of the Goddess*, 174.
30. I refer to all participants by pseudonyms. Alana is a Reclaiming Witch who took Dianic training. She is home-schooling her children in order to prevent conservative indoctrination and to give them a more active appreciation of nature.
31. Lavender is a Reclaiming Witch engaged with her neighbourhood Unitarian Universalist church and a proud Raging Granny activist.
32. River is a long-time Reclaiming member and social justice activist. She helps organize regional Witchcamps.
33. See for example, the excellent discussion of historians' psychoanalysis of Kramer in Smith, 'The Flying Phallus and the Laughing Inquisitor', 85–117.
34. Murray, *Witch-Cult*; Murray, *God of the Witches*; Michelet, *Sorciere*; Summers, *History of Witchcraft and Demonology*; Summers, ed., introduction to his 1928 edition of the *Malleus maleficarum* [1487].
35. Purkiss, *Witch in History*, 63–4.
36. Bechdel, *Are You My Mother?*, 186.
37. For discussion of 'symbolic', 'mytho-poeic' history among esoteric groups in Britain, see Luhrmann, *Persuasions of the Witches' Craft*, 238–44.
38. Budapest, *Grandmother Moon*, 57.
39. Starhawk writes, 'Feminist consciousness raising is a process based on sound magical principles. If we speak to each other as equals, not about abstract theories but about concrete realities of our experience, we will see the common forces that have shaped our lives.' Starhawk, *Spiral Dance*, 28.
40. Wittig, *The Guérillères*, 95. Early goddess spirituality literature repeatedly references the quote in full, or just the last two lines. For example, see Daly, *Gyn/Ecology*, 47; Christ, 'Why Women Need the Goddess', 277; Goldenberg, 'Feminist Witchcraft', 213.
41. Purkiss *Witch in History*; Hutton *Triumph of the Moon*, 342–5. Margot Adler calls on fellow Pagans to abolish use of the nine mil-

lion number: 'it serves no end to perpetuate the miscalculation; it's time to put away the exaggerated numbers forever'. Adler, 'A Time for Truth'.

42. Gage, *Woman, Church and State*, 107. For background on the invention and cultural circulation of the number prior to Gage's publication, see Behringer, 'Neun Millionen Hexen', 664–85. According to his research, this figure first emerged in an anti-Catholic polemic.

43. Daly, *Gyn/Ecology*, 183; Daly, *Pure Lust*, 16.

44. Starhawk, *Spiral Dance*, 20; Dworkin, *Woman Hating*, 130; Budapest, *Holy Book of Women's Mysteries*, 239. Budapest earlier gives the number as 'eleven million women, men and children', xxiii.

45. Several authors toss in combinations of reasonable caveats: that incomplete records make the actual number impossible to know, that the lower estimates do not include those killed before the early modern period and leave out women who died in jail before they were officially sentenced. Daly, *Gyn/Ecology*, 183; Dworkin, *Woman Hating*, 129–30; Starhawk, *Spiral Dance*, 214, Starhawk, *Dreaming the Dark*, 187.

46. Starhawk and Hilary Valentine, *The Twelve Wild Swans*, 283.

47. *Burning Times*.

48. E.g. Dworkin, *Woman Hating*, 149; for analysis, see Purkiss, *Witch in History*.

49. Dworkin, *Woman Hating*; Daly, *Gyn/Ecology*, 78; Starhawk, *Spiral Dance*; Starhawk, *Dreaming the Dark*; Budapest, *Holy Book of Women's Mysteries*.

50. For example, Budapest writes of how easy it was for her to recover ancient women's rituals from cultures that use a lunar calendar, such as those in the Middle East and Asia: 'All I had to do was push aside the patriarchal camouflage and find the gentle moon behind it all.' Budapest, *Grandmother Moon*, xiii.

51. Purkiss, *Witch in History*, 30–58; Luhrmann, *Persuasions of the Witches' Craft*, 239–44.

52. Fedele, *Looking for Mary Magdalene*; Eller, *Living in the Lap of the Goddess*. For an analysis of this practice in a community largely different from Witches, see Bender, *New Metaphysicals*.

53. Lyndal Roper astutely demonstrates this process: Roper, *Oedipus and the Devil*; Roper, *Witchcraze*. For a primary-source reflection

on this process, see the letter of Johannes Junius, burgomaster caught up in the Bamberg trials, to his daughter, Veronica, collected in Kors and Peters, eds, *Witchcraft in Europe 400–1700*, 348–53.

54. For example, see Larner, *Witchcraft and Religion*; Brauner, *Fearless Wives and Frightened Shrews*; Clark, *Thinking with Demons*. In contrast, see E.J. Kent's chapter, this volume.
55. Jackson, 'Witches, Wives and Mothers', 63–83.
56. Reis, *Damned Women*.
57. E.g. that the Black Goat of the satanic sabbat was a perversion of the Horned God of the Pagans or that the promiscuous orgies were misunderstandings of the Great Rite.
58. *Burning Times*. Chris Bishop conclusively demonstrates that most of these objects are nineteenth-century 'reconstructions' based on fantasy alone. Chris Bishop, 'The "Pear of Anguish"', 591–602.
59. Magliocco, 'Pagan Fundamentalism', accessed 21 Sept. 2015. See also Hutton, 'Paganism and Polemic', 103–17; Hutton, 'Writing the History of Witchcraft', 239–62.
60. Adler, 'A Time for Truth'.
61. Vowell, 'God Will Give You Blood to Drink', 41.
62. Charlie is well into retirement and pursuing his PhD. Witnessing his father's physical abuse of his mother and feeling that Christianity condoned it drove him from Catholicism as a child. He is a priest in Alexandrian Wicca.
63. Daly, *Gyn/Ecology*; Starhawk, *Dreaming the Dark*, xxv–xxvi; Budapest, *Holy Book of Women's Mysteries*, xxvi.
64. Reddy, *Navigation of Feeling*, 129.
65. Starhawk, *Truth or Dare*, 3.
66. Reddy, *Navigation of Feeling*, 128.
67. Purkiss, *Witch in History*, 15.
68. Ahmed, *The Cultural Politics of Emotion*, 170; Eustace, 'Emotion and Political Change'; Reddy *Navigation of Feeling*; Scott 'Sexulality'.
69. Ina is a long-time participant in theatre and interested in feminist labour issues. Her Witchcraft includes political activism and during the discussion, she, Lavender, Alana and River talked about actions they had done that were inspired by stereotypes of witches' spells.
70. Starhawk quoting ritual magician Diane Fortune: *Spiral Dance*, 28.

CHAPTER 15

Afterword: Passions in Perspective

Malcolm Gaskill

'Allegory of Discord' is an engraving from 1670 by the German artist Melchior Küsel (Fig. 15.1). For Küsel to personify negative emotions— envy, spite, rage—with a stereotypical witch was perhaps an obvious choice. After all, these were the emotions associated with witches. Though not specifically identified as a witch, the figure commanding the scene is a post-menopausal woman, her face is lined by age, her breasts withered. Whether flying to the sabbat or cooking up spells, this is how Küsel's artistic contemporaries imagined witches: as rebels against society and nature whose life fluids of menstrual blood and milk life had dried up, and who now destroyed what others had. Here she breaches the peace of the community by provoking men and women to fight, feeding the flames of violent anger with her bellows. Even the Olympian gods, depicted in celestial repose, will be set at odds by this wrecker of charity and harmony. Two decades earlier, the dramatist Ben Jonson had used the same character in a masque, 'a malicious fury' who arrives on stage in a storm and 'by the invocation of malignant spirits ... put most of the world into discord'.[1]

M. Gaskill
University of East Anglia

© The Author(s) 2016
L. Kounine, M. Ostling (Eds.), *Emotions in the History of Witchcraft*, DOI 10.1057/978-1-137-52903-9_15

Fig. 15.1 Melchior Küsel, *Allegory of Discord*, 1670, etching, Harvard Art Museums/Fogg Museum, Anonymous fund for the acquisition of prints older than 150 years, S11.136.1 (Photo: Imaging Department © President and Fellows of Harvard College)

We should remember, however, that these metaphysical creations had analogues in real life. In the year that Jonson's masque was performed, 1646, a hundred miles away at Upwell in Norfolk, a village that knew nothing of allegories, ordinary people were dealing with their own flesh-and-blood manifestation of discord. Her name was Ellen Garrison. Robert Parsons, a butcher, sold her a pig on condition that his wife agreed. But Katherine

Parsons demurred, and when Garrison came to collect there was a row. She 'clapte her hand uppon the table & swoare twice or thrice that she would make her glad to lett her have the pigg', and departed. An hour or so later, Katherine was 'extremely tormented all over as if some were pulling her into peeces', and fearing for her life gave Garrison the pig. But things did not improve. Within a month the Parsons' children, one aged seven, the other six months, were dead. Katherine Parsons, beside herself with grief and fury, went to a magistrate, fearlessly swearing on oath that Ellen Garrison, a woman long suspected of witchcraft, had murdered her children. Neighbours rallied round, the men to watch the suspect to see if she was visited by demonic familiars, the women to search her body for the places where those familiars fed.[2]

The essays in this collection, like the story of Ellen Garrison, demonstrate that the witch, as well as being a scapegoat for society, a spiritual enemy of religion, and a political symbol of rebellion, was a tangible projection of intangible emotions. Like Küsel's hag, the 'real' witches identified by early modern people represented negative feelings that everyone recognized. Suspects were, to quote one historian, 'tangled up in their neighbours' darkest emotions'.[3] Unlike Küsel's hag, however, witches were identified less by appearance than by behaviour. Suspected witches really did unleash hostility upon their neighbours, which in turn both reflected and bred more hostility.[4] Nor was this just a matter of communities at war. The accusation of Ellen Garrison happened during the English Civil War, a traumatic schism. If the body politic was the macrocosm of discord, the witch's body was its corrupted microcosm. Tributaries of emotion in England's parishes fed rivers of high political passion.[5]

One might imagine a kind of emotional economy, local and national, where feelings were both capital to be stored and currency to be spent. Here witchcraft offers valuable insights because it exemplifies a range of emotional transactions as people moved in and out of uneasy proximity with one another. Magic and emotion went together, provoking and resolving disputes, complicating and rationalizing relationships, making something solid and actionable from unspoken unease. To detect bewitchment usually presented an opportunity for redress. Robin Briggs describes how the victim's anger needed to subside if the witch was to be induced to reverse her spell.[6] Conflicting with such strategies was the state's wish that people should use the law rather than fighting illegal magic with illegal magic. As Richard Bovet wrote in 1684, folk 'often become Witches, by endeavouring to defend themselves against Witchcraft'.[7] But the law was slow and dispassionate, and people were swept up by an urgent need to resist witches on their own magical and emotional plane.

To have substance, emotions must have either occupied a visible space or been expressed verbally or physically; abstract emotions, disconnected from human activity, have little historical meaning. In different ways, all the contributors demonstrate this. The body is important: emotions are embodied. Imbalance in the four humours of Galenic medicine caused melancholy and a predisposition to witchcraft, or at least delusions about the world of the witches. Charles Zika suggests that Jacques de Gheyn's phantasmagoria of the sabbat, and similar artworks, were expressions of scepticism rather than credulity. We see not what the artist believed but what the deluded witch, and perhaps also her accusers and interrogators, believed.[8] Humours needed to flow, but in witches they had stopped. One sign was the witch's alleged inability to shed tears, which as Zika indicates was caused by an impeded flow of liquid—or 'fluxes'—in the distempered body.[9]

The body was both a capsule and a crucible for emotions, a transmitter and receiver, and an arena for the struggle between good and evil. And where should spiritual battles be fought except in hearts and minds? Tamar Herzig argues that the infamous *Malleus maleficarum* 'construed the female heresy of witchcraft as an inherently physical, as opposed to doctrinal, heresy'.[10] Women's struggle to control their passions, it was believed, made them vulnerable to diabolic temptation. Here, then, we see the body, emotions, and witchcraft neatly connected. Charles Zika and Rita Voltmer both describe how suspects' bodies were thought to betray guilt through a malevolent gaze or inability to shed tears.[11] But it was the tortured body where investigations were most thorough and the results most significant: pain, jurists reasoned, would raise the confession from deep within, whereas spotless Christians had nothing to hide, nor would they confess falsely as God would give them strength to remain silent. The body was, of course, just a wrapper for the immortal soul. 'Like a fearless martyr', writes Voltmer, 'an innocent person fought not for bodily intactness, but for his or her soul's purity'.[12] Flesh, unstable and unreliable, was both a barometer of truth and a barrier to uncovering it.

The witch's body was also an arsenal of emotion and emotional expression. Her words, for instance, were deeds. Well chosen, with the right tone, volume, and accompanying gesture, language focused the witch's anger upon individual enemies, refining a general emotion into a specific threat—not merely describing but doing. Emotions, then, were weapons.

Valerie Kivelson explains how in Russia emotions were the engines driving magical spells and curses. She also notes that William Reddy's concept of the 'emotive'—an expression of emotion that effects change—had long been familiar to witchcraft historians, who see feelings not as 'interior dispositions but rather agents, powers that reach out an act in the exterior world'.[13] However sociologically structural and anthropologically functionalist Alan Macfarlane's study of English witchcraft accusations is, it relies on two clusters of emotion: hope followed by disappointment and resentment in beggars, and the guilt and fear of those who refused beggars alms and then suspected them of magical vengeance.[14]

Some witches were accused of making maleficent charms, the most iconic being the pin-studded wax effigy. What turned these objects into magical missiles were the negative emotions with which their creators imbued them. An awareness in the intended victim that these weapons had been unleashed could have profound psychological and somatic consequences, explained by what Edward Bever calls 'the neurobiology of emotional aggression'.[15] Extreme fear can cause adverse chemical changes in the body, not unlike a humoral disequilibrium. Witchcraft really did harm people, argues Bever, through 'a combination of overt or subliminal communication of hostility and psychophysical influences on disease'— or, as Valerie Kivelson puts it, 'emotions can be deadly'.[16] Such deadly emotions sometimes took the form of diabolic familiar—demons in animal form usually understood just as intermediaries between Satan and the witch. But as Charlotte-Rose Millar shows, familiars were also physical extensions of the furious yet impotent self. They were vectors of emotion, animated in the mind of the witch as hatred directed at an adversary, and received as fear and horror.[17] Richard Denton, a blacksmith at Upwell, watched Ellen Garrison in 1646. He was shocked by what he saw. To appreciate the emotion present that night, one should imagine an intimate room where Garrison sits before her captors, dimly lit by hearth, rushlight, or candle. Her body had already been searched, so the watchers knew the devil's imps must be nearby. Suddenly, Denton recalled, 'he sawe a thing in [the] likenesse of a Beetle Runneing in the roome (where they watcht) Rownde aboute the Chayer where shee satt and under her ffeete, and imediately after it went much faster then ever he sawe any thinge before'.[18]

The clear link between emotions and witchcraft, and the way that witches embodied emotions, leads us to gender. Witchcraft was a weapon of the weak, and women the weaker vessel. Not all participants in an accusation made as explicit a connection between female passions and diabolism as that in the *Malleus maleficarum*, but similar prejudices were engrained in men and women alike. If the ideal woman was gentle, nurturing and sub-missive, then the witch was her anti-type. According to Charles Zika, de Gheyn's drawing *Three Witches in an Archway* may have been intended to invert the tenderness of the *Pièta*, 'figuring these tearless women who give vent to their merciless savagery by violating and mutilating Christian bod-ies rather than feeling compassion for them'.[19] At the same time, as Laura Kounine makes clear, witchcraft was not governed by fixed gender rules. Nor were the emotions linked to witchcraft limited to lust and envy, with their feminine associations.[20] Men, too, made sense as witches. However recognizable the image of Melchior Küsel's hag, accusers were not bound by stereotypes.[21] It is debatable whether male witches were feminized by the label 'witch', but they definitely offended some social ideal, even at a subliminal level.[22] E.J. Kent notes the similarity between male witches and tyrants: both had chaotic, transgressive constitutions shaped by emotion not reason. 'The tyrant is a man who has failed to govern his body', writes Kent, 'and has descended into a monstrous state of masculine tyranny.'[23] The paths of different political anxieties about husbands and wives, sub-jects and monarchs, governors and governed, converged in patriarchy.

As historical categories, both gender and emotion should be seen in terms of action and setting. The household is a good place to begin. By focusing on emotion, these essays encourage us to think of witchcraft sus-picions in terms of domestic intimacy, not as paranoia about the menac-ing scapegoat on the edge of the community. Peter Geschiere describes the intense emotions of people packed together with limited means of escape: 'the dark side of kinship'.[24] To sense hostility here might be to fear for one's life, triggering an emotional counter-attack. At the same time, people need to draw close to others in order to share a sense of mutual self-confidence. Valerie Kivelson illustrates this with the example of love in Russia. Love requires trust, trust makes one vulnerable, so love creates danger.[25]

From the gendered, emotional body to the intimacy of the household leads us to communities, whose core values can be expressed in emotional terms—Sarah Ferber refers to a 'politics of emotion'.[26] Like households, these were meant to be secure enclosures of charity and cooperation; too often, however, they were not. Peter Geschiere shows how witch-craft 'seems to be about the terrible realization that precisely the inner sphere, where solidarity and trust should reign, is a hotbed of jealousy and aggression'.[27] Witchcraft is an excellent way of seeing Barbara Rosenwein's 'emotional communities' in action.[28] If an accusation went to law, the passions of the community were replayed in the courtroom. Legal hearings reified the witch, focusing blurred images in a forum sanctified by sacred and secular ideology. We might share Rita Voltmer's opinion of courtrooms as emotional communities in their own right, with their own standards and codes of expression.[29]

These essays also encourage us to reflect on the history of emotions more generally: Reddy's 'emotives' and 'emotional regimes', Rosenwein's 'emotional communities', and the 'emotionology' of Peter and Carol Stearns.[30] Witchcraft also illustrates tensions between emotional essentialism—the idea that emotions are universal—and social constructionism, which holds that the meaning of emotions consists in the cultural forms of their manifestation.[31] Edward Bever argues that fear and anxiety were basic emotions linked to stress, and that stress caused illness—the sort of illness attributed to witchcraft. The modern mind grasps this easily, whereas it fails to understand the belief that witches derived power from Satan. Sarah Ferber endorses the idea of 'emotionology', highlighting the ways in which 'agencies and institutions ... have established the means to understand emotions and behaviours related to magic, witchcraft and demonology', associating the latter with 'mental illness and extreme emotion'.[32] Even basic emotions need to be situated in official, administrative, legal, and institutional contexts.

Historians of emotions depend upon workable methodologies. Related to the essentialist–constructionist divide is the way that historians differ about whether we can really extract emotions. Charlotte-Rose Millar suggests that witchcraft pamphlets do not contain 'historical truth' but only evidence of what early modern people believed.[33] Legal records may be even more problematic. Rita Voltmer argues that the archives contain only *representations* of emotions, and that scribes and inquisitors 'reinterpreted de facto expressed feelings', leaving only stereotypical images and distorted echoes.[34] Emotions were standardized because 'they were meant to stabilize a legal, and thus a political and religious truth'.[35] Historians need to decode evidence of emotions, but even then may only get so far. Michael Ostling is more optimistic, proposing that we can recover more than just 'emotional representations' but authentic emotions, especially if we look beyond envy, wrath and fear, where 'occasional genuine glimpses of the gentler emotions', such as loyalty and affection, lie.[36]

Legal archives are uniquely valuable for the history of emotions. For all their problems of distortion and unrepresentativeness, records of crime cut through a layer of public conduct into private lives beneath, before finally reaching a mental and emotional core. Here the implicit and concealed become the explicit and revealed. Perhaps because of its heinousness and the scarcity of proofs, witchcraft trials, more than most criminal proceedings, exposed early modern beliefs, ideas, assumptions, suspicions, and prejudices. Deep emotions, often relating to dreams and fantasies, surfaced from the subconscious and were recorded as proofs. Like Rita Voltmer, Michael Ostling cautions against treating the confessions of tortured women as pure products of their inner lives, yet adds, 'the only thing worse than misconstruing the voices of accused witches would be to ignore them in light of the methodological problems they raise'.[37] This echoes the methodology of Lyndal Roper's work, which pays careful attention to women's words and the deep psychic currents of anxiety and desire they reveal.[38]

The memory of the 'witch-craze' owes much to the idea that delusion and zeal were to blame. As Laurel Zwissler relates, the 'Burning Times' equip feminist and Pagan commentators with 'an intimate martyrology which both explains emotional dissatisfaction with present conditions and motivates political action for future change'.[39] Witches are thus co-opted to serve the present, with scant regard for understanding them in the past. But if we set aside an apparent absence of reason, it remains the case that witchcraft accusations also stemmed from familiar emotions erupting in a harsh social and economic environment. The challenge lies in imagining how we might feel to live that life, and in using empathy historically. We risk anachronism if we get inner lives wrong—even a kind of ventriloquism, as we substitute our subjects' thoughts for our own.

I have five recommendations. First, we need to historicize emotions, beginning by assuming change over time. We shouldn't be too quick to identify with universal emotions, but neither should we succumb to what Sarah Ferber calls the 'persistent tendency ... to presume emotions to do with belief in demons are atavistic'.[40] As Stuart Clark has shown, in its own time demonology was logical and progressive, like inquisitorial procedure, which by eliminating superstitious ordeals, girded faith in human ability to determine truth.[41] Second, we need to think about subjectivity and what it says about interior states.[42] It is vital to understand witchcraft as witchcraft, and to listen to voices in texts. As Peter Geschiere suggests, we must 'take people's experiences as seriously as possible and not ignore them as rationalizations of some sort of "real" issue'.[43] We don't have to endorse supernatural beliefs and interpretations, only respect them; otherwise we limit our chances of discovering what was going on. Recent research into the embodiment of emotion as seen in the cultural embeddedness of dreams illustrates this well.[44]

My third and fourth recommendations are practical. Historians of emotions need to build on empirical foundations. They should be cautious yet optimistic, and use evidence creatively to the limits of its usefulness, inspired by interdisciplinary interpretative models. They might also consider documents in appropriate contexts of space and time. Apparently isolated accusations invariably belonged to complex webs of hostility and suspicion, affinity and alliance. Detailed case studies of German trials prove the point.[45] The significance of laconic English depositions can be enhanced by contextual research. Cases from the Court of Star Chamber involving witchcraft already describe much of this context, revealing that friction over witchcraft was just one strand in a whole web of local tensions spun over many years.[46]

My final recommendation also relates to context. We need to seal in meaning, easily lost if we strip out events for analysis. As Rita Voltmer insists, many trial records were 'carefully fabricated stories which must be interpreted within the legal framework of their original setting'.[47] Beyond the legal, we need to consider as many spheres of existence as possible, and peg emotions at an appropriate level. Cultural historians risk raising to a self-consciousness that which in its own time was unconscious or unexamined. No one deliberately deployed emotions as weapons—that is, by a choice they might have explained to themselves or others. What makes for good historical analysis does not necessarily describe past experience authentically. Nor should we assume that early modern people had a singularly coherent sense of 'the self', but rather a multifaced interiority that varied and shifted with their relationships to environment, from household to community to cosmos.[48]

Early modern people carried secret feelings to the grave; but from another perspective historians, with their commanding view of the past, know things they did not. Emotions were part of cognition, but they ran ahead of thinking, bypassing self-conscious reflection, impelling people in extremis to act decisively. The way that rage and terror over-rode natural inhibitions about going to law against witches is a case in point, well illustrated by the denunciation of Ellen Garrison in 1646.[49] A contemporary description of anger helps us to imagine how Katherine Parsons may have felt and appeared: 'a vehement heat of the minde, which brings palenesse to the countenance, burning to the eyes, and trembling to parts of the body'.[50] At one level, this transmutation was a loss of control, an infraction of Peter and Carol Stearns's 'emotional standards'; at another, however, the social utility of emotions is more apparent. Bold, furious interventions by people like Katherine Parsons were socially risky yet potentially profitable, achieving exactly the kind of change in circumstances that human evolution had intended for unbridled passions.

NOTES

1. Petherbridge, *Witches and Wicked Bodies*, 27.
2. Cambridge University Library (CUL), EDR E44/3; E12 1647/1–2. See also Gaskill, *Witchfinders*, 231–2.
3. Wilby, *Cunning Folk and Familiar Spirits*, 45.
4. This idea runs through Briggs, *Witches and Neighbours*.
5. Elmer, *Witchcraft, Witch-Hunting and Politics*, esp. ch. 3; Stoyle, *Black Legend of Prince Rupert's Dog*.
6. Briggs, this volume.
7. Bovet, *Pandaemonium* [1684], 87.
8. Zika, this volume. For more on this, see Zika, *Appearance of Witchcraft*.
9. Rublack, 'Fluxes', 1–16.
10. Herzig, this volume, 22.
11. Zika, this volume; Voltmer, this volume.
12. Voltmer, this volume, 100. See in addition Silverman, *Tortured Subjects*.
13. Kivelson, this volume, 132. On 'emotives' see Reddy, *Navigation of Feeling*; Scheer, 'Are Emotions a Kind of Practice?' 193–220.
14. Macfarlane, *Witchcraft in Tudor and Stuart England*.
15. See Bever's chapter, this volume.
16. Bever, this volume, 194; Kivelson, this volume, 132.
17. Millar, this volume.
18. CUL, EDR E12 1647/2.
19. Zika, this volume, 53.
20. Kounine, this volume.
21. Scribner, 'Is a History of Popular Culture Possible?' 183–4; Rowlands, 'Witchcraft and Old Women', 50–89.
22. For some contrasting interpretations, see: Kent, *Cases of Male Witchcraft in Old and New England*; Apps and Gow, *Male Witches in Early Modern Europe*; Schulte, *Man as Witch*.

23. Kent, this volume, 215.
24. Geschiere, this volume, 215.
25. Kivelson, this volume.
26. Ferber, this volume, 233.
27. Geschiere, this volume, 215.
28. Rosenwein, *Emotional Communities*. See also Gaskill, 'Little Commonwealths II' (forthcoming).
29. Voltmer, this volume.
30. Stearns and Stearns, 'Emotionology', 813–36. See also Plamper, *History of Emotions*; Rosenwein, *Generations of Feeling*.
31. Historians tend to be social-constructionists. See Harré, 'An Outline of the Social Constructionist Viewpoint', 2–14; Gergen, 'History and Psychology', 15–29; Shweder and Haidt, 'Cultural Psychology of the Emotions', 397–414.
32. Ferber, this volume, 241.
33. Millar, this volume, 175.
34. Voltmer, this volume, 107.
35. Ibid., 98.
36. Ostling, this volume, 159.
37. Ibid., 165.
38. Roper, *Witch-Craze*.
39. Zwissler, this volume, 250.
40. Ferber, this volume, 236.
41. Clark, *Thinking with Demons*; Langbein, *Prosecuting Crime in the Renaissance*.
42. Rublack, 'Interior States and Sexuality'.
43. Geschiere, this volume, 226.
44. Plane, *Dreams and the Invisible World*.
45. Notable examples include Robisheaux, *Last Witch of Langenburg*; Rublack, *The Astronomer and the Witch*.
46. Ewen, *Witchcraft in the Star Chamber*.
47. Voltmer, this volume, 103.
48. Davis, 'Boundaries and the Sense of Self'. See also Kounine, *Imagining the Witch* (forthcoming), esp. ch. 3.
49. The high acquittal rate was a deterrent to going to law, so Parsons may have needed emotion to take appropriate action. Even then, one indictment was rejected on a technicality and the jury acquitted Garrison on the other: Gaskill, *Witchfinders*, 235–6.
50. Smith, *The Mysterie of Rhetorique Unvail'd* [1657], 168.

BIBLIOGRAPHY

ARCHIVAL SOURCES

Archivio Generale dell'Ordine dei Predicatori, Rome.
Archivio Storico Diocesano, Ferrara.
Archiwum Państwowe w Lublinie (APL).
Cambridge University Library (CUL).
Departmental Archives Meurthe-et-Moselle, Nancy.
Hauptstaatsarchiv Stuttgart.
Landeshauptarchiv Koblenz.
Rossiiskii Gosudarstvennyi Arkhiv Drevnikh Aktov (RGADA), Moscow.
Stadtbibliothek Trier.

WORKS ORIGINALLY PUBLISHED BEFORE 1800

Anon. 1566. *The Examination of John Walsh*. London: Printed by John Awdely.
Anon. 1589. *The Apprehension and Confession of Three Notorious Witches. Arreigned and by Justice Condemned and Executed at Chelmes-forde, in the Countye of Essex* [etc.]. London: E. Allde.
Anon. 1612a. *The Life and Death of Lewis Gaufredy*. London: n.pub.
Anon. 1612b. *The Witches of Northampton-shire. Agnes Browne. Joane Vaughan. Arthur Bill. Hellen Jenkenson. Mary Barber. Witches* [etc.]. London: Printed by Tho: Parfoot, for Arthur Johnson.

© The Author(s) 2016
L. Kounine, M. Ostling (eds.), *Emotions in the History of Witchcraft*, DOI 10.1057/978-1-137-52903-9

Anon. 1619. *The Wonderful Discoverie of the Witchcrafts of Margaret and Phillip Flower, Daughters of Joan Flower neere Bever Castle* [etc.]. London: Printed by G. Eld for I. Barnes.

Anon. 1628. *A Briefe Description of the Notorious Life of John Lambe.* London: n. pub.

Anon. 1635. *Witchcrafts Strange and Wonderfull: Discovering the Damnable Practices of Seven Witches, Against the Lives of Certaine Noble Personages, and Others of this Kingdome* [etc.]. London: Printed by M.F. for Thomas Lambert.

Anon. 1642. *A Magazine of Scandall, or, A Heape of Wickednesse of Two Infamous Ministers, Consorts, One Named Thomas Fowkes of Earle Soham in Suffolk* [etc.]. London: Printed for R.H.

Anon. 1643. *A Most Certain, Strange and True Discovery of a Witch. Being Taken by Some Parliament Forces, as She Was Standing on a Small Planck Board and Sayling on It Over the River of Newbury* [etc.]. N.p.: Printed by John Hammond.

Anon. 1645. *Signes and Wonders from Heaven. With a True Relation of a Monster Borne in Ratcliffe Highway, at the Signe of the Three Arrows, Mistris Bullock the Midwife Delivering Here Thereof* [etc.]. London: Printed by I. H.

Anon. 1652. *The Tryall and Examination of Mrs Joan Peterson.* London: Printed for G. Horton.

Anon. 1662. *The Power of Witchcraft, Being a Most Strange but True Relation of the Most Miraculous and Wonderful Deliverance of One Mr. William Harrison, of Cambden in the County of Glocester, Steward to the Lady Nowel* [etc.]. London: Printed for Charls Tyns.

Anon. 1681. *Strange and Wonderful News from Yowel in Surry; Giving a True and Just Account of One Elizabeth Burgiss, Who Was Most Strangely Bewitched and Tortured at a Sad Rate.* London: Printed for F. Clarke, Seignior.

Anon. 1682a. *A True and Impartial Relation of the Informations Against Three Witches, viz., Temperance Lloyd, Mary Trembles, and Susanna Edwards* [etc.]. London: Printed by Freeman Collins.

Anon. 1682b. *The Tryal, Condemnation, and Execution of Three Witches viz. Temperance Floyd, Mary Floyd, and Susanna Edwards.* London: Printed for J. Deacon.

Anon. 1682c. *Witchcraft Discovered and Punished/or, the Tryals and Condemnation of Three Notorious Witches, Who were Tried/the Last Assizes, Holden at the Castle of Exeter, in the County of Devon.* N.p.: n.pub.

Anon. 1687. *The Life and Conversation of Temperance Floyd, Mary Lloyd, and Susanna Edwards Three Eminent Witches, Lately Condemed at Exeter Assizes.* London: Printed by J.W.

Anon. 1689. *Great News from the West of England. Being a True Account of Two Young Persons Lately Betwitch'd in the Town of Beckenton in Somerset-shire* [etc.]. London: Printed by T.M.

Anon. 1714 [1639]. *Czarownica powołana, abo krotka nauka y prestroga z strony czarownic* Gdańsk: Jan Daniel Stoll.

Aubrey, John. 1784 [1696]. *Miscellanies Upon Various Subjects*. London: W. Ottridge.

Berry, L.E. 2007. *Geneva Bible: A Facsimile of the 1560 Edition*. Peabody: Hendrickson Bibles.

Binsfeld, Peter. 1590. *Tractat Von Bekantnuß der Zauberer und Hexen: Ob vnd wie viel denselben zu glauben*. Trier: Bock.

Binsfeld, Peter. 2004. *Tractat von Bekanntnuß der Zauberer und Hexen*, ed. Hiram Kümper. Wien: Mille Tre Verlag.

Bodin, Jean. 1581. *De Magorum Daemonomania: Vom außgelassnen Wütigen Teuffels-Heer allerhand Zaubereyen Hexen...* Trans. Johann Fischart. Straßburg: Bernhart Jobin.

Bodin, Jean. 1995. *On the Demon-Mania of Witches*. Trans. Randy A. Scott and Ed. Jonathan L. Pearl. Toronto: Centre for Reformation and Renaissance Studies.

Bovet, Richard. 1684. *Pandaemonium, or the Devil's Cloyster*. London: J. Walthoe.

Camerarius, Joachim. 1605. De ecclesiis fratrum in Bohemia et Moravia narratio historica. In *Historica narratio de fratrum orthodoxorum ecclesiis in Bohemia, Moravia et Polonia*, ed. Ludwig Camerarius. Heidelberg: Typis Voegelinianis.

Carmichael, J. 1591. *Newes from Scotland*. London: n.pub.

Cotta, John. 1616. *The Triall of Witch-Craft, Shewing the True and Right methode of the Discovery with a Confutation of Erroneuous Wayes*. London: George Parslowe.

D.J. 1698. *King Charles I. No Such Saint, Martyr or Good Protestant*. London: n.pub.

de Hollanda, Francisco. 1998. *Diálogos em Roman (1538): Conversations on Art with Michelangelo Buonarroti*, ed. G.D. Folliereo-Metz and W. Drost. Heidelberg: Winter.

Dekker, Thomas, John Ford, and William Rowley. 1658 [1621]. *The Witch of Edmonton*.

del Rio, Martin. 1600. *Disquisitionum magicarum: libri sex*. Louvain: Gerardus Rivius.

del Rio, Martin. 2000. *Martin del Rio: Investigations into Magic*. Trans. and Ed. P.G. Maxwell-Stuart. Manchester: Manchester University Press.

Goodcole, Henry. 1621. *The Wonderfull Discoverie of Elizabeth Sawyer a Witch, Late of Edmonton*. London: William Butler.

Grillando, Paolo. 1536. *Tractatus de hereticis et sortilegiis, omnifariam coitu... eorumque poenis*. Lyons.

Guazzo, Francesco Maria. 1988 (1626). *Compendium Maleficarum*. Trans. E. Ashwin, 2nd ed. New York: Dover.

Institoris, Henricus. 1482. *Epistola contra quendam conciliistam archiepiscopem videlicet Crainensem et adversus citationem et libellum infamie ipsius quem contra sanctissimum dominum nostrum dominum Sixtum papam IIII modernum summum pontificem edidit*. N.p. [Strasbourg].

Institoris, Henricus. 1486. *Malleus maleficarum.* Speyer: Peter Drach.

Institoris, Henricus. n.d. [1493]. *Tractatus novus de miraculoso eucharistie sacramento.* N.p [Augsburg].

Institoris, Henricus. 1496. *Tractatus varii cum sermonibus plurimis contra quattuor errores novissime exortos adversus divinissimum eucharistie sacramentum.* Nuremberg: Anton Koberger.

Institoris, Henricus. 1499. *Opusculum in errores Monarchie.* Venice: Jacobus de Leucho.

Institoris, Henricus. 1501a. *Sancte Romane ecclesie fidei defensionis clippeum adversus Waldensium seu Pickardorum heresim.* Olomouc: Konrad Baumgarten.

Institoris, Henricus (ed.). 1501b. *Stigmifere virginis Lucie de Narnia aliarumque spiritualium personarum feminei sexus facta admiracione digna.* Olomouc: Konrad Baumgarten.

Institoris, Henricus. 1928. [Heinrich Kramer and James Sprenger]. *Malleus maleficarum.* Ed. and Trans. Montague Summers. London: Rodker.

Institoris, Henricus. 2006. *Malleus maleficarum.* Ed. and Trans. Christopher S. Mackay, 2 vols. Cambridge: Cambridge University Press.

Institoris, Henricus. 2009. *The Hammer of Witches: A Complete Translation of the Malleus maleficarum.* Trans. and Ed. Christopher Mackay. Cambridge: Cambridge University Press.

James VI and I. 1597. *Daemonologie, In Forme of a Dialogue, Divided into Three Books.* Edinburgh.

Kałowski, Marcin. 1723. *Informacya o początkach y dalszym progressie Cudownego Mieysca Łagiewnickiego.* Kalisz: Drukarnia kolegium księży Jezuitów.

Kramer, Heinrich. See Institoris, Henricus.

Lancre, Pierre de. 1613. *Tableau de l'inconstance des mauvais anges et demons,* 2nd ed. Paris.

Marchocka, Anna Maria (Mother Teresa). 1939. *Autobiografia mistyczna m. Teresa od Jezusa karmelitanki bosej (Anny Marii Marchockiej) 1603–1652.* Poznań: Księgarnia Uniwersytecka Jana Jachowskiego.

Marlowe, Christopher. 1990. The Tragicall Historie of Dr. Faustus. In *The Complete Works of Christopher Marlowe,* ed. by Roma Gill, 5 vols. Oxford: Clarendon Press.

Mather, Cotton. 1693. *Wonders of the Invisible World: Being an Account of the Tryals of Several Witches Lately Executed in New-England.* Boston: n.pub.

Misoda, B. 1649. *The Divels Delusions or A Faithfull Relation of John Palmer and Elizabeth Knott Two Notorious Witches Lately Condemned at the Sessions of Oyer and Terminer in St. Albans* [etc.]. London: Printed for Richard Williams.

Moravus, Augustinus. 1500. *Tractatus de secta waldensium.* Olomouc: Konrad Baumgarten.

Nider, Johannes. 1475. *Formicarius.* N.p., n.d. [Cologne: Ulrich Zell].

Numagen, Peter. 1657. *Tertia editio invectiva responsalis sub nomine archiepiscopi Craynensis per Petrum Trevirensem contra Henricum Institoris formata.* In Johannes Heinrich Hottinger, *Historiae Ecclesiasticae Novi Testamenti seculum XV*, vol. 4. Zürich: Johannes Henrich Hambergeri.

Phillips, John. 1566. *The Examination and Confession of certaine Wytches at Chelmsford in the countie of Essex.* London: Willyam Powell for Willyam Pickeringe.

Rémy, Nicolas. 1598. *Daemonolatria: Das ist Von Vnholden und Zauber Geistern.* Frankfurt: Palthenius.

Rémy, Nicolas.1930. *Demonolatry.* Ed. Montague Summers, Trans. E.A. Ashwin. London: John Rodker (repr. Mineola, 2008).

Scot, Reginald. 1584. *The Discoverie of Witchcraft.* London: William Brome.

Scot, Reginald. 1609. *Ondecking van Toverij.* Trans. Thomas Basson. Leiden: Thomas Basson.

Smith, John. 1657. *The Mysterie of Rhetorique Unvail'd.* London: George Eversden.

Starowolski, Szymon. 1682 [1645]. *Świątnica Pańska zawierająca w sobie kazania na czterdzieści świąt całego roku.* Kraków: Krzystof Schedel.

Swizralus, Januarius [pseud.]. 1843 [1614]. Peregrinacya dziadowska. In *Pomniki do historii obyczajów w Polsce z XVI i XVII wieku*, ed. J.I. Kraszewski. Warszawa: S. Orgelbrand.

Szymonowic, Szymon. 1964 [1614]. *Sielanki i pozostałe wierze polskie Szymona Szymonowica*, ed. Janusz Pelc. Wrocław: Zakład Narodowy im. Ossolińskich.

W.W. 1582. *A True and Just recorde, of the Information, Examination and Confession of All the Witches, Taken at S. Oses in the countie of Essex* [etc.]. London: Thomas Dawson.

Weyer, Johann. 1991 [1583]. *Witches, Devils, and Doctors in the Renaissance.* Ed. George Mora and Trans. John Weber. Binghamton: Medieval & Renaissance Texts & Studies.

Weyer, Johann. 1998 [1583]. *On Witchcraft: An Abridged Translation of Johann Weyer's 'De praestigiis daemonum'.* Ed. Benjamin G. Kohl and H.C. Erik Midelfort and Trans. John Shea. Asheville: Pegasus Press.

WORKS ORIGINALLY PUBLISHED AFTER 1800

Adler, Margot. 1986. *Drawing Down the Moon: Witches, Druids, Goddess Worshipers, and Other Pagans in America Today.* Boston: Beacon Press.

Adler, Margot. 2015. A Time for Truth: Wiccans Struggle with Information that Revisions Their History. Last modified September 2000. http://www.belief-net.com/Faiths/Pagan-and-Earth-Based/2000/09/A-Time-For-Truth.aspx. Accessed 23 Sept 2015.

Adolphs, Ralph and Michael Spezio S. Anders, G. Ende et al. 2006. Role of the Amygdala in Processing Visual "Social Stimuli". In *Understanding Emotions*, ed. S. Anders, G. Ende et al. Amsterdam: Elsevier.

Ahmed, Sara. 2004. *The Cultural Politics of Emotion*. New York: Routledge.

Alia-Klein, Nelly, Rita Z. Goldstein, Dardo Tomasi, et al. 2009. Neural Mechanisms of Anger Regulation as a Function of Genetic Risk for Violence. *Emotion* 9(3): 385–396.

Almond, Philip. 2011. *England's First Demonologist: Reginald Scot and 'The Discoverie of Witchcraft'*. London: I. B. Taurus.

American Psychiatric Association. 2013. Dissociative Disorders. In *Diagnostic and Statistical Manual of Mental Disorders*, 5th ed. Arlington: American Psychiatric Publishing.

Anders, Silke, Gabriele Ende, et al. (eds.). 2006. *Understanding Emotions*. Amsterdam: Elsevier.

Anglo, Sydney. 1992. Melancholia and Witchcraft. In *The Literature of Witchcraft, Volume 4 of Articles on Witchcraft, Magic, and Demonology*, ed. B.P. Levack. New York: Garland.

Apps, Lara, and Andrew Gow. 2004. *Male Witches in Early Modern Europe*. Manchester: Manchester University Press.

Armstrong, W.A. 1946. The Elizabethan Conception of the Tyrant. *Review of English Studies* 22(87): 161–181.

Armstrong, W.A. 1948. The Influence of Seneca and Machiavelli on the Elizabethan Tyrant. *Review of English Studies* 24(93): 19–35.

Atwood, Craig D. 2009. *The Theology of the Czech Brethren from Hus to Comenius*. University Park: Pennsylvania State University Press.

Audisio, Gabriel. 1999. *The Waldensian Dissent: Persecution and Survival, c. 1170–1570*. Trans. Claire Davison. Cambridge: Cambridge University Press.

Bähr, Andreas. 2013. *Furcht und Furchtlosigkeit. Göttliche Gewalt und Selbstkonstitution im 17. Jahrhundert*. Göttingen: V & R unipress.

Bailey, Michael D. 2002. The Feminization of Magic and the Emerging Idea of the Female Witch in the Late Middle Ages. *Essays in Medieval Studies* 19: 120–134.

Bailey, Michael D. 2003. *Battling Demons: Witchcraft, Heresy and Reform in the Late Middle Ages*. University Park: The Pennsylvania State University Press.

Bailey, Michael D. (ed.). 2010. Forum: Contending Realities: Reactions to Edward Bever. *Magic, Ritual, and Witchcraft* 5(1): 81–121.

Bammer, Leila R. 2000. *Excluded from Suffrage History: Matilda Joslyn Gage, Nineteenth Century American Feminist*. Westport: Greenwood Press.

Barry, Jonathan. 1996. Keith Thomas and the Problem of Witchcraft. In *Witchcraft in Early Modern Europe: Studies in Culture and Belief*, ed. J. Barry, M. Hester, and G. Roberts. Cambridge: Cambridge University Press.

Barry, Jonathan. 2012. *Witchcraft and Demonology in South-West England, 1640–1789*. Basingstoke: Palgrave Macmillan.

Barry, Jonathan, Marianne Hester, and Gareth Roberts (eds.). 1996. *Witchcraft in Early Modern Europe: Studies in Culture and Belief*. Cambridge: Cambridge University Press.

Bartolomucci, Alessandro, Paola Palanza, Tania Costoli, Elisa Savani, Giovanni Laviola, Stefano Parmigiani, and Andrea Sgoifo. 2003. Chronic Psychosocial Stress Persistently Alters Autonomic Function and Physical Activity in Mice. *Physiology and Behavior* 80(1): 57–67.

Bechdel, Alison. 2012. *Are You My Mother?: A Comic Drama*. Boston: Houghton Mifflin Harcourt.

Behringer, Wolfgang. 1987. Meinungsbildende Befürworter und Gegner der Hexenverfolgung (15. bis 18. Jahrhundert). In *Hexen und Zauberer: Die grosse Verfolgung – ein europäisches Phänomen in der Steiermark*, ed. H. Valentinitsch. Graz: Leykam.

Behringer, Wolfgang. 1997. *Witchcraft Persecutions in Bavaria: Popular Magic, Religious Zealotry and Reason of State in Early Modern Europe*. Trans. J.C. Grayson and David Lederer. Cambridge: Cambridge University Press.

Behringer, Wolfgang. 1998. Neun Millionen Hexen: Entstehung, Tradition und Kritik eines populären Mythos. *Geschichte in Wissenschaft und Unterricht* 49: 664–685.

Behringer, Wolfgang. 2004. *Witches and Witch-Hunts: A Global History*. Cambridge: Polity.

Behringer, Wolfgang. 2006. Malleus Maleficarum. In *Encyclopedia of Witchcraft*, ed. R.M. Golden, vol. 3. Santa Barbara: ABC-CLIO.

Behringer, Wolfgang. 2007. Demonology 1500–1660. In *The Cambridge History of Christianity, Vol. 6: Reform and Expansion 1500–1660*, ed. R. Po-Chia Hsia. Cambridge: Cambridge University Press.

Bell, Catherine. 2009. Ritual. In *The Blackwell Companion to the Study of Religion*, ed. R.A. Segal. Malden: Wiley-Blackwell.

Bender, Courtney. 2010. *The New Metaphysicals: Spirituality and the American Religious Imagination*. Chicago: University of Chicago Press.

Berkowitz, Leonard. 2012. A Different View of Anger: The Cognitive-Neoassociative Conception of the Relation of Anger to Aggression. *Aggressive Behavior* 38(2): 322–333.

Bever, Edward. 2000. Witchcraft Fears and Psychosocial Factors in Disease. *The Journal of Interdisciplinary History* 30(4): 573–590.

Bever, Edward. 2006a. Disease. In *Encyclopedia of Witchcraft*, ed. R.M. Golden, vol. 1. Santa Barbara: ABC-CLIO.

Bever, Edward. 2006b. Magic and Religion. In *Encyclopedia of Witchcraft*, ed. R.M. Golden, vol. 3. Santa Barbara: ABC-CLIO.

Bever, Edward. 2008. *The Realities of Witchcraft and Popular Magic in Early Modern Europe: Culture, Cognition, and Everyday Life*. Basingstoke: Palgrave Macmillan.

Bever, Edward. 2010. The Critiques and *The Realities. Magic, Ritual, and Witchcraft* 5(1): 113–121.

Bever, Edward. 2012. Current Trends in the Application of Cognitive Science to Magic. *Magic, Ritual, and Witchcraft* 7(1): 3–18.

Bever, Edward. 2013. Popular Witch Beliefs and Magical Practices. In *The Oxford Handbook of Witchcraft in Early Modern Europe and Colonial America*, ed. B.P. Levack. Oxford: Oxford University Press.

Biesel, Elisabeth. 1997. *Hexenjustiz, Volksmagie und soziale Konflikte im lothringischen Raum*, Trierer Hexenprozesse. Quellen und Darstellungen 6. Trier: Spee.

Bishop, Chris. 2014. The "Pear of Anguish": Truth, Torture and Dark Medievalism. *International Journal of Cultural Studies* 17(6): 591–602.

Blackwell, Jeannine. 2000. German Narratives of Women's Divine and Demonic Possession and Supernatural Vision, 1555–1800: A Bibliography. *Women in German Yearbook: Feminist Studies in German Literature and Culture* 16(1): 241–257.

Blécourt, Willem de. 2000. The Making of the Female Witch: Reflections on Witchcraft and Gender in the Early Modern Period. *Gender & History* 12(2): 287–300.

Blécourt, Willem de. 2013. Sabbath Stories: Towards a New History of Witches' assemblies. In *The Oxford Handbook of Witchcraft in Early Modern Europe and Colonial America*, ed. B.P. Levack. Oxford: Oxford University Press.

Boddice, Rob. 2014. The Affective Turn: Historicizing the Emotions. In *Psychology and History: Interdisciplinary Explorations*, ed. C. Tileaga and J. Byford. Cambridge: Cambridge University Press.

Boddy, Clive. 2011. *Corporate Psychopaths*. New York: Palgrave Macmillan.

Borman, Tracy. 2014. *Witches: James I and the English Witch-Hunts*. London: Vintage.

Bornstein, Daniel. 1998. Spiritual Kinship and Domestic Devotions. In *Gender and Society in Renaissance Italy*, ed. J.C. Brown and R.C. Davis. Essex: Longman.

Boyer, Paul, and Stephen Nissenbaum. 1974. *Salem Possessed: The Social Origins of Witchcraft*. Cambridge, MA: Harvard University Press.

Brauner, Sigrid. 1995a. Cannibals, Witches, Shrews and the "Civilizing Process". In *"Neue Welt"/"Dritte Welt": Interculturelle Beziehungen Deutschlands zu Latinamerika und der Karibik*, ed. S. von Bauschinger and S.L. Cocalis. Tübingen: Francke.

Brauner, Sigrid. 1995b. *Fearless Wives and Frightened Shrews. The Construction of the Witch in Early Modern Germany*. Amherst: University of Massachusetts Press.

Brayman Hackel, Heidi. 2005. *Reading Material in Early Modern England: Print, Gender and Literacy*. Cambridge: Cambridge University Press.

Breen, Louise A. 2001. *Transgressing the Bounds: Subversive Enterprises among the Puritan Elite in Massachusetts, 1630–1692*. Oxford: Oxford University Press.

Briggs, Robin. 1984. Witchcraft and Popular Mentality in Lorraine, 1580–1630. In *Occult and Scientific Mentalities in the Renaissance*, ed. B. Vickers. Cambridge: Cambridge University Press.

Briggs, Robin. 2002. *Witches and Neighbours: The Social and Cultural Context of European Witchcraft*, 2nd ed. Oxford: Blackwell Publishing.

Briggs, Robin. 2007. *The Witches of Lorraine*. Oxford: Oxford University Press.

Briggs, Robin. 2013. Witchcraft and the Local Communities: The Rhine-Moselle-Region. In *The Oxford Handbook of Witchcraft in Early Modern Europe and Colonial America*, ed. B.P. Levack. Oxford: Oxford University Press.

Brock, Peter. 1957. *The Political and Social Doctrines of the Unity of Czech Brethren in the Fifteenth and Early Sixteenth Centuries*. The Hague: Mouton.

Broedel, Hans Peter. 2003. *The Malleus Maleficarum and the Construction of Witchcraft: Theology and Popular Belief*. Manchester: Manchester University Press.

Broedel, Hans Peter. 2013. Fifteenth-Century Witch Beliefs. In *The Oxford Handbook of Witchcraft in Early Modern Europe and Colonial America*, ed. B.P. Levack. Oxford: Oxford University Press.

Brooks, Peter. 2005. Narrative in and of the Law. In *A Companion to Narrative Theory*, ed. J. Phelan and P.J. Rabinowitz. Oxford: Oxford University Press.

Brzezińska, Anna. 1996. Accusations of Love Magic in the Renaissance Courtly Culture of the Polish-Lithuanian Commonwealth. *East Central Europe* 20–23(1): 117–140.

Budapest, Zsuzsanna E. 1991. *Grandmother Moon: Lunar Magic for Our Lives, Spells, Rituals Goddesses, Legends, and Emotions under the Moon*. San Francisco: HarperSanFrancisco.

Budapest, Zsuzsanna E. 1999. *The Holy Book of Women's Mysteries: Feminist Witchcraft, Goddess Rituals, Spellcasting & Other Womanly Arts, 20th Anniversary Edition*. Oakland: Wingbow Press.

Burckhardt, Jakob. 1852. *Erzbischof Andreas von Krain und der letzte Concilsversuch in Basel 1482–84*. Basel: Schweighauser.

Burr, George Lincoln (ed.). 1896. The Witch Persecutions. In *Translations and Reprints from the Original Sources of European History*, vol. 3. Philadelphia: University of Pennsylvania Press.

Bushnell, Rebecca W. 1990. *Tragedy of Tyrants: Political Thought and Theatre in the English Renaissance*. Ithaca: Cornell University Press.

Caciola, Nancy. 2003. *Discerning Spirits: Divine and Demonic Possession in the Middle Ages*. Ithaca/London: Cornell University Press.

Camerlynck, Elaine. 1983. Féminité et sorcellerie chez les théoriciens de la démonologie à la fin du Moyen Age: Étude du *Malleus Maleficarum*. *Renaissance and Reformation* 19: 13–25.

Cameron, Euan. 2000. *Waldenses: Rejections of Holy Church in Medieval Europe*. Oxford: Blackwell.

Campbell, Lorne. 2009. The New Pictorial Language of Roger van der Weyden. In *Roger van der Weyden 1400–1464: Master of Passions*, exhibition catalogue. Zwolle: Waanders; Leuven: Davidsfonds.

Cannon, Walter B. 1942. 'Voodoo' Death. *American Anthropologist* 44(2): 169–181.

Carré, Justin, Kelly Murphy, and Ahmad Hariri. 2013. What Lies Beneath the Face of Aggression? *Social Cognitive and Affective Neuroscience* 8(2): 224–229.

Carter, C. Sue. 2007. Neuropeptides and the Protective Effects of Social Bonds. In *Social Neuroscience: Integrating Biological and Psychological Explanations of Social Behavior*, ed. E. Harmon-Jones and P. Winkielman. New York: The Guilford Press.

Cegna, Romolo. 1965. I valdesi di Moravia nell'ultimo medioevo. *Rivista di storia e letteratura religiosa* 1: 392–423.

Chakrabarti, Bhismadev, and Simon Baron-Cohen S. Anders, G. Ende et al. 2006. Empathizing: Neurocognitive Developmental Mechanism and Individual Differences. In *Understanding Emotions*, eds. S. Anders, G. Ende et al. Amsterdam: Elsevier.

Christ, Carol. 1979. Why Women Need the Goddess: Phenomenological, Philosophical, and Political Reflections. In *Womanspirit Rising: A Feminist Reader in Religion*, ed. C.P. Christ and J. Plaslow. San Francisco: Harper and Rowe.

Christian Jr., William A. 1973. Holy People in Peasant Europe. *Comparative Studies in Society and History* 15: 106–114.

Christian Jr., William A. 2012. Provoked Religious Weeping in Early Modern Spain. In *Crying in the Middle Ages: Tears of History*, ed. E. Gertsmann. New York: Routledge.

Clark, Stuart. 1983. French Historians and Early Modern Popular Culture. *Past & Present* 100: 62–99.

Clark, Stuart. 1990. Protestant Demonology: Sin, Superstition, and Society (c. 1520–c. 1630). In *Early Modern European Witchcraft: Centres and Peripheries*, ed. B. Ankarloo and G. Henningsen. Oxford: Clarendon Press.

Clark, Stuart. 1991. The "Gendering" of Witchcraft in French Demonology: Misogyny or Polarity? *French History* 5(4): 426–437.

Clark, Stuart. 1997. *Thinking with Demons: The Idea of Witchcraft in Early Modern Europe*. Oxford: Oxford University Press.

Clark, Stuart (ed.). 2001. *Languages of Witchcraft. Narrative, Ideology and Meaning in Early Modern Culture*. New York: St. Martin's Press.

Clark, Stuart. 2002. Witchcraft and Magic in Early Modern Culture. In *Witchcraft and Magic in Europe, Vol. 4: The Period of the Witch Trials*, ed. B. Ankarloo, S. Clark, and W. Monter. London: The Athlone Press.

Confino, Alon, Ute Frevert, Uffa Jensen, Lyndal Roper, and Daniela Saxer. 2010. Forum: History of Emotions. *German History* 28(1): 67–80.

Corrigan, John. 2014. Religion and Emotions. In *Doing Emotions History*, ed. S.J. Matt and P.N. Stearns. Urbana, Chicago, and Springfield: University of Illinois Press.

Cowdell, Scott. 2012. Hard Evidence for Girardian Mimetic Theory? Intersubjectivity and Mirror Neurons. In *Violence, Desire, and the Sacred, Vol. I: Girard's Mimetic Theory Across the Disciplines*, ed. S. Cowdell, C. Fleming, and J. Hodge. New York: Continuum.

Cressy, David. 1980. *Literacy and the Social Order: Reading and Writing in Tudor and Stuart England*. Cambridge: Cambridge University Press.

Cressy, David. 2000. Agnes Bowker's Cat: Childbirth, Seduction, Bestiality and Lies. In *Travesties and Transgression in Tudor and Stuart England: Tales of Discord and Dissension*, ed. D. Cressy. Oxford: Oxford University Press.

Daily Mail Reporter. 2013. "I've Rid the World of 160,000 Demons", Says Catholic Church's Leading Exorcist as He Calls on the Pope to Allow All Priests to Perform the Ritual. *Daily Mail*, May 28.

Daly, Mary. 1978. *Gyn/Ecology: The Metaethics of Radical Feminism*. Boston: Beacon.

Daly, Mary. 1984. *Pure Lust: Elemental Feminist Philosophy*. Boston: Beacon.

David, Ransel. 1988. Character and Style of Patron-Client Relations in Russia. In *Klientelsysteme im Europa der frühen Neuzeit*, ed. A. Mączak. Munich: R. Oldenbourg.

Davis, Natalie Zemon. 1986. Boundaries and the Sense of Self in Sixteenth-Century France. In *Reconstructing Individualism: Autonomy, Individualism and the Self in Western Thought*, ed. T.C. Heller, M. Sosna, and D.E. Wellbery. Stanford: Stanford University Press.

Davis, Natalie Zemon. 1987. *Fiction in the Archives: Pardon Tales and Their Tellers in Sixteenth Century France*. Stanford: Stanford University Press.

Davy, Barbara Jane. 2007. *Introduction to Pagan Studies*. New York: Alta Mira.

De Lange, Albert. 2008. La fin tragique des vaudois au nord des Alpes à la lumière du destin de Friedrich Reiser. *Revue d'histoire et de philosophie religieuses* 88(1): 3–19.

Decety, John. 2007. A Social Cognitive Neuroscience Model of Human Empathy. In *Social Neuroscience: Integrating Biological and Psychological Explanations of Social Behavior*, ed. E. Harmon-Jones and P. Winkielman. New York: The Guilford Press.

Delumeau, Jean. 1978. *La peur en occident XIVe-XVIIIe siècles: Une cité assiégée*. Paris: Fayard.

Dewey, Melvil. 2004. *A Classification and Subject Index for Cataloguing and Arranging the Books and Pamphlets of a Library* [1876; Dewey Decimal Classification], June 4, 2004 [EBook #12513]. Facsimile reprinted by Forest Press Division Lake Placid Educational Foundation. Accessed at Project Gutenberg, http://www.gutenberg.org/files/12513/12513-h/12513-h.htm, 8 Feb 2016.

di Simplicio, Oscar. 2002. Witchcraft and Infanticide. *Acta Histriae* 10(2): 411–442.

Dillinger, Johannes. 2000. Annäherung an das Fremde. In *Incubi Succubi. Hexen und ihre Henker bis heute. Ein historisches Lesebuch zur Ausstellung*, ed. R. Voltmer and F. Irsigler. Luxembourg: Publications du Musée d'Histoire de la Ville de Luxembourg.

Dillinger, Johannes. 2009. *'Evil People': A Comparative Study of Witch Hunts in Swabian Austria and the Electorate of Trier*. Trans. Laura Stokes. Charlottesville: University of Virginia.

Dixon, Thomas. 2015. *Weeping Britannia: Portrait of a Nation in Tears*. Oxford: Oxford University Press.

Dolan, Frances E. 2013. *True Relations: Reading, Literature and Evidence in Seventeenth-Century England*. Philadelphia: University of Pennsylvania Press.

Donaghue, John. 2013. *Fire under the Ashes: An Atlantic History of the English Revolution*. Chicago: University of Chicago Press.

Doty, Kathleen L. 2007. Telling Tales. The Role of Scribes in Constructing the Discourse of the Salem Witchcraft Trials. *Journal of Historical Pragmatics* 8(1): 25–41.

DSM5.org. 2010. Proposed Revisions. *Diagnostic and Statistical Manual (DSM 5)*. http://www.dsm5.org/ProposedRevisions/Pages/proposedrevision.aspx?rid=436#. Accessed 10 Sept 2010.

During, E.H., F.M. Elahi, O. Taieb, M.R. Moro, and T. Baubet. 2011. A Critical Review of Dissociative Trance and Possession Disorders: Etiological, Diagnostic, Therapeutic, and Nosological Issues. *The Canadian Journal of Psychiatry* 56(4): 235–242.

Durrant, Jonathan B. 2007. *Witchcraft, Gender and Society in Early Modern Germany*. Leiden: Brill.

Dworkin, Andrea. 1974. *Woman Hating*. New York: Penguin.

Dydek, Zbigniew. Czary w procesie inkwizycyjnym w Rzeszowie w XVIII wieku. *Rocznik Wojewówdztwa Rzeszwoskiego* (1964/1965 1968): 383–401.

Echols, Alice. 1989. *Daring to Be Bad: Radical Feminism in America 1967–1975*. Minneapolis: University of Minnesota Press.

Eco, Umberto. 1994. *Reflections on The Name of the Rose*. Trans. William Weaver. London: Minerva.

Eisner, Manuel. 2003. Long-Term Historical Trends in Violent Crime. *Crime and Justice* 30: 83–142.

Eller, Cynthia. 1995. *Living in the Lap of the Goddess: The Feminist Spirituality Movement in America*. Boston: Beacon.

Eller, Cynthia. 2011. *Gentlemen and Amazons: The Myth of Matriarchal Prehistory, 1861–1900*. Berkeley: University of California Press.

Elliott, Dyan. 1997. The Physiology of Rapture and Female Spirituality. In *Medieval Theology and the Natural Body*, ed. P. Biller and A.J. Minnis. Woodbridge: York Medieval Press.

Elliott, Dyan. 2004. *Proving Woman: Female Spirituality and Inquisitional Culture in the Later Middle Ages*. Princeton: Princeton University Press.

Elliott, Dyan. 2010. Flesh and Spirit: The Female Body. In *Medieval Holy Women in the Christian Tradition, c. 1100-c. 1500*, ed. A. Minnis and R. Voaden. Turnhout: Brepols.

Elmer, Peter. 2016. *Witchcraft, Witch-Hunting and Politics in Early Modern England*. Oxford: Oxford University Press.

Elster, Jon. 1999. *Strong Feelings: Emotion, Addiction, and Human Behavior*. Cambridge: The MIT Press.

Eshuis, Rik, Kenny Coventry, and Mila Vulchanova. 2009. Predictive Eye Movements Are Driven by Goals, Not by the Mirror Neuron System. *Psychological Science* 20(4): 438–440.

Eustace, Nichole. 2014. Emotion and Political Change. In *Doing Emotions History*, ed. S.J. Matt and P.N. Stearns. Urbana, Chicago, and Springfield: University of Illinois Press.

Evans, Sara. 1979. *Personal Politics: The Roots of Women's Liberation in the Civil Rights Movement and the New Left*. New York: Knopf.

Evans, Richard J. 1996. *Rituals of Retribution. Capital Punishment in Germany 1600–1987*. Oxford: Oxford University Press.

Evans-Pritchard, E.E. 1965 [1937]. *Witchcraft, Oracles and Magic Among the Azande*. Oxford: Clarendon Press.

Ewen, C.L'Estrange (ed.). 1929. *Witch Hunting and Witch Trials. The Indictments for Witchcraft from the Records of 1373 Assizes Held for the Home Circuit A.D. 1559–1736*. London: Kegan, Paul, Trench, Trubner & Co.

Ewen, C. L'Estrange (ed.). 1984. *Witchcraft and Demonianism*, 2nd ed. New York: AMS Press.

Faraone, Christopher A. 1999. *Ancient Greek Love Magic*. Cambridge: Harvard University Press.

Favret-Saada, Jeanne. 1977. *Les mots, la mort, les sorts*. Paris: Gallimard.

Favret-Saada, Jeanne. 1980. *Deadly Words: Witchcraft in the Bocage*. Trans. Catherine Cullen. Cambridge: Cambridge University Press.

Favret-Saada, Jeanne. 2009. *Désorceler*. Paris: Seuil, Éditions de l'Olivier.

Fedele, Anna. 2013. *Looking for Mary Magdalene: Alternative Pilgrimage and Ritual Creativity at Catholic Shrines in France*. Oxford: Oxford University Press.

Ferber, Sarah. 2004. *Demonic Possession and Exorcism in Early Modern France*. London: Routledge.

Ferber, Sarah, and Adrian Howe. 2005. The Man Who Mistook His Wife for a Devil: Exorcism, Expertise and Secularisation in a Late Twentieth-Century Australian Criminal Court. In *Dämonische Besessenheit: Zur Interpretation eines kulturhistorischen Phänomens*, ed. H. de Waardt, J. Schmidt, and D. Bauer. Bielefeld: Verlag für Regionalgeschichte.

Ferracuti, S., and M. Civita DeMarco. 2004. Ritual Homicide During Dissociative Trance Disorder. *International Journal of Offender Therapy and Comparative Criminology* 48(1): 59–64.

Ferracuti, S., R. Sacco, and R. Lazzari. 1996. Dissociative Trance Disorder: Clinical and Rorschach Findings in Ten Persons Reporting Demon Possession and Treated by Exorcism. *Journal of Personality Assessment* 66(3): 525–539.

Firat, Rengin, and Steven Hitlin. 2012. Neuroscience and the Difficult Art of Building Interdisciplinary Bridges. *Contemporary Sociology* 41(6): 780–783.

Frankfurter, David. 2014. The Social Context of Women's Erotic Magic in Antiquity. In *Daughters of Hecate: Women and Magic in the Ancient World*, ed. K.B. Stratton and D.S. Kalleres. New York: Oxford University Press.

Frick, David. 2014. The Witches of Wilno: Constant Litigation and Conflict Resolution. *Slavic Review* 73(4): 881–902.

Fudge, Erica. 2003. *Brutal Reasoning: Animals, Rationality, and Humanity in Early Modern England*. Ithaca: Cornell University Press.

Gage, Matilda Joslyn. 1980 [1893]. *Woman, Church and State*. Watertown: Persephone Press.

Gallese, Vittorio. 2007. Before and Below "Theory of Mind": Embodied Simulation and the Neural Correlates of Social Cognition. *Philosophical Transactions of the Royal Society B: Biological Sciences* 362(1480): 659–669.

Gardner, Gerald. 1954. *Witchcraft Today*. London: Rider.

Gardner, Gerald. 1959. *The Meaning of Witchcraft*. London: Aquarian.

Gaskill, Malcolm. 2000. *Crime and Mentalities in Early Modern England*. Cambridge: Cambridge University Press.

Gaskill, Malcolm. 2005. *Witchfinders: A Seventeenth-Century English Tragedy*. London: John Murray.

Gaskill, Malcolm. 2008. Witchcraft, Emotions, and Imagination in the English Civil War. In *Witchcraft and the Act of 1604*, ed. J. Newton and J. Bath. Leiden: Brill.

Gaskill, Malcolm. forthcoming. Little Commonwealths II: Communities. In *The Cambridge Social History of England, 1500–1750*, ed. K. Wrightson. Cambridge: Cambridge University Press.

Gauvard, Claude. 1991. '*De grace especial': crime, état et société en France à la fin du moyen âge*. Paris: Presses de la Sorbonne.

Gehm, Britta. 2000. *Die Hexenverfolgung im Hochstift Bamberg und das Eingreifen des Reichshofrates zu ihrer Beendigung*. Hildesheim: Georg Olms Verlag.

Gergen, Kenneth J. 1998. History and Psychology: Three Weddings and a Future. In *An Emotional History of the United States*, ed. P.N. Stearns and J. Lewis. New York: New York University Press.

Gertsman, Elina. 2012. Introduction. "Going They Went and Wept": Tears in Medieval Discourse. In *Crying in the Middle Ages: Tears of History*, ed. E. Gertsmann. New York: Routledge.

Geschiere, Peter. 1982. *Village Communities and the State: Changing Relations Among the Maka of Southeastern Cameroon Since the Colonial Conquest*. London: Kegan Paul International.

Geschiere, Peter. 1997. *The Modernity of Witchcraft: Politics and the Occult in Postcolonial Africa*. Charlottesville: University of Virginia Press.

Geschiere, Peter. 2013. *Witchcraft, Intimacy and Trust: Africa in Comparison*. Chicago: University of Chicago Press.

Gibson, Joan. 1992. Could Christ Have Been Born a Woman? A Medieval Debate. *Journal of Feminist Studies in Religion* 18(1): 65–82.

Gibson, Marion. 1999. *Reading Witchcraft: Stories of Early English Witches*. London: Routledge.

Gibson, Marion. 2000. *Early Modern Witches: Witchcraft Cases in Contemporary Writing*. London: Routledge.

Gibson, Marion. 2001. Understanding Witchcraft? Accusers' Stories in Print in Early Modern England. In *Languages of Witchcraft. Narrative, Ideology and Meaning in Early Modern Culture*, ed. S. Clark. New York: St. Martin's Press.

Golden, Richard (ed.). 2006. *Encyclopedia of Witchcraft: The Western Tradition*. 4 vols. Santa Barbara: ABC-CLIO.

Goldenberg, Naomi. 1982. Feminist Witchcraft: Controlling Our Own Inner Space. In *The Politics of Women's Spirituality: Essays by the Founding Mothers of the Movement*, ed. Charlene Spretnak. New York: Anchor.

Goodare, Julian (ed.). 2013. *Scottish Witches and Witch Hunters*. Basingstoke: Palgrave Macmillan.

Goodich, Michael E. 2007. *Miracles and Wonders: The Development of the Concept of Miracle, 1150–1350*. Aldershot: Ashgate.

Grandjean, Didier, Tanja Bänziger, and Klaus Scherer. 2006. Intonation as an Interface Between Language and Affect. In *Understanding Emotions*, ed. S. Anders, G. Ende et al. Amsterdam: Elsevier.

Guldon, Zenon. 1962. Proces czarownicy we wsi Staniszewo w 1695 r. *Studia z dziejów kościoła katolickiego* 2(1): 150–161.

Haliczer, Stephen. 1991. The Jew as Witch: Displaced Aggression and the Myth of the Santo Niño de la Guardia. In *Cultural Encounters: The Impact of the Inquisition in Spain and the New World*, ed. M.E. Perry and A.J. Cruz. Berkeley: University of California Press.

Hamburger, Jeffrey. 1998. *The Visual and the Visionary: Art and Female Spirituality in Late Medieval Germany*. New York: Zone.

Harmon-Jones, Eddie. 2007. Asymmetrical Frontal Cortical Activity, Affective Valence and Motivational Direction. In *Social Neuroscience: Integrating Biological and Psychological Explanations of Social Behavior*, ed. E. Harmon-Jones and P. Winkielman. New York: The Guilford Press.

Harmon-Jones, Eddie, and Piotr Winkielman. 2007. A Brief Overview of Social Neuroscience. In *Social Neuroscience: Integrating Biological and Psychological Explanations of Social Behavior*, ed. E. Harmon-Jones and P. Winkielman. New York: The Guilford Press.

Harré, Rom. 1986. An Outline of the Social Constructionist Viewpoint. In *The Social Construction of Emotions*, ed. R. Harré. Oxford: Blackwell.

Harris, Marvin. 1989 [1974]. *Cows, Pigs and Witches: The Riddles of Culture*. New York: Vintage Books.

Hayward, Rhodri. 2009. Enduring Emotions: James L. Halliday and the Invention of the Psychosocial. *Isis* 100(4): 827–838.

Heberlein, Andrea, and Ralph Adolphs. 2007. Neurobiology of Emotion Recognition: Current Evidence for Shared Substrates. In *Social Neuroscience: Integrating Biological and Psychological Explanations of Social Behavior*, ed. E. Harmon-Jones and P. Winkielman. New York: The Guilford Press.

Hennenlotter, Andreas, and Ulrike Schroeder. 2006. Partially Dissociable Neural Substrates for Recognizing Basic Emotions: A Critical Review. In *Understanding Emotions*, ed. S. Anders, G. Ende et al. Amsterdam: Elsevier.

Herzig, Tamar. 2006. Witches, Saints, and Heretics: Heinrich Kramer's Ties with Italian Women Mystics. *Magic, Ritual, and Witchcraft* 1(1): 24–55.

Herzig, Tamar. 2010. Flies, Heretics and the Gendering of Witchcraft. *Magic, Ritual, and Witchcraft* 5(1): 51–80.

Herzig, Tamar. 2013. *Christ Transformed into a Virgin Woman: Lucia Brocadelli, Heinrich Institoris, and the Defense of the Faith*. Rome: Edizioni di Storia e Letteratura.

Hille, Iris. 2009. *Der Teufelspakt in frühneuzeitlichen Verhörprotokollen:Standardi sierung und Regionalisierung im Frühneuhochdeutschen*. Berlin/New York: Walter de Gruyter.

Holbrook, Colin, Andrew Galperin, Daniel M.T. Fessler, Kerri L. Johnson, Gregory A. Bryant, and Martie G. Haselton. 2014. If Looks Could Kill: Anger Attributions Are Intensified by Affordances for Doing Harm. *Emotion* 14(3): 455–461.

Holeton, David R. 1996a. Church or Sect? The *Jednota Bratrská* and the Growth of Dissent from Mainline Utraquism. *Communio viatorum* 38(1): 5–35.

Holeton, David R. 1996b. The Bohemian Eucharistic Movement in its European Context. In *Bohemian Reformation and Religious Practice 1*, ed. Zdeněk V. David and David R. Holeton. Prague: Academy of Sciences of the Czech Republic.

Honeybone, Michael. 2008. *Wicked Practise & Sorcerye: The Belvoir Witchcraft Case of 1619*. Buckingham: Baron.

Howe, Adrian, and Sarah Ferber. 2005. Delivering Demons, Punishing Wives: False Imprisonment, Exorcism and Other Matrimonial Duties in a Late 20th-Century Manslaughter Case. *Punishment & Society* 7(2): 123–146.

Hults, Linda C. 2005. *The Witch as Muse: Art, Gender, and Power in Early Modern Europe*. Philadelphia: University of Pennsylvania Press.

Hutcherson, Audrey (ed.). 2012. *Psychology of Victimization*. New York: Nova Science Publishers.

Hutton, Ronald. 1999. *The Triumph of the Moon: A History of Modern Pagan Witchcraft*. Oxford: Oxford University Press.

Hutton, Ronald. 2000. Paganism and Polemic: The Debate over the Origins of Modern Pagan Witchcraft. *Folklore* 111(1): 103–117.

Hutton, Ronald. 2002. The Global Context of the Scottish Witch-hunt. In *The Scottish Witch-hunt in Context*, ed. J. Goodare. New York: Manchester University Press.

Hutton, Ronald. 2004. Anthropological and Historical Approaches to Witchcraft: Potential for a New Collaboration? *Historical Journal* 47(2): 413–434.

Hutton, Ronald. 2010. Writing the History of Witchcraft: A Personal View. *The Pomegranate* 12(2): 239–262.

Iacoboni, Marco. 2007. The Quiet Revolution of Existential Neuroscience. In *Social Neuroscience: Integrating Biological and Psychological Explanations of Social Behavior*, ed. E. Harmon-Jones and P. Winkielman. New York: The Guilford Press.

Jackson, Louise. 1995. Witches, Wives and Mothers. *Women's History Review* 4(1): 63–83.

Jackson, Michael. 1999 [1989]. The Witch as a Category and as a Person. In *The Insider/Outsider Problem in the Study of Religion: A Reader*, ed. R. McCutcheon. London: Cassell.

Jackson, Allison and Bruce Crosson. 2006. Emotional Connotation of Words: Role of Emotion in Distributed Semantic Systems. In *Understanding Emotions*, ed. S. Anders, G. Ende et al. Amsterdam: Elsevier.

Jensen, Karin, Ted J. Kaptchuk, Irving Kirsch, Jacqueline Raicek, Kara M. Lindstrom, Chantal Berna, Randy L. Gollub, Martin Ingvar, and Jian Kong. 2012. Nonconscious Activation of Placebo and Nocebo Pain Responses. *Proceedings of the National Academy of Sciences of the United States of America* 109(39): 15959–15964.

Jerouschek, Günter. 1992. 500 Years of the *Malleus Maleficarum*. In *Malleus Maleficarum 1487 von Heinrich Kramer (Institoris). Nachdruck des Erstdruckes von 1487 mit Bulle und Approbatio*, ed. G. Jerouschek. Hildesheim/Zurich/New York: Georg Olms Verlag.

Johns, Andreas. 2004. *Baba Iaga: The Ambiguous Mother and Witch of the Russian Folktale*. New York: Peter Lang.

Johnstone, Nathan. 2006. *The Devil and Demonism in Early Modern England*. Cambridge: Cambridge University Press.

Judson, Richard. 1973. *The Drawings of Jacques de Gheyn II*. New York: Grossman.

Kaczmarczyk, Kazimierz. 1901. Proces o czarostwo w r. 1688 i 1689. *Lud* 7: 302–322.

Kamensky, Jane. 1997. *Governing the Tongue: The Politics of Speech in Early New England*. New York: Oxford University Press.

Kantorovich, Iakov Abramovich. 1990. *Srednevekovye protsessy o ved'makh (reprint of 1899 edition)*. Moscow: Kniga.

Karant-Nunn, Susan. 2009. *The Reformation of Feeling: Shaping the Religious Emotions in Early Modern Germany*. New York: Oxford University Press.

Karpiński, Andrzej. 1995. *Kobieta w mieście polskim w drugiej połowie XVI i w XVII wieku*. Warszawa: Instytut Historii Polskiej Akademii Nauk.

Kassinove, Howard (ed.). 1995. *Anger Disorders: Definition, Diagnosis, and Treatment*. Washington, DC: Taylor and Francis.

Kassinove, Howard, and Denis G. Sukhodolsky. 1995. Anger Disorders: Basic Science and Practical Issues. In *Anger Disorders: Definition, Diagnosis, and Treatment*, ed. H. Kassinove. Washington, DC: Taylor and Francis.

Kent, E.J. 2013. *Cases of Male Witchcraft in Old and New England, 1592–1692*. Brepols: Turnhout.

Kent, E.J. forthcoming. *Setting Up Satan's Kingdom: Male Witchcraft Confessors, Salem 1692*.

Keysers, Christian, and Valeria Gazzola. 2006. Toward a Unifying Neural Theory of Social Cognition. In *Understanding Emotions*, ed. S. Anders, G. Ende et al. Amsterdam: Elsevier.

Kivelson, Valerie. 2013. *Desperate Magic: The Moral Economy of Witchcraft in Seventeenth-Century Russia*. Ithaca: Cornell University Press.

Klaniczay, Gábor. 1997. Miraculum and Maleficium: Reflections Concerning Late Medieval Female Sainthood. In *Problems in the Historical Anthropology of Early Modern Europe*, ed. R. Po-Chia Hsia and R.W. Scribner. Wiesbaden: Harrassowitz.

Klaniczay, Gábor. 2003. The Process of Trance, Heavenly and Diabolic Apparitions. In Johannes Nider's *Formicarius*. *Collegium Budapest Discussion Paper Series* 65: 2–81.

Klaniczay, Gábor. 2008. Learned Systems and Popular Narratives of Vision and Bewitchment. In *Witchcraft Mythologies and Persecutions*, ed. G. Klaniczay and É. Pócs in collaboration with E. Csonka-Takács. Budapest/New York: CEU Press.

Klassen, Chris. 2006. The Colonial Mythology of Feminist Witchcraft. In *Between The Worlds: Readings in Contemporary Neopaganism*, ed. S. Ried. Toronto: Canadian Scholars Press.

Knack, Jennifer, and Tracy Vaillancourt. 2011. Evidence of Altered Cortisol Levels across Child Maltreatment, Intimate Partner Abuse, and Peer Victimization. In *Psychology of Victimization*, ed. A.N. Hutcherson. New York: Nova Science Publishers.

Koeniger, Albert Maria. 1923. *Ein Inquisitionsprozess in Sachen der täglichen Kommunion*. Bonn/Leipzig: Schröder.

Kohl, Benjamin G. and H.C. Erik Midelfort. 1998. Introduction to *On Witchcraft: An Abridged Translation of Johann Weyer's 'De praestigiis daemonum'*, ed. B.G. Kohl and H.C. Erik Midelfort. Asheville: Pegasus Press.

Kok, Jan Piet Filedt. 1990. Jacques de Gheyn II: Engraver, Designer and Publisher, parts 1 and 2. *Print Quarterly* 7: 248–281, 370–396.

Kok, Jan Piet Filedt, Marfolein Leesberg and Ger Luijten (eds.). 2000. *The De Gheyn Family*, 2 vols. Rotterdam: Sound & Vision Interactive; Amsterdam: Rijksprentenkabinet.

Kors, Alan Charles, and Edward Peters (eds.). 2001. *Witchcraft in Europe 400–1700: A Documentary History*. Philadelphia: University of Pennsylvania Press.

Kotkov, Sergei Ivanovich, A.S. Oreshnikov, and I.S. Filippova (eds.). 1968. *Moskovskaia delovaia i bytovaia pis'mennost' XVII veka*. Moscow: Nauka.

Kotz, Sonja A., Martin Meyer, and Silke Paulmann. 2006. Lateralization of Emotional Prosody in the Brain: An Overview and Synopsis on the Impact of Study Design. In *Understanding Emotions*, ed. S. Anders, G. Ende et al. Amsterdam: Elsevier.

Kounine, Laura. 2013. The Gendering of Witchcraft: Defence Strategies of Men and Women in German Witchcraft Trials. *German History* 31(3): 295–317.

Kounine, Laura. 2016. The Witch on Trial: Narratives of Conflict and Community in Early Modern Germany. In *Cultures of Conflict Resolution in Early Modern Europe*, ed. S. Cummins and L. Kounine. Farnham: Ashgate.

Kounine, Laura. forthcoming. *Imagining the Witch: Emotions, Gender and Selfhood in Early Modern Germany*. Oxford: Oxford University Press.

Kudielka, Brigitte, Dirk Hellhammer, and Clemens Kirschbaum. 2007. Ten Years of Research with the Trier Social Stress Test—Revisited. In *Social Neuroscience: Integrating Biological and Psychological Explanations of Social Behavior*, ed. E. Harmon-Jones and P. Winkielman. New York: The Guilford Press.

Lakoff, George, and Mark Johnson. 2003 [1980]. *Metaphors We Live By*. Chicago: The University of Chicago Press.

Langbein, John H. 1974. *Prosecuting Crime in the Renaissance: England, Germany, France*. Cambridge, MA: Harvard University Press.

Larner, Christina. 1984. *Witchcraft and Religion: The Politics of Popular Belief*. London: Blackwell.

Lawless, Elaine J. 2009 (1988). "The Night I Got the Holy Ghost..": Holy Ghost Narratives and the Pentecostal Conversion Process. In *Sacred Realms*, ed. R. Warms, J. Garber and R.J. McGee. New York: Oxford University Press.

Leland, Charles Godfrey. 1990 [1899]. *Aradia, Gospel of the Witches*. Custer: Phoenix.

Lembke, Sven. 2000. Folter und gerichtliches Geständnis. Über den Zusammenhang von Gewalt, Schmerz und Wahrheit im 14. und 15. Jahrhundert. In *Das Quälen des Körpers. Eine historische Anthropologie*, ed. P. Burschel. Köln: Böhlau.

Lesses, Rebecca. 2014. "The Most Worthy of Women is a Mistress of Magic": Women as Witches and Ritual Practitioners in *I Enoch* and Rabbinic Sources. In *Daughters of Hecate: Women and Magic in the Ancient World*, ed. K.B. Stratton and D.S. Kalleres. New York: Oxford University Press.

Lester, David. 1972. Voodoo Death: Some New Thoughts on an Old Phenomenon. *American Anthropologist* 74(3): 386–390.

Levack, Brian P. (ed.). 2004a. The Confession of Niclas Fiedler at Trier, 1591. In *The Witchcraft Sourcebook*. London: Routledge.

Levack, Brian P. (ed.). 2004b. The Confession of Johannes Junius at Bamberg 1628. In *The Witchcraft Sourcebook*. London: Routledge.

Levack, Brian P. (ed.). 2013a. *The Oxford Handbook of Witchcraft in Early Modern Europe and Colonial America*. Oxford: Oxford University Press.

Levack, Brian P. 2013b. Witchcraft and the Law. In *The Oxford Handbook of Witchcraft in Early Modern Europe and Colonial America*, ed. B.P. Levack. Oxford: Oxford University Press.

Lewis, Michael, Jeannette Haviland-Jones, and Lisa Barrett (eds.). 2008. *Handbook of Emotions*. New York: The Guilford Press.

Loewenstein, David. 1992. "An Ambiguous Monster": Representing Rebellion in Milton's Polemics and *Paradise Lost*. *Huntington Library Quarterly* 55(2): 295–315.

Loomba, Ania. 2005. *Colonialism/Postcolonialism*, 2nd ed. New York: Routledge.

Löwensteyn, Machteld. 1986. Helse hebzucht en wereldse wellust: Een iconografische interpretate van enkele heksenvoorstellingen van Jacques de Gheyn II. *Volkskundig Bulletin* 12: 241–261.

Löwensteyn, Machteld. 2011. "A Singular Design": A Newly Discovered Drawing by Jacques de Gheyn II. *Burlington Magazine* 153(1295): 81–85.

Luhrmann, T.M. 1989. *Persuasions of the Witches' Craft: Ritual Magic in Contemporary England*. Cambridge, MA: Harvard University Press.

Macfarlane, Alan. 1970. *Witchcraft in Tudor and Stuart England*. New York: Harper and Row.

Macfarlane, Alan. 1999. *Witchcraft in Tudor and Stuart England: A Regional and Comparative Study*, 2nd ed. London: Routledge.

Macha, Jürgen, et al. 2005. *Deutsche Kanzleisprache in Hexenverhörprotokollen der Frühen Neuzeit*. Berlin/New York: Walter de Gruyter.

Maclean, Ian. 1980. *The Renaissance Notion of Woman: A Study in the Fortunes of Scholasticism and Medical Science in European Intellectual Life*. Cambridge: Cambridge University Press.

Magliocco, Sabina. 2004. *Witching Culture: Folklore and Neo-Paganism in America*. Philadelphia: University of Pennsylvania Press.

Magliocco, Sabina. 2013. 'Pagan Fundamentalism?' *The Wild Hunt: A Modern Pagan Perspective*. Last modified 9 Feb 2013. http://wildhunt.org/2013/02/sabina-magliocco-pagan-fundamentalism.html.

Maikov, L. 1992. *Velikorusskie zaklinaniia: Sbornik L. N. Maikova*, ed. A.K. Baiburin. St. Petersburg: Izd-vo Evropeiskogo doma.

Marchal, Claude. 1997. *La Prévôté de Bruyères aux XVIe et XVIIe siècles: population, économie et société*, 2 vols. Villeneuve d'Ascq: ANRT.

Marker, Gary, and Rachel May. 2001. *The Lives of a Russian Noblewoman: The Memories of Anna Labzina*. DeKalb: Northern Illinois University Press.

Martin, Lauren. 2002. The Devil and the Domestic: Witchcraft, Quarrels and Women's Work in Scotland. In *The Scottish Witch-Hunt in Context*, ed. J. Goodare. Manchester: Manchester University Press.

Matt, Susan J., and Peter N. Stearns (eds.). 2014. *Doing Emotions History*. Urbana, Chicago, and Springfield: University of Illinois Press.

Maxwell-Stuart, P.G. 2001. *Witchcraft in Europe and the New World, 1400–1800*. Basingstoke: Palgrave.

McNamara, Jo Ann. 1993. The Rhetoric of Orthodoxy: Clerical Authority and Female Innovation in the Struggle with Heresy. In *Maps of Flesh and Light: The Religious Experience of Medieval Women Mystics*, ed. U. Wiethaus. Syracuse: Syracuse University Press.

McNamer, Sarah. 2010. *Affective Meditation and the Invention of Medieval Compassion*. Philadelphia: University of Pennsylvania Press.

Meij, A.W.F.M. (ed.). 1986. *Jacques de Gheyn II, 1565–1629: Drawings*. Rotterdam: Museum Boymans-van Beuningen. Exhibition catalogue.

Meyer, Birgit. 1999. *Translating the Devil: Religion and Modernity Among the Ewe in Ghana*. Edinburgh: Edinburgh University Press.

Meyer, Birgit. 2010. Aesthetics of Persuasion: Global Christianity and Pentecostalism's Sensational Forms. *South Atlantic Quarterly* 9: 741–763.

Michelet, Jules. 1862. *La sorcière*. E. Dentu: Paris.

Michelet, Jules. 1939. *Satanism and Witchcraft: A Study in Medieval Superstition*. New York: Citadel Press.

Midelfort, H.C. Erik. 1972. *Witchhunting in Southwestern Germany 1562–1684. The Social and Intellectual Foundations*. Stanford: Stanford University Press.

Millar, Charlotte-Rose. 2015. Sleeping with Devils: The Sexual Witch in Seventeenth-Century England. In *Supernatural and Secular Power in Early Modern England*, ed. M. Harmes and V. Bladen. Farnham: Ashgate.

Millar, Charlotte-Rose. 2016. The Non-Human World: Familiars. In *Emotions in Early Modern Europe: An Introduction*, ed. S. Broomhall. London: Routledge.

Millar, Charlotte-Rose. forthcoming 2017. *The Devil is in the Pamphlets: Witchcraft in Early Modern England*. London: Routledge.

Moeller, Katrin. 2007. *Dass Willkür über Recht ginge. Hexenverfolgung in Mecklenburg im 16. und 17. Jahrhundert*. Bielefeld: Verlag für Regionalgeschichte.

Molnàr, Amedeo. 1982. Autour des polémiques antivaudoises du début du XVIᵉ siècle. In *I Valdesi e l'Europa*, Torre Pellice: Società di Studi Valdesi.

Monks, Claire P., and Iain Coyne (eds.). 2011a. *Bullying in Different Contexts*. Cambridge: Cambridge University Press.

Monks, Claire P., and Iain Coyne. 2011b. An Overview of Bullying and Abuse Across Settings. In *Bullying in Different Contexts*, ed. C.P. Monks and I. Coyne. Cambridge: Cambridge University Press.

Monter, William and Edward Peters. 2006. Rémy, Nicolas. In *Encyclopedia of Witchcraft*, ed. R.M. Golden, vol. 4. Santa Barbara: ABC-CLIO.

Motta, Franco. 2016. Evidence, Truth and Sovereignty in Late 16th Century Demonological Literature. *Forum historiae iuris*, http://www.forhistiur. de/2016-04-motta/?l=en.

Muchembled, Robert. 1989. *La violence au village: sociabilité et comportements populaires en Artois du XVe au XVIIe siècle*. Turnhout: Brepols.

Muchembled, Robert. 2012. *A History of Violence: From the End of the Middle Ages to the Present*. Cambridge: Polity.

Muir, Edward. 2005. *Ritual in Early Modern Europe*, 2nd ed. Cambridge: Cambridge University Press.

Müller, Josef. 1963–1966. Bohemian Brethren. In *The New Schaff-Herzog Encyclopedia of Religious Knowledge*, vol. 2. Grand Rapids: Baker.

Murray, Margaret A. 1921. *The Witch-Cult in Western Europe: A Study in Anthropology*. Oxford: Oxford University Press.

Murray, Margaret A. 1931. *The God of the Witches*. London: Faber and Faber.

Murray, Margaret A. 1954. *The Divine King of England: A Study in Anthropology*. London: Faber and Faber.

Nagy, Piroska. 2000. *Le don des larmes au Moyen Âge: un instrument spirituel en quête d'institution (Ve–XIIIe siècle)*. Paris: A. Michel.

Neiworth, Julie J. 2009. Thinking About Me: How Social Awareness Evolved. *Current Directions in Psychological Sciences* 18(3): 143–147.

Niehaus, Isak. 2013. *Witchcraft and a Life in the New South Africa*. Cambridge: Cambridge University Press.

Normand, Laurence, and Gareth Roberts (eds.). 2000. *Witchcraft in Early Modern Scotland: James VI's Demonology and the North Berwick Witches*. Exeter: University of Exeter Press.

Norris, Catherine J., and John T. Cacioppo. 2007. I Know How You Feel: Social and Emotional Information Processing in the Brain. In *Social Neuroscience: Integrating Biological and Psychological Explanations of Social Behavior*, ed. E. Harmon-Jones and P. Winkielman. New York: The Guilford Press.

Norton, Mary Beth. 2002. *In the Devil's Snare: The Salem Witchcraft Crisis of 1692*. New York: Alfred A. Knopf.

Novombergskii, N. Ia. 1906. *Koldovstvo v Moskovskoi Rusi XVII veka. Prilozhenie*, vol. 2. Moscow: Iazyki slavianskoi kul'tury.

O'Callaghan, Michelle. 1998. "Talking Politics": Tyranny, Parliament, and Christopher Brooke's *The Ghost of Richard the Third* (1614). *Historical Journal* 41(1): 97–120.

Ochsner, Kevin N. 2007. How Thinking Controls Feeling: A Social Cognitive Neuroscience. In *Social Neuroscience: Integrating Biological and Psychological Explanations of Social Behavior*, ed. E. Harmon-Jones and P. Winkielman. New York: The Guilford Press.

Oestmann, Peter. 1997. *Hexenprozesse am Reichskammergericht*. Köln: Böhlau.

Oldridge, Darren. 2000. *The Devil in Early Modern England*. Stroud: Sutton.

Online Computer Library Center, Dewey® Services. 2015. Dewey Decimal Cataloguing System (current). http://www.oclc.org/dewey/resources/summaries/default.htm#100.

Opitz-Belakhal, Claudia. 2006. *Das Universum des Jean Bodin: Staatsbildung, Macht und Geschlecht im 16. Jahrhundert*. Campus: Frankfurt am Main.

Opitz-Belakhal, Claudia. 2009. Witchcraft Studies from the Perspective of Women's and Gender History. *Magic, Ritual, and Witchcraft* 4(1): 90–99.

Ostling, Michael. 2011. *Between the Devil and the Host: Imagining Witchcraft in Early Modern Poland*. Oxford: Oxford University Press.

Ostling, Michael. 2014. Witches' Herbs on Trial. *Folklore* 125(2): 179–201.

Paré, Ambroise. 1982. *On Monsters and Marvels*. Trans. Janis Pallister. Chicago/London: University of Chicago Press.

Park, Jiyoung, Shinobu Kitayama, Hazel R. Markus, Christopher L. Coe, Yuri Miyamoto, Mayumi Karasawa, Katherine B. Curhan, Gayle D. Love, Norito Kawakami, Jennifer Morozink Boylan, Carol D. Ryff. 2013. Social Status and Anger Expression: The Cultural Moderation Hypothesis. *Emotion* 13(6): 1122–1131.

Patton, Christine, and John Stratton Hawley (eds.). 2004. *Holy Tears: Weeping in the Religious Imagination*. Princeton: Princeton University Press.

Pazdro, Z. 1900. Proces o 'perepiczkę'. *Lud* 6: 268–276.

Pearl, Jonathan L. 1995. *Introduction to Jean Bodin, On the Demon-Mania of Witches*. Ed. J.L. Pearl, trans. R.A. Scott. Toronto: CRRS.

Perrie, Maureen. 2013. The Tsaritsa, the Needlewomen and the Witches: Magic in Moscow in the 1630s. *Russian History* 40: 297–314.

Peskowitz, Miriam. 1997. Unweaving: A Response to Carol P. Christ. *Journal of Feminist Studies in Religion* 13(1): 137–143.

Petersohn, Jürgen. 2004. *Kaiserlicher Gestandter und Kurienbischof: Andreas Jamometić am Hof Papst Sixtus' IV. (1478–1481). Aufschlüsse aus neuen Quellen*, Monumenta Germaniae Historica: Studien und Texte, 35. Hannover: Hahnsche Buchhandlung.

Petherbridge, Deanna. 2013. *Witches and Wicked Bodies*. Edinburgh: National Galleries of Scotland.

Pike, Sarah M. 2001. *Earthly Bodies, Magical Selves: Contemporary Pagans and the Search of Community*. Berkeley: University of California Press.

Pike, Sarah M. 2004. *New Age and Neopagan Religions in America*. New York: Columbia University Press.

Pilaszek, Małgorzata. 2008. *Procesy o czary w Polsce w wiekach XV-XVIIII*. Kraków: Universitas.

Plamper, Jan. 2010. The History of Emotions: An Interview with William Reddy, Barbara Rosenwein, and Peter Stearns. *History and Theory* 49: 237–265.

Plamper, Jan. 2015. *The History of Emotions: An Introduction*. Oxford: Oxford University Press.

Plane, Ann Marie. 2014. *Dreams and the Invisible World in Colonial New England: Indians, Colonists, and the Seventeenth Century*. Philadelphia: University of Pennsylvania Press.

Pollmann, Judith. 1999. *Religious Choice in the Dutch Republic: The Reformation of Arnoldus Buchelius, 1565–1641*. Manchester: Manchester University Press.

Poor, Sara S. 2004. *Mechthild of Magdeburg and Her Book: Gender and the Making of Textual Authority*. Philadelphia: University of Pennsylvania Press.

Purkiss, Diane. 1995. Women's Stories of Witchcraft in Early Modern England: The House, the Body, the Child. *Gender and History* 7: 408–432.

Purkiss, Diane. 1996. *The Witch in History: Early Modern and Twentieth Century Representations*. New York: Routledge.

Purkiss, Diane. 2001. Sounds of Silence. Fairies and Incest in Scottish Witchcraft Stories. In *Languages of Witchcraft. Narrative, Ideology and Meaning in Early Modern Culture*, ed. S. Clark. New York: St. Martin's Press.

Purkiss, Diane. 2005. *Literature, Gender and Politics During the English Civil War*. Cambridge: Cambridge University Press.

Purkiss, Diane. 2006. Fairies. In *Encyclopedia of Witchcraft*, ed. R.M. Golden, vol. 2. Santa Barbara: ABC-CLIO.

Quaife, Geoffery Robert. 1987. *Godly Zeal and Furious Rage: The Witch in Early Modern Europe*. New York: St. Martin's Press.

Randall, Peter. 2001. *Bullying in Adulthood*. New York: Routledge.

Ray, Rebecca D., Frank H. Wilhelm, and James J. Gross. 2008. All in the Mind's Eye? Anger Rumination and Reappraisal. *Journal of Personality and Social Psychology* 94(1): 133–145.

Read, Donna. 1989. *The Goddess Remembered*. Montreal: National Film Board of Canada.

Read, Donna. 1990. *The Burning Times*. Montreal: National Film Board of Canada.

Read, Donna. 1993. *Full Circle*. Montreal: National Film Board of Canada.

Reddy, William M. 1999. "Emotional Liberty": Politics and History in the Anthropology of Emotions. *Cultural Anthropology* 14(2): 256–288.

Reddy, William M. 2001. *The Navigation of Feeling: A Framework for the History of Emotions*. Cambridge: Cambridge University Press.

Reeser, Todd W. 2006. *Moderating Masculinity in Early Modern Culture*. Chapel Hill: University of North Carolina Press.

Reiman, Martin, and Philip G. Zimbardo. 2011. The Dark Side of Social Encounters: Prospects for a Neuroscience of Human Evil. *Journal of Neuroscience, Psychology, and Economics* 4(3): 174–180.

Reis, Elizabeth. 1997. *Damned Women: Sinners and Witches in Puritan New England*. Ithaca: Cornell University Press.

Říčan, Rudolf. 1992. *The History of the Unity of the Brethren: A Protestant Hussite Church in Bohemia and Moravia*. Trans. C. Daniel Crews. Bethlehem: The Moravian Church in America.

Riezler, Sigmund. 1896. *Geschichte der Hexenprozesse in Bayern. Im Lichte der allgemeinen Entwickelung dargestellt*. Stuttgart: J. G. Cotta.

Rigby, Ken. 2002. *New Perspectives on Bullying*. London: Jessica Kingsley.

Roach, Marilynne. 2004. *The Salem Witch Trials: A Day-by-Day Chronicle of a Community Under Siege*. Lanham: Taylor Trade Publishing.

Robbins, Paul. 2000. *Anger, Aggression, and Violence*. Jefferson: McFarland.

Robisheaux, Thomas. 2009. *The Last Witch of Langenburg: Murder in a German Village*. New York: W. W. Norton.

Robisheaux, Thomas. 2013. The German Witch Trials. In *The Oxford Handbook of Witchcraft in Early Modern Europe and Colonial America*, ed. B.P. Levack. Oxford: Oxford University Press.

Robisheaux, Thomas. 2004. "The Queen of Evidence": The Witchcraft Confession in the Age of Confessionalism. In *Confessionalization in Europe, 1555–1700. Essays in Honor and Memory of Bodo Nischan*, ed. J.M. Headley, H.J. Hillerbrand, and A.J. Papalas. Aldershot: Ashgate.

Rob-Santer, Carmen. 2003. Le *Malleus Maleficarum* à la lumière de l'historiographie: Un *Kulturkampf? Médiévales* 44: 155–172.

Roper, Lyndal. 1994. *Oedipus and the Devil: Witchcraft, Sexuality and Religion in Early Modern Europe*. London: Routledge.

Roper, Lyndal. 2004. *Witch Craze: Terror and Fantasy in Baroque Germany*. New Haven: Yale University Press.

Roper, Lyndal. 2006. Witchcraft and the Western Imagination. *Transactions of the Royal Historical Society* 16(6): 117–141.

Roper, Lyndal. 2012. *The Witch in the Western Imagination*. Charlottesville: University of Virginia Press.

Rosen, Barbara. 1991. *Witchcraft in England, 1558–1618*, 2nd ed. Amherst: University of Massachusetts Press.

Rosenthal, Bernard. 1993. *Salem Story: Reading the Witch Trials of 1692*. New York: Cambridge University Press.

Rosenthal, Bernard (ed.). 2009. *Records of the Salem Witch-Hunt*. New York: Cambridge University Press.

Rosenwein, Barbara H. 2002. Worrying About Emotions in History. *The American Historical Review* 107(3): 821–845.

Rosenwein, Barbara H. 2006. *Emotional Communities in the Early Middle Ages*. Ithaca: Cornell University Press.

Rosenwein, Barbara H. 2016. *Generations of Feeling: A History of Emotions, 600–1700*. Cambridge: Cambridge University Press.

Rossi, Maura. 2011. Effects of Bullying Victimization from Childhood to Young Adulthood. In *Psychology of Victimization*, ed. A.N. Hutcherson. New York: Nova Science Publishers.

Rountree, Kathryn. 2004. *Embracing the Witch and the Goddess: Feminist Ritual Makers in New Zealand*. New York: Routledge.

Rowlands, Alison. 2001. Witchcraft and Old Women in Early Modern Germany. *Past & Present* 173: 50–89.

Rowlands, Alison. 2003. *Witchcraft Narratives in Germany: Rothenburg, 1561–1652*. Manchester: Manchester University Press.

Rowlands, Alison. 2013. Witchcraft and Gender in Early Modern Europe. In *The Oxford Handbook of Witchcraft in Early Modern Europe and Colonial America*, ed. B.P. Levack. Oxford: Oxford University Press.

Royzman, Edward, Pavel Atansov, Justin F. Landy, Amanda Parks, and Andrew Gepty. 2014. CAD or MAD? Anger (Not Disgust) as the Predominant Response to Pathogen-Free Violations of the Divinity Code. *Emotion* 14(5): 892–907.

Rublack, Ulinka. 2002. Fluxes: The Early Modern Body and the Emotions. *History Workshop Journal* 53: 1–16.

Rublack, Ulinka. 2013. Interior States and Sexuality in Early Modern Germany. In *After the History of Sexuality: German Geologies with and Beyond Foucault*, ed. Scott Spector, Helmut Puff, and Dagmar Herzog. New York: Berghahn Books.

Rublack, Ulinka. 2015. *The Astronomer and the Witch: Johannes Kepler's Fight for His Mother*. Oxford: Oxford University Press.

Ruff, Julius R. 2001. *Violence in Early Modern Europe: 1500–1800*. Cambridge: Cambridge University Press.

Rummel, Walter. 1991. *Bauern, Herren und Hexen. Studien zur Sozialgeschichte sponheimischer und kurtrierischer Hexenprozesse 1574–1664*. Göttingen: V & R unipress.

Ryle, Gilbert. 1949. *The Concept of Mind*. London: Hutchinson.

Ryle, Gilbert. 1971. The Thinking of Thoughts: What is "Le Penseur" Doing?. In *Collected Papers*. London: Hutchinson.

Sabean, David W. 1984. *Power in the Blood: Popular Culture and Village Discourse in Early Modern Germany*. Cambridge: Cambridge University Press.

Salomonsen, Jone. 2002. *Enchanted Feminism: Ritual, Gender, and Divinity Among the Reclaiming Witches of San Francisco*. New York: Routledge.

Sauter, Marianne. 2010. *Hexenprozess und Folter. Die strafrechtliche Spruchpraxis der Juristenfakultät Tübingen im 17. und beginnenden 18. Jahrhundert*. Bielefeld: Verlag für Regionalgeschichte.

Scarry, Elaine. 1985. *The Body in Pain: The Making and Unmaking of the World*. Oxford: Oxford University Press.

Scharff, Thomas. 2000. Seelenrettung und Machtinszenierung. Sinnkonstruktioen der Folter im kirchlichen Inquisitionsverfahren des Mittelalters. In *Das Quälen des Körpers. Eine historische Anthropologie*, ed. P. Burschel, G. Distelrath, and S. Lembke. Köln: Böhlau.

Scheer, Monique. 2012. Are Emotions a Kind of Practice (and Is That What Makes Them Have a History)? A Bourdieuan Approach to Understanding Emotion. *History and Theory* 51(2): 193–220.

Schiewer, Hans-Jochen. 1996. Auditionen und Visionen einer Begine. Die "Selige Schererin": Johannes Mulberg und der Basler Beginenstreit. Mit einem Textabdruck. In *Die Vermittlung geistlicher Inhalte im deutschen Mittelalter*, ed. T.R. Jackson, N.F. Palmer, and A. Suerbaum. Tübingen: Niemeyer.

Schild, Wolfgang. 2001. Der gefolterte weibliche Körper. In *Frieden und Krieg in der Frühen Neuzeit*, ed. K. Garber and J. Held. München: Fink.

Schlecht, Joseph. 1903. *Andrea Zamometić und der Basler Konzilsversuch vom jahre 1482*. Paderborn: Schöningh.

Schneider, Manfred. 1996. Die Beobachtung des Zeugen nach Artikel 71 der "Carolina": der Aufbau eines Codes der Glaubwürdigkeit 1532-1850. In *Geschichten der Physiognomik. Text – Bild – Wissen*, ed. R. Campe and M. Schneider. Freiburg im Breisgau: Rombach.

Schneider, Manfred. 2007. Forum internum – forum externum. Institutionstheorien des Geständnisses. In *Sozialgeschichte des Geständnisses. Zum Wandel der Geständniskultur*, ed. J. Reichertz and M. Schneider. Wiesbaden: Verlag für Sozialwissenschaften.

Schneider, Manfred. 2008. Tränen vor Gericht. In *Tränen*, ed. B. Söntgen and G. Spiekermann. München: Fink.

Schnell, Rüdiger. 2009. Ansätze und Irrwege historischer Emotionsforschung. In *Emotionen! Émotions! 16. Jahrestagung des Brackwerder Arbeitskreises/XVIe colloque annuel du "Brackwerder Arbeitskreis"*. Reader: DHI Paris, 20–21 Nov. 2009.

Schnell, Rüdiger. 2015. *Haben Gefühle eine Geschichte? Aporien einer History of Emotions*. Göttingen: V & R unipress.

Schnyder, André. 1993. *Malleus Maleficarum. Kommentar zur Wiedergabe des Erstdrucks von 1487*. Göppingen: Kümmerle Verlag.

Schröder, Alfred. 1929. Die tägliche Laienkommunion in spätmittelalterlicher Auffassung. *Archiv für die Geschichte des Hochstifts Augsburg* 6: 609–629.

Schulte, Rolf. 2009. *Man as Witch: Male Witches in Central Europe*. Trans. Linda Froome-Döring. Basingstoke: Palgrave Macmillan.

Schuster, Peter. 2016. *Verbrecher, Opfer, Heilige. Eine Geschichte des Tötens*, 2nd ed. Stuttgart: Klett-Cotta.

Schwaninger, Adrian, Christian Wallraven et al. 2006. Processing of Facial Identity and Expression: A Psychophysical, Physiological, and Computational Perspective. In *Understanding Emotions*, ed. S. Anders, G. Ende et al. Amsterdam: Elsevier.

Scott, Joan Wallach. 2011. Sexularism: On Secularism and Gender Equality. In *The Fantasy of Feminist History*, ed. J.W. Scott. Durham: Duke University Press.

Scribner, Robert. 1989. Is a History of Popular Culture Possible? *History of European Ideas* 10: 175–191.

Sell, Aaron, John Tooby, and Leda Cosmides. 2009. Formidability and the Logic of Human Anger. *Proceedings of the National Academy of Sciences of the United States of America* 106(35): 15073–15078.

Serpell, James. 2002. Guardian Spirits or Demonic Pets: The Concept of the Witch's Familiar in Early Modern England, 1530-1712. In *The Animal-Human Boundary: Historical Perspectives*, ed. A.N.H. Creager and W.C. Jordan. Rochester: University of Rochester Press.

Seymour, Mark. 2012. Emotional Arenas: From Provincial Circus to National Courtroom in Late Nineteenth-Century Italy. *Rethinking History* 16(2): 177–197.

Sharpe, James. 1996. *Instruments of Darkness: Witchcraft in England 1550–1750*. London: Hamish Hamilton.

Sharpe, James. 2006. Familiars. In *Encyclopedia of Witchcraft*, ed. R.M. Golden, vol. 2. Santa Barbara: ABC-CLIO.

Shweder, Richard A., and Jonathan Haidt. 2000. The Cultural Psychology of the Emotions: Ancient and New. In *The Handbook of Emotions*, 2nd ed, ed. M. Lewis and J.M. Haviland-Jones. New York: The Guilford Press.

Siegel, Allan, and Jeff Victoroff. 2009. Understanding Human Aggression: New Insights from Neuroscience. *International Journal of Law and Psychiatry* 32(4): 209–221.

Siever, Larry J. 2008. Neurobiology of Aggression and Violence. *The American Journal of Psychiatry* 165(4): 429–442.

Silverman, Lisa. 2001. *Tortured Subjects: Pain, Truth and the Body in Early Modern France*. Chicago: University of Chicago Press.

Sincaceur, Marwan, Gerben A. van Kleef, Margaret A. Neale, Hajo Adam, and Christophe Haag. 2011. Hot or Cold: Is Communicating Anger or Threats More Effective in Negotiations? *Journal of Applied Psychology* 96(5): 1018–1032.

Smilianskaia, E.B. 2002. Zagovory i gadaniia iz sudebno-sledsvennykh materialov XVIII veka. In *Otrechennoe chtenie v Rossii XVII–XVIII vekov: Publikatsiia tekstov*, ed. A.L. Toporkov and A.A. Turilov. Moscow: Indrik.

Smilianskaia, E.B. 2003. *Volshebniki, bogokhul'niki, eretiki: Narodnaia religioznost' i 'dukhovnye prestupleniia' v Rossii XVIII veke*. Moscow: Indrik.

Smith, Moira. 2002. The Flying Phallus and the Laughing Inquisitor: Penis Theft in the "Malleus Maleficarum". *Journal of Folklore Research* 39(1): 85–117.

Spanos, Nicholas P. 1978. Witchcraft in Histories of Psychiatry: A Critical Analysis and an Alternative Conceptualization. *Psychological Bulletin* 85(2): 417–439.

Spivak, Gayatri Chakravorty. 1988. Can the Subaltern Speak? In *Marxism and the Interpretation of Culture*, ed. C. Nelson and L. Grossberg. Chicago: University of Illinois Press.

Spufford, Margaret. 1981. *Small Books and Pleasant Histories: Popular Fiction and Its Readership in Seventeenth-Century England*. London: Methuen.

Starhawk. 1989 [1979]. *The Spiral Dance*. San Francisco: HarperSanFrancisco.

Starhawk. 1990 [1987]. *Truth or Dare: Encounters with Power, Authority, and Mystery*. San Francisco: HarperSanFrancisco.

Starhawk. 1997 [1982]. *Dreaming the Dark: Magic, Sex and Politics*. Boston: Beacon.

Starhawk, and Hilary Valentine. 2000. *The Twelve Wild Swans: A Journey to the Realm of Magic, Healing and Action: Rituals, Exercises and Magical Training in the Reclaiming Tradition*. San Francisco: HarperSanFrancisco.

Stearns, Peter N. 2008. History of Emotions: Issues of Change and Impact. In *Handbook of Emotions*, ed. M. Lewis, J.M. Haviland-Jones, and L. Feldman Barrett. New York: The Guilford Press.

Stearns, Peter N., and Carol Z. Stearns. 1985. Emotionology: Clarifying the History of Emotions and Emotional Standards. *American Historical Review* 90: 813–836.

Steinberg, Mark D. 2008. Melancholy and Modernity: Emotions and Social Life in Russia Between the Revolutions. *Journal of Social History* 41(4): 813–841.

Stephens, Walter. 1998. Witches Who Steal Penises: Impotence and Illusion in *Malleus Maleficarum*. *Journal of Medieval and Early Modern Studies* 28(3): 495–529.

Stephens, Walter. 2001. Incredible Sex: Witches, Demons, and Giants in the Early Modern Imagination. In *Monsters in the Italian Literary Imagination*, ed. K. Jewell. Detroit: Wayne State University Press.

Stephens, Walter. 2002. *Demon Lovers: Witchcraft, Sex, and the Crisis of Belief.* Chicago: University of Chicago Press.

Stone, Valerie E. 2007. An Evolutionary Perspective on Domain Specificity in Social Intelligence. In *Social Neuroscience: Integrating Biological and Psychological Explanations of Social Behavior*, ed. E. Harmon-Jones and P. Winkielman. New York: The Guilford Press.

Stout, Rowland. 2014. Ryle's Conceptions of Emotional Behaviour. In *Ryle on Mind and Language*, ed. D. Dolby. Basingstoke: Palgrave Macmillan.

Stoyle, Mark. 2011. *The Black Legend of Prince Rupert's Dog: Witchcraft and Propaganda During the English Civil War*. Liverpool: Liverpool University Press.

Sullivan, Erin. 2013. The History of the Emotions: Past, Present, Future. *Cultural History* 2(1): 93–102.

Summers, Montague. 1926. *The History of Witchcraft and Demonology*. London: Kegan Paul.

Supreme Court of New South Wales, Regina v Penetito Mika; Regina v Siniue Sagato [2000] NSWSC 852. http://www.austlii.edu.au/au/cases/nsw/supreme_ct/2000/852.html. Accessed 1 Oct 2015.

Swan, Claudia. 1999. The *Preparation for the Sabbath* by Jacques de Gheyn II. The Issue of Inversion. *Print Quarterly* 16: 327–339.

Swan, Claudia. 2005. *Art, Science, and Witchcraft in Early Modern Holland: Jacques de Gheyn II (1565–1629)*. Cambridge: Cambridge University Press.

Swan, Claudia. 2013. Diagnosing and Representing Witchcraft: Medico-Philosophical Theories of the Imagination in the Context of Artistic Practice in the Netherlands ca. 1600. In *Imagination und Sexualität: Pathologien der Einbildungskraft im medizinischen Diskurs der frühen Neuzeit*, ed. S. Zaun, D. Watzke, and J. Steigerwald. Frankfurt am Main: Vittorio Klostermann.

Szyszkowski, Władysław. 1913. Pierwiastek ludowy w poezyi polskiej XV i XVI w. (I). *Lud* 19: 104–152.

Tanaka-Matsumi, Junko. 1995. Cross-Cultural Perspectives on Anger. In *Anger Disorders: Definition, Diagnosis, and Treatment*, ed. H. Kassinove. Washington, DC: Taylor and Francis.

Taylor, Charles. 1989. *Sources of the Self: The Making of the Modern Identity*. New York: Cambridge University Press.

Taylor, Shelley E., and Gian C. Gonzaga. 2007. Affiliative Responses to Stress: A Social Neuroscience Model. In *Social Neuroscience: Integrating Biological and Psychological Explanations of Social Behavior*, ed. E. Harmon-Jones and P. Winkielman. New York: The Guilford Press.

Thomas, Keith. 1973. *Religion and the Decline of Magic*. Harmondsworth: Penguin Books.

Thomas, Keith. 1983. *Man and the Natural World*. London: Allen Lane.

Thomas, Keith. 1986. The Meaning of Literacy in Early Modern England. In *The Written Word in Translation*, ed. G. Baumann. Oxford: Oxford University Press.

Thürlemann, Felix. 2012. The Paradoxical Rhetoric of Tears: Looking at the Madrid *Descent from the Cross*. In *Crying in the Middle Ages: Tears of History*, ed. E. Gertsmann. Routledge: New York.

Timbers, Frances. 2014. *Magic and Masculinity: Ritual, Magic and Gender in the Early Modern Era*. New York: I.B. Taurus.

Topalovic, Elvira and Hille Iris. 2016. 'Perspektivierung von Wirklichkeit(en) im Hexenprozess' in historicum.net, URL: https://www.historicum.net/purl/11j/.

Toporkov, Andrei. 2005. *Zagovory v russkoi rukopisnoi traditsii XV-XIX vv*. Moscow: Indrik.

Toporkov, Andrei. 2008. Russian Love Charms in a Comparative Light. In *Charms, Charmers and Charming: International Research on Verbal Magic*, ed. J. Roper. Basingstoke: Palgrave Macmillan.

Toporkov, Andrei (ed.). 2010. *Russkie zagovory iz rukopisnykh istochnikov XVII-pervoi poloviny XIX v*. Moscow: Indrik.

Toporkov, Andrei. 2013. Verbal Charms Against Authorities and Judges in Seventeenth- and Eighteenth-Century Russia. *Russian History* 40: 532–539.

Touber, Jetze. 2009. Articulating Pain: Martyrology, Torture, and Execution in the Works of Antonio Gallonio (1556–1605). In *The Sense of Suffering. Constructions of Physical Pain in Early Modern Culture*, ed. J.F. van Dijkhuizen and K.A.E. Enenkel. Leiden/Boston: Brill.

Trevor-Roper, H.R. 1967. The European Witch-Craze of the Sixteenth and Seventeenth Centuries. In *Religion, the Reformation, and Social Change*. London: Macmillan.

Uchino, Bert N., Julianne Holt-Lunstad, Darcy Uno, Rebecca Campo, and Maija Reblin. 2007. The Social Neuroscience of Relationships: An Examination of Health-Relevant Pathways. In *Social Neuroscience: Integrating Biological and Psychological Explanations of Social Behavior*, ed. E. Harmon-Jones and P. Winkielman. New York: The Guilford Press.

Uruszczak, Wacław. 1994. Proces czarownicy w Nowym Sączu w 1670 roku. Z badań nad miejskim procesem karnym czasów nowożytnych. In *Historia*

Prawa. Historia Kultury. Liber Memorialis Vitoldo Maisel, ed. E. Borkowska-Bagieńska and H. Olszewski. Poznań: Printer.

van Dijk, Eric, Gerben A. van Kleef, Wolfgang Steinel, and Ilja van Beest. 2008. A Social Functional Approach to Emotions in Bargaining: When Communicating Anger Pays and When It Backfires. *Journal of Personality and Social Psychology* 94(4): 600–614.

Van Gent, Jacqueline. 2009. *Magic, Body and the Self in Eighteenth-Century Sweden*. Leiden: Brill.

van Hasselt, Carlos (ed.). 1985. *Le Héraut du dix-septième siècle. Dessins et gravures de Jacques de Gheyn II et III*. Paris: Institut Néerlandais. Exhibition catalogue.

van Honk, Jack, and Dennis Schutter. 2007. Vigilant and Avoidant Responses to Angry Facial Expressions: Dominance and Submission Motives. In *Social Neuroscience: Integrating Biological and Psychological Explanations of Social Behavior*, ed. E. Harmon-Jones and P. Winkielman. New York: The Guilford Press.

van Regteren Altena, I.Q. 1983. *Jacques de Gheyn: Three Generations*. Trans. Mary Charles, 3 vols. Boston/The Hague: M. Nijhoff Publishers.

Vauchez, André. 1999. Between Virginity and Spiritual Espousals: Models of Feminine Sainthood in the Christian West in the Middle Ages. *The Medieval History Journal* 2(2): 349–359.

Vobr, Jaroslav. 1986. *Catalogus librorum ab a. MDI ad a. MDXX typis impressorum, qui in Scientiarum bibliotheca publica Brunensi asservantur*. Brno: Scientiarum bibliotheca publica Brunensis, 5 vols.

Vogelaar, Christiaan, et al. (eds.). 2011. *Lucas van Leyden en de Renaissance*, Exhib. Cat. Leiden/Antwerp: Museum De Lakenhal/Ludion.

Voltmer, Rita. 2004. *... ce tant exécrable et détestable crime de sortilège*. Der 'Bürgerkrieg' gegen Hexen und Hexenmeister im Herzogtum Luxemburg (16. und 17. Jahrhundert)'. Hémecht. Revue d'Histoire Luxembourgeoise. *Zeitschrift für Luxemburger Geschichte* 56: 57–92.

Voltmer, Rita. 2005a. Henker, Heiler, Hexenbanner – Hexenmeister? Der Fall des Echternacher Scharfrichters und Wasenmeisters Caspar Back (17. Jahrhundert). In *Porträt einer europäischen Region. Der Rhein-Maas-Raum in historischen Lebensbildern*, ed. F. Irsigler and G. Minn. Trier: Kliomedia.

Voltmer, Rita (ed.). 2005b. *Hexenverfolgung und Herrschaftspraxis*. Trier: Paulinus Verlag.

Voltmer, Rita. 2006a. Germany, North and Northwest. In *Encyclopedia of Witchcraft*, ed. R.M. Golden, vol. 2. Santa Barbara: ABC-CLIO.

Voltmer, Rita. 2006b. Luxembourg, duchy of. In *Encyclopedia of Witchcraft*, ed. R.M. Golden, vol. 3. Santa Barbara: ABC-CLIO.

Voltmer, Rita. 2008. Von den Kindern des Saturn und dem Kampf mit dem Schicksal – Lebenswege und Überlebensstrategien kleiner Leute im Spiegel von Strafgerichtsakten. In *Arme und ihre Lebensperspektiven in der Frühen Neuzeit*, ed. S. Schmidt. Frankfurt: Peter Lang Verlag.

Voltmer, Rita. 2009. Witch-Finders, Witch-Hunters or Kings of the Sabbath? The Prominent Role of Men in the Mass Persecutions of the Rhine-Meuse Area (Sixteenth-Seventeenth Centuries). In *Witchcraft and Masculinities in Early Modern Europe*, ed. A. Rowlands. Basingstoke: Palgrave Macmillan.

Voltmer, Rita. 2010. Behind the "Veil of memory": About the Limitations of Narratives. *Magic, Ritual and Witchcraft* 5(1): 96–102.

Voltmer, Rita. 2012. Hexenpolitik im Saarraum? Zu Stand und Perspektiven landes- und kulturgeschichtlicher Hexenforschung in einer "passiven Geschichtslandschaft". In *Historische Blicke auf das Land an der Saar. 60 Jahre Kommission für Saarländische Landesgeschichte und Volksforschung*, ed. B. Kasten. Saarbrücken: Kommission für Saarländische Landesgeschichte und Volksforschung e.V.

Voltmer, Rita. 2015. Judge's Lore? The Politico-Religious Concept of Metamorphosis in the Peripheries of Western Europe. In *Werewolf Histories*, ed. W. de Blécourt. Basingstoke: Palgrave Macmillan.

Voltmer, Rita. 2016. Im Bann des "Planetendämons" Saturn – Zu astrologischen Deutungen des Späten Mittelalters und der Frühen Neuzeit. *Spee Jahrbuch* 21(22): 115–150.

Voltmer, Rita. forthcoming. Witch Trials. In *The Oxford Illustrated History of Witchcraft and Magic*, ed. O. Davies. Oxford: Oxford University Press.

Voltmer, Rita, and Kobayashi Shigeko. 2011. Supplikationen und Hexereiverfahren im Westen des Alten Reiches – Stand und Perspektiven der Forschung. *Kurtrierisches Jahrbuch* 51: 247–269.

Voltmer, Rita, et al. 2015. Stimmen der Frauen? Gerichtsakten und Gender Studies am Beispiel der Hexenforschung. In *Frauen – Männer – Queer. Ansätze und Perspektiven aus der historischen Genderforschung*, ed. A. Conrad. St. Ingbert: Röhrig Universitätsverlag.

von Heusinger, Sabine. 2000. *Johannes Mulberg OP (+1414): Ein Leben im Spannungsfeld von Dominikanerobservanz und Beginenstreit*. Berlin: Akademie Verlag.

Vowell, Sarah. 2003. *The Partly Cloudy Patriot*. New York: Simon and Schuster.

Walinski-Kiehl, Robert. 2004. Males, "Masculine Honour" and Witch-Hunting in Seventeenth-Century Germany. *Men and Masculinities* 6(3): 254–271.

Ward, Jamie. 2015. *The Student's Guide to Cognitive Neuroscience* , 3rd ed. London/New York: Psychology Press.

Wawrzeniecki, Marjan. 1897. Proces o czary w Nieszawie roku 1721. *Wisła* 11: 646–654.

Wiens, Stefan. 2006. Subliminal Emotion Perception in Brain Imaging: Findings, Issues, and Recommendations. In *Understanding Emotions*, ed. S. Anders, G. Ende et al. Amsterdam: Elsevier.

Wilby, Emma. 2005. *Cunning Folk and Familiar Spirits: Shamanistic Visionary Traditions in Early Modern British Witchcraft and Magic*. Brighton: Sussex Academic.

Wilde, Manfred. 2003. *Die Zauberei- und Hexenprozesse in Kursachsen*. Köln: Böhlau.

Wildgruber, Dirk, H. Ackermann, B. Kreifelts, T. Etholfer, et al. 2006. Cerebral Processing of Linguistic and Emotional Prosody: fMRI Studies. In *Understanding Emotions*, ed. S. Anders, G. Ende et al. Amsterdam: Elsevier.

Williams, Gerhild Scholz. 2013. Demonologies. In *The Oxford Handbook of Witchcraft in Early Modern Europe and Colonial America*, ed. B.P. Levack. Oxford: Oxford University Press.

Williams-Krapp, Werner. 1990. *Dise ding sint dennoch nit ware zeichen der heiligkeit*. Zur Bewertung mystischer Erfahrungen im 15. Jahrhundert. *Zeitschrift für Literaturwissenschaft und Linguistik* 80: 61–71.

Williams-Krapp, Werner, Ulla Williams, et al. 2004. Die Dominikaner im Kampf gegen weibliche Irrtümer: Eberhard Mardachs 'Sendbrief von wahrer Andacht' (mit einer Textedition). In *Deutsch-Böhmische Literaturbeziehungen: Germano-Bohemica. Festschrift für Václav Bok zum 65. Geburtstag*, ed. H.-J. Behr. Hamburg: Kovac.

Willis, Deborah. 1995. *Malevolent Nurture: Witch-Hunting and Maternal Power in Early Modern England*. Ithaca: Cornell University Press.

Winkler, John J. 1990. The Constraints of Desire: Erotic Magical Spells. In *The Constraints of Desire. The Anthropology of Sex and Gender in Ancient Greece*, ed. J.J. Winkler. New York: Routledge.

Wirtschafter, Elise Kimerling. 2003. *The Play of Ideas in Russian Enlightenment Theater*. DeKalb: Northern Illinois University Press.

Wiślicz, Tomasz. 2001. *Zarobić na duszne zbawienie. Religijność chłopów małopolskich od polowy XVI do końca XVIII w*. Warszawa: Wydawnictwo Neriton/Instytut Historii Polskiej Akademii Nauk.

Wiślicz, Tomasz. 2012. *Upodobanie: Małżeństwo i związki nieformalne na wsi polskiej XVII-XVIII wieku*. Wrocław: Chronicon Wydawnictwo.

Wiśniewska, Halina. 2003. *Świat płci żeńskiej baroku zaklęty w słowach*. Lublin: Wydawnictwo UMCS.

Wittig, Monique. 1972. *The Guérillères*. London: Picador.

Woronczak, Jerzy. 1972. Procesy o czary przed poznańskim sądem miejskim w XVI wieku. *Literatura Ludowa* 16(3): 49–58.

Wróbel, Elżbieta Elena. 2002. *Chrześcijańska rodzina w Polsce XVI XVII wieku. Między ideałem a rzeczywistością*. Kraków: Wydawnictwo Naukowe Papieskiej Akademii Teologicznej.

Wyschogrod, Edith. 1998. *An Ethics of Remembering. History, Heterology, and the Nameless Others*. Chicago: University of Chicago Press.

Yang, Zixu, and Eddie M.W. Tong. 2010. The Effects of Subliminal Anger and Sadness Primers on Agency Appraisals. *Emotion* 10(6): 915–922.

Zagolla, Robert. 2007. *Folter und Hexenprozess. Die strafrechtliche Spruchpraxis der Juristenfakultät Rostock im 17. Jahrhundert*. Bielefeld: Verlag für Regionalgeschichte.

Zakrzewska-Dubasowa, Mirosława (ed.). 1947. *Procesy o czary w Lublinie w XVII i XVIII w.* Lublin: Nakład. Polskiego Towarzystwa Ludoznawczego.

Zaller, Robert. 1993. The Figure of the Tyrant in English Revolutionary Thought. *Journal of the History of Ideas* 54(4): 585–619.

Zaller, Robert. 1998. Breaking the Vessels: The Desacralization of the Monarchy in Early Modern England. *Sixteenth Century Journal* 29(3): 757–778.

Zaller, Robert. 2007. *The Discourse of Legitimacy in Early Modern England.* Stanford: Stanford University Press.

Zeman, Jarold K. 1977. *The Hussite Movement and the Reformation in Bohemia, Moravia and Slovakia (1350–1650): A Bibliographical Study Guide (with Particular Reference to Resources in North America).* Ann Arbor: Michigan Slavic Publications.

Zika, Charles. 2003a. *Exorcising Our Demons: Magic, Witchcraft and Visual Culture in Early Modern Europe.* Boston/Leiden: Brill.

Zika, Charles. 2003b. Fears of Flying. Representations of Witchcraft and Sexuality in 16th-Century Germany. In *Exorcising Our Demons: Magic, Witchcraft and Visual Culture in Early Modern Europe,* ed. C. Zika. Boston/Leiden: Brill.

Zika, Charles. 2007. *The Appearance of Witchcraft: Print and Visual Culture in Sixteenth-Century Europe.* London: Routledge.

Zwissler, Laurel. 2007. Spiritual, but Religious: "Spirituality" Among Religiously Motivated Activists in North America. *Culture and Religion* 8(1): 51–69.

Zwissler, Laurel. 2011. Second Nature: Contemporary Pagan Ritual Borrowing in Progressive Christian Communities. *Canadian Woman Studies/les cahiers de la femme,* Special Issue: 'Feminism, Activism and Spirituality' 29(1 & 2): 16–23.

Index

Note: Page numbers followed by "n" denote footnotes

© The Author(s) 2016
L. Kounine, M. Ostling (eds.), *Emotions in the History of
Witchcraft*, DOI 10.1057/978-1-137-52903-9